Birth of The Byzantine Army 476-641 CE

Volume 1: Still Late Roman?

Philippe Richardot

Helion & Company Limited
Unit 8 Amherst Business Centre
Budbrooke Road
Warwick
CV34 5WE
England
Tel. 01926 499 619
Email: info@helion.co.uk
Website: www.helion.co.uk
X, formerly Twitter: @helionbooks
Facebook: @HelionBooks
Visit our blog https://helionbooks.wordpress.com/

Published by Helion & Company 2025
Designed and typeset by Mary Woolley, Battlefield Design (www.battlefield-design.co.uk)
Cover designed by Paul Hewitt, Battlefield Design (www.battlefield-design.co.uk)

Text © Philippe Richardot 2025
Maps by George Anderson © Helion & Company 2025
Illustrations © Philippe Richardot unless otherwise credited

Every reasonable effort has been made to trace copyright holders and to obtain their permission for the use of copyright material. The author and publisher apologise for any errors or omissions in this work and would be grateful if notified of any corrections that should be incorporated in future reprints or editions of this book.

ISBN 978-1-804518-28-1

British Library Cataloguing-in-Publication Data.
A catalogue record for this book is available from the British Library.

All rights reserved. No part of this publication may be reproduced, stored in a retrieval system, or transmitted, in any form, or by any means, electronic, mechanical, photocopying, recording or otherwise, without the express written consent of Helion & Company Limited.

For details of other military history titles published by Helion & Company Limited contact the above address or visit our website: http://www.helion.co.uk.

We always welcome receiving book proposals from prospective authors.

Publisher's Note
All dates, unless specifically specified otherwise, are CE

Contents

Acknowledgements		v
Chronology		vi
Birth of The Byzantine Army 476-641 : Volume 1, Still Late Roman?		xvii
Introduction		xix
1	The Emperor as Commander of the Armies	27
2	Major Commands	79
3	The tough job of being a general	100
4	The Chain of Command of a Field Army	128
5	A Professional Army	163
6	A Double Standard Regular Army	193
7	Mercenaries and Barbarian *Foederati*	227
Notes to colour plates		253
Bibliography		256

Acknowledgements

I want to express my friendly gratitude to David Wilson and to the Numerus Invictorum Reenactment Group for their respective help, and to my old and trusted friend Etienne Le Baube.

Chronology

476 Romulus Augustulus, last Emperor of the West, overthrown by Odoacer *Generalissimo* and Patrician, then new King of Italy. Siege of Constantinople and restoration of Emperor Zeno by Isaurian troops. Elimination of the usurper Basiliscus.

478 Mutiny of Theodoric Strabo, Ostrogothic King settled in Thrace, against Eastern Roman Empire.

479 Usurpation of Marcian, son of the Western Emperor Anthemius, in Byzantium, put down by Illus the Patrician, Emperor Zeno restored again. Thrace, Rhodope, Macedonia and New Epirus raided by Ostrogothic Prince Theodoric the Amal. Siege and fall of Epidamnos/Dyrrachium (today Durrës in Albania) by Theodoric the Amal.

480 Ostrogothic King Theodoric Strabo attacked by Bulgars, at the request of Emperor Zeno.

481 Byzantium spared by Theodoric Strabo in exchange for ransom. Dalmatia conquered by Odoacer.

482 Siege and fall of Larissa in Thessaly by Theodoric the Amal.

484 Theodoric Strabo assassinated near Philippi in Thrace; Theodoric the Amal new King of the Ostrogoths. Samaritan revolt put down by Emperor Zeno.

485 War and truce concluded between Emperor Zeno and King Vakhtan I Gorgasali of Georgia. Construction of a Romano-Byzantine fortress on Tzanic territory by Longinus, Emperor's Zeno brother.

487 Moesia raided by Theodoric the Amal.

488 Theodoric the Amal sent by Emperor Zeno to Italy against the usurper Odoacer.

491–518 Anastasius I Emperor.

492–497 Rebelled Isaurians pacified by Romano-Byzantines.

492 Battle of Kotyaion won by Masters of Soldiers, John Gibbo 'the Hunchback' and John the Scythian, over Isaurian rebels.

493 Odoacer killed by Theodoric the Amal (later 'the Great') who becomes new King of Italy.

493 or 494 Unlocated battle in Thrace won by Bulgars over Julian, Master of the Soldiers to Illyricum who is killed in battle. Heruls driven out of Moravia by Lombards.

CHRONOLOGY

498 Euphratensis raided by Lakhmid Bedouins and Palestine raided by Ghassanids. Both repelled by Eugenios, Duke of Euphratensis or Osrhoene, and Romanus, Duke of Palestine.

499 Battle of the River Tzurta won by Bulgars over Aristus, Master of the Soldiers to Illyricum.

502–532 Thirty Years' War between Romano-Byzantines and Sassanid Persians. War is considered split into two phases: the Anastasian War 502–506 and the Justinian War 526–532.

502 Iberian Kingdom (modern eastern Georgia) invaded and King Vakhtang I Gorgasali killed by Persians.[1] Siege and capture of Theodosiopolis of Armenia and Martyropolis (today Erzurum and Silvan in Turkey) by the Sassanid Persian King Kavadh I. Battle of Bismideon, (today Tell-Besmai west of Mardin in Turkey) won the Persians over Olympios, Duke of Mesopotamia. Carrhae's region in Osrhoene raided by Lakhmid Bedouins. Thrace raided by Bulgars.

502–503 Siege, and fall, of Amida by the Persian King Kavadh I.

503 Siege of Amida by Masters of the Soldiers Present Patricius and Hypatius. Siege and battle of Nisibis (today Nusaybin in Turkey) on the Persian border by Flavius Areobindus Dagalaifus, Master of the Soldiers to the East; Persian relief army routed but Nisbis remained in Persian hands. Battle of Apadna won by King Kavadh I over Patricius and Hypatius. Sieges of Constantina/Constantia of Osrhoene and of Edessa, present-day Viranşehir in Turkey and Şanlıurfa in Turkey, by Persians. Northern Persia threatened by Huns at the request of Anastasius I. Arabia Petraea, Palestine and eastern Egypt raided by Lakhmid Bedouins.

504 Arzanene in Persarmenia and Jebel Sinjar raided by Flavius Areobindus Dagalaifus Master of the Soldiers to the East. Amida regained by Romano-Byzantines after negotiations.

505 Siege of Sirmium (today Sremska Mitrovica in Serbia) taken by Ostrogothic General Pitzia from Gepids, a Germanic tribe. Battle of Horreum Margi or Margoplanum (Ćuprija in Serbia) won by Ostrogoth Count Pitzia and Gepid "cattle thieves'" leader Mundo over Sabinian the Younger, Master of the Soldiers to Illyricum and his Bulgar *foederati*. Construction of the Dara fortress on the border with Persia by Romano-Byzantines. Lazica raided by Tzani.

508 Frankish King Clovis honoured with the title of Consul by Anastasius I. Romano-Byzantine naval expedition against Taranto held by Ostrogoths.

512 Heruls settled as *foederati* in Singidunum (today Belgrade in Serbia) by Anastasius I.

513 Armenian rebellion.

513–518 Rebellion led by Vitalian Count of the *Foederati* against Anastasius I.

---

1 At this period, Spain was called in Latin Hispania, Iberia was the Roman and Early Byzantine name for present-day Georgia.

515 Naval Battle of Bytharia won over rebel Vitalian the Thracian by the Praetorian Prefect Marinus of Syria. Armenia, Cappadocia and Lycaonia raided by Sabir Huns.

517 Balkans raided by Slavs. Long Walls erected by Anastasius I in order to protect Byzantium suburbs.

518–527 Justin I Emperor.

518 Vitalian the Thracian reconciled with the new Emperor.

520 Vitalian the Thracian assassinated shortly after being appointed Consul.

524–525 King Tzath I of Lazica and King Gourgen of Iberia revolt against Persians with the help of Hun mercenaries paid by Justin I.

526–532 Iberian War between Romano-Byzantines and Persians.

526 Persarmenia raided by Masters of the Soldiers Sittas and Belisarius. Syria raided by Lakhmid Bedouin King, al-Mundir III ibn al-Nu'man.

527 Unlocated battle in Persarmenia won by Persarmenian Generals and brothers Narses and Aratius Kamsarakan over Sittas and Belisarius. Siege of Nisibis and sudden retreat by Libelarius who was then replaced as Master of the Soldiers to the East by Belisarius.

527–565 Justinian I Emperor.

528 Ghassanid pro-Roman Bedouin tribe attacked by Lakhmid Bedouin King al-Mundir III ibn al-Nu'man, Romano-Byzantine reprisals. Unlocated battle won over Persian-allied Huns by Boa, Queen of the Sabir Huns. Scythia, Moesia and Thrace raided by Bulgar Huns. Two battles won over Justin Master of the Soldiers to Moesia who is killed in battle, then Masters of the Soldiers to Moesia and to Illyricum, Constantiolus and Askum the Hun, captured by Bulgars. Battles of Thannuris (today Tell Tunainir in Syria) and of Mindouos (the modern hamlet of Kasriahmethayro) won by Persian General Xerxes over Belisarius.

529 Region of Antioch (today Antakya in Turkey) raided by Lakhmid King al-Mundir III ibn al-Nu'man. Bulgar Hunnic raid repulsed by Mundo, Master of the Soldiers to Illyricum.

530 Battle of Dara won by Belisarius, Master of the Soldiers to the East over Persian General Perozes. Battles of Theodosiopolis and of Satala won by Sittas, Master of the Soldiers Present, over Persian General Mermeroes/Mihr-Mihroe. Slavic raid in Illyricum and Bulgar raid in Thrace both repelled by Mundo, Master of the Soldiers to Illyricum.

531 First Battle of Callinicum won by Persian General Azarethes over Belisarius. Siege and fall of Abgersaton fortress in Osrhoene by Persians. Romano-Byzantine Lazica and Anatolia raided by Sabir Huns. Two failed sieges of Martyropolis by Persians.

531–533 Slavic raids from Antes and Sklavenes repelled by Chilbudius, Master of the Soldiers to the Thraces.[2]

---

2   Latin often used the plural to designate a whole region as for the rank of Dux Britanniarum, 'Duke of the Britains'.

CHRONOLOGY

532 'Eternal Peace' concluded between Persians and Romano-Byzantines. Nika revolt against Justinian I in Byzantium suppressed by Belisarius.

533–534 Vandal War, destruction of the Vandal Kingdom of Africa by Belisarius.

533 Battles of Ad Decimum and Trikamaron won by Belisarius, Master of the Soldiers to the East, over Vandal King Gelimer.

534–535 Moors revolt.

534 Battle of Mammes won by Solomon, Master of the Soldiers to Africa, over Moors. Unlocated battle north of the Danube won by Sklavenes over Chilbudius, Master of the Soldiers to the Thraces.

535–562 Gothic War in Italy between Romano-Byzantines and Ostrogoths.

535 Battle of Mount Bourgaon won by Solomon, Master of the Soldiers to Africa, over Moors. Sicily invaded by Belisarius. Siege and fall of Panormus (modern Palermo) by Belisarius. Dalmatia conquered from Ostrogoths by Mundo Master of the Soldiers to Illyricum. Battle of the River Iatrus in Moesia, now River Yantra, Bulgaria, won over Bulgar raiders by Sittas, Master of the Soldiers to the Thraces.

536 Romano-Byzantine troops mutiny in Byzantine Province of Africa (roughly today's Libya) led by Stotzas, a 'common soldier'. Siege and fall of Naples, then occupation of Rome by Belisarius. Eastern borders of Egypt and province of Euphratensis in Northern Syria raided by Saracens from the Arabian Peninsula. Dalmatia invaded by Ostrogoths. Battle of Salona won over them by Mundo who was killed in the battle. Dalmatia reconquered by Constantianus Patrician, Count of the Stable, and new Master of the Soldiers to Illyricum.

537 Battle of Skalai Beteres won over Stotzas' mutineers in Africa by Germanus cousin of Justinian I. John Cottistis mutiny at Dara. Battle of Scardon won over the Ostrogothic General Uligisal by Constantianus, Patrician and Count of the Stable. Siege of Salona by Uligisal and Asinarius.

537–538 Siege of Rome victoriously defended by Belisarius against Ostrogoth King Vitiges.

538 Narses the Eunuch sent with reinforcements to Belisarius in Italy. Ariminium (today Rimini) occupied by Romano-Byzantines. Siege of Rimini by Vitiges. Battle of Ticinum (present-day Pavia) won over Ostrogoths by Mundilas, Romano-Byzantine commander. Liguria and Mediolanum (today Milan) occupied by Romano-Byzantines. Sieges and fall of Urbinum and Urbs Vetus (today Urbino and Orvetio in central Italy) by Belisarius. Frankish King Theudebert I's intervenes in Italy but forced to retreat by outbreak of dysentery. Battle of Oinochalakon won by Armenian rebels over Sittas, Master of the Soldiers Present.

538–539 Siege and destruction of Milan by Ostrogoths and Burgundians.

539 Romano-Byzantines defeated by the Gepids on the Danube. Double Battle of Tortona won over Ostrogoths then Romano-Byzantines by Franks. Battle won by the Gepids over Calluc, Master of the Soldiers to Illyricum who was killed in battle. Siege and fall of Faesulae (today

Fiesole in Tuscany) by Cyprian and Justin. Siege and fall of Auximum (today Osimo) by Belisarius.

540 'Eternal Peace' breached by the Persian Sassanid King Khosrow I, invasion of Mesopotamia, siege and destruction of Sura, ransoming of Hierapolis of Syria, capture of Beroea of Syria (today Aleppo) and sacking of Antioch. Siege and fall of Ravenna, capture of King Vitiges by Belisarius. Belisarius recalled from Italy to fight the Persians. Illyricum and Thrace raided by Kutrigur Huns without any opposition. Solomon campaigns against the Moors in the Aures Mountains.

540–562 Romano-Byzantine-Persian War.

541–557 Lazic War between Romano-Byzantines and Persians.

541 Battle of Treviso won by the ephemerous Ostrogothic King Ildibad over Vitalius, Master of the Soldiers to Illyricum, and Heruls. King Gubazes II of Lazica defects to the Persians when Khosrow I invaded his country. Siege and fall of Petra fortress in Lazica (today Tsikhisdziri in Georgia) by Persians. Siege and fall of Verona to Romano-Byzantines then successfully counter-attacked by Totila, new Ostrogothic King. Siege and fall of Sisauranon to Belisarius.

542 Battles of Faventia and of Mucellium (modern Faenza and Mugello valley) won by Totila over Romano-Byzantines. Siege and fall of Callinicum, razed to the ground and its population deported by Persian King Khosrow I.

542–543 Siege and fall of Naples by Totila.

543 Battle of Anglon (near modern Dvin in Armenia) won by Persians over Martin, Master of the Soldiers to the East.

543–547 Desert Moors revolt against Romano-Byzantines.

544 Battles of Theveste and Cillium won by the Moors over Solomon, Master of the Soldiers to Africa, who is killed in battle. Belisarius sent to Italy against Ostrogoths. Thrace raided by Antes. Siege of Edessa by Persian King Khosrow I.

545 Battle of Thacia in Africa won by John the Son Sisiniolus' loyal troops over over the rebel Stotzas, whos is killed in battle. Five-year Peace concluded with Persians by Justinian I.

545–546 Siege of Rome by Totila who partly destroyed the city walls. Thrace raided by Sklavenes.

546 Assassination of Areobindus, Governor of the Province of Africa Proconsularis by secessionist Guntharith, Duke of Numidia, who was himself subsequently murdered.

546–547 Moors pacified by John Troglita, Duke of Libya.

546–562 War between Ghassanids and Lakhmids.

547 Battle of Marta won by Syrtes tribes led by Carcasan over John Troglita, Duke of Libya. Battle of the Fields of Cato won by Troglita over Syrtes tribes. Rome reoccupied by Belisarius. Campania reconquered by Totila. Rebellious Gepids and Heruls pacified by Romano-Byzantines.

548 Siege and fall of Ruscianum (today Rossano, in Calabria) by Totila. Belisarius blockaded in south of the Italian peninsula. Veneto invaded by Franks. Battle in Veneto won by Lombard Prince Ildiges over

Lazarus, Master of the Soldiers. Illyricum raided by Sklavenes. King Gubazes II of Lazica's demand for help against Persians. Siege of Persian-held Petra fortress in Lazica by Dagistaheus, Master of the Soldiers to Armenia.

548–549 Siege and fall of Perusia (today Perugia in Umbria) by Totila.

549 Belisarius recalled to Constantinople. Battle of Laureate in Dalmatia won by Ostrogothic General Indulf over Romano-Byzantines. Illyricum, and Thrace raided by Sklavenes. Battle of the River Phasis, Persian General Phabrizus defeated by Dagisthaeus and Gubazes II.

549–550 Siege and fall of Rome by Totila.

550 Illyricum, Dalmatia and Thrace raided by Sklavenes. Battle of Adrianople, Scholasticus the Eunuch defeated by Sklavenes. Illyricum raided by Kutrigur Huns. Battle of Tanais (present-day River Don) won by Utigur Huns and Tetraxite Goths sent by Justinian I over Kutrigurs. Battle of the River Hippis or Mocherisis won by Dagisthaeus and Gubazes II over Persian General Chorianes, who was killed in the battle. Rome and Sicily reconquered by Totila. Renewal of the Five-Year Peace with Persians, in exchange for 2,600 pounds of gold.

550–551 Siege and fall of Petra fortress in Lazica, destroyed by Bessas, master of the soldiers to Armenia.

551 Truce between Romano-Byzantines and Persians. Ostrogothic naval operations south of the Adriatic and sacking of Corfu. Naval Battle of Sena Gallica (today Senigallia) won by John, the nephew of Vitalian, and Valerian, Master of the Soldiers, over the Ostrogothic Generals Indulf and Gibal. Sicily reconquered by Romano-Byzantines. Corsica and Sardinia invaded by Ostrogoths. Illyricum raided by Sklavenes. Third war between Lombards and Gepids. Athanagild rebelled against Visigothic King Agila and called on Byzantium for help.

552 Battle of Taginae/Tadinae or Busta Gallorum (today Gualdo Tadino and Sassoferrato) won by Narses the Eunuch over Totila, who died from wounds received. Siege and fall of Rome to Narses the Eunuch. Late 552/early 553, Battle of Mons Lactarius (today Monti Lattari south of Naples) won by Narses the Eunuch over Teias the last Ostrogothic King. Romano-Byzantine landings in Malaga and at other Spanish coastal towns.

553 Italy invaded by Franks. Battle of Rimini won by Narses the Eunuch over the Franks. Siege and fall of the Telephis Fortress in Lazica by Persian General Mermeroes.

554 Battle of the Volturnus or of Casilinum (current River Volturno in Capua), won over Franks and Alemanni by Narses the Eunuch. Battle of Yawm Halima near Chalcis (today Qinnasrin) won over Lakhmid King al-Mundhir III ibn al-Nu'man, who was killed in action, by Ghassanid King al-Harith ibn Jabalah. Siege and fall of Nesos fortress in Lazica by Persian General Mermeroes. Small Romano-Byzantine expeditionary force landed in Spain.

554–555 Siege and fall of Compsa (today Conza della Campania) by Narses the Eunuch.

554–567 Sporadic war between the Visigothic King of Spain Athanagild and Romano-Byzantine coastal cities.

555 Narses the Eunuch campaign south of the Po. Lazic War, siege and Battle of Onoguris won by Persian General Nachoragan over Martin, Master of the soldiers to Armenia, and Bouzes.

556 Siege and Battle of Phasis in Lazica (today Poti in Georgia) won over Persian General Nachoragan by Martin, Master of the Soldiers to Armenia.

557 Lazic War, truce between Romano-Byzantines and Persians.

556–557 Misimian revolted against Romano-Byzantines.

558 Revolt of the Tzani or Zanz, subsequently put down by Romano-Byzantines.

559 Greece and Chersonese of Thrace raided by Kutrigur Huns, led by Zabergan, and Sklavenes. Siege of Byzantium by Zabergan. Battle of Melanthius (modern Hoşköy Belediyesi) won over Zabergan by Belisarius who then retired.

562 Last Ostrogothic resistance north of the Po crushed by Narses the Eunuch. 'Fifty-Year Peace' or Treaty of Dara concluded with Persians: Lazica returned to Romano-Byzantine rule. Obaisipolis (Odyssus?) and Anastasiopolis in Thrace raided by Huns.

563–565 Moors revolt against Romano-Byzantines.

565–578 Justin II Emperor.

567 Battle of the Field of Asfeld won by the Lombards and Avars over the Gepids.

568 Veneto conquered by Lombards.

569 Liguria conquered by Lombards.

569–579 Moorish rebellion against Romano-Byzantines.

570 Baza region and the city of Malaga reconquered from Romano-Byzantines by Visigothic King of Spain Leovigild. Thrace raided by Avars then repulsed by Count Tiberius. Siege and fall of Benevento by Lombard Duke Zotto.

570–571 Three battles won over Praetorian Prefect of Africa Theodore, Masters of the Soldiers Theoctistus then Amabilis – all killed in action – by Moorish King Garmul.

571 Siege and fall of Sidonia in Spain, reconquered from Romano-Byzantines by Visigothic King of Spain Leovigild.

572–591 War between Romano-Byzantines and Persians initiated by Justin II.

572 Persian province of Arzanene raided by Romano-Byzantines. Battle of Sarmathon/Sargathon (present-day Qasr Serijihan) in Syria won over Persian General Varaman by Marcian the Patrician, Master of the Soldiers to the East.

573 Failed campaign of Marcian the Patrician, Master of the Soldiers to the East. Siege of Nisibis by Marcian the Patrician. Siege and fall of Dara, Ghassanids submit to Persian King Khosrow I.

574–575 War in Mesopotamia between Persians and Romano-Byzantines.

CHRONOLOGY

574 Battle of Khalamakhik won over Persians by rebellious Persarmenians. Truce concluded between Romano-Byzantines and Persians.

576 Unlocated battle in Italy won over Baduarius, Master of the Soldiers, by Lombards. The Zans or Tzani, a Caucasian tribe, Suans pacified by Romano-Byzantines. Thrace raided by Sklavenes. Battle of Melitene won over Persian King Khosrow I by Justinian, Master of the Soldiers to the East.

577 Unlocated battle in Armenia won over Justinian, Master of the Soldiers to the East, by Persian General Tamkhosrow.

577–579 Campaign against rebel Moors by Gennadius, Master of the Soldiers to Africa.

578 Unlocated battle in Italy won over Romano-Byzantines by Lombards. Thrace and Greece raided by Sklavenes. Sklavene lands raided by Avars at the request of Justin II. Coastal cities of Betica reconquered from Romano-Byzantines by Visigothic King of Spain Leovigild.

578–582 Tiberius II Constantine Emperor.

578–580 War between Persians and Romano-Byzantines in Mesopotamia.

578–579 Siege of Rome by Lombards finally paid to abandon siege by Pope Pelagius II.

579 Pacification of Moors and King Garmul killed by Gennadius, Master of the Soldiers to Africa.

580–603 War interspersed with truces between Romano-Byzantines and Avars.

580–582 Siege and fall of Sirmium by the Avars, after a two-year blockade.

581 Campaign in Mesopotamia of Maurice Master of the Soldiers to the East and Ghassanid King al-Mundir III ibn al-Harith. Second Battle of Callinicum won over Maurice, Master of the Soldiers to the East, by Persians. Siege of Naples by Lombard Duke Zotto.

581–583 Ghassanid revolt against Byzantine rule after unfair arrest of al-Mundir III ibn al-Harith.

582 Battle of Constantina in Osrhoene won over Persian Generals Adarman and Tamkhosrow (latter killed) by Maurice, Master of the Soldiers to the East.

582–602 Maurice Emperor.

583 Northern Illyricum and Thrace raided by Avars.

584 Balkans raided by Sklavenes. Battle of the River Erginia won by Comentiolus the Thracian Master of the Soldiers to the Thracians, over Sklavenes.

585–590 War between Persians and Romano-Byzantines.

585 Persian Arzanene province raided by Philippicus, Master of the Soldiers to the East. Thrace raided by Sklavenes. Battle of Ansinon won against them by Comentiolus the Thracian.

586–588 War between Romano-Byzantines and Avars in the Balkans.

586 Istria raided by Lombards. Enclave at the island of Como conquered from Romano-Byzantines by Lombard King Authari. Northern Balkans raided and siege of Thessaloniki by Sklavenes and Avars. Battle of Solachon in Mesopotamia won over Persian General Kardarigan by Philippicus, Master of the Soldiers to the East. Persian province of Arzanene raided by Philippicus. Siege of Tigranocerta (also called Chlomaron or Cholimma) by Philippicus relieved by a Persian Army.

587–588 Siege of Rome by the Lombards.

587 Balkans raided by Avars then repulsed by Comentiolus the Thracian. Avars taught by a Byzantine prisoner how to construct siege machines. Persian territory raided by Heraclius the Elder, second in command to the Master of the Soldiers to the East.

588 Easter mutiny at Monocarton over pay. Battle of Heraclea won by Avars over Priscus, military pay master to the Thraces. Rebellious Moors pacified again by Gennadius. Battle of Martyropolis in Armenia won by Germanus, Duke of Phoenice Libanensis against Persian General Marouzas, killed in action.

589 Balkans raided by Sklavenes. Eastern Army mutinies but pacified by Philippicus, Master of the Soldiers to the East. Battle of Sisauranon won against Persians by Comentiolus the Thracian, appointed during the autumn new Master of the Soldiers to the East.

590 Siege and fall of Benevento and of Reggio by Lombard King Authari. Peace concluded between Romano-Byzantines and Persians. New Sassanid Persian King Khosrow II political refugee in Syria. Dara fortress returned to Emperor Maurice by the King of the Persians in order to get his help against usurper Bahram VI Chobim.

591 Battle of Blarathon, near Lake Urmia in Iran, won by Khosrow II over Persian rebels. Peace concluded between Romano-Byzantines and Persians.

593–596 War between Romano-Byzantines and Sklavenes.

593 Central Italy partly reconquered from Lombards by Romanus Patrician and *Exarch* of Ravenna. Siege and fall of Perugia by Lombard King Agilulf; Maurice, Lombard Duke of Perugia allied with the Empire, killed. Thrace raided by Sklavenes then liberated by Peter the Kouropalates, Master of the Soldiers. Campaign against Sklavenes by Priscus, Master of the Soldiers to the Thracians.

594 Campaign of Peter the Kouropalates against Sklavenes along Middle Danube.

595–602 War between Romano-Byzantines and Avars.

595 Siege and fall of Singidunum by Avars then liberated by a Romano-Byzantine amphibious operation led by Godwin. Dalmatia raided by Avars.

597 Moesia raided by Avars. Siege of Thessaloniki by the Sklavenes.

598 Siege of Tomi (now Constanța in Romania) by Avars. Battle of Shipka Pass won against Avars by Romano-Byzantines. Truce concluded between Romano-Byzantines and Avars.

599 Istria raided by Sklavenes. Priscus's and Comentiolus the Thracian's joint campaign against Avars, Gepids and Sklavenes along Middle Danube.

600 Thrace raided by Avars. Daughter of Lombard King Agilulf captured by the *Exarch* of Ravenna. Istria raided by Sklavenes.

CHRONOLOGY

601 Siege and fall of Padua razed to the ground by Lombard King Agilulf.
602 'Eternal Peace' concluded between Romano-Byzantines and Persians. Istria raided by Lombards and Sklavenes. Siege and fall of Monselice by Lombards. Romano-Byzantine Danube army mutiny. Emperor Maurice beheaded.
602–610 Phocas Emperor.
603–630 Last war between Romano-Byzantines and Persians.
603 Siege and fall of Cremona and of Mantua by Lombards, helped by Sklavenes sent by the Khan of Avars. Rebellion of Narses Strategos, ex-Master of the Soldiers to the East. Battle of Edessa won over Germanus, Master of the Soldiers to the East, by Persian King Khosrow II and Narses Strategos.
604 Siege of Thessaloniki by Sklavenes. Battle of Constantina won by Persians over Germanus, Master of the Soldiers to the East, who died from wounds.
604–605 Siege and fall of Dara fortress by Khosrow II.
605 Siege and fall of Bagnoregio and of Orvieto by Lombards. Truce concluded between Romano-Byzantines and Lombards. Edessa reconquered from Narses Strategos by Domentziolus the Younger, Master of the Soldiers to the East. Battle of Arzamon (today the River Gümüş Çay, Turkey-Syria) won by Persian King Khosrow II against Leontius the Syrian, Master of the Soldiers to the East,.
606 Truce between Romano-Byzantines and Lombards renewed.
607 Battle of Theodosiopolis of Armenia won over Domentziolus the Younger by Persians.
608 Rebellion of Heraclius the Elder, *exarch* of Africa.
609 Egypt conquered by Niketas, general of Heraclius the Elder. Unlocated battle in Cappadocia won by Persians over Sergius, Master of the Soldiers to the East, who was killed in battle.
610 Syria invaded. Sieges and fall of Emesa, current Homs in Syria and of Antioch by Persians. Phocas deposed and executed after Heraclius the Younger landing in Byzantium with the African army.
610–641 Heraclius I Emperor.
611–612 Ill-fated campaign of Priscus, Master of the Soldiers to the East, against Persians.
611 Istria raided by Sklavenes. Siege and fall of Caesarea of Cappadocia, modern Kayseri in Turkey, by Persian General Shahín. Battle of the River Halys (today Kızılırmak in Turkey) won over Romano-Byzantines by Persians.
612 Priscus recalled to Constantinople and replaced with Philippicus as Master of the Soldiers to the East. Syrian border raided by Saracens. Battle of Caesarea won over Persian General Kesruan by the Master of the Soldiers to the East Niketas the son of Gregory.
613 Battles of Damascus and Antioch won over Heraclius by Persian Generals Shahrbaraz and Shahín.

614 Siege and fall of Jerusalem by Persian General Shahrbaraz. True Cross sent to Ctesiphon capital of the Persian Empire. Shore of the Bosphorus temporary reached at Chalcedon by Persian General Shahín.

615 Siege and fall of Salona by Avars. Northern Greece raided and siege of Thessaloniki by Sklavenes. Palestine raided by Arab tribes. Two battles won over Romano-Byzantine troops in Spain and loss of cities to Visigothic King Sisebuth.

616 Peace concluded in Byzantium with Visigoths of Spain.

617 Siege of Thessaloniki by Avars and Sklavenes.

619 Siege and fall of Alexandria of Egypt to Persians.

621–631 Last Byzantine cities in Spain retaken by the Visigothic King Svinthila.

622–625 First campaign of Heraclius against Persians.

622 Siege and fall of Ganzak, destroyed along with the Zoroastrian Temple of Fire Adhur Gushnasp, by Heraclius.

623 Byzantium suburb raided by Avars.

624 Rhodes raided by Persians.

626 Siege of Byzantium by Avars, Sklavenes and by a Persian fleet. Battle of Satala won over Persian General Shahín by Theodore Trithyrios the Sakellarios.

626–627 Surprise winter attack on Sharbaraz's headquarters in Persarmenia by Heraclius, balance of morale changed in favour of Romano-Byzantines.

627–629 Heraclius' second campaign against Persians.

627 Battle of Nineveh won by Heraclius against Persian General Rahzadh.

628 Persian King Khosrow II overthrown and executed by his son Siroes.

629 Siege and fall of Jerusalem retaken from Persians by Heraclius. Peace between Romano-Byzantines and Persians.

630 Battle of Mothous/Mouta/Mu'ta won over Muslim Arabs by Romano-Byzantines. Siege and fall of Singidunum by Sklavenes, then siege of Thessaloniki.

634–640/642 Palestine and Syria conquered by Islamic Arabs.

634 Battles of Dâthín, Ajnadayn and Fahl in Palestine and Syria won over Romano-Byzantines by Muslim Arabs.

635 Siege and fall Damascus by Muslim Arabs.

635–636 Mesopotamia conquered by Muslim Arabs.

636 Battle then siege of Emesa won over Romano-Byzantines by Muslim Arabs.

637 Battle of the Yarmuk won over Romano-Byzantines by Muslim Arabs.

637–652 Persia invaded by Muslim Arabs.

638 Siege and fall of Jerusalem by Muslim Arabs. Siege of Emesa by Romano-Byzantines. Siege and fall of Antioch by Muslim Arabs.

639–646 Egypt conquered by Muslim Arabs.

639 Siege of Salona razed to ground by Sklavenes. Armenia raided by Muslim Arabs.

641 Death of Heraclius, then Alexandria taken by Muslim Arabs.

Birth of The Byzantine Army 476-641

Volume 1: Still Late Roman?

Philippe Richardot is a specialist in military history and the author of eleven books and nearly 200 articles. His main subject of study is the late Roman army and the warriors of the early Middle Ages, but he also places himself in the broader perspective of comparative military history. A graduate of the regional sessions of the Hautes Etudes de l'Armement and the Institut des Hautes Etudes de la Défense nationale (France), he has also been a member of the Scientific Committee of the Centre d'Histoire et de Prospective Militaires de Lausanne-Pully (Switzerland) and research director at the Institut für vergleichende Tactik in Vienna-Postdam (Austria-Germany). He has written regularly for the Revue Militaire Suisse for nearly three decades, and for three years directed dissertations at the Ecole de Guerre (Paris).

Very Late Roman Army or brand new Byzantine one? That is the question! When the Western Roman Empire disappeared, only the Eastern Empire retained an emperor. Without a Roman tradition army in the East, there would be no more empire at all, but how did it manage to adapt until the advent of Islam?

Introduction

> Army of Rome, surest hope to restore the situation, courage, glory and extreme relief of the world, full of the confidence of the Empire and laurel of our work.
> General John Troglita to his army in 546, Corippus, *Johannis*, I, v.522–523

The great paradox of the times we are about to explore was the fact Emperors who were self-titled as 'Roman' ruled from Constantinople (today Istanbul), when the city of Rome was no more the capital of any Empire or Kingdom. However, they were not viewed as 'Romans' by everyone at the time. In a letter dating to 468, the Gallic Senator and future bishop Sidonius Apollinaris was talking about the *Graecus Imperator* (Greek Emperor).[1] This purely Western vision was not widely shared in the eastern part of the former Roman Empire. In his *Latin Chronicle* for the year 472, Count Marcellinus named the capital of the East as Constantinople, i.e. Constantine's city, but he referred to its inhabitants as *Byzantii* (Byzantines) according to the ancient Greek name of the city, Byzantion or Byzantium. In addition, he never spoke of any Empire but instead of *res publica*, which is more conveniently translated as 'state'.[2] It was a politically correct way of writing for someone living under the rule of the Eastern Roman Empire. The Roman Empire had been divided into two parts for military reasons since the death of Theodosius I in 395.

The year 476 was fateful as the last emperor of the Western Roman Empire, Romulus Augustulus (Little Augustus), a fourteen-year-old boy and the son of one of Attila's secretaries, was deposed without violence by Odoacer, a barbarian condottiere. This event resulted from the flawed integration of barbarian mercenaries, known as *foederati* in Latin or *phoideratoi* in Greek, into the dangerous arena of Roman civil war. Thus, the Western Roman Empire ended without glory whereas its Eastern counterpart continued to exist for centuries.[3] From a legal standpoint, however, the true end

---

1 Sidonius Apollinaris, *Ep.*, I, 7.
2 Marcellinus Comes, *Chr.*, a. 472.
3 H. Börm, *Westrom. Von Honorius bis Justinian* (Stuttgart: Kohlhammer, 2013).

came about with the dissolution of the Western Roman state by a legal act, namely the Justinian's *Constitutio Pragmatica* (Pragmatic Sanction) of 13 August 554. This extended the laws from Constantinople to the recently reconquered Italy, reducing it to a mere provincial prefecture.[4] Byzantium's rule over Rome did not restore old Roman ways but destroyed it and the millenary Senate in the wake. *Sic friat crustulum.*

As with many subjects, historians today do not agree on when the transitional era between late antiquity and the early middle ages ended.[5] The Empire of Rome nor was built in a day, but did not die in a day either. Since 324, by the will of Constantine I the Great and by the terms of law, Byzantium or Constantinople was the capital of a continuing Roman state preserving the legitimate power of command or *imperium*. This Empire endured because some populations still believed in it. However, these populations now lived in the Eastern Mediterranean, and most of them were Greek speaking. As with Count Marcellinus, Latin speakers predominated in the region of Illyricum, which covers present-day Croatia, Bosnia, and Serbia. Some of them who immigrated to Thrace formed an important military clan in the first half of the sixth century, producing no fewer than three Byzantine Emperors: Anastasius I, Justin I and Justinian I.[6] They considered themselves the only and legitimate 'Roman' rulers.

By the late sixth century, the main generals of Emperor Maurice, like himself, used purely Latin names: Priscus, Comentiolus, Celer, only Philippicus had a Greek name. But to be a 'Roman' was not then necessarily linked to Latin speaking. All Latin or Greek literary sources from the sixth century, historians such as Procopius, Agathias and Theophylact Simokatta or a poet such as Corippus, felt a strong sense of belonging to the Roman Empire.[7] When Corippus recounted John Troglita's North African campaign of 546–547, he proudly referred to 'the Roman Army' never to a 'Greek Army', let alone a 'Byzantine Army'. He purposely used expressions such as 'Latin cohorts', 'Latin armies', 'Latin cause' or 'Roman youth' and 'Roman Army'.[8] While Corippus was a North African of a Latin culture,

---

4   *Nov. J.*, 149.
5   A. Cameron, *The Mediterranean World in Late Antiquity AD 395–600* (London: Routledge, 1993), pp.6–7.
6   B. Croke, *Count Marcellinus and His Chronicle* (Oxford: Oxford University Press, 2001), pp.6–7 (the Roman world as Marcellinus knew it; Illyrians at Constantinople).
7   A. Cameron, *Agathias* (Oxford: Oxford University Press, 1970). D. Brodka, *Die Geschichtesphilosophie in der spätantiken Historiographie. Studien zu Prokopios, Agathias von Myrina und Theophylaktos Simokates* (Frankfurt am Main: Peter Lang, Studien un Texte zur Byzantinistik, 5, 2004); J. D. C. Frendo, *History and Panegyric in the Age of Heraclius: The Literary Background to the Composition of the Histories of Theophylact Simocatta*, DOP, 42 (1988), pp.143–156.
8   Corippus, *Joh*, I, v. 81 (Roman Army); VI, v. 345 (Latin cohorts); v. 347 (Latin cause); VIII, v. 200 (Latin armies); VI, v. 360 (Roman youth). E. Burck, 'The Die Iohannis des Corippus' in E. Burck (ed.), *Das römische Epos* (Darmstadt: Buchgesellschaft, 1979), pp.379–399.

INTRODUCTION

in other words a Southern Roman, Procopius was an Eastern Roman from Caesarea in Palestine and reported Justinian's wars in the Greek language.[9] He called Byzantium's inhabitants *Byzantioi* (Byzantines) and described the Empire's citizens and soldiers as *Rhômaioi* (Romans).[10] Imperial pride was linked to the still magic name of 'Roman', even among the numerically overwhelming Greek-speaking people.

As a sign of the confusion of the times, the Latin *Chronicle of 754* written in Spain did not hesitate to record that Heraclius, after his victory over Persians in 628, celebrated a triumph in 'Rome' – in fact Byzantium, the last capital of the Roman state.[11] Culture of the early Byzantine Empire was still bilingual. The chronicler Agathias gives us a glimpse of the double name of a miserable hamlet in what is now Georgia: it was a pottery market the Latins called Ollaria, whereas the Greek named it Chytropôlia.[12] This example provides a clearer picture of the split between Latinity and Romanity dividing the Latins of the West from the Greeks of the East, although all being 'Roman'. Early Byzantines were mostly Greek-speaking Romans. In fact, the Greek language never ceased to be the *lingua franca* of the eastern Mediterranean even during Roman rule. As far back as the early fourth century, and even earlier, many documents of the Eastern Roman Army were written in Greek. Nevertheless, Justinian I wrote his *Code* in Latin, thereby demonstrating his Imperial legitimacy by continuing Rome's political institutions.[13] Like Rome, Constantinople had a senate with the monumental setting of a basilica, capitol and statuary, and the whole decorum of political legitimacy.[14] Rome in Byzantium was no more than an assumed legal fiction, an administrative structure surviving for itself.

Romano-Byzantine seems an appropriate term to describe this dual allegiance as long as Latin retained a legal and military role. Justinian I's claim to Roman legitimacy was not some antiquarian nostalgia, but a pragmatic way to assert his power. All poetry apart, his ambition was crudely geopolitical: rolling back the barbarian hordes from borders and achieving nearly total control of the Mediterranean Sea. So, the difference between Romans and barbarians was something fluid: was a Roman the one who could claim being born in an Imperial province, bearing allegiance

---

9   Procopius' *Wars* or *History of the Wars* are divided into eight books as follow: Books I-II *The Persian War (Bellum Persicum)* from 527 on, III-IV *The Vandal War (Bellum Vandalum)* in Africa, V-VII *The Gothic War (Bellum Goticum)* in Italy, VIII untitled as *Gothic War* but on all theatres up to 553. Agathias was the continuator of Procopius.

10 Procopius, *BG*, V, 15, 14 (Βυζάντιοι). The term Ῥωμαῖοι is used countless times to designate the army but also the inhabitants of Rome, V, 15, 11; ô is for omega, o for omicron.

11 *Chr. 754*, 4.

12 Agathias, *Hist.*, II, 20, 5.

13 M. Maas, *John Lydus and the Roman Past. Antiquarianism and Politics in the Age of Justinian* (London: Routledge, 1992).

14 A. Cameron, *The Mediterranean World*, p.20.

to the Emperor, the way to talk, to be dressed and cut your hair, the lifestyle, and the behaviour towards moderation and discipline.[15] For instance, Chilbudius, although of a Germanic origin, spoke fluent Latin or Greek and was general of Thrace. After he died in 534 his name was taken over by a Slav who sought to usurp his identity and probably also spoke Latin or Greek.[16] Nevertheless, the real genuine Roman, according to Procopius, and Ammianus two centuries before him, was the professional soldier who fought for the Empire, a hard task to handle.

The Eastern Roman Empire had to defend a land spanning three continents but geographically unified by the Mediterranean Sea. The Empire's wealth made it a tempting target for its warlike barbarian neighbours. At a peace conference held in Dara *c.* 581–582, a Persian ambassador named Andigan stressed this uneasy strategic situation to Zachariah his Romano-Byzantine colleague:

> We are well aware that the Roman Empire, which has many enemies to contend with, is fighting in different parts of the world and its forces are divided by wars with almost every barbarian nation, while of course the Romans know that our people are at war with no one but the Romans. While the Romans are sure to win when they fight a few tribes or our Kingdom alone, we will win for sure since we have no enemy other than the Romans and we fight only one war at a time.[17]

The Empire's borders were being overrun by hordes of ravenous barbarians, consequently theatres of war and adversaries were becoming increasingly diverse. In the north, the Danube River formed a natural border against the nomadic horse archers from the steppes known as the Scythians, an indiscriminate grouping formed by Huns, Bulgars, Turks and Avars: 'The Scythian nations are one and the same, in terms of their way of life and their primitive organisation, comprising many peoples.'[18] The other enemies on this much disputed frontier were the Slavs, then known as Sklavenes and Antes. Slavic migrations throughout the sixth and seventh centuries were no less a turmoil than the Germanic from previous eras. They brought about a major geopolitical upheaval in Europe whose consequences are still visible.[19] The Slavs emerged from their forests and marshes to relentlessly clash with the Romano-Byzantine Empire. Militarily brave and politically

---

15   D. A. Parnell, 'A Prosopographical Approach to Justinian's Army', *Medieval Prosopography*, 27, 1 (2012), pp.4–6.
16   Procopius, *BG*, VII, 14, 36. References to Procopius' Books include numeration of the *History of Wars*, so VII is the third Book of *Bellum Gothicum*, 'the Gothic War'.
17   Menander Protector, *Fragm.* 26.1.
18   Maurice, *Strategikon*, XI, 2, 4–5.
19   P. J. Heather, *Empires and barbarians. Migration, Development and the Birth of Europe* (London: Macmillan, 2009), pp.29–30.

undisciplined they 'refused to be subjugated or even governed.'[20] They settled in Imperial Illyricum, which was later named Yugoslavia, literally 'the Country of the Southern Slavs'. With the exception of the Avars in the 620s, all these elusive northern barbarians proved to have little capacity for siege warfare. The Danubian area suffered their perpetual attacks, while Greece and Byzantium formed two separate 'funnels' where these returning invaders were trapped.

The strongly fortified city of Byzantium was strategically situated between Europe and the Orient. Its ports were the convenient outlet for a rich trade and for a war fleet capable of stopping invaders from the sea. Encircling Byzantium required land and naval resources, something that few powers could achieve at the time and certainly not the steppe or forest hordes.

To the east, the most constant enemy was the Persian Sasanian dynasty, a kind of evil doppelganger of the Romano-Byzantine Empire. The Persians gave the Romans the taste for rich embroidered tunics and heavy cavalry armour and the custom for kneeling before monarchs. To be fair, since the third century the Persians had mostly been the aggressors. Despite their countless attacks Anatolia formed a tough barren mountainous bastion against them. It abutted Armenia to the east, a no less hilly region but then divided between Roman and Persian authority. It was not only an invasion entry route for the Persians, but also a hotbed of anti-fiscal revolts. Byzantium's Empire also maintained a bridgehead further north-east in Lazica, on the coast of today's Georgia, another point of friction with the Persians, who were trying to reach Byzantium via the Black Sea. The Romano-Byzantines controlled the Levant region and the Northern Syrian border to the south of Anatolia. The upper reaches of the 'Fertile Crescent' were a rich agricultural region and a tempting target. For this reason, Roman Mesopotamia, now southern Turkey, was the main area of contact and cause of conflict with the Persians. Wars there lasted several years, involving huge numbers of troops, because the Persians had all the skills of land warfare and knew how to build, defend and attack fortifications. Roman and early Byzantine sources depicted the Persians as a slave army led by a tyrant, but in fact they were a disciplined force. They rarely reached the Levant region, where a string of coastal cities stretched across Phoenicia and Palestine.

The south-eastern desert between the Rivers Jordan and Euphrates was occupied by the Ghassanids, a friendly Christian Bedouin tribe. Although sometimes raided by inimical Bedouins named Lakhmids, this area was almost a quiet front until Muhammad's lieutenants decided otherwise. Facing south, Egypt faced south and formed a kind of strategic island. A mere *gendarmerie*-like force was enough to protect it from raids launched by Saharan nomads. Romano-Byzantine authority vanished in the Western Desert as far as Cyrenaica, where the port areas were under control.

---

20 Maurice, *Strategikon*, XI, 2, 3–4.

The Moors resided in the desert and further west, as far as the distant Atlas Mountains. They were turbulent neighbours, or sometimes allies, and they fielded large mobile armies, lightly equipped, keen to set ambushes but not very strong in open battle. In waging these guerrilla wars which they always lost, they sought for revenge and looting rather than for conquest. Their main objective was to raid Libya, a Romanised area including present-day Tripolitania and Tunisia. Until 533 this place was occupied by a Germanic people, the Vandals, who had evolved from being pirates in the fifth century to becoming a regular Kingdom ruling in the Roman way but then too weak to defend itself.[21] According to Byzantine accounts, the Vandals were known as 'fair-haired barbarians' and likened to the Goths, Franks and other Lombards: 'although their spirits are bold and reckless, their bodies are soft, incapable of suffering calmly. They fear the heat, the cold, the rain, the lack of food, especially wine, and when a battle is postponed.'[22]

Initially, the Empire's western European borders with the Ostrogothic Kingdom of Italy stood in Dalmatia. The conquest of North Africa and Italy could allow Byzantium's Empire to close the Eastern Mediterranean and cut itself off from the Germanic Kingdoms ruling the West. As a consequence, the pretended 'reconquest' of Africa and Italy resulted in two near-fatal duels with the Vandals and the Ostrogoths between 533 and 562. Once North Africa and Italy were 'reconquered', Byzantium reached his peak size in the Mediterranean. From then, the Western Mediterranean was still bordered by two vast Germanic Kingdoms, those of the Franks in Gaul and the Visigoths in Spain. These kingdoms were built on late Roman geographical and administrative bases and had long since adopted Roman weapons and mastered siege warfare. They were 'nuts too hard to crack' and too far away to handle.[23] Here the limits of Byzantium's military power stopped.

A vast, discontinuous area with various enemies to defend against – that was the Imperial military challenge. This strategic situation created the need for multiple tactical styles to deal with. Could Byzantium's Army, heir to the Eastern Roman Army, still fight as it did in late antiquity? The big question was how to organise and equip it in order to defeat a vast array of differing enemies. These included light, mobile cavalry archers like the Huns; ultra-heavy horsemen with the best armour of the time, like the Avars; infantry expert at ambushes and armed with effective and poisonous javelins, like the Slavic tribes; evasive Moorish and Saracen bands; There were also warlike Caucasian and Armenian mountain peoples, who were equally eager to serve or betray the Romano-Byzantines; Ostrogothic horsemen who mastered the spear and were well supported by foot archers; and,

---

21   C. Courtois, *Les Vandales et l'Afrique* (Paris: Arts et Métiers graphiques, 1955).
22   Maurice, *Strategikon*, XI, 3, 25–29.
23   Ph. Richardot, *L'Âge des guerriers ou l'aube du Moyen Âge 476–711* (Le Rove: Centre Littéraire d'Impression Provençal, 2016), pp.504–640.

INTRODUCTION

finally, innumerable Persians with disciplined infantry, siege engines, and heavy, iron-clad *clibanarii*. The other problem was to defend cities against all these peoples or to take cities previously fortified in the Roman style. We must not forget the need to fight at sea from time to time. No other army by then moved on so many fronts in such a short period. In these eminently warlike 'Dark Ages', the Romano-Byzantine military was not unworthy of its Roman ancestor. It was able to control the Eastern Mediterranean, Balkans and Near East with rudimentary resources compared with those of today's powers, which are no longer capable of such a feat. Byzantium was the Rome that not surrender for a nearly 900 years.

We have few direct witnesses to tell the story, quite 'a tale told by an idiot, full of sound and fury'. The main historical source for the 530s–540s Justinianic wars is obviously the Greek historian Procopius, a member of Belisarius' staff, his jural adviser, and most probably an intelligence officer. His eight-book *History of Wars* begins with the Persian Wars, followed by Vandal and Ostrogothic Wars.[24] His successor Agathias was less involved in military affairs and only recorded a narrative of Italy and Lazica for the years 552–559. Corippus, the Libyan grammarian and schoolmaster who wrote the last Latin epic in verse about General John Troglita pacifying the Moors, witnessed the events and was acquainted with the names of the officers and of the battles fought. Perhaps like Procopius he took part to the military expedition in some sort of administrative position. Nevertheless, his poetry remains suspicious of it sublimating reality.[25] These authors, whether historians or poets, all deal with the reign of Justinian I. Theophylact Simocatta was contemporary to the 580–590s wars in the Balkans and Near East, which he described with accuracy but was not a witness. The main source for tactics is the *Strategikon*, a late sixth-century military treatise attributed to, or commissioned by, the Emperor Maurice, sometimes erroneously confused with a certain Urbicius or Urbikios. It was the first of a long list of Byzantine military treatises.[26] It provides accurate

---

[24] Procopius *BP*, I, 12, 23 (Belisarius's *xymboulos* or *symboulos*, σύμβουλος since first Persian campaign). G. Greatrex, 'Perceptions of Procopius in Recent Scholarship', *Histos*, 8 (2014), pp.76–121.

[25] B. Baldwin, 'The Career of Corippus', *CQ* 28 (1978), pp.195–212; Y. Modéran, 'Corippe et l'occupation Byzantine de l'Afrique: Pour une nouvelle lecture de la Johannide', *Antiquités Africaines*, XXII (1986), pp.195–212; P. Galland-Hallyn, 'La *Johannide* (*De Bellis Libycis*). Corippus et le sublime dans la 'dernière' épopée romaine' in J. Droin, A. Roth (eds), *La croisée des études libyco-berbères: mélanges offerts à Paulette Galand-Pernet et Lionel Galand* (Paris: Geuthner, 1993), pp.73–87; V. Zarini, 'Images de guerre dans la poésie officielle de l'Antiquité tardive: l'exemple de la Johannide de Corippe', *Images romaines*, Études de littérature ancienne, IX (1998), pp.161–173; E. Kern, '*Non ignota cano*: histoire et mémoire dans 'la dernière épopée Romaine', la *Johannide* de Corippe', *Schedæ*, fasc.1 (2007), pp.97–106.

[26] A. Dain, 'Les stratégistes byzantins', Collège de France, *Centre de recherche d'histoire et civilisation de Byzance, Travaux et Mémoires*, 2, (1967), pp.317–392. *Id*., 'Urbicius ou Maurice', *REB*, 26 (1968), pp.123–136.

details and sets a sound tactical overview of the Empire's numerous enemies. But to a larger extent this is a book of proposals mixed with contemporary facts, written in the same manner as the *Maréchal* de Saxe's *Mes Réveries* of the eighteenth century. Other sources are mixed Byzantine and Oriental Christian historians most of whom lived after events they were reporting. The Latin historians from the Western Germanic Kingdoms were, of course, focused on their own ethnic group, and give poor information on the Byzantine Army. Jordanes was historian of the Goths and himself from a Gothic origin but was writing in Byzantium.[27] Only later Arabic sources show the other side of the hill but most were regrettably fading into epics.[28] Other sources – such as inscriptions, contracts and inventories on *papyri*, laws, ruins and archaeological artefacts – are dry and sketchy. but they furnish unique details that fit into the grand narrative of history.

It is time to march along with Romano-Byzantine soldiers, but before, let's pay tribute to the Emperor.

---

27 W. A. Goffart, *The Narrators of barbarian History AD 550–800. Jordanes, Gregory of Tours, Bede and Paul the Deacon* (Princeton NJ: Princeton University Press, 1988).

28 T. Khalidi, *Arabic historical though in the Classical* Period, Cambridge Studies in Islamic Civilisation (Cambridge, Cambridge University Press, 2004) pp.62–64; R. Paret, 'The Legendary Futūḥ Litterature' in F. M. Donner, *The Expansion of the Early Islamic State*, The Formation of the Classical Islamic World (London: Routledge, 2007), pp.163–176.

1

The Emperor as Commander of the Armies

> [Justinian I] never showed any sign of anger or wrath towards those who had offended him, but it was with a placid face, without batting an eyelid, and in a gentle voice that he ordered the massacre of thousands of completely innocent people, the destruction of cities, and the confiscation of all property for the public treasury.
>
> Procopius, *Anecdota*, XIII, 2.

As commander-in-chief, the Emperor had to rule over and defend territories spanning vast distances. Situation reports and orders took days or even weeks to arrive. He was therefore informed late, and his instructions were likely to be out of step with the evolving situation. Although he was the head of the army and was martially depicted on coins with cuirass and helmet, the Emperor delegated actual military action to skilful, or not, generals. Extremely few Emperors risked their lives on the battlefield, but the salvation of the Empire always depended on their army. Sixth-century or seventh-century Greek sources did not term the Emperor as *Imperator*, *Augustus* or *Caesar*, but as a *Basileus* or *Autokratôr* (King or Autocrat). In the same way, his soldiers did not defend a so-called Empire but *ta Rhômaiôn pragmata* (the [public] affairs of the Romans).[1] If you keep that in mind, the early Byzantine way of thinking will be better understood.

---

1 Βασιλεύς. Αὐτοκράτωρ is often found in official texts. Procopius, *BV*, IV, 16, 13, (τά Ῥωμαίων πυράματα).

Zeno, the Isaurian *Generalissimo* who Took the Purple and Saved the Eastern Roman Empire

The first Emperor in the Romano-Byzantine tradition was Zeno the Isaurian, ruling from 474 to 491. Originating from Isauria, an unsettled, semi-Barbaric province in the south of Asia Minor, his real name was Tarasis or Tarasicodissa, which was considered unsuitable for a political career. Adept at arms and professional soldier Zeno made his mark thanks to the Isaurian clan from the Imperial Guard and became the son-in-law of Emperor Leo I. He evidently also had a talent for palace intrigue, as demonstrated by the Greek name he adopted and his fortunate marriage. He soon became head of the armies, with the bombastic title of *Magister Militum Praesentalis* (Master of the Soldiers Present – on Emperor's side), a *generalissimo*. Following his victory over the Huns in 466, he ushered in a rare decade of peace.

During 474, he became co-Emperor with his son, Leo II, who was aged only four but who did not survive an illness the following year. Afterwards, Zeno found himself sole Emperor with no real dynastic legitimacy, which earned him the enmity of the aristocratic families of the East and the short-lived usurpation of the *generalissimo* Basiliscos. This insurgency was accompanied by the massacre of Isaurians in Byzantium and gained support from Theodoric Strabo, leader of the Ostrogoths settled as *foederati* in Thrace (475–476). Exiled for some time to his own lands, Zeno was even besieged in the town of Sbidē by two Isaurian Masters of the Soldiers, Illus the Patrician and Trocundes, both sent by the usurper Basiliscos. Longinus, Zeno's brother, was captured. However, Zeno managed to turn the situation around by bribing Illus and Trocundes, winning them over to his cause, and he was now able to march on Constantinople with a large force of Isaurians. In his way, at Nicaea in Bithynia, stood the field Army of the East commanded by the usurper's nephew, Armatus in Latin or Harmatios in Greek. But once again Zeno's secret weapon was negotiation and bribery. He sent Illus and Trocundes to Armatus, promising him the lifetime title of Master of the Two Militias, or supreme *generalissimo*, and that of *Caesar* for his son. Armatus shamelessly betrayed his uncle and made a diversion to avoid Zeno's Isaurian troops. In August 476, Zeno laid siege to Constantinople. The Senate and the population rallied behind him because of their hatred for Basiliscos' Monophysist heresy as well as his rapacious fiscal policy. Once Basiliscos had been eliminated, Zeno simply got rid of Armatus, of course.[2]

---

2   Malchus, *Fragm.*, 7 and 8. John of Antioch, *Fragm.*, 210; Theophanes Confessor, *Chrgr.*, AM 5967, 121; Anonymus Valesianus, *Exc.*, IX, 42–44; Evagrius Scholasticus, *HE*, III, 7; John Malalas, *Chrgr.*, XV, 5–8; S. Williams & G. Friell, *The Rome That Did Not fall: The Survival of the East in the Fifth Century* (London: Routledge, 1999), pp.183–184.

THE EMPEROR AS COMMANDER OF THE ARMIES

Zeno's main contribution to the survival of the Eastern Roman Empire was his gentle ousting of the Ostrogothic *foederati*. In 478, when the two rival branches of the Ostrogoths opportunistically offered him their services, the Senate of Byzantium warned Zeno that the treasury did not have the money to pay them and was already struggling to supply the regular soldiers.[3] At first, Zeno tried to push Theodoric the Amal, who came from Pannonia, against Theodoric Strabo in Thrace, but the two Ostrogothic chiefs were not so stupid and soon reconciled. Zeno then assembled the regular army, much to the satisfaction of the soldiers, who were still jealous of these barbarian *foederati*. Against all odds, no major battle occurred. His 'natural cowardice', according to Malchus, led Zeno to send the army back to their winter quarters to their great displeasure. He promised Theodoric Strabo the well-paid rank of Count of *Scholarii*, commander of the two *Scholae Palatinae* elite units which were the backbone of the Imperial Guard. He even appointed him to one of the two posts of Master of the Soldiers Present, and offering to settle the arrears pay for his 13,000 men. But he failed to keep his word because he had no money.

On the other hand, Zeno left nothing for Theodoric the Amal who had no choice but to plunder Thrace for food. The negotiations led to a series of reciprocal betrayals, and prompted the Ostrogoths to plunder Stobi, Macedonia's main city, and to occupy Epidamnos, formerly the Roman Dyrrachium,.[4] From 478 to 481, the Balkans were ravaged by both Ostrogothic forces while the regular army could only defend certain fortified towns. It attempted, unsuccessfully, to ambush Theodoric Strabo who supported a new usurper named Marcian, the son of the Western Emperor Anthemius, in 479. In fact, these undesirable Ostrogothic migrants did not want to overthrow Roman rule, but rather wanted simply to receive regular pay as mercenaries; they had families to feed and a military reputation to sustain. The next year, Theodoric Strabo even came to the walls of Constantinople but without any result. Soon afterwards the Bulgars led a proxy war against him at the request of Emperor Zeno. Finally, Theodoric Strabo was assassinated by a javelin near Philippi in 481. *Qui fecit cui prodest*, but sources do not incriminat Zeno. Theodoric the Amal then became the sole King of all the Ostrogoths then assembled in Thrace, after which he came to terms with Zeno. Money must had been found somewhere!

While his Isaurian origins had initially made Zeno unsympathetic in the eyes of Constantinople's aristocracy and populace, now his interventions in the religious sphere made him downright unpopular. Nevertheless, he had the laudable intention of putting an end to the public unrest caused by the dispute of the monophysites opposed to the supporters of the dual nature of Christ, which was reaffirmed by the Council of Chalcedon. In 482, Zeno proposed an edict of reconciliation, known as the Henotic Act, or

---

3 Malchus, *Fragm.*, 15.
4 Malchus, *Fragm.*, 18–20.

Henotikon, which avoided specifying the nature of Christ – he succeeded only in winning the enmity of both camps. Supporters of the dual nature of Christ utterly rejected the text. In 484, religious opposition led to civil war and to a new usurpation, taking us out of late antiquity and into more of the cultural and mental universe of the Byzantine middle ages. The Chalcedonians brought to power Leontius, an Isaurian fellow like Zeno, supported by his compatriot Illus, Master of the Soldiers to the East, who changed sides again. The usurper was also supported by the prayers of the Patriarchs of Alexandria and Antioch, and by Verina, the former Empress. Leontius even had the spiritual support of Pope Felix III from Rome, who was hostile to the Henotic Act and who issued an anathema against Acacius, the Patriarch of Constantinople, marking the beginning of the so-called Acacian schism, which lasted until 518.

Zeno was not beaten; to deal with this new rebellion he first consolidated his position to the very east of Anatolia and, *c.* 485, he arranged for a close relative's daughter to marry the Iberian (today Georgian) King Vakhtang I Gorgasali. Zeno eventually met him to conclude an alliance and restored the Imperial borders in Lazica, 'the land between the River Egrisi [current Rioni] and the Klisura [border from Saberdzneti to Sakartvelo]'. Zeno sent his brother Longinus to build a fortress among the restless Tzani, or Zans, whose territory (now in north-eastern coastal Turkey) was contiguous to Lazica, Persarmenia and Roman Armenia. By doing so Zeno secured an alliance with the Iberian Kingdom which provided a buffer zone between Imperial-controlled Lazica and Persian territory. He demonstated that *he* was the real Emperor and trapped Leontius from the east. He also replaced the unreliable Illus with a popular general, John the Scythian, rallying to his cause most of the Eastern Army troops. Zeno's last military support surprisingly came from the capricious Theodoric the Amal and his *foederati*.

Finally defeated, Leontius, Illus and Verina took refuge in the fortress of Papirios on the Black Sea, where the former Empress died shortly afterwards, and where her accomplices held out until 488 before being captured and executed.[5] Thereafter, Theodoric the Amal was no longer a help but a financial burden. The same year, or in 489, Zeno commissioned Theodoric to eliminate the barbarian warlord Odoacer who had established himself as King in Italy and had seized Dalmatia. Thus, Zeno found out a subtle way of shifting the threat to the ex-Western Roman Empire without having to pay more. This idea made Zeno the saviour of the Eastern Roman Empire. According to what is known about Theodoric the Amal, who would become 'the Great', he was certainly not the Zeno's dupe but he could not resist the opportunity to make himself King of Italy, a fate preferable to that of an unpaid mercenary.

---

5   Procopius, *Aed.,* III, 6, 23 (Longinus' fortress); G. Greatrex, *Rome and Persia at War, 502–532* (Cambridge: Francis Cairns, 2006), p.128.

THE EMPEROR AS COMMANDER OF THE ARMIES

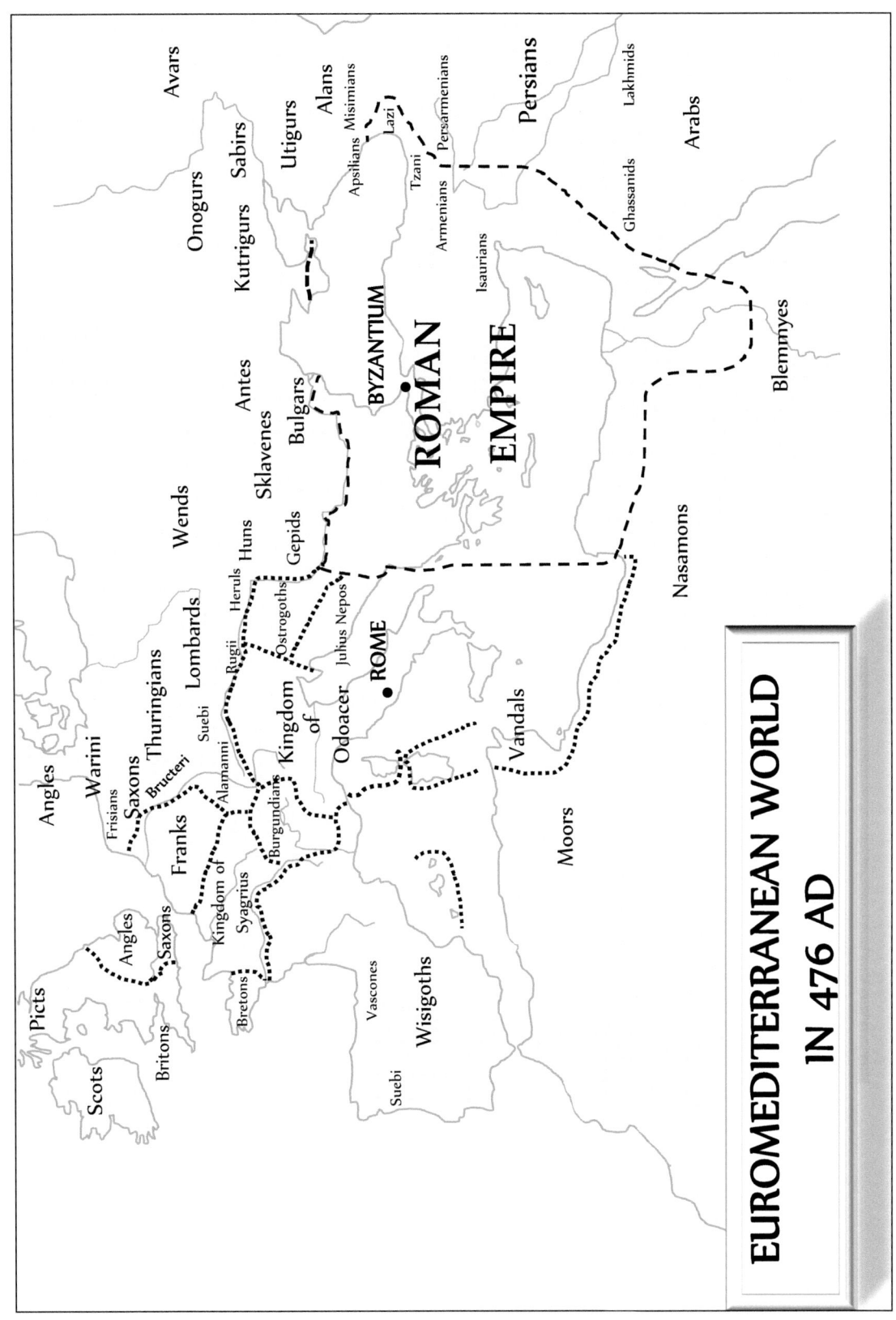

Around 489, in a last-ditch attempt to both please the monophysites and the Chalcedonians Zeno persecuted the Nestorian heresy by closing down their school in Edessa and forcing its last adherents to flee to the Persians.[6]

Zeno died of dysentery or epilepsy on 9 April 491, without a male heir. His brother Longinus, disliked by Constantinople's senators and high-ranking officials, was unable to win any votes, and thus ended the clan of the Isaurians.

The Illyrian Clan Takes Power

The Illyrian clan now imposed his own candidates, from Anastasius I to Justinian I. Their home region was Illyricum, a land laying in northern Greece between the Adriatic Sea and today's Bulgaria. In the absence of a legitimate successor to the throne the choice was submitted to Aelia Ariadne, widow of Zeno and eldest daughter of Leo I. It was proceeded to do so on the wise proposal of the eunuch Urbicius, *Praepositus Sacri Cubiculi* (Attendant to the Sacred Bedchamber), chamberlain by title but a sort of general secretary. Ariadne's choice was not a military man but an apparently unglamorous senior civil servant in his sixties. Despite his age, Anastasius I had a longer reign than his predecessors, ruling from 491 to 518. Born in Dyrrachium, his natural language was Latin, but few details are known about his family.[7] Before ascending to the throne, he simply held the rank of *decurion* of the silentiaries, whose task was primarily to keep silent the people in the Emperor's presence. Sources described him as tall, bald, intelligent, calm and generous.[8] He was a Monophysite, and therefore appeared as an abominable heretic to many, since Byzantium's citizens generally held to the dual nature of Christ, backed by the Council of Chalcedon and by the Pope. The Patriarch of Byzantium therefore opposed his accession and asked him to uphold the decisions of the Council of Chalcedon, which Anastasius apparently accepted. To secure his quite unstable new position, Anastasius married his benefactress Ariadne a month after his coronation.

His second problem was to protect himself from the wrath of the Isaurians.[9] The Isaurian military clan became irritated at losing power and at the exile of Longinus the late Emperor Zeno's brother, in Thebaid. Longinus had even to take vows. Consequently, Isaurian soldiers caused some unrest at the Byzantium hippodrome. But when Anastasius I expelled

---

6   A. Cameron, B. Ward-Perkins, M. Whitby (eds), *Late Antiquity: Empire and Successors, AD 425–600*, The Cambridge Ancient History, 14 (Cambridge: Cambridge University Press, 2008), pp.51–52.

7   Procopius of Gaza, *Panegyric of the Emperor. Anastasius I*, PG, 87, 1865, col. 2796–2797; Evagrius Scholasticus, *HE*, III, 29.

8   A. H. M. Jones, J. R. Martindale, J. Morris, *PLRE*, 2 (1980), pp.79–80.

9   Ph. Richardot, *La fin de l'Armée Romaine 284–476, 3e édition revue et augmentée avec une traduction de la Notitia Dignitatum* (Paris: Economica, 2005), p.218.

all the Isaurians from the capital, civil war broke out. In 492, an Isaurian army marched on Byzantium but was defeated at Kotyaion by John Gibbo 'the Hunchback' and John the Scythian. The rebels continued to fight bitterly in their bare mountains until 498, when John Gibbo captured their last leaders, Longinus of Selinus (not to be confunded with Longinus the Zeno's brother) and Indes, who were beheaded after being exhibited at Anastasius' triumph. But it was not enough to gain popularity. Mainly for religious reasons, Anastasius I was disliked in Constantinople and Antioch, where uprisings took place and were bloodily put down. To calm the growing popular discontent, in 498 Anastasius I abolished the tax known as *collatio lustralis*, in Greek *chrysargyron*. He also remitted taxes in regions affected by invasions or disasters. However, like all his predecessors and successors, he had to meet the costs of war. He also proclaimed several military edicts. The first was aimed at combating fraud and known as the Military Decree from Perge in Pamphylia. The second reformed supplies in Cyrenaica or Libya Pentapolis, an edict of which three incomplete copies can be found in Ptolemais, Taucheira-Tocra and Apollonia-Sôsouza. The last edict concerned the Near East specifying the dukes' pay and the limits of their administration, then setting the timetable for the payment of troops by officers known as *erogatores*. Four copies of this edict survive today, at Bosra and Imtan in Syria, at Qasr al-Hallabat in Jordan and at Jerusalem.[10]

Since the 490s, the Great Moravia south of the Danube was the western boundary of the Empire, with the Ostrogoths, now masters of Italy and Dalmatia, trying to cross it. Additionally, after Zeno's death, the Bulgars were increasingly no longer mercenaries or *foederati* but unwelcome raiders. In 493 and 499 they defeated and killed two Masters of the Soldiers to the Thraces, Julian and Aristus. But in 505, the Bulgars became *foederati* again. They and the Master of the Soldiers to Illyricum Sabinian the Younger were defeated by the Ostrogothic Count Pitzia and the Gepid Mundo at Horreum Margi (now Ćuprija in Serbia). This city, which defended the Great Moravia, then known as the Margus, remained in Imperial hands. In 510 Anastasius I recognised to Theodoric the Amal, now called 'the Great' since he was King of Italy, the possession of Sirmium (present-day Sremska Mitrovica in Serbia) an important Pannonian city still inhabited by so-called Romans. Two years later, Anastasius I allowed the Heruls to settle 50km east of Sirmium at Singidunum. Anastasius I's intention was to

---

10   F. Chamoux, 'Une nouvelle copie de l'édit d'Anastasius Ier sur la Cyrénaïque', *Comptes rendus des séances de l'Académie des Inscriptions et Belles-Lettres*, 99-3, 1955, pp.333–334 (fragment found at Apollonia, which completes the one found at Ptolemais in 1825); F. Onur, 'The Anastasian Military Decree from Perge in Pamphylia: Revised 2nd Edition', *Gephyra*, 14 (2017), pp.133–212; I. Arce, D. Feissel, Th. M. Weber-Karyotaki, 'The Anastasius Edict Project: A Preliminary Report. Part 1 – The Epigraphic Evidence' in C. Sebastian Sommer & S. Matešic (eds), *Limes*, XXIII, Sonderband 4 / II, *Proceedings of the 23rd International Congress of Roman Frontier Studies, Ingolstadt, (2015), Akten des 23. Internationalen Limeskongresses in Ingolstadt 2015* (Mainz: Nünnerich-Asmus Verlag, 2018), pp.673–681.

create a buffer zone against the Ostrogoths, but he soon had to take action against the Heruls who were raiding the Empire's border area.[11] He also took advantage of a temporary respite to build a chain of fortifications along the Danube and in Thrace. Following the failure of the Illyrian Army to cope with the unreliable Bulgars and the indomitable Ostrogoths, Anastasius I was probably the one who strengthened the cavalry as it was later seen in action under Justinian I.

Anastasius I resolutely pushed the Persians into war. In 502, he refused to lend money to Kavadh I previously ruined by a civil war. To take revenge the angry Persian King invaded the Iberian Kingdom, killed Vakhtang I Gorgasali, seized Theodosiopolis of Armenia and Martyropolis (current Silvan in Kurdish Eastern Turkey). In 505, understanding the war was going badly for Byzantium, the Tzani or Zans raided Imperial territory in Lazica. Despite all of these setbacks, Anastasius I found in Transcausus an unexpected ally in Ambazuces, King of the Sabir Huns who invaded the Persian northern lands, maybe at his own request but not for free. Ambazuces offered him no less than the Caspian Gates, also known as the Gates of Alexander – the mountain passes between Parthia and Media called today as the Dariel Pass. However, Anastasius declined the deal; he had no regular troops to occupy this place, and he probably understood it was a 'Pass too far'. Moreover, the Caspian Gates were the northern axis of invasion to Persia and were of little strategic interest for a western power.

According to Procopius, Anastasius I mustered the strongest army ever against the Persians and sent it to the Mesopotamian border. At the request of his generals, he had a fortress built there in the village of Dara, or Daras, a name that the current village has retaken after having been called for a long time Oğuz. Probably as a provocation, he named it from his own name Anastasiopolis.[12] It was then a strategic position facing the Persian border fortress of Nisibis, (current Nusaybin in Turkey) lost by the Romans in 363. To fully understand this gesture, it is worthwhile to remember that until then the rival outposts were 200km apart: Amida (the current Diyarbakir in south-east Turkey) and Nisibis. Thus, Anastasius I moved his new outpost 120km eastwards, to a location just five hours or 18km distant from Nisibis on the Persian border. This move was historically similar to the Cuba crisis in 1962, when the Soviets brought their missiles at the US gates! The conflict came to a favourable end for the Romano-Byzanties in 506, and afterwards a period of armed peace lasted until 525.

No doubt to strengthen his position in the eastern provinces, Anastasius I introduced a Monophysite liturgy from 511, but which aroused strong opposition in Byzantium and the Balkans. In November 512, fires were started around the city and statues of the Emperor were smashed. The angry population offered the purple to Flavius Areobindus Dagalaifus, a former Consul and Master of the Soldiers who was half-barbarian. He

---

11 Marcellinus Comes, *Chr.*, a. 512.
12 (Pseudo-)Zachariah Rhetor, *HE*, VII, 6.

THE EMPEROR AS COMMANDER OF THE ARMIES

prudently declined. Anastasius I restored public order in a move as bold as it was unexpected: he went to the hippodrome, the official venue for both sporting and political events, and bluntly offered to abdicate. The rebels calmed down for fear of the chaos. From 513 to 518, the *foederati* and the Balkan Army mutinied under the command of Count Vitalian the Thracian.[13] These mutineers, reinforced by peasants who were hostile to Anastasius I's religious reforms, held the northern parts of the Empire: Thrace, Scythia and Moesia as far as Odyssus (now Varna in Bulgaria).[14] After Marinus the Syrian, the Praetorian Prefect, won a naval battle at the gates of Byzantium in Bytharia, Vitalian was repulsed but still posed a threat. Anastasius I celebrated this victory with a religious procession and thanksgiving in St Michael's church, maybe prematurely because that same year, the Sabir Huns devastated the provinces of Asia Minor as far as Cappadocia. The only help the Emperor could provide was to compensate the victims and rebuild fortifications in major cities.[15] In 517, with most of the Imperial forces near Byzantium tied up in the civil war, the Sklavenes were free to plunder a wide area stretching from Macedonia and Thessaly to Thermopylae and Epirus, between the Aegean Sea and the Adriatic Sea. Anastasius I gave the prefect of Illyricum 1,000 pounds of gold to pay the ransoms. However, this was not enough, and the Sklavenes burnt the prisoners alive in their houses or executed them in front of the cities.[16]

In the same year, Anastasius I's last strategic decision was to build the Long Walls to protect Byzantium's outer suburbs. His death at the age of 90 put an end to the conflict with Vitalian the Thracian. Anastasius bequeathed a public treasury with full coffers of 320,000 pounds of gold after having earned a strong reputation for avarice.[17] The succession opened a crisis that was quickly resolved among the palace troops – the era of the Praetorian Guard seemed to returned. Hypatius, one of the three militarily active nephews of Anastasius I, was proclaimed Emperor by the *Scholarii*, Palace guards from the *Scholae Palatinae*. But he was almost killed by their rivals, the *Excubitores*, who wanted to bring to power Justin, their own Count. Hypatius, saved at the last minute by Justinian, Justin's nephew, preferred to concede. Adding to the confusion, the eunuch Amantius, *Praepositus Sacri Cubiculi*, had entrusted Justin with a sum of money to persuade the

---

13 S. Williams & G. Friell, *The Rome That Did Not Fall*, pp.114-116; C. Morrisson (ed.), *Le monde Byzantin. L'Empire Romain d'Orient (330-641)* (Paris: Nouvelle Clio, 2006), p.26.
14 John Malalas, *Chrgr.*, XVI, 16.
15 Marcellinus Comes, *Chr.*, a. 515; John Malalas, *Chrgr.*, XVI, 17.
16 Marcellinus Comes, *Chr.*, a. 517 (Getae for Sklavenes); Theophylact Simocatta, *HU*, III, 4, 7 (*'As for the Getaen that is to say the herds of Skavenes'*).
17 *Chr. Paschale*, a. 517 *pro incerte* (walls qualified as 'Anastasian'). Procopius, *Anecdota*, XIX, 5 and 7. John the Lydian, *De Magistratibus*, III, 52, 5. A. Cameron et al (eds), *Late Antiquity: Empire and Successors*, p.55.

Excubitores to proclaim his nephew, Theocritus, as Emperor. But Justin wisely used the money to his advantage, and got rid of the troublemakers.[18]

Justin I (Emperor, 518–527) was an Illyrian whose family emigrated to Thrace. His story recalled that of Emperor Maximinus Thrax three centuries before. A pig and ox farmer of low extraction, Justin embarked on a military career. Of high stature, he became *Excubitor* or Imperial Guard, rose through the ranks as *tagmatarchias* (*tagmatarch*, a squadron or regiment commander), then *komēs* (count) a few years before attaining the Imperial dignity.[19] As a military man, he was not content with just parading around the palace gates and slavishly lurking awaiting a promotion. During a battle he received an arrow in the stomach which caused to him a permanent ulcer. Procopius said he was old and illiterate when he took power, and his adviser Proclos even signed for him with a stamp dipped in ink bearing the Latin inscription for 'we have read.'[20] Malalas described him as: 'Medium height, broad chest, short, completely grey hair, strong nose, ruddy complexion, presence. He was a war veteran but illiterate.'[21] Not lacking political skill, Justin executed a number of palace plotters who were planning to overthrow him and concluded a peace with Vitalian the Thracian by promoting him to the rank of *generalissimo*. Two years later, he raised him to the rank of Consul and then, after a race in the hippodrome, had him assassinated.[22] In 524–525, King Tzath I of Lazica and King Gourgen of Iberia rebelled against the unfair Persian rule. Emperor Justin I saw the golden opportunity of a proxy war against the hereditary Persian enemy and paid Hunnic Hehptalites mercenaries from North Caucasus to reinforce the rebels. But the idea was not good as Persian intelligence probably found out about the Romano-Byzantine undercover activities. Tensions with the Persians resumed in 525 with skirmishes in Armenia and a threatened invasion of Mesopotamia.[23] Justin I avoided conflict with the Persians, informing the Persian King Kavadh I of the duplicity of Zilgibi, the leader of the Huns Hehptalites, who received money from both parties. As a mark of gratitude and as a mark of good will, Kavadh abandoned his project of military campaign.[24] This action, like earlier ones, showed that Justin relied on a good intelligence service and preferred indirect strategy to open struggle. Considering the economy of forces used by him, he was undoubtedly the most skilful of the Emperors of the sixth century. He bequeathed his nephew chests full of gold and an efficient army.

---

18 Evagrius Scholasticus, IV, 1 and Constantine VII Porphyrogenitus, *De Ceremoniis*, I, 93, (seizure of power). Procopius, *BV*, I, 11, 1 (elimination of Anastasius I's family members).
19 Procopius, *Anecdota*, VI, 10.
20 Procopius, *Anecdota*, VI, 11 (elderly, illiterate); 13–15 (Proclos, stamp).
21 John Malalas, *Chrgr.*, XVII, 1 (description); 23 (wound).
22 John Malalas, *Chrgr.*, XVII, 6 (*magister militum praesentalis*), 8 (consulate and assassination).
23 G. Greatrex, *Rome and Persia at War*, pp.139–149.
24 John Malalas, *Chrgr.*, XVII, 10.

THE EMPEROR AS COMMANDER OF THE ARMIES

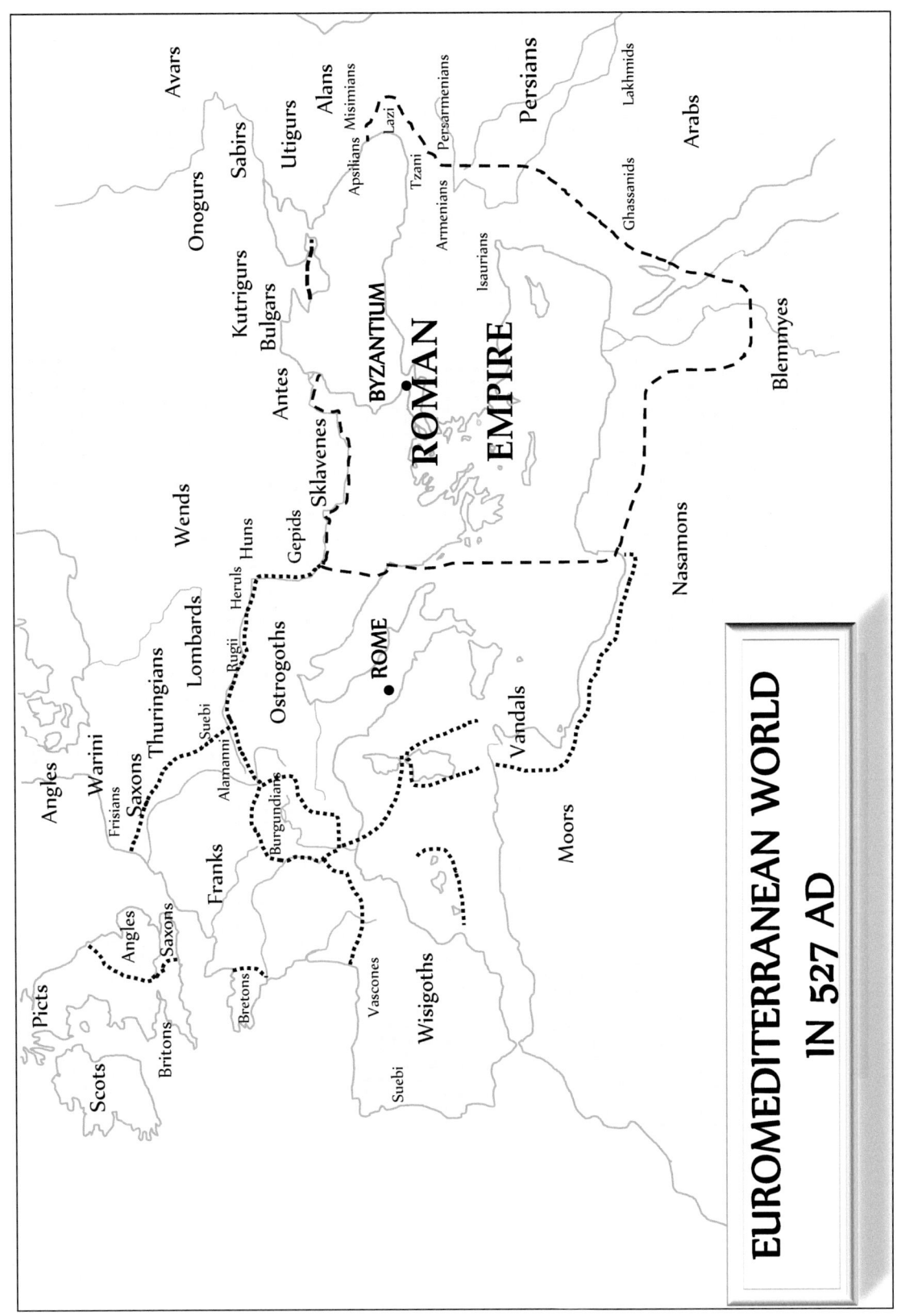

Justinian I, great Emperor or megalomaniac?

> In the name of Our Lord Jesus Christ, Emperor Caesar Flavius Justinian, Alamanic, Gothic, Frankish, Germanic, Antic (Antes, Slavic people), Alanic, Vandal, African, pious, fortunate and the most renowned Conqueror and Triumphant since Augustus.[25]

As this pompous half-bogus praise relating to victories over countless peoples proclaimed, Justinian I (ruled 527 to 565) was the most famous Byzantine Emperor. Flavius Petrus Sabbatius Justinianus to give him his full Latin name was the nephew and adopted son of Justin I. Born in Tauresium (also called Bederiana), a small Illyrian town in today's Macedonia, he was 45 years old when he took the purple. He had previously held the title of *Caesar* for just four months but had always exercised political influence during his uncle's reign. 'He was small in appearance, with a broad torso, strong nose, fair complexion, short hair, round face, handsome, with hair pulled back, red, greying hair and beard.'[26] The magnificent mosaic from Basilica of San Vitale in Ravenna pictures a very different, if stereotypical, portrait of him as glabrous with brown hair. Procopius depicted him as a suspicious, thieving tyrant, married to an authoritarian and unfaithful woman who was the daughter of a bear-showman and sold her charms in her teens: the infamous and glorious Empress Theodora. While history textbooks still extol the Latin Code of Justinian, Procopius turned its promoter into the disorganiser of Roman law, reigning in defiance of laws and magistrates.[27] Between 535 and 541, with the help of John of Cappadocia who acted as his prime minister, Justinian I tried to reduce the senior provincial administration to save money and limit corruption. This reduction in size of bureaucracy made him unpopular with Procopius, Agathias and John Lydus, whose career prospects may have suffered as a result. Justinian tried to abolish the dioceses system by giving more power to the provincial governors, but finally he returned to it after he dismissed John of Cappadocia.[28] In 541, he put an end to the traditional annuality of consulship, thereby destroying a part of Roman and Ancient world. The new court etiquette revealed the monarch's megalomania and it easy to see why those who had to bend felt resentful. In public ceremonies, while the senators bowed and the others knelt, all had to lie down to kiss the Imperial feet of Justinian and Theodora. Perhaps Justinian only wanted to humiliate the arrogance of some officials, for Procopius noted later, in quite a contradiction, that Justinian was informal, affable and approachable.

---

25   *CJ*, I, 27 (address to Archelaüs, Praetorian Prefect of Africa, 13 April, 534).
26   John Malalas, *Chrgr.*, XVIII, 2.
27   Procopius, *Anecdota*, XIV, XXI and XXVIII.
28   A. H. M. Jones, *The Later Roman Empire, 284–602. A Social, Economic and Administrative Survey*, Oxford, Blackwell, vol. 1 (1964), p.376.

We definitively cannot believe him when he said of the Emperor: 'He was extraordinarily foolish and looked quite like a stupid donkey ready to follow.'[29] The great policy of reconquest and the splendour of Hagia Sophia in Byzantium were not the deeds of a mad man.[30]

Although not devoid of military experience, Justinian I's soldiering career was limited to the Imperial palace. He first became a guard in the *Scholarii*, or *Scholarioi*, in 518, then served as a *candidatus*, a member of this ultra-select corps, and in 519 was promoted to count (of *domestici*?) and head of aides-de-camp. He was appointed the following year to Master of the Soldiers Present, that is *generalissimo*.[31] It was a great help to him to be the Emperor's nephew. As Emperor, Justinian I has been, bluntly speaking, no more than a conqueror by proxy and an order-giver sitting on his gilded throne in Byzantium. His role was to find the right general and assign him a mission, without interfering in the conduct of the campaign. Given the distance of 2,200 kilometres between Rome or Carthage and Byzantium, this was the wisest way to command. Of course, Justinian I had maps and itineraries at his disposal to define a Mediterranean-wide strategy. Unlike the Philosopher-Emperor, Marcus Aurelius three centuries before him, Justinian never exposed his life to war. He relied on Belisarius and others to lead campaigns. He sent reinforcements, recalled and replaced generals who were in trouble, but did not provide them with the financial resources necessary to support the war, as Procopius noted regarding the second campaign in Italy.[32] Later Napoleon was no different when he launched his armies into Spain with years behind in pay. But like Napoleon, Justinian believed in order and imposed on Belisarius the model of military organisation for the newly 'Roman' Africa. He also had forts built in Balkan area and in Mesopotamia. Procopius even wrote a book on this matter. Justinian was impervious to bad news in war and persisted in his intent to achieve his goals – his military genius was stubbornness.

Justinian I's approach to war was to take one step at a time. War with Persians had started again in 526 and the following year he inherited it along with the Imperial Purple. This conflict is known as the Iberian War – Iberia equating to present-day Georgia. It was both the battlefield and the prize. This new Persian war diverted the elite troops stationed around Byzantium, then weakened the defences of the Moesia and Scythia regions near the Eastern Danube. The Huns took this opportunity to devastate these regions and inflict two crushing defeats. The first battle resulted in the death of Justin, Master of the Soldiers to Moesia, although his colleague Baduarius managed to escape. Then, in a second disastrous fight, Constantiolus, the new Master of the Soldiers to Moesia, was captured alongside his colleague Askum the Hun, commanding the troops in Illyricum. The former was

---

29   Procopius, *Anecdota*, VIII, 3.
30   A. Cameron, *The Mediterranean World*, pp.104–127 (Justinian and reconquest).
31   A. H. M. Jones, J. R. Martindale, J. Morris, *PLRE*, 2 (1980), p.646 (on Justinian).
32   Procopius, *Anecdota*, V, 4.

returned under ransom but the latter was not.[33] Nevertheless, concentrating his main effort against Persians, Justinian I ended the Iberian War in 532. He had previously suffered two setbacks in attempting to fortify the Mesopotamian border at Thannuris and Mindouos. Then he had gained two major victories – won by Belisarius at Dara and by Sittas at Satala. Afterwards, he received two severe blows when Belisarius was crushed at Callinicum, followed by the dramatic fall of Abgersaton Fort, in Osrhoene. The heroic defence of Martyropolis against the Persians closed this series of actions in a more optimistic way. It was an all-in indecisive and balanced result. Incidentally, hearing of the appalling losses suffered by his troops, Kavadh I suffered a stroke that paralysed his right side, and he died soon after, on 13 September, after having his son crowned.[34] The new King of Kings (the form that the Sassanids used), Khosrow I, thought it was better to conclude with Justinian I what was known as the 'Eternal Peace', in fact a bombastic name for an eight-year armistice. Justinian I agreed to pay a one-off disguised tribute of 110 *centenaria* for the defence of the Caspian Gates, it was presented as a sort of military alliance in order for Justinian to save face. Justinian also agreed to move the headquarters of the Duke of Mesopotamia back from Dara to Constantia.[35] Justinian's only gain was the peace with Persia; it was not a victory, but the Emperor had free his hands to send his army elsewhere.

The following year, Belisarius destroyed the Vandal Kingdom in North Africa – 'Libya' for the Greeks, more or less today's Tunisia. But why did Justinian I start a conquest strategy with a province so far away? Theodora was originally born from Libya and she may have felt concerned about events from there. Moreover, circumstances had been favourable for military intervention since 529, because the Moors had rebelled and had inflicted a series of setbacks on the Vandals, causing Gelimer's usurpation of the crown. All those events were putting an end to the *Pax Vandalica*. Additionally, the coastal and urban populations still fell themselves to be Roman as Latin speakers, which remained true until Muslim conquest.[36] The poet Corippus declared that, from this time onwards, an era of insecurity began, with massacres, fires and rapine unleashed by the Moors. Corippus is grateful to Justinian I for having freed the Libyans (Romans from Libya) from the Moors, but made no negative mention of the Vandals.[37] Their internal difficulties gave to Justinian the appetising possibility of conquering an Africa that had formerly been Rome's breadbasket.

---

33 John Malalas, *Chrgr.*, XVIII, 21.
34 John Malalas, *Chrgr.*, XVIII, 68.
35 G. Greatrex, *Rome and Persia at War*, pp.151–212 (military campaigns); p.213 (Eternal Peace).
36 J. Conant, *Staying Roman. Conquest and Identity in Africa and the Mediterranean, 439–700* (Cambridge: Cambridge University Press, 2012).
37 Corippus, *Joh*, III, 191–194 (terror); 281–285 (gratitude for Justinian); Y. Modéran, *Les Maures et l'Afrique romaine (IVe-VIIe siècle)*, (Rome: PEFR, 2003), p.565.

THE EMPEROR AS COMMANDER OF THE ARMIES

In Byzantium, the crowds were enthusiastic for a military intervention in Africa, although the Praetorian Prefect John of Cappadocia objected, arguing that Byzantium was too far away from Carthage. However, he objected in vain, as a bishop persuaded the Emperor to liberate the Christians from the Arian heresy of the Vandals.[38] This reconquest of Africa almost took on the air of a crusade before its time. It was also a strategic pivot, as the Eastern Roman Empire then looked westwards.

Justinian I enjoyed a geopolitical advantage at the time, the first wave of the great Germanic invasions had stabilised and the western kingdoms were not militarily aggressive towards the Eastern Roman Empire. To support Justinian I's project in Africa, the Ostrogothic Kingdom of Italy provided logistical rest harbours and supplies in Sicily for the invading fleet from Byzantium. But never feed a crocodile.

After some sort of *Blitzkrieg* over Africa and a triumph offered to Belisarius in Byzantium, Justinian I then turned his attention to Ostrogothic Italy, which was probably the main objective of his opportunistic reconquest policy, even though it was actually an ally. He took the decision because by then the Ostrogothic Kingdom has fallen in complete chaos, with the premature death of the young King Athalaric and the subsequent murder of Queen Amalasuntha. It is worthwhile to say that Amalasuntha was killed by Theodahad her cousin, husband and co-ruler. Justinian I used the pretext of defending Ostrogoth dynastic rights against the murderer. He had no idea that he was embarking on long war that would last from 535 to 562, nearly the rest of his life. He formally declared war in April 535.

Insofar as it is his own, the strategic plan of the invasion reveals several qualities: an encircling manoeuvre with a pincer attack on Dalmatia and Sicily, and a letter inviting the Franks to attack the Ostrogothic lands in southern Gaul. In execution of this plan, Mundo, the Master of the Soldiers to Illyricum invaded Dalmatia and took Salona. The Ostrogoths preferred to run away as the walls of the town of Salona were derelict and in no defenceable condition. Nevertheless, Mundo was killed in a skirmish near Salona and the Imperial troops withdrew. The northern pincer attack was thus a failure. The southern pincer attack in Sicily, however, was a success. As two years earlier, Belisarius had already passed through Sicily to attack Vandal Africa, with material assistance from the Ostrogoths, his return to Sicily had been interpreted as simply a return to Byzantium. Once the initial surprise has passed, Belisarius' success was due to the defection of Sinderith, the Ostrogothic military governor in Syracuse, and of his troops. It was a powerful psychological warning to King Theodahad, who became frightened and secretly sent an ambassador to tell Justinian that he was ready to cede Sicily.

In May 535, Theodahad with the Senate of Rome asked Justinian not to attack Italy: 'Thine am I already in love, if thou send none of thy soldiers

---

38 Procopius, *Anecdota*, XII, 30 (Libyan origin of Theodorea); *BV*, III, 6 (crowd); 7–17 (John); 18–19 (bishop).

to lacerate my limbs.'[39] This gesture was interpreted as a sign of weakness by Justinian I. The ongoing conquest of Sicily by Belisarius was a military walkover. Only Panormus (today Palermo) resisted for some time, and Sicily was in Belisarius' hands by late December 535.

Today the year 536 is cited by some historians as the worst year in history to be alive due to climate crisis. Procopius wrote:

> And it came about during this year that a most dread portent took place. For the sun gave forth its light without brightness, like the moon, during the whole year, and it seemed exceedingly like the sun in eclipse, for the beams it shed were not clear nor such as it is accustomed to shed. And from the time when this thing happened men were free neither from war nor pestilence nor any other thing leading to death.[40]

Nevertheless, this probable volcanic winter did not interfere with military operations in Italy which were relentless. No supply problems were mentioned by Procopius, and neither panic nor millenarist crisis amongst populations or soldiers.

Although Belisarius had half as many men as for the invasion of Africa, he was able to land unopposed on the Italian peninsula. On Easter (23 March) 536, luck passed into the hands of Theodahad as a mutiny forced Belisarius to return to Africa and during his absence a second mutiny broke out among the troops abandoned in Sicily. In April, Belisarius managed to restore discipline but the delay gave Theodahad time to send troops to successfully retake Salona and to gather a relief army in Bruttium under the command of Ebrimuth, his son-in-law.[41] In June Belisarius crossed over into Italy and seized the unwalled and undefended Rhegium (today Reggio Calabria), where he was welcomed as a liberator by the inhabitants. This time again, treachery and defection helped the Byzantine cause. Ebrimuth fled to Belisarius, abandoning his own army, and was rewarded by Justinian who made him a Patrician.

A new pincer attack was then launched against Italy. Theodahad was hesitating heading north-eastwards or southwards, and did nothing. In Dalmatia, the Patrician and Count of the Stable Constantianus restored the situation with a large fleet and an army which disembarked near Salona. In the southern arm of the pincer Belisarius took Naples after a 20-day siege in November. The road to Rome was open. Shortly after this, Theodahad's unwillingness to help Naples led to his being assassinated while he was

---

39 Cassiodorus, *Variae*, XI, 13.
40 Procopius, *BV*, IV, 14, 5–6; A. Gibbons, 'Why 536 was the "worst year to be alive"' in *Science Magazine*, 362 (2018), pp.733–734.
41 Jordanes, *Getica*, XL, 308; Procopius, *BG*, V, 5, 5–12 (Palermo); Marcellinus, *Chr.*, a. 536 (Ebrimuth).

THE EMPEROR AS COMMANDER OF THE ARMIES

withdrawing from Rome to Ravenna. Like most of the Italian cities, Rome was occupied without a fight in late December. Bribery rather than the sword was a possible reason for Belisarius's first successes. The other reason was that after the Romano-Byzantine Army's swift conquest of the Vandal Kingdom Belisarius had certainly acquired a reputation of invincibility. So the Ostrogoths were led into inaction and avoided pitched battle. At the very beginning of the Gothic War, their army had not been ready to wage a large-scale war.

Beyond Rome, Empire's resources were insufficient to take the north of Italy, and three years were necessary to send Belisarius forces comparable to the expedition he led against the Vandals.[42] The occupation and pacification of Africa required troops that Belisarius lacked to conquer Italy. It might be said that in some ways Justinian I had crushed Vandals with a club and then beaten the Ostrogoths to death with a stick. After Theodahad's assassination, under the iron rule of Vitiges the Ostrogoths revealed themselves to be a tough nut to crack and were now supported by the Suevi, by the Rugians all settled in Danube area and maybe by some Gepids.[43] The Gothic War proved to be not as easy as that against the Vandals, because the Ostrogoths now relied on a number of fortified cities and good Roman-style administration, moreover central Italy is mountainous countryside, difficult for an army to deal with. In addition, the conquest of Italy was also that of Dalmatia, which was accompanied by restoration of the Northern Illyricum *limes*, in other words a massive distraction of human and financial resources and Justinian had to 'scrape the bottom of the barrel.' With sporadic Moorish unrest and military mutiny, Africa was fast becoming a quagmire, and as a consequence the situation was worsening in Italy.

In 537, the new King Vitiges gained the initiative over the bogged down Romano-Byzantines. He first sent Uligisal with an army into Dalmatia, but who was beaten by Patrician and Count of the Stable Constantianus at the Battle of Scardon. But Uligisal was quickly reinforced by Suevi troops led by Asinarius, and unsuccessfully besieged Constantianus in Salona for some months. To meet Belisarius in central Italy Vitiges mustered a large army including heavily armoured cavalry on armoured horses.[44] He was strong enough to besiege Belisarius in Rome for a year, 537 to 538, but without any result. The real war had begun.

Belisarius's from Sicily to Mediolanum (today Milan) Belisarius's positions were overstretched while Ariminium, modern Rimini was besieged by the Ostrogoths a direct threat to the possible line of communication

---

42 W. Treadgold, *Byzantium and its Army, 284–1081* (Stanford: Stanford University Press, 1995), p.60.
43 A. H. M. Jones, J. R. Martindale, J. Morris, *PLRE*, 3b (1992), pp.1382–1386 (Vitigis).
44 Procopius, *BG*, V, 16, 11 (150,000 strong army of Vitiges with super-heavy cavalry; a highly exaggerated number); 12 (Suevi reinforcements); 13 (Scardon), 14–18 (siege of Salona).

BIRTH OF THE BYZANTINE ARMY 476-641 CE VOLUME 1: STILL LATE ROMAN?

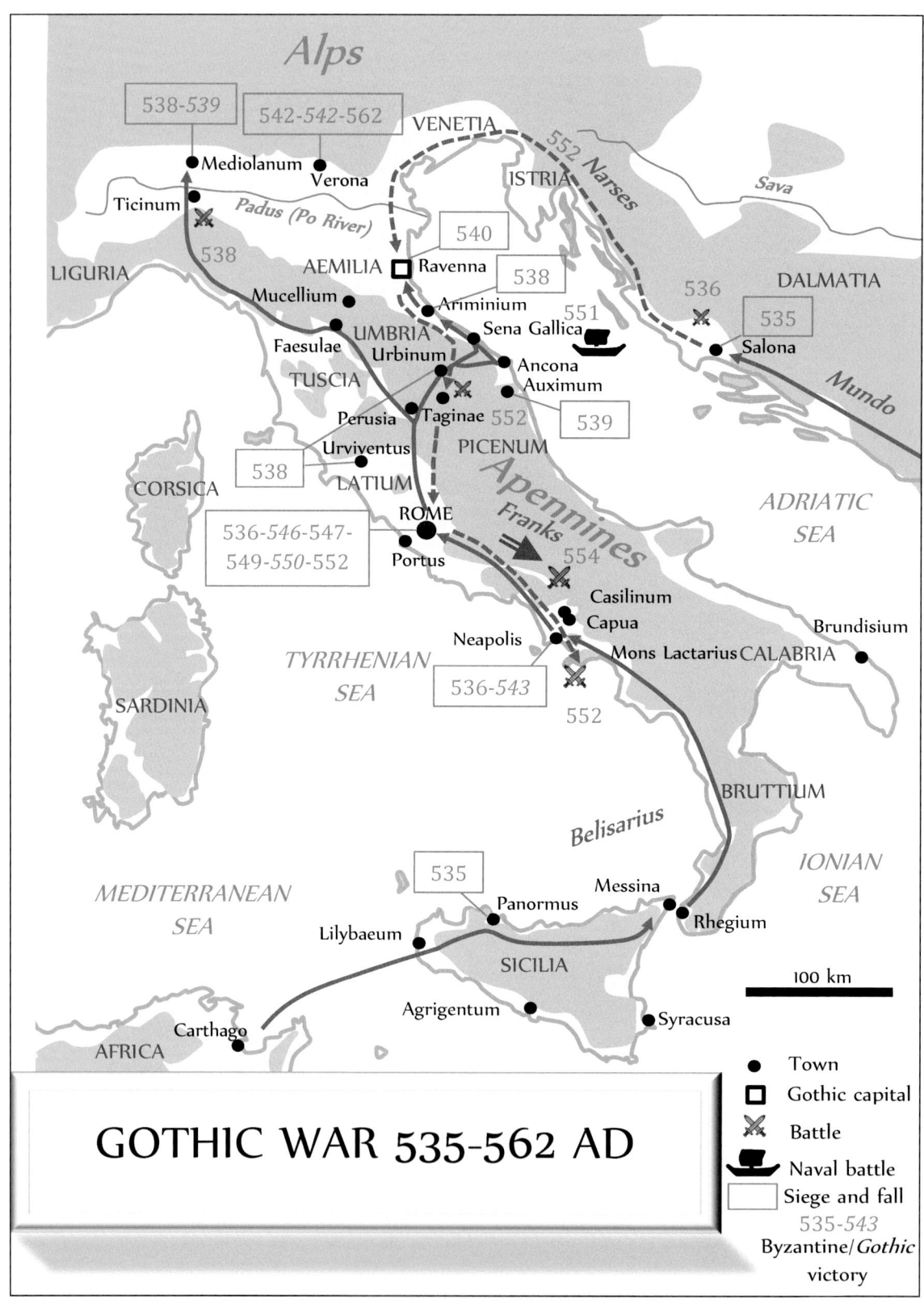

with Illyricum, a line already cut by Uligisal in Dalmatia. Then Belisarius's strategy was focused on controlling the road network in central Italy, especially the Via Flaminia from Rome over the Apennine Mountains up to Ariminium and to Ancona. From Ariminium the Via Popilia led directly to Ravenna, the principal city of the Ostrogothic Kingdom. In other words, Belisarius was set on a defensive posture – never the best position for an aggressor.

To get out of this strategic quagmire, in June 538 Justinian I sent Narses the Eunuch from Ancona with an army to reinforce Belisarius. It was a bad idea because the two men did not get along and the command of the army was divided in two, each selfishly retaining command of their own troops. They nevertheless moved to help Rimini, but soon after that their cooperation blurred, and Belisarius was left on his own when he besieged Urbinum (modern Urbino). In addition, the Frankish King Theudebert I generously paid to be an ally of Justinian I invaded northern Italy, but for only a short time because his men were struck by dysentery. Afterwards, changing his mind, or more probably being bribed by Vitiges, he changed sides. Theudebert I's 10,000 Burgundians sent as expeditionary corps allowed the Ostrogoths to retake Milan, which was reduced to ashes at the start of 539.[45] This war had escalated, and the destruction of Milan was a loud and clear warning to the Italian cities that had joined the Imperial cause.

During this time, Belisarius and Narses the Eunuch had been divided on what to do next: the relief of Milan or the siege of Auximum or Auximus, (today Osimo near the Adriatic coast). Almost eight months and 11,000 men proved necessary for Belisarius to take this hilly fortress that Auximus was. At the same time the city of Faesulae (present-day Fiesole in Tuscany) was successfully besieged by Cyprian and Justin controlling the Via Cassia and the head of the Via Annia that led to Ravenna over the Apennines. Nevertheless, Justinian had to reassert Belisarius' authority by recalling Narses the Eunuch, whose insubordination had caused the loss of Milan. The following year mixed good and bad news. Probably by the spring, Kutrigur Huns devastated the Balkan area from Illyricum to the outskirts of Byzantium just north of the Ionian Gulf. No battle was recorded simply because no field army was available there. The Danubian border was wide open to invasion.[46]

As the Empire's difficulties became evident, in early spring 540 Khosrow I King of the Persians opportunistically broke the quite ill-named 'Eternal Peace'. He was encouraged to do so by an Ostrogothic embassy sent by Vitiges, who recommended a pincer attack against the Empire. Khosrow was confirmed in this by other emissaries from the rebellious Armenians

---

45 According to contemporary sources although this is probably an exaggeration for effect.
46 Procopius, *BP*, II, 4, 1–6.

who promised him their own support plus that of the Lazians.[47] The Persians demolished or bypassed the Romano-Byzantine border fortresses and raided Antioch, the greatest city in the East. Fortunately to Justinian I, some good news came from Italy. After capturing Ravenna, the former capital of both the Western Roman Empire and the Ostrogoths, Belisarius could be urgently recalled to repel the invading Persians. At this occasion, Justinian showed his pettiness by denying him this time the customary triumph, even though he was bringing to Byzantium the defeated King Vitiges, with his wife and his treasury. Procopius explained this as pure jealousy.[48] Undoubtedly an element of fear was also present, as a victorious general in the Roman tradition could be a potential usurper. By contrast, Justinian was a generous victor towards Vitiges, granting him the title of Patrician and estates in Asia, while keeping him in Byzantium where he died two years later. Nevertheless, the war in Italy was not ended, as the Ostrogoths did not give up. Vitiges was soon succeeded by the ephemerous Ildibad then Eraric, both murdered. Quite surprisingly Eraric was a Rugian noble. As he had proposed to recognise Justinian I's suzerainty over Italy, the Ostrogothic nobles who had elected him allowed him to reign for only five months until October 541. It was time for Totila, or Baduila of his real Gothic name, the nephew of Ildebad to take power.[49]

Meanwhile Justinian I showed very poor judgement in his control of reconquered Italy. He sent a greedy *logothete*, a paymaster-general, who plundered the country and angered the soldiers depriving them of the necessary supplies. Additionally, Justinian failed to appoint a theatre commander, but left several general officers in charge who proved incapable of coordinating their efforts much like Napoleon's *maréchals* in Spain.

After Belisarius' departure, the Ostrogoths became active again and in late 541, the besieged city of Verona fell to the Romano-Byzantines by bribery. However, while the Romano-Byzantines were quarrelling over the booty, Totila launched a lightning counter-attack and retook the city. After having reached their maximum advance on the Po plain, the Romano-Byzantines were now withdrawing to central Italy like a shrinking flood.

From then on, bit by bit, Justinian I's strategy derailed. The situation drastically changed and he had to fight on four very different fronts: Italy, Danube, the East plus intermittent unrest in North Africa. He also had to deal with plague, which had begun in Egypt in 541 and struck Byzantium

---

47 Procopius, *BP*, II, 2, 1–12 (Ostrogothic emissaries); 3, 31–56 (Armenian emissaries); *BG*, VI, 22, 17–20 (Ostrogothic emissaries).
48 Procopius, *BG*, VI, 18, 27–28 (letter); 22, 4 (Narses is recalled); VII, 1, 3 (jealousy). On the Armenian name of Narses: it was borne by a brother officer of Aratios, by the eunuch *generalissimo* in Italy and rival of Belisarius, by Narses the Persarmenian who rallied in 530 and was defeated and killed at the Battle of Anglon in 543, by the master of the soldiers who rebelled against Phocas in 602.
49 A. H. M. Jones, J. R. Martindale, J. Morris, *PLRE*, 3b (1992), pp.1328–1332 (Totila/Baduila).

THE EMPEROR AS COMMANDER OF THE ARMIES

the following year.[50] The year 542 was bad for the Romano-Byzantine military in Italy: Totila won two battles against superior forces at Faventia then Mucellium (current Faenza in Emilia and Mugello valley in Tuscany, 30km northeast of Florence). In 543, after stabilising the situation with the Persians, Belisarius was replaced as Master of the Soldiers to the East by a competent former subordinate, Martin, who had fought in Africa and Italy. By this year, when negotiations were due to end the conflict with the Sassanid Persians, Justinian I learned that their army had been hit by an epidemic. Exaggerating the situation to himself and thus misguided, he ordered Martin to invade Persarmenia. Poorly coordinated, the invading Romano-Byzantine Army of the East was split into three corps. One of the corps commanders, Peter of Arzanene attacked a believed to be defenceless territory. Not wanting to miss out on the potential plunder, the rest of the army joined in and marched disorderly along dry mountainous roads to the newly fortified village of Anglon (near today's Dvin in Armenia). Although 30,000-strong, the Romano-Byzantines came up bit by bit against only 4,000 Persians but in full battle array. When the Romano-Byzantine right wing was pushed back, the whole army panicked and ignominiously fled in rout. Weapons were thrown away, horses died of exhaustion in a long desperate flight, and the Persians went on an easy massacre, as well as taking a large number of prisoners. Anglon was the worst Romano-Byzantine defeat of the sixth century and the least well known, a real *damnatio memoriae*. The unfortunate commander-in-chief of this disaster was Martin. Although a veteran, he had hastened to follow his subordinate Peter who had left first early in the day, with the intent of keeping the loot for himself. The terrain was steep and a reconnaissance had reported that the Persians were entrenched, but Martin agreed with his generals to engage in battle because they would have been ashamed to retreat. Only the right wing composed of Heruls fought with some honour although much misfortune, while the rest of the army just watched the scene. Their leader who had defected from the Persians in 530 was Narses Kamsarakan, he was fatally wounded with a javelin to the head and his body was recovered by his brother Isaac. The retreat of the Heruls that he commanded led the entire army to be routed.[51] Total casualties are unknown, but the butcher's bill must have been severe. Afterwards, Martin remained in command of the East, probably because Justinian, influenced by inaccurate intelligence, felt guilty for having ordered him to invade Persarmenia. The following year, Martin paid a ransom to lift the siege Edessa, defended by Peter of Arzanene, against the Persians. A reminder that war is racket!

To re-establish the situation in Italy, during the spring of 542 Justinian I had finally appointed Maximinus, an officer devoid of any military experience, as praetorian prefect with full authority. Having left Byzantium,

---

50 M. Meier, 'Prokop, Agathias, die Pest und das Ende der antiken Historiographie', *Historiche Zeitschrift*, 278 (2004), pp.281–310.
51 Procopius, *BP*, II, 25, 5–34 (Anglon).

Maximinus halted his fleet in Epirus, overcome by fear. Justinian then realised his mistake and ordered Demetrius, as general, to support him. He had to wait for Belisarius's return. But Belisarius's second campaign in Italy was a failure, marked in 543 by the fall of Naples, followed in 546 by the loss of Rome. As Totila partially destroyed its circuit-walls, Rome was abandoned by many of its inhabitants and lost his strategic value. Belisarius would reoccupy this empty shell in 547.

In late 548, Belisarius, who had promised the Emperor that he would not ask for funds, wrote to him that he had been unable to obtain the necessary subsidies from Italy.[52] Justinian I was infuriated by this demand and wanted to replace him. The same year, Theodora who was a close friend to Belisarius's wife had died, and Belisarius lost her support.

The chronology is unclear for the years 548–551, but the vacuum in command is obvious. To replace Belisarius, Justinian I first appointed his cousin Germanus, who had been successful in Africa and over the Antes, but problems in Illyricum prevented this promotion. So Justinian sent the Patrician Liberius, an old man not without military experience as he was wounded near Arles when fighting the Visigoths, at the time he was in the service of the Ostrogothic Kings. Nevertheless, the Emperor changed his mind while Liberius was at sea en route, and replaced him with Artabanes the Arsacid. Again changing his mind, Justinian I once again gave the supreme command in Italy to his cousin Germanus, but who unexpectedly died before leaving for the campaign during the autumn 551 at Serdica (now Sofia, Bulgaria). Thus, John, the nephew of Vitalian, was appointed although he quickly became disliked by the other officers, so in late 551 Justinian I finally had no choice but to designate Narses the Eunuch.[53] In this waltz of command on the Italian front, the Emperor shows the attitude of a frantic gambler. This episode demonstrates that it was not simple to find an able and trustworthy general.

Justinian I was perhaps not the all-powerful tyrant we imagine him to be today. He had to deal with the rival factions within the court in order to keep his crown and his head. Otherwise why did he not replace Belisarius with John Troglita? Why did he call on the Armenian Prince Artabanes the Arsacid who, a year earlier, had plotted to overthrow him? Why did he rely twice on Germanus, who was to take the throne as a result of this 'Armenian plot'? Admittedly, Justinian forgave them, showing himself to be less vindictive than Procopius implied.[54] Justinian nevertheless took some

---

52 Procopius, *Anecdota*, IV, 39 (broken promise to Justinian); *BG*, VII, 12, 6 (letter).
53 Procopius, *BG*, VI, 2 (three named military governors plus others); VII, 1, 20–33 (Alexander of Byzantium logothete); 6, 9–10 (Maximinus); 6, 13 (Demandrios); 35, 1 (Belisarius is recalled); 36, 6 (Liberius); 37, 6–7 (refusal of peace); 37, 24–27 (Germanus then Liberius); 39, 7 5 (Liberius); 8 (Artabanes); 9 (Germanus); 40, 10 (John nephew of Vitalian); VIII, 21, 6 (Narses).
54 To avoid any confusion with another Artabanes, Artawan in Armenian, this study uses the name of his dynastic family Aršakouni, the Arsacids in our historiography, A. H. M. Jones, J. R. Martindale, J. Morris, *PLRE*, 2 (1980), pp.125–130; Chr.

precautions: Artabanes was only given command of the army from Thrace, with the sole task of liberating Sicily, and Germanus was given a command without troops, only Liberius was taking with himself 'a considerable army made up of infantry units'.[55] Old, as he began his career under Odoacer, and himself an Italian, Liberius was a defector to the Empire who for most of his life had served the Ostrogothic state in the highest positions including Praetorian Prefect of Italy. It was undoubtedly his knowledge of the Ostrogothic administrative machinery and his aristocratic connections that led Justinian I to appoint him to this mission.[56] Nevertheless once Liberius had landed in Palermo he had been replaced with Artabanes. He probably stayed in Sicily as a political counsellor. C. 552 Liberius intervened in the civil war tearing the Visigoths of Spain apart. It is unclear whether he did it at the request of the rebel Athanagild or King Agila, but Justinian I's authorisation was necessary in both cases. Liberius seized a piece of Spain, probably in Baetica, north of the current Straits of Gibraltar.[57]

Although Totila had reconquered four-fifths of Italy as far as Calabria, Justinian I refused the peace and alliance he was offered. On 16 January 550, Rome was lost for the second time due to the betrayal of the Isaurians. It was held by only 3,000 men under Diogenes, a *bucellarius* officer. The Romano-Byzantines were now on the back foot. They only controlled a handful of coastal Adriatic fortresses defending the access to Ravenna and Totila even invaded Sicily, their main strategic base for the Italian campaign.

This lengthy reconquest of Italy calls for several comments. Over a period of 27 years the best troops were worn out and succeeded one another there. The Italian populations frankly did not support their supposed 'liberators' except in the south where they received a warm welcome. Noble families from southern Italy supported the reconquest, probably because they had wheat to sell eastwards. Byzantine military difficulties in central and northern Italy were largely caused by the cities' loyalty to the Ostrogothic monarchy, which had wisely continued the Roman administration.[58] Moreover, central Italians distrusted these eastern intruders, and when the Imperial Army reached Picenum, the population fled and did not return until they were sure that Belisarius' army was not attacking them but the

---

Sandtipani, *Continuité des élites à Byzance durant les siècles obscurs. Les princes caucasiens et l'Empire du VIe au IXe siècle* (Paris: de Boccard, 2006), pp.106, 130 (family of general Artabanes).

55 Procopius, *BG*, VII, 39, 6.
56 J. J. O'Donnell, 'Liberius the Patrician', *Traditio*, 31, 1981, pp.31–72. A. H. M. Jones, J. R. Martindale, J. Morris, *PLRE*, 2 (1971), p. 677–681.
57 Jordanes, *Getica*, LVIII, 303 (Athanagild called for help); J. Fossella, 'Waiting Only for a Pretext: A New Chronology for the Sixth Century Byzantine Invasion of Spain', *Estudios bizantinos*, 1 (2013), pp.31–38 (according to him, the Romans landed only in 544 when Athanagild was then on the throne).
58 J. Moorhead, 'Italian loyalties during Justinian's Gothic War', *REB*, 53 (1983), pp.575–596.

Goths.⁵⁹ For many Italians, the Imperial troops were undoubtedly not 'Romans' just only a bunch of Greeks, Armenians, Huns and rough-hewn Latin Balkan troops with exorbitant demands because they had to live off the land. By contrast, as a true King Totila brought relief to Roman aristocratic families ruined by war, such as the widow of the poet Boethius.⁶⁰ Procopius considered the Italo-Romans, and particularly the inhabitants of Rome, as some sort of museum custodians devoid of any real patriotism.⁶¹ But a fact worth remembering to avoid easy over criticism: Ancient Rome itself took at least three centuries to gain control of the peninsula and Sicily.

The bogging down of best Imperial troops in Italy was detrimental to the Danube frontier, which formed a fourth and poorly defended front. If the Gepids stood rather pacific because they were paid as *foederati*, the Huns and Slavs did not. These restless peoples launched many raids across the River Danube inflicting 'irreparable damages upon the Romans' according to Procopius whose dating is foggy but could be dated firstly from the late 520s. From 531 to 534, Chilbudius, appointed as general of Thrace, successfully forestalled the Slavs' incursions until he was killed by the Sklavenes who opposed him en masse when he raided northern Danube with too few troops. After his death, the Slavic crossings became incessant.⁶² Between 545 and 551, they ravaged Thrace and Illyricum, reached Byzantium. The good news came from the Persians with whom Justinian concluded a five-year truce in 545, renewed in 550. But, to the great anger of Procopius, this peace was paid for with 2,600 pounds in gold with a penalty for 18 months of delay.⁶³ But it was certainly a lower price than fighting the war. Unfortunately, the Moors rose in revolt in Africa from 546 to 549, and it took all the skill of John Troglita with a newly-raised army to put an end to the revolt. Meanwhile Justinian I did not give up on his long-lasting Italian project, and a high turnover of generals proved necessary there as Belisarius was by then in disgrace.

However, it was another senior official Narses the Eunuch who broke the deadlock in Italy. Appointed commander-in-chief, he spent the whole of 551 in Illyricum building up a large army. By April 552, the Franks blocked his path in Veneto and Totila flooded the area between Verona and Ravenna. The unstoppable Narses arrived in Ravenna on the 6 June, following the coast and using floating bridges. He decisively defeated King Totila at Taginae, then his successor Teias at Mons Lactarius. He also repelled the Frankish and Alemannic invasion of 553–554. But it is

---

59 Procopius, *BG*, VI, 1 and 6.
60 Procopius, *BG*, VII, 20, 27–31.
61 M. E. Stewart, 'The Danger of the Soft Life: Manly and Unmanly Romans in Procopius' Gothic War', *Journal of Late Antiquity*, 10.2 (2017), p.487.
62 Procopius, *BG*, VII, 14, 2 (Antes, Skavenes and Huns); 3–5 (Chibuldius); 6 (incessant crossings).
63 Procopius, *BG*, VIII, 15, 17.

THE EMPEROR AS COMMANDER OF THE ARMIES

worthwhile to remember that these invaders were stopped 200km south Rome on the River Volturnus (today the Volturno).

Defeating the Franks enabled Justinian to promulgate the Pragmatic Sanction on 13 August 554, which placed Italy under Imperial law but retained certain specific features, such as the weights and measures to the Roman Senate. In northern Italy, the Ostrogoths continued to hold several cities, such as Pavia and the smal town of Compsa (today Conza della Campania), which Narses the Eunuch spent several months besieging between 554 and 555. The resumption of the endless conflict with the Persians in Lazica in 555–557 reopened the eastern front. The overall situation was getting near catastrophic in 559, when the Huns unexpectedly arrived at the gates of Byzantium, while the best troops were still engaged in Italy or were garrisoning Lazica. Although ageing and retired, Belisarius managed to push back the Hunnic horde with an improvised army. By 562, the last Ostrogothic strongholds, Verona and Brescia, fell to Narses the Eunuch and a 'Fifty-Year Peace' was concluded with the Persians. When he died three years later, Justinian I had fulfilled all his objectives.

It is perhaps time to assess the outcome of Justinianic turmoil. The conquest of Africa, a region rich in wheat, and of Italy, cradle of the Empire, were flattering achievements for Justinian, but at what cost? Procopius accused him of having caused the deaths of 5,000,000 people in Africa, of having depopulated Italy and allowed the invasion of Illyricum and Thrace, causing the loss of 200,000 Roman civilians with each incursion.[64] There are many criticisms of real or so-called tyrants in ancient historians, but only Procopius dared to write an entire book just to denigrate an Emperor with his *Secret History*, cautiously published after Justinian's death. Procopius wrote: 'That he was not a human being but, as has been said, a demon in human form, could be proved by assessing the magnitude of the evils he inflicted on men.'[65] Procopius gave a cataclysmic death toll almost comparable to a world war. It is difficult to assess the financial losses, but they were probably significant, particularly in Italy. Papal revenue from the rich province of Picenum was cut by 77 percent between the late fifth century and 556.[66] Securing the Balkans would undoubtedly have been better than this interminable Italian expedition, whose efforts were rendered partially futile by the imminent Lombard invasion. Despite its promising name, the 'Fifty-Year Peace' with the Persians resulted only in a truce lasting less than 10 years. Procopius also accused Justinian I of having broken the Imperial Post Office, destroyed the foreign intelligence service and worsened the living conditions of the soldiers.[67] This portrait in evil

---

64 Procopius, *Anecdota*, XVIII, 8 (Africa); 21 (Europe).
65 Procopius, *Anecdota*, XVIII, 1.
66 P. Llewellyn, *Rome in the Dark Ages* (London: Constable and Company Ltd, 1993), p.80.
67 Procopius, *Anecdota*, XXIV (military personnel); XXX (Imperial mail and foreign espionage).

BIRTH OF THE BYZANTINE ARMY 476-641 CE VOLUME 1: STILL LATE ROMAN?

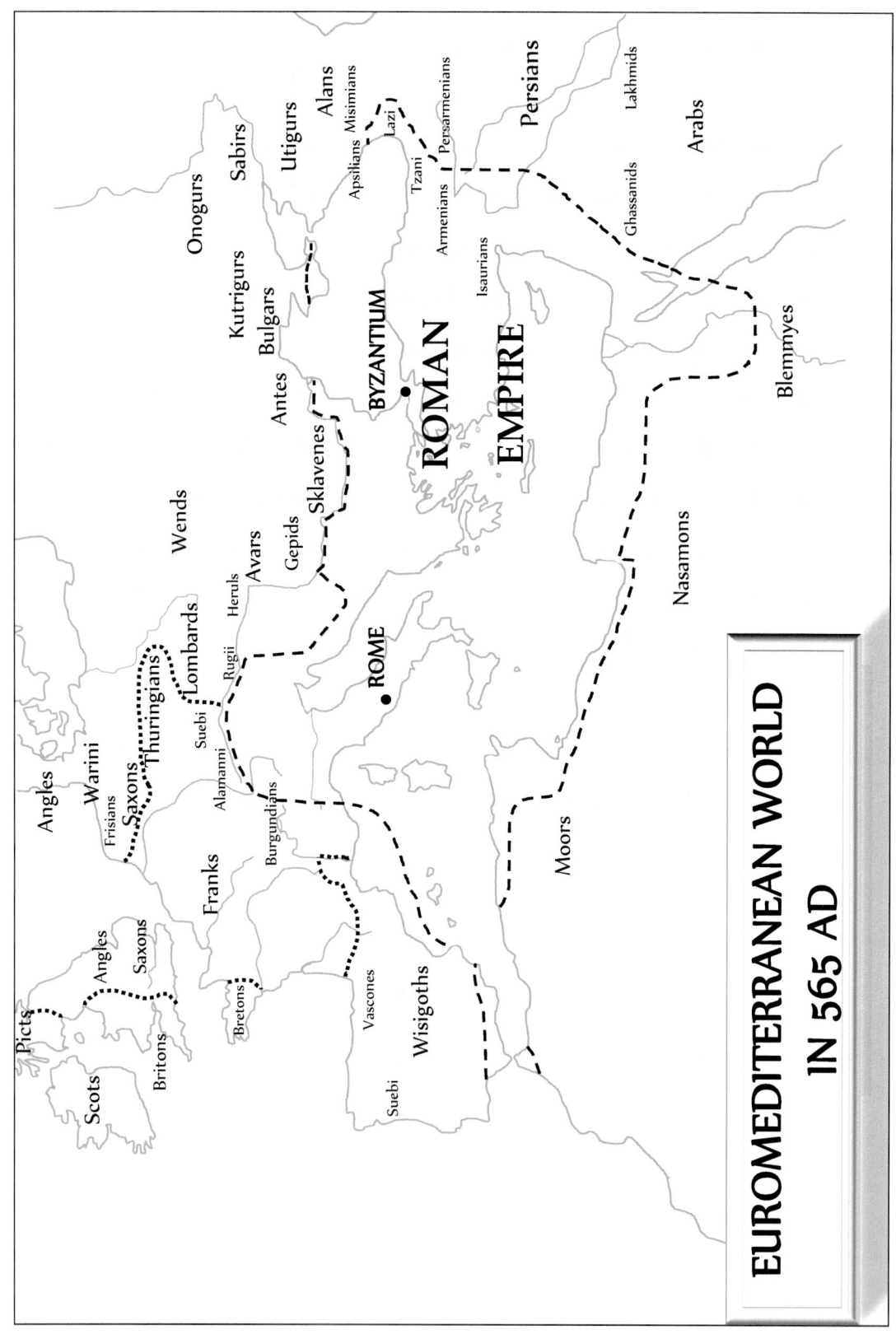

THE EMPEROR AS COMMANDER OF THE ARMIES

deserves to be examined. It was with the army bequeathed by Justin I that Justinian concluded his swift and victorious wars against the Persians and Vandals from 528 to 533. After that, his troops struggled for almost 30 years to conquer Italy, a sign of declining military effectiveness. The resulting deterioration in their living conditions led the soldiers into a number of mutinies. Justinian I bequeathed his successor a larger Empire but a weaker army. His military effort was nonetheless prodigious: victorious wars against the Persians, massive restoration of Balkan border, the annexation of Africa with the Western Mediterranean islands, and the conquest of Italy and Dalmatia. Justinian I was the only Byzantine ruler who tried to conquer new territories. He was successful despite the plague that broke out in Egypt at late 541, before sweeping through Byzantium and the rest of the Empire. More than the Justinianic wars this plague may have led to oliganthropy and price inflation which a law from 544 attempted to combat.[68] Depopulation in the northern Balkan region seems to have eased its colonisation by the Slavs 50 years later.

Justin II, the Emperor Demented but not so Mad

Justin II, who reigned from 565 to 578, was a nephew of the previous Emperor, Justinian I, proving nepotism is not a irrelevant word. He was formerly an official, with the title of *kouropalates* (anglicised as curopalate, was a court title meaning '[the one] in charge of the palace'), and had no military experience. But his immense wealth and that of his wife, a niece of Theodora, rallied much support, as he repaid the forced loans that Justinian I had demanded of the wealthy and his wife even repaid some debts. In 566, he celebrated his consulship sumptuously, to the satisfaction of the people. The beginning of his dull reign was marked by the reoccupation of Sirmium in 567 after 126 years of barbarian occupation, mainly by the Gepids. This victory was due to the sudden invasion of Pannonia by a new steppe people called the 'Western Huns' by Theophanes: The Avars, who first crushed the Gepids.[69] This enabled the frontier to extend as far as the River Sava, providing better protection to Illyricum. Subsequently, Justin II had to face the hydra of war on three fronts – in Europe, Africa and Asia.

Justin II's reign unwillingly marked a strategic turning point for the Empire, as the second phase of the period of the great invasions began with the arrival of the Lombards in Italy in 568. They were an enemy that Byzantium would never be able to subdue. This was perhaps the result of the clumsiness of Justin II and his wife, who humiliatingly dismissed the Narses the Eunuch. In an attempt at revenge, it is said the latter secretly called on the Lombards to invade the Italian peninsula, which he was defending with a small number of troops. Whether the accusation was malicious or not,

---

68   A. Cameron et al (eds), *Late Antiquity: Empire and Successors*, p.77.
69   Theophanes Confessor, *Chrgr.*, AM 6117, 315.

the Lombards and their Saxon allies took most of the Veneto and Milan the following year after Narses the Eunuch was dismissed. The question arises of how a Nordic people which had barely been heard of, could beat the first military power of Europe. In 570, a Lombard Duchy was formed around Benevento, which waged war for 20 years against the Empire's possessions to the south of Italy. Only Ravenna, backed by the Adriatic Sea, resisted, but in 572 the road linking it to Rome was blocked. The military response was initially weak, if not ineffective, no doubt because the army was worn out and the coffers empty. From 569 the Moors in Africa rebelled again under the very competent leadership of King Garmul, who until 571 successively defeated and killed all generals sent against him: the Praetorian Prefect Theodore, the Masters of the Soldiers Theoctistus then Amabilis.[70] Probably unable to collect sufficient financial resources, Justin II refused to honor the annual tribute to the Persians in 572, which had been regularly paid since the ill-named 'Fifty-Year Peace' of 562. The official reason for not paying was the construction of a Mazdaist Temple of Fire in Persarmenia, provoking a revolt among the predominantly Christian populations, since in the treaty of 562, the Byzantines had asked the Persians not to persecute the Christians. Byzantine refusal led to a 19-year conflict with Persians from 572 to 591, although interrupted by truces. At the beginning of this conflict, Justin II became angry with his Ghassan ally al-Mundir III ibn al-Harith, who asked him for gold. Consequently, he ordered Marcian the Patrician, in command of the East, to assassinate al-Mundir, an order that wisely was not carried out.[71]

Justin II shared the reins of power with his wife Sophia, who had the rank of *Augusta*, or Empress Consort. He had a son with her, who died in 565, and a daughter whom he married to Baduarius the Kouropalates. The state could have been ruled normally had the Emperor not suffered from fits of dementia from December 573, when he learned that the Persians had taken the fortress of Dara, formerly known as Anastasiopolis. It was the second defeat of the year after the failure of the siege of Nisibis, where Marcian's army had been routed by the Persian King. The psychological shock was too much for Justin II, and his wife took the initiative of negotiating with the Persian King through a doctor named Zachariah. By paying a large amount of gold, a truce was agreed for the following year.[72] The political situation was far from ideal. A madman and a woman were at the head of the Empire in a world of male predatory warriors.

In 574, Sophia wisely suggested to her husband that, according to the Roman tradition, he should take on an adopted son and then proclaim him *Caesar*, i.e. second Emperor and putative heir. Sophia proposed no other than

---

70 A. H. M. Jones, J. R. Martindale, J. Morris, *PLRE*, 3a (1992), p.504.
71 John of Ephesus, *HE*, VI, 3–4.
72 John of Ephesus, *HE*, VI, 5 (detailed account from the siege of Dara); Theophylact Simocatta, *HU*, III, 11, 2 (fall of Dara); 3 (madness and negotiations). Menander Protector, *Fragm.*, 37–38 (negotiations started by Sophie).

Tiberius, commander of the Imperial bodyguards as Count of *Excubitores*. It was a clever idea capable of discouraging any possible *pronunciamento* from Tiberius, who in addition was reputed to be close a friend to Justin II. As a sign of his joyful ascent, the *Caesar* Tiberius distributed the treasure of Narses the Eunuch to the poor. He also remitted the cash taxes for 575, but not those paid in kind, which proved to be vital for the military needs of the provinces.[73] He negotiated an extension of the truce with the Persians and, at the same time, recruited 'a multitude of soldiers' from the Balkans.[74] The Imperial Treasury's coffers were full. The war against Persians then regained strength and vigour, with alternating victories and defeats. In 575, Justinian, Master of the Soldiers to the East, captured 34 elephants from Khosrow I. He brought these back to Byzantium as the symbols of defeated Persian military power to celebrate Justin II's triumph in a most Roman way.[75] Two years later, the same Justinian was defeated and killed by the Persians in Armenia.

As a true niece of Theodora, Sophia tried to seduce Tiberius the new *Caesar*, forgetting that he had four children a wife and was younger than her. However, her charms had no effect on him. Perhaps influenced by Sophia's scheming, in 576 Justin II sent his son-in-law Baduarius the Kouropalates to fight the Lombards in Italy. The details are unclear, but Baduarius was killed in battle – one does not become a capable general simply by the will of his mother-in-law[76] Justin II, still suffering from madness and as far as he governed, was unable to stabilise the degrading situation in Italy. Moreover, Italy was not his main concern. In 577, he was faced with the Persians then more threatening because of their recent victories in Armenia and Mesopotamia. The Empire needed a new general in the East. Tiberius probably encouraged Justin II to choose Maurice, who had succeeded him as Count of *Excubitores*. It is easy to assume that Tiberius and Maurice, both *Excubitores*, were acquainted. With this new military command, Maurice also attained the dignity of Patrician. Meanwhile, the Army of the East was so badly battered that Maurice was unable to intervene immediately. He had first to recruit troops from Cappadocia and Syria. In fact, until mid-summer, the Persians took the initiative and captured several border towns, including Amida, a key town in Mesopotamia. Once his army was mustered, in 578 Maurice counter-attacked successfully, forcing the Persians to retreat. This eastern strategy clearly sacrificed Italy to the Lombards who during the same year took Classis, the military port of Ravenna, and marched on Rome. At the time, the Avars were still allies, helping the Empire repel the Sklavenes. It was also true that Justin paid them tribute.

---

73 *Nov. J.*, 163.
74 Theophylact Simocatta, *HU*, III, 12, 3 (negotiations); 4 (recruitment). Evagrius Scholasticus, *HE*, V, 14 (recruitment from Balkans).
75 John of Biclaro, *Chr.VT*, 35 (24 elephants captured). Paul the Deacon, *HL*, III, 12 (triumph).
76 A. H. M. Jones, J. R. Martindale, J. Morris, *PLRE*, 3a (1992), p.64.

Justin II died on 4 October 578 and Tiberius became full Emperor. This was the end of Sophia's influence, who Tiberius ironically called his 'mother', and his reign continued rather than began.

Tiberius II Constantine, the First Greek-Speaking Emperor

Even though he had assumed a large part of the power for four years, Tiberius II Constantine (Emperor, 578–582) did not have time to become a great ruler, but with him came the end of the Illyrian clan. He was a man of Thracian origin, and the first fully Greek-speaking Byzantine Emperor.[77] During his short reign, Tiberius II Constantine was hampered by the strategic dilemma of a war on soon four fronts, Africa, Italy, the East and the Balkans. He was luckily served by some good generals. The first attested was Gennadius who was appointed Master of the Soldiers to Africa in 578. He had to deal with the long-lasting Moorish rebellion; a task promptly fulfilled the following year costing the life of the defeated King Garmul. At the same time, Tiberius II deliberately and symbolically sacrificed central Italy when, in 578, he refused the City of Rome's accession gift of 3,000 pounds of gold, suggesting to the senators that they should use this sum for their own defence. The Eternal City was by then a giant ruined museum difficult to defend and too far from the sea lanes to be easily reinforced. A few months before his accession, the Lombards had taken Classis, the port of Ravenna and in 579 they besieged Rome. To cope with this imminent danger, on the advice of the Emperor the new Pope, Pelagius II, requested military assistance from the Franks. Finally, Pelagius II paid a generous tribute to the Lombards to lift the siege. In the same year, Tiberius II retook Classis, a harbour strategically more important than Rome, which was no longer worth defending.

The second supposedly able general to serve Tiberius II was Maurice, who was also a native Greek speaker like the Emperor. The author, or sponsor, of the first Byzantine tactics manual, the *Strategikon*, Maurice recommended an ideal mobile army of 24,000 infantry and 10,000 cavalry. Imbued by Hellenistic tacticians, he wanted cavalry or infantry phalanxes. As with the Roman Vegetius's work, this highly theoretical treatise is confined to training, a table of organisation, armament, discipline and tactics, but unlike Vegetius no considerations about siege and naval warfare. For both of these authors, strategy boils down to the art of the general in the field. Although not nostalgic, Maurice's treatise is similar to *Maréchal de Saxe's Rêveries* in the sense that it proposed an overall reorganisation and

---

77 John of Ephesus, *HE*, III.5–10. Gregory of Tours, *HF*, V.30; M. Whitby, 'The successors of Justinian' in A. Cameron et al (eds), *Late Antiquity: Empire and Successors*, p.95.

THE EMPEROR AS COMMANDER OF THE ARMIES

new armament.[78] As a general, Maurice was the armed hand of Tiberius II. In 581, then Master of the Soldiers to the East, he attempted to strike at the heart of the Persian Empire. His intention was to repeat the bold manoeuvre Emperor Julian had done in 363: a straight attack from the Osrhoene south-eastwards to Ctesiphon, the Persian capital, along the Euphrates that protected the army's left flank and provided a convenient riverine path for logistics. Such an operation required considerable resources, which only the Emperor could authorise. Although Maurice was not killed in the operation, as Julian had been, it was a complete failure. As he marched on Sassanid Mesopotamia and Ctesiphon, he was stopped by the breaking of the bridge over the Euphrates and, above all, the Persians had crossed into Roman Mesopotamia and were ravaging Osrhoene in his rear. With his base threatened and his march blocked, Maurice had no choice but to retreat. He had suffered a strategic defeat without suffering a tactical setback, but someone needed to be responsible for this disaster and, in bad faith, Maurice accused his Ghassanid ally al-Mundir III ibn al-Harith of having delivered his plans to the enemy and went to Byzantium to convince Tiberius II. Invited to explain himself al-Mundir III ibn al-Harith was treacherously arrested and exiled to Sicily provoking an anti-Byzantine reaction from his tribe.

In the Balkans, the Slavs resumed the offensive in 581. From then on, the Empire also had to fight the Avars, whose Khan Bayan captured Sirmium in Pannonia around June/July 582 after a two-year siege. The departure of the best troops towards the East could not have escaped the vigilance of barbarian spies and Persian gold may have convinced Bayan to intervene. Tiberius II Constantine had deliberately sacrificed Europe to the Eastern front. As a result, the capture of Sirmium, key to the defence of Illyricum, brought down the Sava barrier, a strategic failure. Against the Persians, in June 582 Maurice won a battle at Constantina of Osrhoene, (today Viranşehir in Turkey) shielding Syria, along with Egypt and Africa, one of the Empire's richest regions.[79] The ageing Tiberius II's main concern was then to select his best general to succeed him. This was not obvious, and he seemed to be hesitating between his son-in-law Germanus, sometimes identified with the Patrician of that name, and Maurice who was engaged to another of the Emperor's daughters. On 5 August, Tiberius II jointly proclaimed Germanus and Maurice as *caesars*, perhaps with the idea of splitting the Empire in two. Finally, he decided in favour of Maurice, whom he proclaimed by 13 August, the symbolic month that owes its name to the first Emperor, and died the following day. His large generosity had left the state coffers empty.

---

78 Maurice, *Strategikon*, XII, B, 8 (ideal army).
79 Theophylact Simocatta, *HU*, III, 18, 1–2. John of Ephesus, *HE*, VI (26 (battle from June 892 AG).

Maurice, another Emperor from the Imperial Guard

Originating from Cappadocia and a Greek speaker, Maurice (Emperor, 582–602) was a notary and a friend of Tiberius, who made him Count of *Excubitores*. He fought against the Persians as Count of the *Foederati* and then Master of the Soldiers to the East.[80] Soon after his accession to the throne, he married Constantina a daughter of Tiberius II Constantine, which placed him into a legitimate line. During his twenty-year reign he had to face the tensest military situation of the sixth century, a war on four fronts against the Persians in the East, in the Balkans against the Slavs and the Avars, while the situation in Italy with the Lombards did not improve and the Moors again rebelled.[81] Documentation about Spain is lacking but the Visigoths seem to have regained ground, and this was a very minor fifth front.

Like his predecessors, Maurice left his generals to their own devices and stayed in the capital. In 582 or 583, he appointed John Mystakon, 'the Mustachian', Master of the Soldiers to Armenia, the Emperor's former subordinate and a Thracian like him. Sent to invade Arzanene, a Persian province, Mystakon was defeated twice and then recalled.[82] But Maurice was fortunate to have a breeding ground of valuable generals: Philippicus, his brother-in-law who replaced Mystakon, Heraclius the Elder, Peter the Kouropalates, his brother Priscus and, to a lesser extent, Comentiolus the Thracian, and Germanus, the former Duke of Phoenicia.[83] Most of them fought the Persians, but had now to contain raids launched by Ghassanid Bedouins, traditional allies turned into adversaries since their King had been imprisoned for religious and unjust reasons. The first of these was Maurice's enmity towards the Ghassanid King al-Mundir II whom he had previously accused of treason to Tiberius II. In 583, led by al-Nu'man VI ibn al-Mundir, the son the imprisoned King, the Ghassanids raided Bosra to the south of present-day Syria and then capital of province of Arabia Petraea. Maurice feigned to open negotiations, but while on his way to Byzantium to find common ground Nu'man was arrested and exiled to Sicily, where his father was. Maurice's Arab policy was a complete disaster, losing the Ghassanids' trust.

---

80   John of Ephesus, *HE*, VI, 26 (friend of Tiberius, notary, Count of *Excubitores*, Master of the Soldiers to the East); W. Treadgold, *A History of the Byzantine State and Society* (Stanford: Stanford University Press, 1997), p.227 (hypothesis of the title of count not attested by the sources).

81   M. Whitby, *The Emperor Maurice and his Historian: Theophylact Simocatta on Balkan and Persian Warfare* (Oxford: Oxford University Press, 1988).

82   A. H. M. Jones, J. R. Martindale, J. Morris, *PLRE*, 3a (1992), pp.679–681 (Ioannes 101).

83   A. H. M. Jones, J. R. Martindale, J. Morris, *PLRE*, 3a (1992), pp.321–325 (Comentiolus 1); 529–530 (Germanus 6) and probably pp.532–533 (Germanus 13); 584–586 (Heraclius 3); 3b, pp. 1009–1011 (Petrus 55); 1022–1026 (Philippicus 3); 1052–1057 (Priscus 6).

THE EMPEROR AS COMMANDER OF THE ARMIES

John Mystakon was replaced in 584 with Philippicus and who continued operations near Nisibis and in Arzanene. Two years later he stopped a Persian invasion at the Battle of Solachon, south of Dara in Mesopotamia. But like Maurice himself when he was a general, he stumbled before Chlomaron the capital of Arzanene and there his army was routed by an incoming relief Persian Army. In 587, Philippicus fell ill and Heraclius the Elder temporarily took command until Priscus was commissioned as the new Master of the Soldiers to the East. Maurice had to face the classic Byzantine dilemma of a war on three fronts without finding out a miraculous solution, but he kept the Empire in being.

In 584, the Avars launched a raid that took them to the Black Sea, past the port of Anchialos, now Pomorie in Bulgaria, and then to the Long Walls of Byzantium. The same year, after three years of continuous pillaging the Sklavenes were defeated by Comentiolus the Thracian on the River Erginia near the Long Walls. They returned to devastate Athens and Corinth in 585, venturing back into Thrace where Comentiolus defeated them again at Ansinon, a fort north-west of Adrianople (now Edirne in Turkey). They again invaded the Empire in 586 while the Avars, after crossing the Danube the following year, reached the Thracian plain. While they were besieging the fort of Appiara (modern Tutrakan in Bulgaria) they were taught how to build siege machines by a Romano-Byzantine prisoner named Busas and thereafter were able to take several cities.[84] In Italy in 584, the Lombards tried again to move towards Rome, but were dissuaded by the Frankish military intervention from King Childebert II of Austrasia, who had received a sum of 50,000 solidi from Maurice for his much-needed help. The geographical link between Ravenna and Rome was restored by fortifying the Via Amerina through Rimini.[85] Notwithstanding this, Rome was besieged by the persistant Lombards during the winter of 587–588. Against the no less obstinate Persians, victories and defeats alternated in Mesopotamia resulting in a stalemate.

Maurice's reign was either marked by his avarice or by the state's very real cash-flow problems, the latter no doubt exacerbated by the continuous raids the Avars, Sklavenes and Huns, launched, inroads which turned into local occupation. The Empire seemed powerless. On two occasions, Maurice reduced the army's pay, in the East in 588 and in Thrace in 594. The subsequent mutinies were calmed by the Patriarch of Antioch and then by the skill of his brother Peter the Kouropalates, who announced that the pay cut would be offset by social measures. Maurice's avaricious nature is well attested in the sources, with Bishop John of Nikiu stating that 'he loved money very much', but John of Ephesus explains that his predecessor Tiberius had emptied the state coffers.[86] More bluntly, the soldiers mutinied at Monocarton during Easter 588 called him a 'shopkeeper', but not before

---

84 Theophylact Simocatta, *HU*, II, 16, 11.
85 A. Cameron et al (eds), *Late Antiquity: Empire and Successors*, p.537.
86 John of Nikiu, *Chr.*, 95, 1 (1883), p.403. John of Ephesus, *HE*, V, 20.

toppling his statues and erasing his portrait from the coins![87] During this mutiny, which lasted a year, only distance protected Maurice in Byzantium, from the wrath of the mutineers stationed in south-east Asia Minor. The Master of the Soldiers to the East Priscus had to take refuge in Edessa. Appointed to the military region of the Thracians, he had to pull back the Avars from Anchialus but was soon defeated near Heraclea on the Sea of Marmara. Elected as their general by the mutinied soldiers the Duke of Phoenice Libanensis Germanus managed to restore discipline. Moreover, during the late summer or autumn at Martyropolis he inflicted he inflicted a painful defeat on the Persians who tried to take advantage of the mutiny by invading Armenia. Thousands of Persians were slaughtered, 3,000 were taken prisoners including the two left and right wings' commanders and 1,000 managed to run away. As a gesture of courtesy, Germanus sent to the Emperor the head of the Persian General Marouzas with all the standards taken from the enemy.[88] This tactful gift led Maurice to pardon Germanus who had been sentenced to death in absentia. By Easter 589 negotiations brought the mutineers back to obedience towards the Emperor. Philippicus took command over the Eastern Army. In the autumn, he fell ill and must be replaced by Comentiolus who won the battle and won a battle at Sisauranon current northern Syria in current northern Syria. In 590, the Persian war was getting better due to the fact of internal discord within the enemy, since the new King Hormisdas IV was overthrown, enucleated then assassinated by an ambitious General and usurper called Bahram VI Chobim. Khosrow II, the son of the deposed King, took refuge in Syria and obtained military assistance from Maurice to regain his throne. In 591 Khosrow II won a decisive battle over the usurper at Blarathon near the ancient city of Ganzak/Gazaca near Lake Urmia in Iran. This led to a peace treaty ending to a nineteen-year war. Although the Empire recovered Dara and Martyropolis and its border from 502, it only gained a truce.

Nevertheless, having a free hand in the east Maurice could devote his army to re-establishing the shattered Danubian border. In 590, for the only time during his reign, he resumed his duties as a general, leading his troops to Anchialos where he could inspect the damage done by the Avars. In the following years, Priscus and Peter the Kouropalates drove the Sklavenes out of the Eastern Balkans or subjugated them as subjects.[89] When Maurice unfairly cut the pay of the Balkan Army in 594, only promises of compensation made by his brother Peter the Kouropalates saved Maurice once again.[90]

In 595, the Avars razed the walls of Singidunum but the city was retaken by Godwin a general of Germanic origin. Nevertheless, the Avars went westwards and ravaged Dalmatia. Three years later, they cornered Priscus

---

87   Theophylact Simocatta, *HU*, III, 2, 8.
88   Theophylact Simocatta, *HU*, III, 4, 1–4 (battle); 5, 8 (Marouzas' head).
89   A. Cameron et al (eds), *Late Antiquity: Empire and Successors*, p.106.
90   Theophylact Simocatta, *HU*, VII, 1, 2–7.

at Tomi (today Constanța in Romania). Sent as a relief force Comentiolus the Thracian was forced to retreat further south through the Shipka Pass to draw the Khan's army towards him. But the Avars penerated as far as the Long Walls and Maurice himself had to command the interposition troops. A fragile truce was concluded. It was broken the following summer in 599, when Priscus and Comentiolus the Thracian went on a brilliant joint campaign to clear the Middle Danube between Viminiacum and the River Tissus (the now River Tisza in the Hungarian plain). At the outset of the campaign Comentiolus fell sick then self-inflicting false wounds, so Priscus had to take over. This time it was not just a defensive campaign but Gepid, Sklavene and Avar lands were raided. At least three large battles were won on the bank opposite Viminiacum, where Priscus held his headquarters. After he had destroyed the Gepid settlements, moving 100km westward Priscus moved up the River Tisza and won two more battles against the Avars. It was a great success and he brought back 19,200 prisoners of war, mainly Sklavenes, Avars and other undefined barbarians. All these were sent to Tomi on the Black Sea, however threatened by Avar ambassadors Maurice weakly agreed to return them to the Khan.[91] In 600, Maurice's impecuniosity was such that he refused to pay the ransoms for the prisoners taken by the Avars. The following year, he again appointed his brother Peter the Kouropalates as Master of the Soldiers to the Thraces.[92] In Italy, he was militarily unable to intervene and Pope Gregory the Great was at loggerheads with him. This Pope, who contested the ancient cultural heritage and banned mythological literary references, even challenged the Patriarch of Byzantium's authority over Illyricum and, undoubtedly not appreciating the Marcianite heresy supported by Maurice, entered into talks with the insatiable Lombards.

The year 602 was politically fatal for Maurice. In February, his bodyguards had to put down a popular riot in Byzantium following a famine that had probably arisen because he had not bought enough public wheat. However, never during this period was a civilian revolt able to overthrow this military regime that the Byzantine Imperium was. In the autumn, Maurice wrote to Peter the Kouropalates to take up his winter quarters with the Army of Thrace among the Sklavenes in present-day Wallachia, to spare the Romano-Byzantine population the logistical burden. In a second letter, he expressly ordered a winter campaign, in keeping with a principle in his treatise according to which the Sklavenes had to be attacked in winter when

---

91 Theophylact Simocatta, *HU*, VIII, 1, 11 (Priscus and Commentiolus forces united at Singidunum); 2, 2 (Viminiacum, Comentiolus sick); 3–12 (first battle opposite Viminiacum); 3, 1–3 (second battle); 4–7 (third battle); 8–10 (first battle on Tissus); 11–12 (Gepids); 13–14 (second battle on Tissus); 15 (prisoners dispatched to Tomi); 4, 1–2 (POW's give up to the Khan).

92 A. H. M. Jones, J. R. Martindale, J. Morris, *PLRE*, 3b (1992), pp.1009–1010. The term Peter the Kouropalates was not coined at the time, but is simply used to distinguish him from the numerous other Peters.

the trees were leafless and ambushes rendered more difficult.[93] Peter the Kouropalates, embarrassed by his brother's avarice, informed his officers. The news did not go down well with the troops who did not want to pass the winter miserably in the half-buried huts of Slavic barbarians or in makeshift barracks, as implied by the order to occupy Wallachia. Thus the Army of Thrace rebelled and tried again to negotiate with Emperor's brother, Peter the Kouropalates. When Maurice refused bluntly, the exasperated army brought one of its own, Phocas, to the Purple. Peter fled to warn Maurice, whose only resource was to arm the Blue Faction, supporters of the chariot race team who dressed in this colour at the hippodrome. In doing so, he turned against him the Green Faction who recognised Phocas. Byzantium rose in revolt and the palace of the praetorian prefecture was burnt down. Maurice tried to escape to Bithynia by boat with his treasure, but he was murdered after his five children were by killed Phocas' soldiers. Their heads were brought back to Byzantium to be displayed for the army in the Hebdomon district.[94] All the work of consolidation in Mesopotamia and reconquest in the Balkans was compromised.

Phocas, the Return to an era of *Pronunciamentos*

Phocas (Emperor, 602–610) was part of the delegation of eight representatives from the Army of Thrace to Peter the Kouropalates in protest against Maurice's plan to winter the army north of the Danube. The embassy failed and Phocas was hoisted on a shield by the troops as a sign of acclamation as new Emperor. Depending on the source, he was either an ordinary centurion or one of the four revolting generals from the Army of Thrace.[95] Actually he was undoubtedly a senior officer or general, count or *merarch*, rather than a *hecatontarch* in charge of 100 men. Simocatta and the *Paschal Chronicle* call him a 'tyrant' and historiography present Phocas as unqualified, lacking experience in politics or in a high military command.[96] However, this unflattering portrait is balanced by the fact that, on 23 November 602, in the church of St John the Baptist in Hebdomon, he was the first Emperor to be crowned in a church and also by a Patriarch, Kyriakos. It was the birth of the coronation of Christian monarchs and a

---

93   Theophylact Simocatta, *HU*, VIII, 6, 2 -10 (mutiny cause); 7, 1–6 (failed negotiations); 9, 3–5 (popular revolt and harson of the palace of Lardys). Maurice, *Strategikon*, 4, 82.

94   Theophylact Simocatta, *HU*, VIII, 7, 7 (Phocas hoisted on a shield). Theophanes Confessor, *Chrgr.*, AM 6094, 290 (death of Maurice).

95   Theophylact Simocatta, *HU*, VII, 7, 7 (centurion; shield). John of Antioch *Fragm.*, 218d.4 (Phocas hoisted on a shield by Blue and Green Factions in Hebdomon district); John of Nikiu, *Chr.*, 102, 9 (1883), p.417 (one of the four leaders of the Thracian army).

96   C. Morrisson (ed.), *Le monde Byzantin*, pp.38–40.

THE EMPEROR AS COMMANDER OF THE ARMIES

powerful political act which could not have been imagined by an idiot.[97] By doing so, Phocas created a tradition that went beyond him and has marked the entire history of Europe. He also invited the Senate to his coronation and cleverly was trying to rely on the support of the Greens, whose parish was Hebdomon. Despite this the support of the Greens would not last long. The following day, he returned to the Roman Imperial tradition by riding triumphantly into the capital on a *quadriga* of white horses, throwing handfuls of gold to the crowds and giving games to the plebs. Shortly afterwards, he organised a triumphal ceremony for his wife Leontia. He also financed Menander the Protector to write a universal history. None of this was a sign of political inexperience or of a lack of culture, any more than the column he had erected in the Roman forum in 608. Phocas mastered political communication well enough to remain in power for eight years. His main failure was diplomatic, when the Persian King Khosrow II refused his ambassadors on the spurious pretext that he was irritated by the murder of Maurice.[98] All misfortunes of Phocas' reign stemmed from this irreconcilable Persian hostility, a simple pretext for war.

A career soldier, Phocas, like most Emperors, preferred to delegate command of an army on campaign. He was ruthless and cruel, but was he more so than any other Emperor? Having all Maurice's sons killed in front of their father does not really speak in Phocas favour. Moreover, he began his reign with a series of purges. As soon as he took power, he had Peter the Kouropalates, *Comentiolus* ex-commander of the Army of Thrace whom Maurice had uselessly charged with defending Byzantium, executed along with George, second in command of Philippicus.[99] Nonetheless, Phocas simply tonsured and exiled Philippicus to the monastery of Chrysopolis, showing a more humane, Christian and political attitude. Phocas kept Priscus alive, one of Maurice's leading generals, and even made him his brother-in-law with the highest position of Count of *Excubitores*. He entrusted other key positions to those closest to him. His brother Domentziolus became *Magister Officiorum* (Master of the Offices) the head of administration, effectively a sort of prime minister.[100] The position of Master of the Soldiers to the East was then withdrawn from a man named Narses, often titled *stratēgos* or *stratēlatēs* in Greek sources, and entrusted to Germanus, former Duke of Phoenicia.[101] Probably angered at being replaced and seeing Phocas

---

97   Theophylact Simocatta, *HU*, VIII, 9, 13 (support from the Greens in the Hebdomon district); 10, 1–7, (appeal to the Senate, coronation); 7–8 (triumphal entry); 9 (ceremony of his wife's triumph); *Chron Pasch*, a. 602 (Patriarch).
98   John of Nikiu, *Chr.*, 103, 9 (1883), p. 419.
99   Theophylact Simocatta, *HU*, VIII, 8, 7 (Comentiolus charged with defending Constantinople); 13, 1 (Peter the Kouropalates executed); 2 (Comentiolus and George). Theophanes Confessor, *Chrgr.*, AM 6095, 221 (Maurice, Peter 'and numerous others' executed).
100 A. H. M. Jones, J. R. Martindale, J. Morris, *PLRE*, 3a (1992), p.417 (Domnitziolus 1).
101 A. H. M. Jones, J. R. Martindale, J. Morris, *PLRE*, 3a (1992), pp. 933–935 (Narses

as a usurper, this Narses Strategos rebelled in Edessa. At his instigation the Persians resumed the war in 602. Two years later, Germanus was defeated and mortally wounded while engaged at Constantina of Osrhoene, caught between the walls of Edessa defended by the rebel Narses Strategos and Khosrow II's army. Phocas gave his command to a eunuch without any military experience, Leontius the Syrian. It is worthwhile to remember that Justinian did the same when entrusting Narses the Eunuch with military command in Italy. Less successful, in 605, Phocas had Leontius imprisoned after his defeat by the Persians at Arzamon, but he did not hold a long grudge, appointing him *Sacellarios* five years later.[102]

To replace Leontius the Syrian as new Master of the Soldiers to the East, Phocas chose his nephew Domentziolus the Younger, already *Kouropalates* and Patrician. He proved no more successful than his two predecessors and was defeated at Theodosiopolis.[103] He nevertheless achieved a real success when the rebel Narses Strategos surrendered to him under the promise of life. Even so the prisoner was burnt at the stake. Sources give Narses Strategos the image of a competent general before his became a traitor. What Phocas did not forgive him for was not the rebelling but probably threatening the Emperor's dynastic legitimacy by supporting the claim of a son of Maurice named Theodosius.[104]

Phocas was discredited by the setbacks he suffered at the hands of the Persians, who once again took Dara, the key border city of Mesopotamia, in 605 after a nine-month siege. Mesopotamia was on the verge of falling into Persian hands but the situation was recovered. Two years later, as Khosrow II was invading Armenia, Phocas sent a relative named Sergius as Master of the Soldiers in this distant province, another fateful choice. It was probably by this time that Phocas entrusted another of his brothers, Comentiolus Phocides, with the rank of Master of the Soldiers to the East.[105] While he was obliged to concentrate his forces in the Near East, the Lombards were eating away at the Exarchate of Ravenna and, on the River Danube, the Avars were holding the Empire to ransom. Phocas' era was coming to a bitter end.

Heraclius, the Last Soldier-Emperor?

The Governor or *Exarch* of Africa was Heraclius the Elder, a more experimented officer than Phocas, an Armenian like Narses Strategos and

---

10).
102 Theophanes Confessor, *Chrgr.*, AM 6096, 292. Sebeos, *Hist.*, 56. A. H. M. Jones, J. R. Martindale, J. Morris, *PLRE*, 3b (1992), p.780 (Leontius 29).
103 A. H. M. Jones, J. R. Martindale, J. Morris, *PLRE*, 3a (1992), pp.417–418 (Domnitziolus 2).
104 A. H. M. Jones, J. R. Martindale, J. Morris, *PLRE*, 3b (1992), pp.933–935 (Narses 10).
105 A. H. M. Jones, J. R. Martindale, J. Morris, *PLRE*, 3a (1992), p.326 (Comentiolus 2).

perhaps a relative of his. Probably judging Phocas incompetent, he rebelled in 608 and sent Bonakis, his best military leader, to occupy Pentapolis in Cyrenaica, which was achieved without a fight. He then ordered his nephews Niketas and Bonakis to occupy Egypt, depriving Byzantium of wheat. After a short battle in the suburbs, the insurgents were supported by the whole city of Alexandria, whose clergy and population hated Phocas. Nevertheless, Phocas was supported by the Blue Faction, the dukes of the interior and the arrival of Bonosus Master of the Soldiers to the East.[106] Bonakis was killed in battle, but Bonosus had to retreat after an unsuccessful attempt to retake Alexandria. All of Egypt then fell into the rebels' hands around the summer of 610.[107]

In the autumn of 610, Heraclius the Younger, the son of the *Exarch* of Africa, landed in Byzantium with barbarian troops from Africa and the supporters of the Greens gathered from the islands.[108] Phocas was betrayed by the only force left to him, the *Exkoubitoroi* of the Imperial Guard commanded by his very pragmatic son-in-law Priscus. Phocas was cruelly executed in October 610. John of Nikiu states that he was castrated and then flayed up to his legs for having raped a woman consecrated to God, before to be burnt alive and his ashes scattered to the wind.[109] Leontius the Syrian was simply clubbed to death. Comentiolus the Phocian, Phocas' brother, who had taken refuge with a few loyal troops in Ancyra (today Ankara) did not resist for long and was assassinated during an embassy led by Philippicus, who had been taken from the monastery for the occasion. Domentziolus the Younger, on the other hand, escaped Heraclius' vendetta through the intercession of Bishop Theodore of Sykeon. As his father died in Carthage during the almost mafia-like events there, the Purple fell to Heraclius the Younger who reigned from 610 to 641. He was to be the last Soldier-Emperor.[110]

Like Maurice, Heraclius was born in Cappadocia but into an important family, which prepared him for the profession of arms, he was perhaps from Armenian origin. Historiography has written a great deal about him, giving rise to the most divergent opinions while his religious and fiscal policies are controversial, as was his second marriage to his niece.[111] His contemporary, the panegyrist George of Pisidia, made Heraclius the ideal blend of the ancient heroes, Achilles, Ulysses and Nestor. But one must be

---

106 A. H. M. Jones, J. R. Martindale, J. Morris, *PLRE*, 3a (1992), pp.239–240 (Bonosus 2).
107 John of Nikiu, *Chr.*, 107 – 109, 1–15 (1883), pp.421–430.
108 John of Nikiu, *Chr.*, 109, 25 (1883), pp.421–430.
109 John of Nikiu, *Chr.*, 110, 6 (1883), pp.432–433.
110 G. J. Reinink, B. H. Stolte (eds), *The Reign of Heraclius (610–641), Crisis and Confrontation* (Leuven: Paris, Dudley MA: Peeters, 2002).
111 W. E. Kaegi, *Heraclius, Emperor of Byzantium* (Cambridge: Cambridge University Press, 2003), pp. I, 5, 12–1, 16, 195 and 201, 216 (controversial religious policies, fiscal changes, second marriage to his niece, forcible baptism of Jews in Africa in 632).

wary of official flatterers. The physical portrait given by George of Pisidia seemed to be more accurate: 'Gifted with great strength, broad-chested, with beautiful, albeit greyish eyes, white skin, blond hair and a long, full beard.'[112] Heraclius was also a cruel man and began his reign by having Phocas' head carried through the streets of Byzantium on a stake, his right hand on a sword and his carcass dragged on his stomach in the dust. He ended his reign by having the Patriarch of Alexandria tortured. During the middle ages, Heraclius was portrayed as the victor over paganism, the defender of the Faith and the precursor of the Crusades. Later, gorgeous novels of chivalry were written in his honour by Gauthier of Arras and Otto von Freising, a way to justify the present by glorifying the past.[113] In more recent times, historians first portrayed him as the brilliant reformer who instituted the military regions known as themes, or as a courageous Emperor struck by fate and hostage to fluid circumstances. Changing their minds, historians strip him of his reputation as a great reformer and turn him into a mere transitional monarch to the Meso-Byzantine period. And so it goes in historiography. In the end, it was the Emperor who carried the heaviest burden. In addition to war, he had to face palace conspiracies, the scandal of the 11 children he had by his niece Martina, the opposition of the Latins and the Orthodox to the Monophysite heresy he embraced.

The first five years of Heraclius's reign were catastrophic, but we have to remember the fact his father died unexpectedly just before he ascended on the throne. In others words, accustomed to obeying his father, Heraclius the Younger was probably not ready to become Emperor. In Asia, the Persians continued imperturbably to build on the momentum created under Phocas and swept into Palestine and Chalcedon between 609 and 615.[114] During this troubled period, Heraclius first delegated the leadership of military operations to experienced generals. The Empire was then put on the defensive by the Persians, who had the strategic initiative and were targeting Anatolia.

Supporting the new Emperor, Priscus became Master of the Soldiers to the East and fought the Persians in the heart of Cappadocia. Nonetheless, he led the campaign of 611–612 rather sluggishly. In 612, he trapped the General Shahín at Caesarea in Cappadocia (modern Kayseri, Turkey), but seems to have objected to the visit when Heraclius came to the army and even refused to receive him, claiming to be ill. He then let Shahín to escape. Afterwards, Heraclius called him back to Byzantium under an honourable pretext, but dismissed him from his position as Count of *Excubitores* and

---

112 George of Pisidia, *De Expeditione Persica*, I, v. 81 (ancient heroes); III, v. 99 and 431 (portrait).
113 Drapeyron L., *L'Empereur Héraclius et l'Empire byzantin au VIIe siècle* (Paris: Ernest Thorin, 1869), p.111 (medieval accounts). S. Luchitskaya, 'L'Empereur Héraclius vu par les chroniqueurs occidentaux du XIIe siècle', *Cahiers de Recherches Médiévales et Humanistes*, 37 (2019), pp.75–96.
114 Marius Aventicensis, *Chr.*, a. 615.

had him put on trial before the Senate for high treason. Finally tonsured in December 612, Priscus died in his monastery the following year. Heraclius reshuffled the deck, his cousin Niketas became Count of the *Excubitores*. The position of Master of the Soldiers to the East previously held by Priscus was given to two men: Philippicus recalled from his forced monastic retirement and Theodore the Kouropalates, Heraclius's brother.[115] Theodore's recall of the elderly Philippicus seems like a surveillance measure. There was probably some familial memory in this appointment because Heraclius the Elder was the trusted *hypostratēgos* of Philippicus during the years 585–587. This whole episode reveals that Heraclius was afraid for his throne, which was undoubtedly at the mercy of a *pronunciamento*.

The war continued disastrously and, in 613, the strategic dam formed by the Mesopotamia and Osrhoene was broken. The Persians took Damascus, then Antioch after twice defeating an Imperial Army near these two major cities, whose populations were then deported. It was a major blow and difficult for Romano-Byzantine Empire to cope with.

In 614, the Persians attacked in two directions. In the south, they reached as far as Jerusalem, where they captured the relic of the True Cross. In the north, they crossed Anatolia again and penetrated as far as Chalcedon on the Asian side of the Bosphorus, 6km from Byzantium. Philippicus did not risk confronting them in a frontal battle, but sneaking in central position he invaded Persarmenia and cut off the supplies of the northern Persian Army, forcing it to retreat from Chalcedon. By doing so, he won a strategic victory that made up for the lack of tactical resources. Philippicus died the following year and by then, all the generals of Maurice's generation had disappeared. This temporary lack of experienced generals was cruelly felt in the Romano-Byzantine camp.

On the other hand, the Persians had two master strategists at their head, Shahrbaraz and Shahín Vahmanzadegan. The latter led the raid on Chalcedon proving Lazica was not a necessary step for the Persians to wet the hooves of their horses in the Bosphorus. Shahrbaraz is not a name and literally means 'Boar of the Empire' it was a boastful Sassanid title for a *generalissimo* who the Greeks called *Sabaros* or *Salbaras*. He had taken Jerusalem, capturing the True Cross. Four years later at the command of Khosrow II, Shahrbaraz repeated the feat of Cambyses, invading Egypt and seizing Alexandria.

In Europe, Heraclius was unable to stem the advance of the Avars, the Kutrigurs and the Sklavenes. Around 615, when the latter formed an alliance with the Avars, the northern Balkans were lost[116]. As news flew quickly across the Mediterranean, King Sisebuth of the Visigoths took advantage of these events to retake the lost coastal cities. In 615, he inflicted

---

115 Nikephoros of Constantinople, *Brev.*, 2, 55–58. *Chr. paschale*, a. 612.
116 Vl. Popović, 'La descente des Koutrigurs, des Slaves et des Avars vers la mer Égée: le témoignage de l'archéologie', *Comptes rendus des séances de l'Académie des Inscriptions et Belles-Lettres*, 122–3 (1978), p.597.

two defeats on the Roman-Byzantines. The following year, at the request of the Patrician Caesarius, a fragile peace was ratified in Byzantium itself.[117] It was a dramatic time for the Romano-Byzantine Empire.

The Empire's efforts had to be concentrated, as Phocas had tried to do but without success. Around 620–621, Heraclius made peace with the Khan of the Avar at a high price. He let the Sklavenes establish themselves along the Velika Morava River, launching unopposed raids as far as Greece. Relatively free on the European front, he brought about a revolution in the high command, taking charge of the army to fight the Persians in 622 and gathering the best troops from Thrace and the East. Beforehand, he ensured political stability by leaving a regency government in Byzantium under his son Heraclius Constantine, the Patriarch Sergius and the Patrician Bonus. Prudence was the hallmark of Heraclius' first campaign against the Persians, as he landed in Bithynia on the southern coast of the Black Sea. There, securing the path to Chalcedon, cautiously he trained his troops throughout the summer before moving into Cappadocia, where he interrupted the lines of communication of Shahrbaraz, who had penetrated into Anatolia and Galatia. This indirect manoeuvre seems to have been inspired by that of Philippicus eight years earlier. Shahrbaraz came to seek Heraclius in Cappadocia but was defeated and retreated. Heraclius again had to convince the Khan of the Avars to respect the truce and sought to negotiate with him personally in 623. Tempers flared and he narrowly escaped capture.[118] Bad news came again in 624 when the Persians, who had seized the ports of Phoenicia, landed on the island of Rhodes and were able to cut off naval communications between Byzantium and Egypt.

Heraclius was on the brink of losing everything between 29 July and 8 August 626 when the Avars, reinforced by the Sklavenes and the Persians led by Shahrbaraz himself, attacked Byzantium in a vast pincer movement. Heraclius had his army divided into three corps, keeping one under his command to fight the Persians in Lazica, the second commanded by his brother Theodore the Kouropalates was to contain Shahín in Anatolia and the third was to garrison Byzantium. The Avars were free to besiege the city walls, while the Persians reaching Chalcedon cut off Heraclius and Theodore. This brilliant encircling plan was foiled by the political incompetence of the Avars and by the Byzantine Fleet, which had no trouble sinking the Sklavene and Persian pirogues. Themselves cut off by the Bosphorus, the two barbarian allies fought two separate sieges against the same city. In the end, logistics prevailed and the Avars with their Slavic vassals withdrew, followed shortly after by the Persians. The withdrawal was hastened by the arrival of one of the three army corps, commanded by Theodore the Kouropalates.

---

117 Ch. Diehl, *L'Afrique Byzantine. Histoire de la domination Byzantine en Afrique (533–709)* (Paris: Ernest Leroux, 1896, p.531.
118 J. Howard-Johnston, 'Heraclius' Persian Campaigns and the Revival of the East Roman Empire 622–630', *War in History*, 6 (1999), pp.1–44.

THE EMPEROR AS COMMANDER OF THE ARMIES

Heraclius, engaged in the East against the Persians, had neither given up nor gained anything. Khosrow II's clumsiness finally gave Heraclius the keys to victory. When Shahrbaraz learned that the King of Kings wanted to cut off his head because of his failure, Heraclius offered him the opportunity to defect. Shahrbaraz hesitated but retreated. Byzantium was saved and the enemy morale broken. At the same time, the other great Persian military commander, General Shahín, was defeated in north-eastern Anatolia by Theodore the Kouropalates. The road to Persia was now open, and Heraclius had the means and the reasons to go on the offensive the next year. This marked a break with the great Imperial strategy, which up until then had been to contain the Persians and favour the status quo along the border.

Ambitiously Heraclius planned to strike at the heart of the Sassanid Empire; it should perhaps be remembered that his father had already fought in Persarmenia and could have mentored him. It was nevertheless a perilous manoeuvre, and the only two Roman Emperors to have tried it, Valerian in 260 and Julian in 363, both lost their lives in the process. For this reason, Heraclius was not going to do as same, but to innovate strategically by attacking the Caucasus from the north. He relied on the Khan of the Khazars, who provided him with a large contingent. Iberia and Albania, today's Georgia and Azerbaijan, were invaded. From there, the army descended through Persarmenia towards Ctesiphon in a risky winter campaign that the Khazars quickly deserted from.

During the winter of 626–627, Heraclius launched a surprise attack on Sharbaraz's headquarters at Archesh, after destroying the Persian vanguard at Salbanon. During this boldly-led campaign Heraclius deserved his mythological name and his reputation as a warrior reached as far as the Franks. Fredegar reported that in a battle, that he neither located nor dated, Heraclius and the Persian King Khosrow II agreed to pit two champions against each other rather than risk their armies in battle. Then Khosrow II sent some sort of new Goliath, so big he frightened the entire Romano-Byzantine Army. Heraclius cut off his head![119] Fredegar may have been influenced by the issue of silver dishes celebrating Heraclius as a new David triumphing over Goliath. Today, the Metropolitan Museum of Art in New York has a complete series of silver dishes on this heroic theme. It probably refers to the single combat between Heraclius and the Persian General Rahzadh at the Battle of Nineveh on Saturday 12 December 627, one of the few dates to have come down to us so precisely, no doubt because of this unusual feat. The Emperor threw Rahzadh down from horseback. Then he killed two other champions before the trumpets sounded the charge. During the ongoing fight, Heraclius' horse was wounded in the thigh by the spear of an infantryman but victory was already achieved.[120] All Byzantine historians confirmed Heraclius' taste for duels before battle.[121]

---

119 Fredegar, *Chr.*, 64 (duel with sword), 65 (portrait).
120 Theophanes Confessor, *Chrgr.*, AM 6118, 318.
121 Sebeos, *Hist.*, 38, 125–126. Theophanes Confessor, *Chrgr.*, AM 6094, 311–312 (this

After having destroyed the Persian Army at Nineveh, Heraclius took Khosrow II's Treasure which had been left in Saqarta.[122] Although he failed to take the Persian capital Ctesiphon, Heraclius looted the royal palace of Dastagird, utterly destroyed the Temple of Fire, an important place for Zoroastrianism, and caused a dynastic crisis among the Sassanids, with Khosrow II being overthrown. However, the Persians still had to be dislodged from the Levantine regions, and in March 629 Jerusalem was liberated. Heraclius was victorious when he concluded the peace treaty in July, obtaining the evacuation of the eastern provinces of the Empire by the Persians and putting an end to the 400-year war with the Sassanids. The True Cross was taken back from the Persians and brought to Byzantium in triumph.[123]

Heraclius succeeded in doing what no 'Roman' Emperor had ever achieved, breaking Persian imperialism. He was one of the rare conquerors who subjugated the Persians as, before him, had the Macedonian King, Alexander the Great, with whom he was incline to compare himself. Nevertheless, Heraclius's victory over Persia was Pyrrhic and left the Empire reeling and his ownl health had deteriorated. Byzantium itself suffered a severe toll during the siege of 626. The Empire's second city, Alexandria, was undoubtedly impoverished from previously being pillaged by the Persians. The tribute paid to the Avars, the cost of waging a war and devastations caused by Persians, Sklavenes and Avars emptied the Imperial Treasury. As a sign of the misery of the times, Byzantium's main aqueduct, devastated by the Avars in 626, was not repaired until 150 years later.[124] Meanwhile, in the distant theatre of Spain, the remaining Byzantine-controlled cities were taken by the Visigothic King Svinthila between 621 and 631.

Moreover, Heraclius was unlucky in that, after achieving this strategic success, he faced a more formidable new threat: the Muslim Arabs. According to Nikephoros of Byzantium and Theophanes Confessor, war was caused with the ending of a tribute paid to the Arab tribes for a desert watch.[125] This harsh period marked the end of Heraclius' career as a Soldier-Emperor, since, at the age of 50, his health was failing. Then he delegated

---

episode is dated earlier as 623–624).

122 Theophanes Confessor, *Chrgr.*, AM 6118, 317–318 (most detailed narrative, Razates is the name by him given to the Persian general; 3'000-strong reinforcements promised by Khosro II); Sebeos, *Hist.*, 34, 113 (allusive); 38, 126 (short narrative, Persian general is called Ročveh, 'the Fortunate'); Movses, II, 11 (1961), p.89 (Persian general Ročveh, 'the Fortunate' gathered and call for reinforcement but he is killed with his troops; short reconstructed monologues); Michael the Syrian, *HU*, XI, 3, t. 2 (1963), p.409 (very short narrative 'Persians were defeated, their learder was killed'; Saqarta). *Chr. 1234*, t. 1 (1937), p.183.

123 C. Zuckerman, 'Heraclius and the Return of the Holy Cross' in C. Zuckerman (ed.), *Constructing the Seventh Century* (Paris: Collège de France/ CNRS/ Centre de recherche d'histoire et civilisation de Byzance, 2013), pp.197–219.

124 A. Cameron et al (eds), *Late Antiquity: Empire and Successors*, p.110.

125 Theophanes Confessor, *Chrgr.*, AM 6123, 336. Nikephoros of Constantinople, *Brev.*, 20, 14–20.

THE EMPEROR AS COMMANDER OF THE ARMIES

command and stationed himself in towns further and further north, depending on the Muslim advance: Edessa, Antioch and then Byzantium.

Military operations against Muslim invaders began when the so-called *'vicarius'* or more appropriately the Duke of Arabia, Theodore, defeated them by surprise east of the River Jordan at the Battle of Mothous (toady Mu'tah) in September 630. Ignoring this minor setback, they returned every year after 632, sent by the first Caliph Abu Bakr al-Siddiq. The Muslim forces also took advantage of the unrest in the Persian Empire to attack it and also to subdue the Bedouin tribes. As a result, in January 634, the old Romano-Byzantine and Persian enemies joined their reduced forces against the invaders, but were defeated at Firad, or Firaz, in Mesopotamia by the General Khalid ibn al-Walid, the best of the Muslim generals.[126] In February 634 the Patrician Sergius lost his life, either at the Battle of Dâthín, near Gaza, or at the Battle of al-Araba, when fighting Amir ibn al-As. By late July, Theodore the Kouropalates faced the latter in what Arab historians call the Battle of Ajnadayn, possibly south-west of Bethlehem.[127] The Muslims were victorious again and Theodore the Kouropalates fled to join his Imperial brother in Edessa. By September, Damascus had to pay tribute to Khalid ibn al-Walid who was coming from the east. Shortly afterwards, the Byzantine troops of Palestine were defeated at Fihl (Pella).

In 635, Heraclius offered his daughter in marriage to the Persian King Yazdgard III and the two monarchs planned a pincer attack against the Muslims for the following year. Thus, in 636 Heraclius assembled a large army at Antioch to defend Syria and Palestine. These forces temporarily recaptured Emesa and Damascus pushing the Muslims back southwards into Arabia Petraea. The best Byzantine forces in the East, under Theodore Trithyrios the Sakellarios, the Armenian General Vahan/Baanes, Niketas the Persian the son of Shahrbaraz and Jabalah the Sheikh of the Ghassanids all converged there. Khalid ibn al-Walid crushed them in August at the Battle of the Yarmuk – the Yarmuk is a tributary of the Jordan near Lake Tiberias.[128] In November, it was the Persians turn to be smashed – at the Battle of al-Qadisiyyah, a hamlet on the western bank of the River Euphrates in Iraq.

From now on Heraclius was unable to prevent the loss of Palestine and then Syria, which he left before or after the Battle of Yarmuk battle, depending on the source. He watched from afar, but without relinquishing his authority. In 638, when the Duke of Osrhoene John Kataias, trapped

---

126 A. I. Akram, *The Sword of Allah: Khalid bin al-Waleed – His Life and Campaigns* (Oxford: Oxford University Press, 2004).

127 W. E. Kaegi, *Byzantium and Early Islamic Conquests* (Cambridge: Cambridge University Press, 1992), pp.88–97; Cl. Lo Jacono, 'La bataille d'Aǧnadain selon Ibn Aʿtam al-Kūfī's Kitab al-futūḥ' in R. Traini (ed.), *Études en l'honneur de Francesco Gabrieli à l'occasion de son quatre-vingtième anniversaire*, vol. 2 (Rome: 1984), pp.447–457.

128 David Nicolle, *Yarmuk 636 AD: The Muslim Conquest of Syria*, Campaign Series 31 (Oxford: Osprey Publishing,1994).

in the stronghold of Edessa, paid an enormous tribute of 100,000 solidi to the Arabs without his approval, Heraclius exiled him and replaced him with Ptolemy.[129] Then incapacitated by dropsy, Heraclius refused to stay in Byzantium preferring the discrete palace of Hieronymus on the Asian shore. He probably did not want his deformed body to be seen rather than because he feared the water as was said. For three years, he retreated there with his wife and niece Martina.

In 639, Heraclius ordered his governors not to pay tribute to the Saracens who, in retaliation, invaded Egypt, a rich but poorly defended province. Some of the population even joined the Saracens, attacked Heraclius' troops and took part in the looting and massacre of civilians. The Patriarch of Alexandria, Cyrus Moukaoukis, proposed to increase the tribute demanded by the Caliph Omar and to conclude a matrimonial alliance by giving him Eudocia, a daughter of Heraclius.[130] Heraclius refused, but his name was no longer feared. Condemned for heresy by the Lateran Council, he died at the age of 66 on 11 February 641.[131]

The loss of Mesopotamia, Osrhoene, Syria, Phoenicia, Palestine and Egypt deprived the Imperial Treasury and the Army of a significant part of their resources. If we take the *Notitia Dignitatum* as an indication, this represents 207 units out of the 467 of the Eastern Roman Empire – just under half of the army.[132] The mould of the Romano-Byzantine Army, ever partly transformed, had been broken! The damage was even greater at sea, as the Phoenician and Egyptian merchant navies and their expertise in shipbuilding fell into the hands of Muslims. Timber too, as the Syrian Levantine region was rich in forests, particularly cedars, which were still the emblems of Lebanon and had already been used a long time before for King Solomon's Temple.[133] This territorial decline meant that Byzantium was to lose its hitherto uncontested naval supremacy, and by the late seventh century the city was within reach of the Arab Fleet.

Heraclius I was the best and the worst. The best because he was the only Emperor to break Persian power, the worst, because no Emperor had ever lost as much territory as he did. He was also a brawler and a lover of war like his illustrious model, Alexander the Great. Nevertheless, his dynasty survived until the beginning of the next century. From 638, he took care to crown two sons born from his two marriages, Heraclonas and Heraclius Constantine, a temporary and awkward pairing.

---

129   Theophanes Confessor, *Chrgr.*, AM 6128, 340 (John Kataias).
130   Michael the Syrian, *HU*, XI, 7, t. 2 (1963), p.425 (Omar came to an agreement with the Patriarch Cyrus, who was disowned by Heraclius, hence the invasion). Iorga N., *Histoire de la vie Byzantine, tome 1, l'Empire œcuménique (527–641)*, Bucarest, edition from the author, (1934), p.170.
131   W. E. Kaegi, (1992), p.67.
132   Ph. Richardot, *La fin de l'Armée Romaine*, p.82.
133   C. Morrisson (ed.), *Le monde Byzantin*, p.194 (wood-rich regions).

THE EMPEROR AS COMMANDER OF THE ARMIES

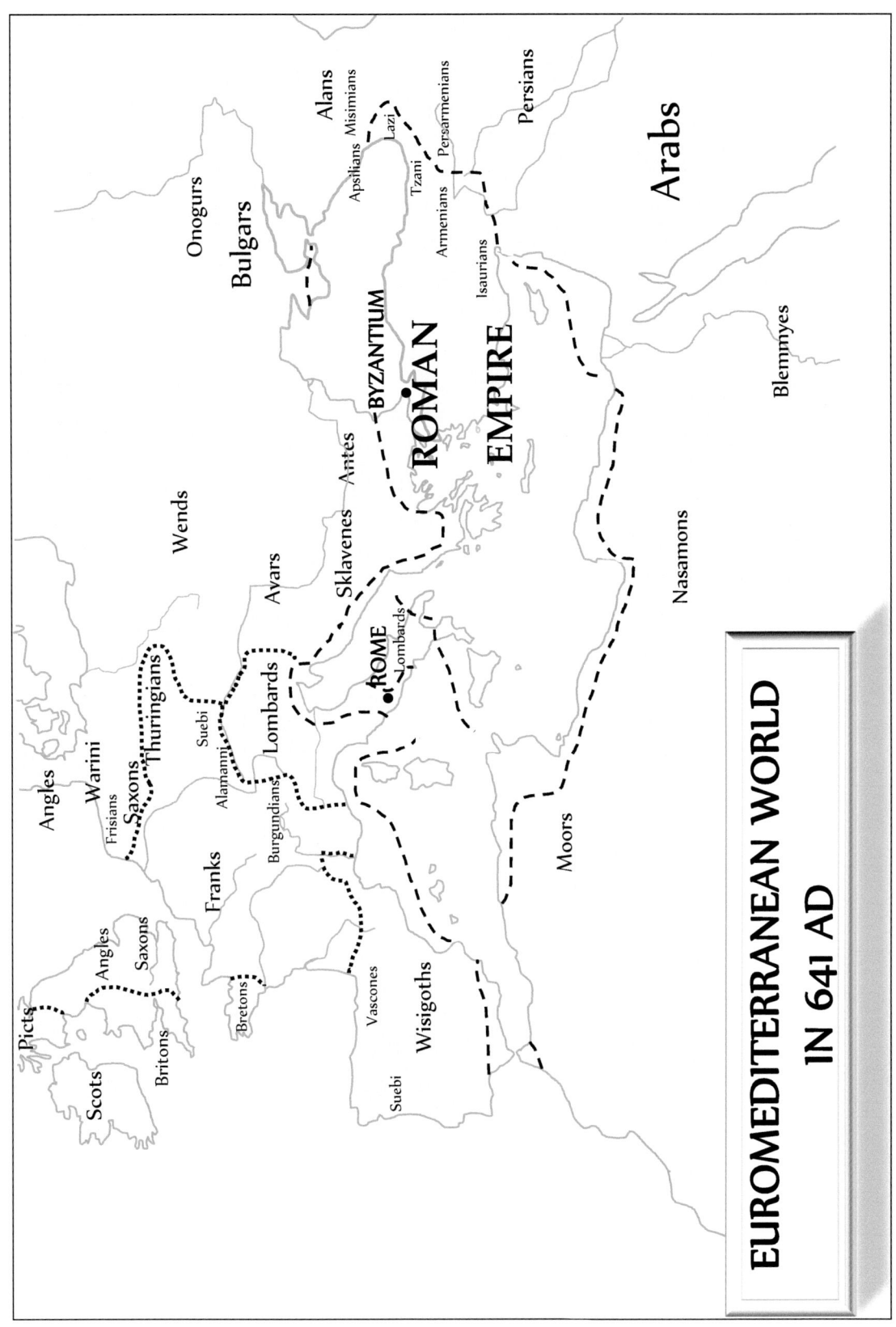

EUROMEDITERRANEAN WORLD IN 641 AD

The Emperor in Military Dress

A fifteenth century manuscript miniature depicts the equestran statue of a Constantinopolitan Emperor and has long been subject of debate over the identity: Theodosius I or Justinian I? If the medieval designer expressly wrote the name Theodosius on the horse, modern scholars prefer to see him as Justinian because the latter had a giant bronze statue made around 542–543, mounted on a column, to commemorate his victory over the Persians.[134] This medieval drawing perfectly suits with a description by Procopius of Justinian's equestrian bronze statue holding an *Orbis Terrarum* and wearing military garb:

> On this horse is mounted a colossal bronze statue of the Emperor, and this statue seems to be inhabited by Achilles, since his costume is known by that name. She wears half-boots and her legs are not covered by leggings. She also wears a breastplate in heroic fashion, a helmet covers her head which gives the impression of moving back and forth, and a bright light shines from it.[135]

The 'breastplate in heroic fashion' or muscled cuirass can be found on most Imperial representations from the period and even on the icons of military saints today. It is worn by both a mounted Emperor and the officer on foot bringing him a Victory statuette as shown on Barberini Ivory, today in the Louvre Museum. This breastplate is wrapped with a harness characteristic throughout the Byzantine period, a band across the torso that joins two others falling from the shoulders. A double row of pteruges, probably of leather, are attached to the cuirass to protect the upper thighs and the upper arms. Only the officer has spalieres, a Byzantine innovation. Both wear a tunic with embroidered long sleeves and a military cloak, *paludamentum* or *chlamys*, held on the right shoulder by a clasp or *kornoukipion*. Their legs are bare with half-boots laced up at the front and leaving the toes uncovered, from the Roman *crepidae*-type. The Emperor's boots are adorned with a lion's head at the top of the half-boot. The Emperor grasps a spear with a ball heel to balance the iron head. The Barberini Ivory is variously supposed to depict Constantine, Zeno, Anastasius I, but more likely Justinian.[136] For war an alternative such as a scale cuirass was perhaps more suitable, eventually with a breast harness and a cord or ribbon tied

---

134 Ph. W. Lehmann, 'Theodosius or Justinian? A Renaissance Drawing of a Byzantine Rider', *The Art Bulletin*, vol. 41, no. 1, March (1959), pp.39–57.
135 Procopius, *Aed.*, I, 2, 5–8.
136 G. Schlumberger, 'L'ivoire Barberini', *Monuments et mémoires de la Fondation Eugène Piot*, 7-1 (1900), pp.79–94; A. P. Kazhdan, A. M. Talbot, A. Cutler, T. E. Gregory, N. P. Ševčenko (eds), 'Barberini Ivory', *The Oxford Dictionary of Byzantium*, vol. 1 (Oxford: Oxford University Press, 1991), p.254.

THE EMPEROR AS COMMANDER OF THE ARMIES

above the belly in the Hellenistic and Roman fashion to designate an officer. Such a cuirass with a triple row of pteruges is worn by a mounted Emperor on the ambo of Henry II, or Ambo Heinrichs II in German, today in the palatine Chapel of Aachen. Dated to the early eleventh century it reuses two sixth-century Coptic ivory panels.[137] For later periods, such as the eleventh and twelfth centuries, Byzantine iconography depicted the Emperor with gilded offensive and defensive weapons.[138] It is likely that they were also gilded during the sixth and seventh centuries.

Unlike Procopius, the aforesaid fifteenth century manuscript depicts an Emperor with an odd peacock feather headgear in the manner of an Indian chief or a Rio carnival dancer. This is known as the toupha or touphion, terms defining a tiara, but various reasons led to interpreting this toupha as a feathered crest.[139] The first known instance of the toupha was a coin minted at Pavia around 315, depicting Constantine I wearing a helmet adorned with pearls and a crest with a double row of peacock feathers bearing the *chi rho* symbol on the band. Constantine is wearing a riveted, scale cuirass but no cloak. A horse's head appears to his right, and on his left he is carrying a shield featuring Romulus and Remus under the Roman she-wolf. A pole supporting a globe with a cross stands above the shield. Late Roman coinage perpetuated this model but with a spear on the right shoulder. The same type was found on a *solidus* of the Ostrogothic King Athalaric. Coins of Anastasius and Justin I also show them as soldier-Emperors, but their helmet has become a diadem with a double row of pearls and a fairly thick curved crest. This model persisted up to the era of Constantine IV (668–685).[140] A 1060s silk artefact, known as the Gunthertuch Tapestry in the Bamberg Diocesan Museum, shows an Emperor on horseback wearing a diadem with pearls and pendants as depicted worn by Justinian in the Ravenna mosaic, while a *Fortuna* to his left brings him a bowl-shaped helmet with a crest of peacock feathers. This seems to solve the enigma of the feather hat, originally a crest on a helmet then a skullcap superimposed on the Imperial tiara occasionally used for parades. The excessive stylisation of figures on coins no doubt misled many people, explaining the switch

---

137 H. Lepie, A. Münchow, *Elfenbeinkunst aus dem Aachener Domschatz* (Pandersberg: Imhof Verlag, 2006), pp.26–58. An Emperor hunting, perhaps with a hidden coat of mail worn under a cloak, is also depicted on seventh-century Coptic ivory panel, in the collection of the Walters Art Museum in Baltimore, reference number 71.1144. Two tapestries, in the Textile Museum in Washington, and in the Cleveland Museum of Art, have very similar representations.

138 M. Parani, Reconstructing the Reality of Images: Byzantine Material Culture and Religious Iconography (11th–15th centuries), (Leiden: Brill, 2003), pp.102–103 (distinction between ceremony and war, gilded artefact).

139 A. P. Kazhdan, A. M. Talbot, A. Cutler, T. E. Gregory, N. P. Ševčenko (eds), 'Toupha', vol. 3 (1991), p.2100 (τοῦφα, τουφίον).

140 W. Hahn, *Moneta Imperii Byzantini*, vol.1, *Von Anastasius I. bis Justinianus I. (491–565)*, vol. 2, *Von Justinus II bis Phocas (565–610)*, vol. 3, *Von Heraclius bis Leo III (610–720)*, (Vienna: Veröffentlichungen der Numismatischen Kommission X = Österr. Akad. der Wiss., phil.-hist. Kl., Denkschriften 148, 1973, 1975 and 1981).

Late Roman Emperor, possibly Justinian, in Armour wearing a Diadem
Late Roman Emperor, possibly Justinian I, on horse triumphing over various enemies from East and West. He is wearing a classical style of armour with leather *subarmalis*, and a thrusting spear with a counterweight, after the Barberini Ivory, Musée du Louvre, Paris.

Fifth-Century or Sixth-Century Byzantine Emperor Anastasius I in Armour
Solidus of Anastasius I, Emperor 491–518. The Emperor's bust is topped with a *toupha*-like crested helmet decorated with pearls, he is wearing scale armour and holding a spear and shield decorated with cavalryman motif.

THE EMPEROR AS COMMANDER OF THE ARMIES

Emperor Constantine I with a Toupha-Crested Helmet
Constantine I, the first Christian Emperor wearing a helmet adorned with a peacock crest and displaying the *chi rho* symbol on the brow. A pole supporting a globe with a cross stands above the shield. In a more pagan way, his shield represents the she-wolf suckling Remus and Romulus the twin brother founders of Rome. After a silver coin minted in Pavia in 315.

Emperor Theodosius or Justinian Crowned with w Toupha
The *toupha* or *tufa* (τοῦφα) or *touphion* (τουφίον) was a peacock crest on a military helmet or a ceremonial cap. Facsimile after a fifteenth century sketch depicting the bronze equestrian statue of Theodosius or Justinian atop a column standing above the Augustaion square in Constantinople.

Emperor Justinian I with A Toupha-Crested Diadem
The Byzantine Imperial *toupha* seems to have been a crested ornament put on a diadem for a triumph. After the portrait of Justinian from the Ravenna basilica on Bishop Gunther (died 1065) tomb's fabric from Bamberg, Germany, showing an allegory of Byzantium offering a *toupha* to either the Emperor John I Tzimiskes (971–976) or the Emperor Basil II (976–1025).

from helmets to diadems, since the late Roman helmets were decorated with cabochons and pearls.[141]

---

141 Ph. Richardot, *La fin de l'Armée Romaine*, p.247.

2

Major Commands

> If, in fact, I am not haranguing you in Carthage but on the battlefield, it is because I do not wish to prevent anyone, if he so wishes, from deserting and going over to the enemy, because everyone can here express his political tastes without any danger.
>
> The Patrician Germanus to his army in Libya, Procopius, *Bellum Vandalum*, IV, 16, 24.

The constantly-at-war army of the sixth and seventh centuries was based on a command structure inherited from the late Roman Empire and which lasted until the Muslim invasion. The initial scheme was a strategic field army garrisoned in or around Byzantium, and regional border commands. Precise military ranks in Latin or their transliteration into Greek are rarely given by sixth-century historians, but can be found in epigraphy and legal texts. The Latin expression to discuss a general was *magister militum*, literally 'master of the soldiers' and translated in this book as master of the soldiers. This type of rank was called a *magisterium* (magistracy).[1] The Hellenised form was *magistros*, although it was barely used by Procopius and other Byzantine historians, it was given once to the ambassador Peter after the success of his mission.[2] An army was called *stratos*, a soldier *stratiôtēs* and a general *stratēgos*.[3] The commander of a field army was sometimes called a *stratēlatēs*.[4]

---

1 *CJ*, XII, 35, 18, 1 (year 492). Marcellinus Comes, *Chr.*, a. 547 (*praesentale magisterium*).
2 Procopius, *BG*, VI, 22, 24.
3 Army, στρατός; soldier, στρατιώτης, general, στρατηγός.
4 Στρατηλάτης.

Generals of the strategic forces

The military legacy of the late Roman Empire can be read from the *Notitia Dignitatum* compiled *c.* 400 and listing all the commands with their assigned units, an incomparable document but with some parts lost.[5] At the top level, commanding the field army were two *generalissimos* known as *magistri militum praesentales* (masters of the soldiers present). The word *praesentalis* means literally 'present' or something perhaps like 'on hand'. This kind of general was 'present at the Emperor's side.' By the 400s, they commanded 69 elite units.[6] Hypothetically the first master was on the European side in Byzantium, the second on the Asian side in Chalcedon, bartely 2km opposite. Their forces were deployed either on the Danube or in the Near East. In 479, under Zeno's reign these two *generalissimos*, named in Greek *stratēgoi peri Basileia* (generals at the Royal Court) still existed along with the *scholôn archonte*s (leaders of the palace guard) in command of the so-called *Scholae Palatinae*.[7] The high command structure was precisely laid down by Procopius for the second year of the Anastasian War against the Persians in 503:

> There were chiefs for each unit and four generals commanded the whole: Aerobindus, the son-in-law of Olybrius who had a short time before ruled over the western part of the Empire and who was general of the East; Celer the chief of the palace guards, a title which the Romans call *magister*. There were also the commanders of the troops in Byzantium, Patricius the Phrygian and Hypatius, the Emperor's nephew. These were the four generals. They were also accompanied by Justin [then Count of *Excubitores* and Emperor to be].[8]

The historian Malalas added to these a civil governor, the Patrician Apion, Praetorian Prefect of the East, but did not mention Justin.[9] The 'commanders of the troops in Byzantium', Patricius the Phrygian and Hypatius were the two Masters of the Soldiers Present leading the strategic forces. In 513, these troops were virtually annihilated in a battle with the rebel Vitalian the Thracian near Akris (now Kaliakra in Bulgaria). As Vitalian was able to mobilise 60,000 supporters, we can assume that the strategic troops were

---

5   Translation of military list into French, Ph. Richardot, *La fin de l'Armée Romaine*, pp.83–141; F. Lot, 'La Notitia dignitatum utriusque imperii ses tares, sa date de composition, sa valeur', *REA* (1936), pp.285–338 (this study is still invaluable today).
6   *Notitia Dignitatum*, OR. V and VI.
7   Malchus, *Fragm.*, 18, 4 (στρατηγοί περί βασιλέα; σχολῶν ἄρχοντες).
8   Procopius, *BP*, I, 8, 1–3.
9   John Malalas, *Chrgr.*, XVI, 9.

severely beaten. Emperor Anastasius I had to pay a ransom of 5,000 pounds in gold to ransom his nephew Hypatius and had to confer on Vitalian the title of Master of the Soldiers to the Thraces.[10] The death of Anastasius I brought Vitalian into the fold of the new Emperor Justin I. Vitalian was then appointed Master of the Soldiers Present along with Justinian, the Emperor to be. An ivory diptych commemorating Justinian's accession to the consulship in 520 gives him the Latin title of *com(es) (et) mag(ister) eqq(uitum) and p(editum) praes(entalis)* (count and master of the cavalry and infantry present). A letter that reached Rome on 18 July 520, from a bishop to Pope Hormisdas, mentioned Justinian and Vitalian simply as *magistri militum*.[11]

In the same year, after the assassination of Vitalian the Thracian, only Justinian I retained this title and when he became Emperor in 527, the position of master of the soldiers present gradually disappeared.[12] Still a few clues in the law of 528 referred to the levying of troops *de praesentalibus et orientalibus* (present and eastern) for the benefit of Armenia.[13] After that, the lack of documentary evidence leaves plenty of room for supposition. In 532, when the *Nika* revolt broke out in Byzantium, the Imperial Guard was almost nonexistent. Public order was restored by the regular troops and the *bucellarii* of Belisarius who were just returning from a war against the Persians. They were helped by a contingent of Heruls led by Mundo, the leader of the Illyrian troops, who was there by chance.[14] This bitter episode highlights the weakness of Byzantium's military structure, which no longer corresponded to the *Notitia Dignitatum*. As the law of 528 explained it the forces *praesentales* (present on the Emperor's side) had been siphoned off for the needs of the war against the Persians and remained in the East. The major command was from then the *magister militum per Orientem* (master of the soldiers to the East).

After 533, the Justinianic reconquests inevitably disrupted the previous Roman system, as it extended the military obligations to territories which, in today's geography, cover Libya, Tunisia, Algerian-Moroccan coastline, Slovenia, northern Croatia and Italy. Even with modern resources, this would require a great deal of manpower and logistics. The initial force used to achieve these conquests was Belisarius's Army of the East, and the troops who embarked with Belisarius and who had previously fought the Persians complained bitterly about the African expedition and wanting to see their

---

10   John of Antioch *Fragm.*, 214ᵉ, 6–10. A. H. M. Jones, J. R. Martindale, J. Morris, *PLRE*, 2 (1971), p. 1173.
11   A. H. M. Jones, J. R. Martindale, J. Morris, *PLRE*, 2 (1980), p.646 (diptych inscription, letter to the Pope); Metropolitan Museum no. 17.190.53, https://www.metdmuseum.org/art/collection/search/464489.
12   C. Zuckerman, 'L'armée' in C. Morrisson (ed.), *Le monde Byzantin. L'Empire romain d'Orient (330–641)*, Paris: PUF, Nouvelle Clio, 2006), p.165.
13   *CJ*, I, 29, 5.
14   Procopius, *BP*, I, 24, 40–41 (*bucellarii* and Heruls); 43–44 (Palace garrison; indecision).

families again.[15] Even after conquering Africa from the Vandals, the law of 534 still gave Belisarius the regional rank of *Magister Militum per Orientem* (Master of the Soldiers to the East).[16] From a geographical point of view, it seems absurd to continue calling the general commanding the troops in Africa with the name of Master of the Soldiers to the East, but from a budgetary point of view, this avoided creating a new post for Africa. For the same reason, Belisarius kept this title until 542, even when he was fighting in Italy.

The rank of master of the soldiers present reappeared in late 546, when the Armenian Prince Artabanes the Arsacid, after his recall from the government of Africa, was appointed '*stratēgos* (general) of the soldiers in Byzantium'. He was also granted the title as Count of the *Foederati*.[17] It was nevertheless an empty title as suggested by an episode that occurred in 559, when the Kutrigur Huns penetrated to the gates of Byzantium which was guarded only by ceremonial troops, the *Scholae* and *Excubitores*, and by factions of chariot race supporters. Just imagine London defended by the Yeomen of the Guard and by football fan clubs! In the emergency Justinian had to summon a retired Belisarius, who was in his sixties and no longer had *bucellarii*! Belisarius collected together 300 veteran infantrymen who had fought with him in the past, plus a host of townsfolk and peasants. Ultimately, launching a surprise attack, they won a victory over what has must be more a body of raiders than a regular army.[18] This miserable episode, like the previous one in 532, clearly showed that Byzantium no longer had a permanent garrison of mobile troops.

From Justinian I onwards Romano-Byzantine Emperors preferred a temporary main theatre commander when the situation was needed over a permanent *generalissimo* such as the former *magistri militum praesentales*. Heraclius I settled it for a time in his own way when he took personal command of the army campaigning against the Persians until 630, but three years later, at the time of the Arab conquest, he was ill and appointed high-ranking dignitaries to replace him. The first was his brother Theodore the Kouropalates, who was beaten; the office of *kouropalates*, was not military in nature but literally the honorific 'Palace Keeper'. It appeared in the late fifth century and from Justinian I onwards was reserved for members of Imperial family, giving access to the position of *generalissimo* during the reign of Maurice and until Heraclius.[19]

---

15   Procopius, *BV*, III (10, 5.
16   *CJ*, I, 27, 2, 36.
17   Procopius, *BG*, VII, 31, 10 (στρατηγός τε τῶν ἐν Βυζαντίῳ στρατιωτῶν καὶ ἄρχοντα τῶν φοιδεράτων). Marcellinus Comes, *Chr.*, a. 547 (rank of *praesentale magisterium*).
18   Agathias, *Hist.*, V, 15, 2 (*scholae* inefficiency); 7 (Belisarius is recalled); 16, 2–3 (heterogeneous forces).
19   A. P. Kazhdan, A. M. Talbot, A. Cutler, T. E. Gregory, N. P. Ševčenko (eds), 'Kouropalates', vol. 2 (1991), p.1157, (κουροπαλάτης).

After the failure of Theodore the Kouropalates, Heraclius appointed the joint command of Vahan (or Baanes) the Armenian and Theodore Trithyrios the Sakellarios. Trithyrios as a former Master of the Soldiers to the East was thus not without military experience. His title of *sac(c)ellarius* or *sakellarios* appeared late in the fifth century. The word is derived from the Latin *saccellus*, a 'small bag'. The Greek term *sakelion* also means 'treasury' and implied financial functions that are well documented for the eighth century and for two centuries earlier in ecclesiastical administration. The *sacellarius* was probably akin to a paymaster-general or comptroller of the armies. There was only one in the Empire[20]. Theophanes used the expression *monostratēgos* (sole general) to refer to the commander-in-chief of a field army. Other examples attest to this rank. In 697, Tiberius III appointed his brother Heraclius as *monostratēgos* for all cavalry matters, and a seal preserved also gave him the title of Patrician. In 717, the *monostratēgos* appointed by the usurper Basil was beheaded along with his benefactor.[21] This was no longer the model of the later Roman Empire, but was already the Byzantine Army.

Generals of the Imperial Guard

During the later Roman Empire, the second highest rank after the generals of strategic armies was that of *magister officiorum*. Head of the administration and armament factories, on paper he commanded the seven *Scholae Palatinae*, whose members were known in Greek as *skolarioi*, plus a *schola* of agents in affairs, *agentes in rebus*. The title of master of the offices lasted until Leo VI the Wise (886–912).[22] From the late fifth century, the master of the offices controlled a new figure known as the count of *Scholarii*, *comes Scholariorum*, the tactical leader of the *Scholae Palatinae*.[23] The chain of command during the Anastasian War does not mention the count of *domestici*, *comes domesticorum*. According to the *Notitia Dignitatum*, the eastern Imperial Guard had two counts of *domestici*, one for the horse *domestici*, and the other for the foot *domestici*, two corps of cadet officers.[24] *c.* 500, sources mention only one count of *domestici* with a rank equivalent to that of count of *Scholarii*. In 508, a retaliatory naval expedition against Ostrogothic Taranto was even commanded by Romanus count of *domestici* and Rusticus count of *Scholarii*[25]. The diptych commemorating Justinian's

---

20 A. P. Kazhdan, A. M. Talbot, A. Cutler, T. E. Gregory, N. P. Ševčenko (eds), 'Sakellarios', vol. 3 (1991), pp.1828–1829, (σακελλάριος).
21 Theophanes Confessor, *Chrgr.*, AM 6190 (Heraclius/Herakleios is entitled μονοστρατηγός); AM 6210 (Basil).
22 C. Morrisson (ed.), *Le monde Byzantin*, pp.98–99.
23 Ph. Richardot, *La fin de l'Armée Romaine*, pp.33–39, 117–141.
24 *Notitia Dignitatum*, OR.I.15; XV; OC.I.3; XIII (*comes domesticorum equitum*); OR.I.16; XV; OC.I.14; XIII (*comes domesticorum peditum*).
25 Marcellinus Comes, *Chr.*, a. 508.

consulship and his rank as master of the soldiers also gives him the title of count, as attested by a letter from 519 received by Pope Hormisdas.²⁶ This could be seen as the title of count of *domestici*, but why not also that of the *Scholarii*? As Procopius judged the palace troops to have little fighting spirit, it would be easy to see this as an honorary distinction, but above all, it was a position of trust.

At the start of the Anastasian War in 503, Procopius mentions a command that does not exist in the *Notitia Dignitatum* and is specific to the Eastern Roman Empire. It was held by Justin, the Emperor to be and then Count of *Excubitores* or *Comes Excubitorum*, in Greek *komēs tôn Exkoubitôv* or *Exkoubitorôn*.²⁷ Created by Leo I, this rank took precedence over the count of *Scholarii*. Those who held this position proved ro have real military qualities: in 570, Tiberius, Count of *Excubitores* and future Emperor, repelled an Avar invasion in Thrace.²⁸ This position was a stepping stone to the Imperial Purple for Justin I, Tiberius II Constantine and Maurice, a feat that the Praetorians had not been able to achieve.²⁹ Nevertheless, the attribution of this rank to Maurice is more assumed than attested. When the *Excubitores* stopped supporting Maurice or Phocas, the fall was likely to come. Counts of the *Excubitores* were often members of the Imperial family. Their names are known for a period stretching from Justin to Armenian Valentin, from 515 to 641. After this period information became scarce, indicating a decline. For the second half of the seventh century, all that is known is the seal of Stephen, Count of the divine *excubiton* (guard), *komēs tou theiou exkoubitou*.³⁰ The rival corps to the *Excubitores* for highest promotions was that of the *spatharii* or *spatharioi* (sword-bearers) a branch from the *cubicularii* (chamberlains). Narses the Eunuch in 570 held the honorific position of *kubikularios* and *protospatharios* (first sword-handler). In 717, Sergius *Stratēgos* of Sicily was also a *protospatharios*. As he was not in a position to take any command of the *spatharioi* in Byzantium, this rank probably could not refer to the head of this corps but to a particular distinction.³¹

The Imperial Guard also had a count of the *foederati*, *comes foederatorum*, in Greek *komēs tôn phoideratôn*.³² The *foederati* in question were regular troops, no longer barbarian allies of uncertain loyalty and were also recruited from the Romano-Byzantines. It is assumed that the

---

26   A. H. M. Jones, J. R. Martindale, J. Morris, *PLRE*, 2 (1980), p.646.
27   Κόμης τῶν ἐξκουβίτων. Theophylact Simocatta, *HU*, III, 11, 4 (Tiberius is said κόμης τῶν ἐξκουβιτώρων).
28   John of Biclaro, *Chr. VT*, 13 (Tiberius).
29   A. Cameron et al (eds), *Late Antiquity: Empire and Successors*, p.291.
30   A. H. M. Jones, J. R. Martindale, J. Morris, *PLRE*, 3b (1992), p.1510.
31   Theophanes Confessor, *Chrgr.*, AM 6063, 244 (Narses); AM 6210, 398 (Sergius). A. P. Kazhdan, A. M. Talbot, A. Cutler, T. E. Gregory, N. P. Ševčenko (eds), 'Protospatharios', vol. 3 (1991), p.1748 (Latin *spatharius*, plural *spatharii*; Greek σπαθάριος, plural σπαθάριοι).
32   Κόμης τῶν φοιδεράτων.

Thracian Vitalian, who revolted against Anastasius I and held the rank of count, probably of the *foederati* because he led barbarians and not regular troops.[33] In 533, during the expedition against the Vandals, their leaders were Dôrotheos, ex-Master of the Soldiers to Armenia, and Solomon, a member of the military corps of *domestici*.[34] Around 574, under Tiberius II, an expedition of 15,000 men was led by Maurice, who was then Count of the *Foederati*, and by a certain Narses who acted as second in command, *Hypostratēgos*. In this study I have referred to him as *Strategos* to avoid any confusion with Narses the Eunuch, who was commander-in-chief during the second part of the Gothic War.[35]

Regional and Border Commands

As in the past, the master of the soldiers to the East was the senior regional command. He defended Empire's largest and richest provinces and had authority over the troops stationed there. From the time of Justinian I onwards, this position was given either to the Emperor's designated successor or to the most capable general in times of crisis. In this way Belisarius was appointed to the position twice. With administrative support from Hermogenes, the Master of the Offices, and additional troops, he repulsed the Persians in 530. The following year, he had up to 20,000 soldiers at his disposal and was able to win the war.[36] Ten years later, Belisarius was recalled from Italy to fight again the Persians who had broken the truce. In 542, he managed to bring Khosrow I back within his borders, but had to retreat due to a lack of troops. A victim of defamatory remarks by his disloyal subordinates, he was recalled to Byzantium.[37] Over the course of the century, military magistracy in the east was consolidated, probably resulting in the disappearance of the masters of the soldiers present. In 578, Tiberius II Constantine appointed Maurice, his *Caesar* and designated successor, as Master of the Soldiers to the East in order to push back the Persians.[38] By this time, the master of the soldiers to the East had become the leading military command in the Empire.

---

33 A. H. M. Jones, J. R. Martindale, J. Morris, *PLRE*, 2 (1980), p.1171. Victor de Tunnuna, *Chr.*, a.510; 511; 514 ('comes' foederatorum?').
34 Procopius, *BV*, I, 11, 3.
35 Theophanes Confessor, *Chrgr.*, AM 6074, 252. W. Treadgold, *Byzantium and its Army*, pp.15–16, 63–64, 73–74 (admiral). J. F. Haldon, *The Byzantine Wars* (Brimscombe Port Stroud: The History Press, 2008, pp.17, 61 (year 577), p.70 (year 578).
36 Procopius, *BP*, I, 13, 5 (insufficient forces in Mesopotamia and Phoenicia); 9 (appointment to the *magisterium* of the Orient); 10 (Hermogenes *magistros*); I, 18, 5 (20,000 soldiers).
37 Procopius, *BP*, II, 21, 34 and *Anecdota*, IV, 1–12 (recall after defamatory reports).
38 John of Biclaro, *Chr.VT*, 49 (Maurice).

The second in rank was the *magister militum per Illyricum* (master of the soldiers to Illyricum). He was in charge of the Western Balkan region of Illyricum, which was particularly vulnerable to invasion and was partly overrun by the Ostrogoths. He was not a King in his province and still had to submit himself to military regulations, and he was also under the jealous scrutiny of the Emperor. Anastasius I reminded a Master of the Soldiers to Illyricum named John that soldiers could not be transferred from one place to another without his consent and that their pay could not be reduced. If transfers were necessary in an emergency, the Emperor and the praetorian prefect had to be notified, specifying the units and places concerned, as the prefect was responsible for logistical matters such as food.[39] The Illyrian chronicler Count Marcellinus gave two unofficial Latin synonyms for this rank: *ductor militiae illyricianae* and the old-fashioned *ductor utriusque militiae illyricianae* (leader of the Illyrian army and leader of the two armies).[40] Procopius preferred unofficially, but speaking his opinion, titles such as *tôn Illyriôn stratēgos* (general of the Illyrias). At the beginning of Justinian I's reign, two barbarian officers were promoted to this regional command. The first was Askum the Hun in 528, after his baptism. Unfortunately for him, he was defeated and captured in a battle by his former compatriots who refused to return him under ransom.[41] From 528 or 529 to 532, this rank was held by Mundo another barbarian general. Ironically, 15 years before his appointment Mundo was the leader of a band of looters and had killed Sabinian the Younger, who held this rank, at the Battle of Horreum Margi.[42]

The third regional command was held by the *magister militum per Thracias* (master of the soldiers to the Thraces). Procopius refers to him as the *Thrakēs stratēgos* (general of Thrace) or the *stratēgos katalogôn epi Thrakēs* (general of the troops in Thrace). This was an uncomfortable and risky position, as two of its holders were killed by the Bulgars: Julian in 493 and Aristus six years later at the Battle of the River Tzurta along with the Counts Nicostratus, Innocent, Tancus and Aquilinus.[43] Chilbudius, another unfortunate holder of this command, was killed by the Sklavenes in 534. His successor, the Armenian Prince Artabanes the Arsacid, unable to oppose the Sklavenes in 549, was sent to Sicily.[44]

The *Notitia Dignitatum* placed the master of the soldiers to the Thraces above the regional dukes, but things were no longer so clear under Justinian I. In 527, Libelarius was promoted from Master of the Soldiers to the Thraces to Duke of Mesopotamia. In theory, this was a demotion, but not necessarily so, given that Mesopotamia was the location of the hottest

---

39   *CJ*, I, 29, 4.
40   Marcellinus Comes, *Chr.*, a. 499 and a.530.
41   John Malalas, *Chrgr.*, XVIII, 21.
42   Marcellinus Comes, *Chr.*, a. 530. Procopius, *BP*, I, 24, 41 (542).
43   Zonaras, *Ep.H*, III, 137 (Julian). Marcellinus Comes, *Chr.*, a. 499 (Aristus).
44   Procopius, *BG*, VII, 14, 2–6 (Chibuldius); 39, 8 (Artabanes).

confrontation with Byzantium's most formidable enemy. Nevertheless, it was a short-lived experience for Libelarius, as after being defeated near the Persian fortress of Nisibis, he was replaced with Belisarius, then simply an officer in the *bucellarii*.[45]

The master of the soldiers to the Thraces was under the sphere of authority of the new *quaestor exercitus*. The economic dilapidation of the Danubian frontier in *Moesia Secunda* and *Scythia* was hampering the supply of garrisons and forced Justinian I to create a new civilian and military region on 18 May 536. In command of this was the *quaestor exercitus* (*quaestor* of the army) and his office was named the *quaestura exercitus*. His sphere of action covered the two Danubian provinces mentioned above, plus the region of Caria in Asia Minor, the Aegean Sea islands and Cyprus. He drew the supplies from Caria and eastern Mediterranean islands to the Danubian garrisons. This also made him an admiral, or rather a maritime officer. His headquarters was at the port of Odessus. The first *quaestor* of the army was Bonus who still held this title in 553 when he was with Narses the Eunuch in Italy where he also took an operational military command.[46] The *quaestura exercitus* was still in existence in the 570s, but its continuity after that time is unclear. The former diocese of Thrace probably remained covering the provinces of Haemimontus, Europa and of Thrace itself. The rank of master of the soldiers to the Thraces persisted. Priscus distinguished himself with the army of Thrace, leading five campaigns against the Avars in 588, 593, 595, 597–598 and 599.[47]

The most important change took place under Justinian I in 528, when the duke of Armenia was replaced with nothing less than a *magister militum per Armeniam* and *Pontum Polemoniacum and gentes* (master of the soldiers to Armenia and the region of Pontum Polemoniacum and amongst peoples). Tzanica and Lazica fell upon his authority according to Agathias. This powerful position was first held by Zita, whom Procopius called Sittas and Theophanes Confessor Tzitas. He had under his command the border guards plus four units taken from the three masters of the soldiers and elsewhere.[48] This relative administrative revolution put Armenia on the map of major commands and strategic concerns.[49] Armenia's strength by 530

---

[45] Procopius, *BP*, I,12, 23 – 24.
[46] Nov. J., 51. W. Treadgold, Byzantium and its Army, pp.15–16, 63–64, 73–74 (naval officer under Justinian reign); A. H. M. Jones, J. R. Martindale, J. Morris, PLRE, 3a (1992), pp.240–241.
[47] Theophylact Simocatta, *HU*, VI, 4, 7 à 5, 16 (1st campaign); 6, 2 à VII, 1, 1 (2nd campaign); VII, 5, 10; 7, 1–5 à 11, 8; 11, 1–9 (3rd campaign); VII, 13, 1–5 (4th campaign); VIII, 1, 11 à 4, 2 (5th campaign).
[48] *CJ*, I, 29, 5 (law of 528). Theophanes Confessor, *Chrgr*., AM 6020, 175 (promotion of Tzitas over dukes and counts, 4 *numeri*). Agathias, *Hist.*, IV, 21, 1 (rank of master of the soldiers to Colchis and Armenia); G. Greatrex & S. N. C. Lieu (eds), *The Roman Eastern Frontier and the Persian Wars, Part II, AD 363–630. A Narrative Sourcebook,* (London: Routledge, 2002), p.83.
[49] John Malalas, *Chrgr*., XVIII, 10 (master of the soldiers to Armenia, dukes).

was estimated at 15,000 men, half of that of the opposing Persian Army.[50] Operational necessities forced the provisional appointment of *magister militum vacans* (vacant master of the soldiers). The term 'vacant' existed in the lower ranks to designate officers who were detached and without specific command.

The masters of the soldiers had under their command border *comites* and *duces* (counts and dukes). Theoretically, a duke was in charge of a province smaller than the count but unlike the Western Roman Empire, the Eastern Roman Empire only had two regional counts. The *Notitia Dignitatum* listed no less than 13 dukes for the Eastern Roman Empire. It assigned each a dedicated number of units varying in size. The numerous border units were smaller than the mobile troops but they had to deal with few nomadic raiders.[51] *c.* 400, there were one-third more troops in the Middle East than in the Euro-Balkan part of the Empire.

Table 1 – The Eastern Regional Commands and their Troops according to the *Notitia Dignitatum* (*c.* 400)

Senior and Regional Commanders in Europe	Number of units	Senior and Regional Commanders in Asia and Africa	Number of units
Count of Domestici on Horse *Comes Domesticorum Equitum*	2	**Master of the Soldiers in the Imperial Presence II** *Magister militum praesentalis II*	35
Count of Domestici on Foot *Comes Domesticorum Peditum*	2	**Master of the soldiers to the East** *Magister Militum per Orientum*	22
Master of the Offices *Magister Officiorum*	8	Duke of Phoenicia *Dux Foenicis*	26
Master of the Soldiers in the Imperial Presence I *Magister militum praesentalis I*	34	Duke of Syria *Dux Syriae*	18
Master of the Soldiers to Thrace *Magister militum per Thracias*	27	Duke of Palestine *Dux Palaestinae*	30
Duke of Scythia (Danube Delta) *Dux Scythiae*	22	Duke of Osrhoene *Dux Osrhoenae*	19
Duke of Moesia II *Dux Moesiae secundae*	24	Duke of Mesopotamia *Dux Mesopotamiae*	17
Master of the Soldiers to Illyricum *Magister Militum per Illyricum*	26	Duke of Arabia *Dux Arabiae*	21
Duke of Moesia I *Dux Moesiae Primae*	26	Duke of Armenia *Dux Armeniae*	26

---

50 Procopius, *BP*, I, 15, 11.
51 Ph. Richardot, *La fin de l'Armée Romaine*, pp.117–141 (translation).

MAJOR COMMANDS

Duke of Riparian Dacia *Dux Daciae Ripensis*	29	**Count to Isauria** *Comes per Isauriam*	2
Sub-Total Europe	**200**	**Count of the Egyptian Frontier** *Comes limitis Aegypti*	31
		Duke of the Libyas *Dux Libyarum*	?
		Duke of Thebaid *Dux Thebaidos*	44
		Unnamed?	?
		Sub-Total Middle East	**291**
		TOTAL	**491**

Sources after 400 are far less precise and give only fragmentary information. The line of command had to be redefined. In 472 a law from Leo I mentioned the dukes of Pentapolis (the western part of Libya was in Vandal hands), and Pontus, the counts of Pamphylia, Lycaonia and Pisidia. These were something new and did not exist in the *Notitia Dignitatum*.[52] Cilicia and Isauria were not border regions but inner insecure areas. To deal with this, Emperor Leo I in 472 instituted a new *comes rei militaris* (military count) in Pamphylia, a province to the west of Cilicia. Twenty years later, in Perge, a legion was attested there.[53] These new counties were regional commands of much lesser importance than the ordinary duchies, even though the title of count was theoretically higher. On 1 January 492, Anastasius I specified to John Master of the Soldiers Present that troops dispatched to the East were to obey the border dukes and him, without answering to the Master of the Soldiers to the East and that they were to be controlled by an aide-de-camp called *ad responsum* (to the answer).[54] This reflects the overcomplexity and inner conflicts of Byzantine administration. Another military edict found at Ptolemais referred to the Libyan Pentapolis.[55] Anastasius I suppressed the *vicarius Thraciarum*, governor of the late Roman diocese of Thrace, replacing him by two vicars instead: one responsible for civil duties and the other with a military charge committed to the Long Walls later called the

---

52 *CJ*, XII, 59, 10 (*officii virorum spectabilium ducum Palaestinae, Mesopotamiae, novi limitis Phoenices, Osrhoenae, Syriae et Augustae Euphratensis, Arabiae et Thebaidis, Libyae, Pentapoleos, utriusque Armeniae, utriusque Ponti, Scythiae, Mysiae primae, secundae, Daciae, Pannoniae, officii virorum spectabilium comitum Aegypti, Pamphyliae, Isauriae, Lycaoniae et Pisidiae*).
53 *CJ*, XII, 59, 10 (edict from 472); F. Onur, 'The Anastasian Military Decree,' pp.133–212.
54 *CJ*, I, 35, 18.
55 Emperor Anastasius edict on Libya Pentapolis, *Die vom Kaiser Anastasius fur Libya Pentapolis erlassenen Formae*, K. E. Zakariä von Lingenthal (ed.), (Berlin: *Monatsberichte der k. Akademie der Wissenschaften zu Berlin*, 1879, pp.134–158.

Anastasian Wall, a buffer zone for Byzantium.[56] In 535, Justinian replaced these two vicars with a *praetor Iustinianus Thraciae* who had to watch over the Long Walls.[57] Following the Kutrigur incursions of 540 and 559, Justinian probably abolished the ineffective office of *praetor Iustinianus Thraciae*.

An inscription found at Gerasa in Arabia and dated 5 August 533 refers to a certain Anastasius as *komētos kai doukos kai archontos* (count and duke and commander).[58] This complicated inscription reveals that, alongside the traditional title of duke, Anastasius was also given the title of count and appointed military governor of Roman Arabia. This demonstrates the maintenance and evolution of Roman titles in the provinces, while Procopius preferred periphrases such as *os tôn ēn Mesopotamía stratiôtôn ērchēn/tôn ēn Mesopotamía katalogôn archon* (he who commands the soldiers in Mesopotamia or chief of the troops in Mesopotamia).[59] Theophylact Simocatta used the Greek term *lochagos* to designate a military duke of Thrace, but this was unofficial and corresponded here to something like 'chief'.[60] Below the rank of duke was that of *vicarius* (vicar), which came from the Hellenised term *bikarios*. It was an administrative function in the fifth century, and around 630–631, a man named Theodore held this rank and, with the help of Arab tribes including the Koraishites, defended the desert approaches to Gaza. He was stationed in the town of Muchea (variously identified as today Ma'âb/Mu'ân/Khierbhat al-Mahna).[61]

Through *Edict* XIII of 539, the innovative Justinian I reorganised Egypt into five duchies: Egypt proper, centred on Alexandria and located to the west of the Nile Delta; Augustamnica, located to the east of the delta; Arcadia, located in the Fayum in Middle Egypt; Thebaid, located around Antinoe in Upper Egypt to the south; and Libya, which actually comprised only Cyrenaica. This reform suppressed the former diocese with his vicar once called *comes limitis Aegypti* (count of the Egyptian frontier). These five duchies were divided into eparchies or districts, which in turn were divided into pagarchies or cantons. An augustal prefect was in charge for the region of Alexandria. The aim of this reorganisation was to exercise better control over the inhabitants, including both bad taxpayers and Monophysite heretics.[62] It was more a police measure than a defensive one.

---

56 J. Wiewiorowski, 'The Defence of the Long Walls of Thrace (Μακρά Τείχη τῆς Θράκης) under Justinian the Great (527–565 AD)', *Studia Ceranea*, 2, (2012), pp.181–194.

57 *Nov J.*, 26.

58 *SEG*, VII, 874 and *JRS*, XVIII, 1928, 170/1, 37. A. H. M. Jones, J. R. Martindale, J. Morris, *PLRE*, 2 (1980), p.62 (κόμητος καὶ δουκὸς καὶ ἄρχοντος; *archontos* is a later Greek word for classical ἄρχων).

59 Procopius, *BP*, II, 14, 12 (ὃς τῶν ἐν Μεσοποταμίᾳ στρατιωτῶν ἦρχεν) and 18, 16 (τῶν ἐν Μεσοποταμίᾳ καταλόγων ἄρχον).

60 Theophylact Simocatta, *HU*, II, 10, 0 (λοχαγός).

61 Theophanes Confessor, *Chrgr.*, AM 6123, 336 (βικάριος).

62 *CJ*, edict XIII. L. Valensi, 'La réorganisation de l'Égypte Byzantine au temps de

In the event of an invasion, these scattered Egyptian forces were going to prove militarily ineffective.

The Conquest of Africa and Italy Creates New Commands

The count of Africa or *comes Africae* existed around 400, but was linked to the Western Roman Empire.[63] Following Belisarius's success over the Vandals, Justinian I recreated the African command, but not as a county any more. He set up an African diocese by the law of 13 April 534. He gave to it a praetorian prefect but without instituting any master of the soldiers. He continued to designate Belisarius as Master of the Soldiers to the East as discussed above. Historical sources give Belisarius's African command generic terms that have nothing official about them. Procopius called his former leader either *stratēgos autokratōr* or *autokratōr pantos tou polemou* (autocrat general or total autocrat of war, i.e. commander-in-chief).[64] The law of 534 also established five military dukes in Africa: Tripolitania, Byzacene, Numidia, Mauritania and Sardinia. These dukes did not come under the authority of the praetorian prefect but under Belisarius. Justinian even asked him to set up a garrison commanded by a tribune at Septem (now Ceuta in Spanish Morocco). His law outlined the military organisation of the duchies. It ordered the reoccupation of Roman era forts by raising troops called *limitanei* (border guards) as in the later Roman Empire. It authorised Belisarius free rein to assess the size of the garrisons, but referred to a now lost appendix in which force format was suggested. The dukes and tribunes were asked to train their troops in the use of arms in order to prevent them marauding and enable them to resist the enemy.[65]

Following Belisarius's departure for Italy, a general succeeded him in Africa, but his exact title is unclear. The most plausible would have been master of the soldiers to Africa. Budgetary reasons may be suspected for not creating this rank but such a situation could not last for long. By 546–547, Prince Artabanes the Arsacid was called by Procopius *Libyēs stratēgos* (general of Libya) and his successor John Troglita was qualified by the poet Corippus as *dux summumque magister militia* (supreme leader and master of the soldiers).[66] This may be an indication for a dedicated master

---

  Justinien Ier', *Bulletin de l'Association Guillaume Budé*, LH-11, (1952), pp.55–71.
63 *Notitia Dignitatum*, OC.XXV.
64 Procopius, *BV*, III, 11, 18 (στρατηγός αὐτοκράτωρ); *BG*, VI, 22, 4 (αὐτοκράτωρ παντός τοῦ πολέμου); A. H. M. Jones, J. R. Martindale, J. Morris, *PLRE*, 2 (1980), p.184 (wide range of general titles).
65 *CJ*, I, 27, 2, 2 (Septem); 4a (reoccupation of the old forts); 5 (free assessment of garrison's size); 7 (mission and recruitement of *limitanei*; lost appendix); 9 (duties of dukes and tribuns); 20–32 (listing the five dukes).
66 Corippus, *Joh*, I, 51 (*dux summumque magister militiae*); I, 127, 131; II, 193; III, 60; IV, 263, 306, 310, 400, 549; V, 11, 589; VI, 8, 25-*sq*.; VII, 52, 73-*sq*.; VIII, 107,

of the soldiers to Africa (which the Greeks called Libya). Nevertheless, historiography dates the institution of a *magister militum Africae* to a later period – between 570 and 582. The very earliest epigraphic mention of this title, held by Gennadius, dates from 6 May 586.[67] When Heraclius the Elder raised the Army of Africa against Emperor Phocas in 608-610, the oldest sources gave him the titles of *patrikios kai strategios Aphrikēs* (patrician and general of Africa), but historiography prefers to give him the title of *exarchos* or *exarch*.[68] The *exarch* was a new magistracy above the praetorian prefect of Africa, who remained in office as head of the administrative services. He had more extensive military and civil powers. The *exarch* of Africa was created during the reign of Emperor Maurice (582–602). Its first mention dates to July 591 and is attributed to the same Gennadius, who previously had pacified the Moorish unrest in 578–579 and in 587 or 588.[69] Another command is quite unclear, that of the parts of Spain wrested from the Visigoths under Justinian I by Liberius. Agathias noted that Imperial troops were garrisoned there around 559.[70] They were probably commanded by a tribune, as at Septem. With the creation of five new duchies in Africa and the elevation of the Duke of Armenia to the rank of master of the soldiers, there should have been around 20 duchies at the time of Justinian I.

When Belisarius was ordered to invade Sicily in 535, he used his title of Master of the Soldiers to the East, undoubtedly because, as with in Africa, he brought with him most of the troops in this command. Furthermore, the government certainly wanted to make substantial savings by not appointing a new master of the soldiers to the East and by not creating a *magister militum per Occidentem* (master of the soldiers to the West), a rank that is nowhere attested.[71] Belisarius was forced to leave almost half of his troops behind to guard Africa. After the first capture of Rome on 9 or 10 December 536, he succeeded in having a friend named Phidelis appointed Praetorian Prefect of Rome, a position hitherto held by the illustrious Cassiodorus, a

---

135-sq. (*magister*). Procopius, *BV*, II, 28, 43 (Λιβύης στρατηγὸς Artabanes); 44–45 (John Troglita) and *BG*, III, 31, 4 (Artabanes) and 7 (John Troglita). A. H. M. Jones, J. R. Martindale, J. Morris, *PLRE*, 2 (1980), p.127 (Artabanes), p.646 (John Troglita).

67   *AE* (1937), n° 148 and 1946, n° 241 (Gennadios); B. Bavant, 'Le duché byzantin de Rome. Origine, durée et extension géographique', *MEFR, Moyen Âge, Temps modernes*, 91, n° 91-1 (1979), p.50, n. 46.
68   Theophanes Confessor, *Chrgr.*, AM 6100, 293 and 6101, 297 (πατρίκιος καὶ στρατηγὸς Ἀφρικῆς and στρατηγὸς Ἀφρικῆς); A. H. M. Jones, J. R. Martindale, J. Morris, *PLRE*, 2 (1980), p.585 (title of exarch, exarchos, ἔξαρχος and periphrases to define the government of Africa).
69   Gregory the Great, *Registrum Epistolarum*, I, 59 (letter mentioning Gennadius, July 591). Ch. Diehl, (1896), pp.466–478.
70   Agathias, *Hist.*, V, 13, 7–8.
71   P. Keating, *Belisarius Military master of the West, Book One: Nika*, (Cambridge: Pegasus Elliot Mackenzie Publishers, 2021). The more convenient title of military master of the West is still unattested.

zealous servant of the Ostrogothic Kingdom.[72] The Gothic War dragged on, losses and desertions ensued and successive reinforcements were brought in. Conquering Africa and Italy was beyond the Empire's capabilities. It took three years, from 535 to 538, to bring reinforcements to Belisarius that were comparable to those of the African expedition. First were sent barbarians from across the Danube, then regular troops assembled in Byzantium made up of Isaurians and Thracian cavalrymen, and finally soldiers commanded by the master of the soldiers to Illyricum with some Heruls.[73] This was called scraping the bottom of the barrel and involved no more than the two major regional commands on the Danube, Illyricum and Thracia, plus the count of Isauria; a quarter of their number in barbarian mercenaries was added to these regular troops. In 540, Belisarius was recalled from Italy to go to the East to fight the Persians.

After his departure, the chain of command in Italy was unclear and provided a strategic opportunity to the Ostrogoths. They elected a new King in the person of Totila, who undoubtedly took advantage of the absence of a unified military command in Italy to regain lost ground. In 544, Belisarius returned to Italy, only to be recalled four years later after the death of Theodora, his wife's friend and the real promoter of his career. In 550, his replacement was finally appointed; Germanus, cousin of Justinian I. We can only suppose he then held the rank of, *magister militum per Italiam* (master of the soldiers to Italy).

Germanus was faced with a dilemma: he had received a lot of money from Justinian I but no troops. He sent his two sons to recruit soldiers in Illyricum and Thrace, who would volunteer to fight in Italy perhaps for a better pay. Germanus was reinforced too by the contingent of Philemuth the Herul, and by his own son-in-law John, the nephew of Vitalian, Master of the Soldiers to Illyricum. Lastly, barbarian mercenaries from the banks of the Danube, probably Sklavenes, were handsomely paid to join him. The Lombard King promised Germanus 1,000 armoured infantry. A large army was thus formed, based on a mercenary model, especially as Germanus had a large personal fortune at his disposal. It was Artabanes then appointed Master of the Soldiers to the Thraces, who was charged with reinforcing Sicily, but with only a small contingent.[74] The premature death of Germanus means that it is impossible to say whether his army was actually deployed,

---

72   Procopius, *BG*, V, 20, 20.
73   Procopius, *BG*, V, 27, 1 (1,600 Huns, Sklavenes, Antes early 537); VI, 5 (1–2 (5,600 men) and 13, 16 (7,000 men including 5,000 led by the general of Illyricum and 2,000 Heruls in 538).
74   Procopius, *BG*, VII, 39, 8 (Artabanes appointed master of the soldiers to Thracians and sent to Sicily); 9 (Germanus received money to recruit an army); 10 (Philemuth the Herul, his son-in-law John nephew of Vitalian then Master of the Soldiers to Illyricum); 16 (mustering a numerous army); 17 (the son Germanus recruited regular soldiers at Byzantium, Thrace and Illyricum who deserted their units); 18 (cavalry units from Thrace mobilised with the Emperor's approval); 19 (Barbarians from Danube area); 20 (Lombards).

but Justinian I agreed beforehand that the two regional commands on the Danube should be stripped in favour of Italy. It was an ordinary solution to deal with shortages. The sources failed to mention who was in charge during the two years following Germanus' death, but finally, in 552, Narses the Eunuch was appointed commander-in-chief to Italy.

On 13 August 554, when most of Italy had been conquered, Justinian I imposed 27 laws by means of the Pragmatic Sanction at the request of Pope Vigilius, which sought to preserve property ownership, the Romano-Ostrogothic tax system and the attribution of the *annona* (i.e. a wheat ration) to physicians, grammarians, teachers of the liberal arts and lawyers. The Pragmatic Sanction also guaranteed the gifts made by Totila's predecessors but cancelled his own and, above all, separated civil and military judges.[75] The Pragmatic Sanction only gave Narses the Eunuch the civil title of *praepositus sacri cubiculi*. The other authority to whom this law was sent was Antiochus, Prefect of Italy. The absence of any military title was in keeping with the old Roman legal principle of *arma cedant toga*, that is 'separating arms from robes'. Narses was nevertheless the main representative of Imperial authority in Italy. After his recall in 568, he was replaced with the Praetorian Prefect Longinus, apparently without military power and who was region ofin office until 584. Italy retained the same administrative divisions as in the Ostrogothic period, divided into 18 provinces.[76] The northern frontier was divided into duchies, which were swept away one after the other by the rapid Lombard conquest.[77] One of these duchies was attested in 574, according to Gregory of Tours, who described then a certain Sisinnius as *magister militum a parte imperatoris* (master of the soldiers in the Emperor's territory), maybe the entire Liguria. This Governor resided at Suze and held the crossing of the Cottian Alps, but did not oppose the retreat of Zaban's Lombards who, after a failed invasion of Gaul, fled before Mummolus's Franco-Burgundian army. It lasted until 576.[78] The Greek title of *exarch* was initially synonymous with prefect, according to Simocatta equating the praetorian prefect to *exarchos tôn praitoriôn*.[79] Towards the end of Tiberius II Constantine's reign or the beginning of Maurice's, it took on a different meaning when he merged civil and military power to create a 'super-governor', a sort of viceroy. A letter from Pope Pelagius II dated 4 October 584 described the Patrician Decius as *Exarch* of Italy.[80] This is the earliest mention of the title, consistent

---

75 *Pragmatica Sanctio pro panditione Vigilii*, Nov. J., App. VII, 2 (revocation of Totila's donations); 11 (extension of the *Justinian Code* to Italy); 5, 8, 13 and 21 (respect for property); 22 (*annonae* maintained); 23 (separation between civil and military justice). B. Bavant, (1979), p.49.
76 Paul the Deacon, *HL*, II, 14–24.
77 B. Bavant, (1979), p.42 (Forum Julii-Friul, Trento, Lake Maggiore, Como, Cottian and Graian Alps, precise but largely conjectural enumeration).
78 Gregory of Tours, *HF*, IV, 44. Paul the Deacon, *HL*, III, 8.
79 Theophylact Simocatta, *HU*, VIII (1, 3 (Ἔξαρχος τῶν πραιτωρίων).
80 Ch. Diehl, *Études sur l'administration Byzantine dans l'exarchat de Ravenne* (568–

with the disappearance of the praetorian prefecture of Rome. It is purely conjectural to use the title of *exarch* before this date. The administrative uncertainty in Italy between 568 and 584 partly explains the rapid conquest by the Lombards in a territory that today bears their name. The Exarchate of Ravenna comprised seven duchies (Veneto, Ferrara, Pentapolis, Rome, Perugia, Naples and Calabria).[81]

These major regional commands needed staffs. In Africa, Germanus, the cousin of Justinian I, had two men he trusted throughout his term of office from 536 to 539: the senators Symmachus, Prefect of the Army responsible for expenditure, and Domnikos, commander of infantry. Areobindos, governor of Libya from 544 until late 545/early 546, had a similar staff under him. Athanasius, who had returned from Italy, was his Praetorian Prefect of Africa, while John and Artabanes the Arsacid who were two experienced Armenian officers, who commanded the troops.[82] No text specifies the detailed composition of these administrative staffs. By way of comparison, the law of 534 set the number of officials serving the praetorian prefect of Africa at 396, and those serving the border dukes at 41.[83] Following the conquest, the Imperial administration in Italy became more militarised, which is consistent with a status of occupation. A study of land transactions shows that around 550, only 10 percent of deeds involved military personnel, while by 600, this figure had risen to 75 percent.[84] This near plundering of land must have made the occupation of Italy very unpopular and explains its short duration.

By the seventh century, the second Imperial stronghold, alongside Ravenna, was Sicily. Perhaps it controlled the province of Bruttium, which corresponds to modern-day Calabria. Byzantine Calabria corresponded to modern-day Apulia, with the city of Otranto as the main port. In 717, a governor called Sergius was also *protospatharios* and *stratēgos* of Sicily, curial and military ranks.[85] By this time the Byzantine administrative era that had really begun.

---

751), (Paris: Ernest Thorin, Bibliothèque des Écoles françaises d'Athènes et de Rome, 53, 1888), p.15 (Justin II), pp.43–44 (Liguria). B. Bavant, (1979), pp.53–54 (Maurice and letter of Pelagius).

81   Ch. Diehl, (1888), pp.6–22 (exarchate birth in 568, but conjectural); 23–30 (duchies).
82   Procopius, *BV*, IV, 16, 1–2; 19, 1 (Germanus); 24, 2 (Areobindos).
83   *CJ*, I, 27, 1, 13 (prefect); 2, 18–35 (dukes).
84   T. S. Brown, Gentlemen and Officers: Imperial Administration and Aristocratic Power in Byzantine Italy, AD 554 – 800 (London: British School at Rome, 1984), pp.82–108 (army's role in society).
85   Theophanes Confessor, *Chrgr.*, AM 6210, 398 (Sergius).

Amalgamation into Themes

From 581 to 615, the network of border guards on the Danube was undermined by incursions from the Sklavenes and the Avars, and then by the Persian occupation in the East between 602 and 615. Ultimately, the Arabs wiped it out between 635 and 641. The reigns of Phocas and Heraclius I were hampered by the worst military events which occurred in this quite bloody time. Historiography from the last century has dated the adoption of a decentralised system known as the *themata* (or 'themes') or military districts to the era of Heraclius. However, the date of this is still a matter of debate, as does the attribution to Heraclius. Today's historians no longer believe in a single reform, but rather in a slow evolution.[86] The very first mention of these themes is to 620, when Heraclius mobilised his army against the Persians. Theophanes the Confessor's use of the term on this occasion is considered anachronistic by some historians, but the debate is ongoing. By 620, the Imperial Army had been defeated by the Persians, and some six years of peace in the Balkans were a welcome respite. Heraclius took advantage of this to create a military force capable of driving the Persians out of Syria, Armenia and Mesopotamia, an ambitious project:

> After travelling to the region of the themes, he assembled his armies and added new recruits. He began by training them and instructing them in military matters. He divided his army into two parts and made them attack each other without bloodshed. He taught them the war cry, martial songs and commands, how to be on their guard, so that they would not be frightened in the event of real war, but would go to the enemy as if it were a game.[87]

Heraclius trained his troops and no doubt according the Roman tradition, but it is not clear whether he created any new units. Later, *c.* 634, to oppose the beginning of the Arab invasion of Palestine and Syria, Heraclius appointed Theodore to the position of *Sakellarios*. This appointment may have been interpreted as a way of comforting the troops with the assurance of being paid.[88] And on the way, it was the sign of a new organisation. Catastrophic territorial changes led the Empire to find new ways for the army. Conquest of the Northern Balkan by the Sklavenes and Avars between 581 and 615 led to the disappearance of what remained of the ancient Danubian limes. The same can be said for the provinces swallowed up by the Arab conquest between 636 and 641, namely Syria, Phoenicia, Palestine and Egypt. A

---

86 C. Morrisson (ed.), *Le monde Byzantin*, p.180.
87 Theophanes Confessor, *Chrgr.*, AM 6113, 303. N. Oikonomidès, 'Les premières mentions des thèmes dans la chronique de Théophane', *Zbornik radova Vizantološkog Instituta*, 16 (1975), pp.1–8.
88 Theophanes Confessor, *Chrgr.*, AM 6125, 337–6126, 338 (Theodore).

number of duchies had ceased to exist and maybe it was then time to create new military districts with a new name – the themes.

The only theme well attested after 641, was known as the *Opsikion*, the Greek version of *obsequium*, 'close guard'; it brought together the old elite troops, *phoideratoi*, *optimatoi* and *boukellarioi*. Headed by a count and located on the other side of the Dardanelles Strait, it housed the army protecting the capital. Its location was a strategic choice, to put it at a safe distance from a surprise attack from the Balkans. The *Opsikion* could quickly disembark in Byzantium or at the rear of a potential besieger. Inland, it covered north-western Asia Minor, i.e. the former provinces of Bithynia, Paphlagonia and northern Galatia. Until the reign of Constantine V (741–775), it was the most powerful army in the Empire.[89] Other provincial themes were created, first in Asia Minor, at an unknown date and their first mention dates from later sources. The *thēma Armeniakôn* (theme of the Armenians) first appeared in 667, stretching from Pontus through Armenia Minor to Cappadocia. The *thēma Anatolikon* (Anatolian theme) was first mentioned in 669 and covered the rest of Asia Minor. Two other themes also appeared. First mentioned in 711, the *thema Thrakēsion* (Thracian theme) covered Thrace in Europe and extended to the Aegean coasts of Asia Minor, controlling Ionia, Lydia and Caria. Its name suggests that it was created using the remains of the *magisterium* of the Thracians or the *quaestura exercitus*.[90] The southern coast of Asia Minor and the Aegean Islands were home to a naval region known as the *Karabesianoi* (Those from the Ships) who fought against Arab naval attacks.[91]

The eighth century military reforms of Constantine V are very far from our subject, but they recreated a substantial intervention force in addition to the *themata*. They serve as a reminder that the Byzantine Imperial Army was not frozen in time and that names that endured for four centuries concealed a fluid reality, just as a Roman Legion in 300BCE was differet from that of 300CE.

---

89 J. F. Haldon, *Byzantine Praetorians: an administrative, institutional and social survey of the Opsikion and tagmata, c. 580–900* (Bonn: Rudolf Habelt, Freie Universität Berlin, Byzantinisch-neugriegechischtes Seminar, *Poikila Byzantina*, 3, 1984). A. P. Kazhdan, A. M. Talbot, A. Cutler, T. E. Gregory, N. P. Ševčenko (eds), 'Opsikion', vol. 3 (1984), pp.1528–1529.
90 L. Amela Valverde, *Varia Historicorum*, I (Seville: Punto Rojo Libros, 2021), p.568 (θέμα Θρᾳκησίων).
91 W. Treadgold, *A History of the Byzantine State* pp.315, 382.

Weaknesses in the Romano-Byzantine Chain of Command

Over criticism has been the historian's privilege since Procopius paved the way for it in his *Anecdota*. The Romano-Byzantine chain of command in the field army had several weaknesses. The first was the absence of a clearly defined second in command, and one example shows this very well. In 536, when Mundo the Master of the Soldiers to Illyricum was killed in a battle near Salona (present-day Solin, Croatia), his army abandoned Dalmatia and returned to their barracks but the Goths did not occupy the abandoned land.[92] The troops of Illyricum were disciplined enough not to panic and to hold their positions, but the chain of command was not sufficiently defined to continue operations. The losses had probably been significant as Mundo' successor, Constantius took 'some time' to assemble a new army in Illyricum.[93]

Obtaining obedience from high-ranking officers was often a problem. Even a successful leader like Belisarius met difficulty in being obeyed by certain officers in Italy. A letter from Justinian was not enough to bring Narses the Eunuch back into line and he arrogantly challenged Belisarius authority. This division led to the loss of Milan in 539. Polyarchy became the common rule after Belisarius departed from Italy. John the nephew of Vitalian, the Patrician Bessas, Constantius and others were initially given commands in Italy, probably in a decentralised manner. Constantius and Alexander had a theoretical pre-eminence over the other nine *archontes* (unit-leaders) under their control, but did not seem to exercise it. They proved so incompetent and greedy that they lost Verona while discussing the distribution of the plunder of the newly occupied city, busier arguing than actually fighting the Ostrogothic counter-attack in 541. Before the disaster at Mugello which occurred the following year, they drew lots to decide who would lead the elite cavalry in the vanguard. The lot fell on John the nephew of Vitalian. Defeated once again, although not pursued, they were unable to rally their men who dispersed into small groups, some of which were so disgusted by their leaders that they joined the enemy.[94]

Like Napoleon's marshals in Spain, the Romano-Byzantine Army leaders sometimes found it difficult to coordinate their efforts and even to get along with each other, a more acute problem when two generals hold the same rank. This was the case with Priscus and Comentiolus the Thracian during the campaign against the Avars in 598. From the previous winter, Priscus and his army had been blockaded by the Avars in the port of Tomi. By March,

---

92 Procopius, *BG*, V, 7, 5 (Mundo get killed); 9 (retreat).
93 Procopius, *BG*, V, 7, 26–27.
94 Procopius, *BG*, VI, 21, 1–41 (loss of Milan); 30, 2 (division of command in Italy); VII, 3, 4 (Alexander and Constantian); 3, 15–22 (Verona); 5, 7 (prize draw); 9–16 (Mugello).

Comentiolus the Thracian had rescued the port of Tomi with a relief army. However, this event did not lead to a combined campaign. Priscus even allowed the Avars to quit the siege and pursue his rescuer, Comentiolus, nearly 500km to the south-east. Comentiolus' army suffered significant losses when it crossed the Shipka Pass in eastern Bulgaria, while retreating after its general unashamedly fled on his own route. It was unable to cover Byzantium city itself, and the Avars went as far as the gates, although no further.[95] Probably summoned by the Emperor, Priscus and Comentiolus the Thracian joined their forces during the summer 599 in order to conduct an efficient campaign against Avars on the Middle Danube.[96] The problem of unity of command is a recurring one in military history.

---

95   Theophylact Simocatta, *HU*, VII, 13, 8–14, 9.
96   Theophylact Simocatta, *HU*, VIII, 4, 3–8.

3

The tough job of being a general

> The best general is not a man from an illustrious family, but a man who can pride himself on his own exploits.
>
> Maurice, *Strategikon*, VIII, 2, 54.

Far from the Emperor and in a variety of different theatres of operation, the general had to encourage the troops to accept discipline and to risk their lives in uncertain battles. His mission was difficult and could have cost him his life. He was threatened by illness, mutinies, betrayal of his lieutenants, distrust of the Emperor and, of course, by the enemy. The salvation of the Empire rested on his shoulders. Putting asides his pompous gilded weapons, pearls and embroidered tunics, needless to say he had not to be a knee trembling coward or a blood phobic. But who was he?

The Character of the Good Romano-Byzantine General

To have a rich father, a powerful uncle or a wife with high social connections was of a paramount importance to becoming a general in this period, but he also needed a solid network of family and friends.[1] During the African campaigns against the Vandals, most of the generals and officers came from regions that were under military threat, such as the Balkans and the Near East.[2] Two psychological types of general stood out: the strategist and the brawler. The former commanded from the rear, like Julius Caesar, while the latter exposed himself to combat, like Alexander the Great. Agathias

---

1   D. A. Parnell, *Justinian's Men: Careers and Relationships of Byzantine Army Officers, ca. 518–610*, New Approaches to Byzantine History and Culture (London: Palgrave Macmillan, 2017).

2   J. Conant, *Staying Roman. Conquest and Identity in Africa and the Mediterranean, 439–700* (Cambridge: Cambridge University Press, 2012), p.202, (Belisarius, Solomon; 207–208, officers).

believed that generals should not fight on the front line alongside ordinary soldiers, and he severely criticised an officer of barbarian mercenaries for doing so:

> Fulcaris, the general of the Heruls, was undoubtedly courageous and no danger could frighten him, but he was adventurous and reckless. As not being instructed in his task properly, he thought that the duty of a general and a leader was not to put in order and keep in order the body of troops, but he threw himself in person into warlike action, showing himself brilliant in battle, rushing forward with ardour, charging with all on the enemies, and it was of this that he boasted and gloried.[3]

This merciless criticism enumerated all the characteristic faults of the barbarian as described in Greco-Roman literature, from technical incompetence to boastfulness. But Agathias was invariably critical of whoever posed as a hero when in command. He commented on the behaviour of Germanus the son of Dorotheos who fought the Huns in 559: 'driven more by an immoderate love of glory than by prudence and restraint, he threw himself mercilessly against the enemies and exposed himself to danger, not by encouraging and giving orders, as a general would do, but by fighting like a simple soldier'[4] As the head had to prevail over the arms, it was not surprising to find among the generals from late fifth and sixth centuries who were physically 'challenged', such as John Gibbo 'the Hunchback', the eunuchs Solomon, Narses and Leontius the Syrian. They were neither incompetent nor unlucky as army commanders.

According to Byzantium's first military treatise, a good general was above all prudent. He had to defeat the enemy through deception, harassment and hunger rather than by risking the uncertain chance of battle. A careful comparison of his forces and those of the enemy allowed him to avoid a disastrous defeat, and it was highly recommended to reconnaître the roads with his own eyes. The general had to be wary when he has just negotiated with the enemy to prevent any surprise attack against his camp. After victory, he was better advised to listen to proposals for peace and conclude it on advantageous terms. Unfavourable battles were not to be fought and the general should not go to bed before planning for the following day. He had to control himself in all circumstances and not to trust anyone who has made him a promise. The best option was to deliberate at length before acting, rather than suffering failure after acting on a whim, and never letting his troops know his plans. He was to know the supply possibilities of a country and occupy the hills before the enemy. He never entered battle without a real advantage. He had to change his appearance frequently when

---

3   Agathias, *Hist.*, I, 14, 4.
4   Agathias, *Hist.*, V, 23, 3.

forming the line of battle or engaging in combat, even when eating or sleeping, so as not to be identified by the enemy. Finally, he remained calm on the alert, cautious in his advice, courteous with his subordinates and won battles not like a wild beast, but by calculation.[5] Maurice, to whom this advice of universal military wisdom is attributed, ended up being cruelly butchered during a putsch – he must have forgotten the advice he gave in his treatise.

Military sedition was a Roman legacy and a Byzantine endemic plague but was no less than for France between 1789 and 1961. Political loyalty was therefore as an essential quality. The most famous generals of Justinian I were all loyal to him, probably because he was grateful to them. It was only earlier under Zeno and Anastasius I, then in the late sixth century that *pronunciamentos* flourished again. One of the main qualities of a general, as of any leader, was and is to see the invisible dangers lurking around him. Solomon proved to be a good general because he won his battles, yet he saw no indication of the mutiny of March 536 that involved two-thirds of the army. Even the *doryphoroi* and *hypaspists* of his personal guard and many of his household servants joined the plot out of a wish to reclaim lands confiscated from the Vandals. Solomon was surprised.[6] His successor, the Patrician Germanus restored the situation because he was psychologically more skilful than the vindictive Solomon. Anyway, the slightest incompetence was unforgivable in an era already difficult even for able generals. During the Persian War of 572–591, the masters of the soldiers to the East succeeded one another, albeit over a period of 19 years: Marcian (572–573), Theodore Tziros (573–575), Justinian (575–578), Maurice (578–582 when he became Emperor), John Mystakon (582–584), Philippicus (584–588), Priscus was driven out by a mutiny (588), Philippicus again (588–589), Comentiolus the Thracian (589–591). There was a limit to favouritism: in event of a serious failure, defeated generals were almost always recalled by the Emperor. Replacement of a general did not mean his career was definitively and entirely ended. After being dismissed in Persia, Priscus and Philippicus were sent to the Balkans. The strategy of rotating generals-in-chief was avoiding exhaustion and the loss of prestige among the troops.

What can be said of a man like John Tzibos, who Justinian appointed general around 535–541 in Lazica? There he had built the city of Petra (today Tsikhisdziri in Georgia). But Procopius' portrait of him is one of the worst: 'A man of obscure and unremarkable lineage, who rose to the rank of general for no other reason than being the most dishonest of men and the most gifted at enriching himself illegally.'[7] His greed compromised the Empire's position in the province, as the Lazi invited the Persians to come

---

5   Maurice, *Strategikon*, VIII, 2, 4; 7; 25; 36; 52; 55; 56; 65; 66; 67; 68; 72; 75; 86; 87; 97.
6   Procopius, *BV*, IV, 14, 23.
7   Procopius, *BP*, II, 15, 9 (portrait); 10 (Petra).

and liberate them. Nevertheless, in 541, when Petra of Lazica was under siege, Tzibos led the Persians to believe that the place was deserted before inflicting heavy losses upon them in a surprise sortie. The next day, when Persians began a full-scale siege, he was killed by an arrow in the neck.[8] The story goes that he was a leader who surprised the Persian King's Army with a small garrison and exposed himself to battle, making him rather a courageous man and a good general. One can assume that he bought his rank but a sharp tongue as Procopius said nothing like this.

Who Remembers Sittas Today?

Although of obscure and maybe Gothic origin, Sittas as Procopius called him, was the husband of Theodora's elder sister and therefore Justinian's brother-in-law.[9] He was the perfect example of a general appointed through favouritism, although he was not unworthy of the task. According to Theophanes Confessor, he was, 'of a warlike temperament and very capable.'[10] His real name was actually Zita, as indicated by a Justinianic law.[11] At the beginning of his career, like Belisarius, he served as an officer of Justinian's bodyguards when the latter and future Emperor was only Master of the Soldiers. In 526, Sittas shared command with Belisarius on two raids into Persarmenia, where he took numerous prisoners and a rich booty, but during the second raid, perhaps in 527, a Persarmenian counter-attack forced them to retreat after a defeat.[12]

In 528, appointed Duke of Armenia, Sittas defeated the ferocious Tzani, modern-day Zans or Chans, a Mingrelian ethnic people from Georgia. Rewarded in 530 with the rank of master of the soldiers present, he distinguished himself in this new role, always fighting on the fringes of the Caucasus, which he knew well. He inflicted two defeats on the Persians in the same year: first launching a bold sortie when defending Theodosiopolis, then he defeated a larger Persian Army at *Satala*.

In 531, the rout of his comrade Belisarius at Callinicum earned him supreme command of operations over Mundo the newly-appointed Master of the Soldiers to the East. He undoubtedly re-established the affairs of the Empire, but the death of the Persian King Kavadh I contributed greatly to the conclusion of the Eternal Peace between the two belligerents. On the strength of this impressive record, Sittas became Patrician and Consul in 535. In the same year, probably after receiving patriciate, he met and

---

8   Procopius, *BP*, II, 17, 4–10 (siege and death); A. H. M. Jones, J. R. Martindale, J. Morris, *PLRE*, 3a (1992), pp.639–640 (Ioannes 20).
9   A. H. M. Jones, J. R. Martindale, J. Morris, *PLRE*, 3b (1992), pp.1160–1163.
10 Theophanes Confessor, *Chrgr*., AM 6020, 175.
11 *CJ*, I, 29, 5.
12 Procopius, *BP*, I, 12, 20 (command shared in the East with Belisarius); 21 (ex-bodyguard as *doryphoros*).

defeated Bulgar raiders near the Iatrus in Moesia (now the River Yantra, Bulgaria).[13] Probably with the title of master of the soldiers present, Sittas was living in Byzantium since the peace established with Persians.[14]

But a peaceful life was not for him, and in 538 an Armenian anti-fiscal revolt led him to be sent there. Sittas entered into successful negotiations, but the Emperor was unwilling to abandon his new tax and angrily forced Sittas to settle the revolt by force. Finally, Sittas was defeated and killed at the Battle of Oinochalakon. The terrain, mountainous and cut by ravines, prevented the deployment of the two opposing armies. A disunited struggle ensued between smaller parties and Sittas made the mistake of pursuing a group of Armenians too far and of not wearing his helmet. Routed by a fierce counter-attack, he was scalped by a blow of a sword then killed with a blow from a lance in the back by Artaban.[15] This premature death opened up the prospect of a great career for Belisarius. The story of Sittas is that of a broken destiny and shows the true danger of being a general. The irony of this death is that it was caused by the revolt of the Armenian Prince Artabanes the Arsacid, also responsible for the death of Acacius Proconsul in Armenia. Artabanes would later occupy the highest military positions, master of the soldiers in Italy, to the Thraces, then present on the Emperor's side.[16] So Sittas' death paved the way for Belisarius.

Belisarius, the Model of a Good General

Vieillard en cuirasse assis au bord d'une rue, son casque tendu par un enfant recueille les piécettes des passants (An old man in cuirass sitting by the side of a street, his helmet held out by a child, collecting coins from passers-by.) Painting by Jacques Louis David, 1781.

Flavius Belisarius more than any other today evokes the good general of Byzantium, while others have sunk into oblivion. His figure has become a motif in classical painting, an expression of abandoned old age and faded glory, according to the legend. His bearded face and medium-length hair are supposedly depicted on a mosaic in the Basilica of San Vitale in Ravenna. But before being an artistic motif, Belisarius was an experienced general who fought on fields as varied as the Near East, North Africa, Italy and Eastern Thrace. His career equated him with the great Roman Generals of the Republican period.

Born in the town of Germania in Thrace in 505, he became an officer in Justinian I's personal bodyguard, *bucellarius*, when the latter was Master of the Soldiers Present. Procopius described him as tall, handsome and

---

13 Marcellinus Comes, *Chr.*, *Addimentum*, a. 535.
14 Procopius, *BP*, II, 3, 8.
15 Procopius, *BP*, II, 3, 15–27 (Oenochalakon); 39 (causes of Armenian rebellion).
16 Procopius, *BV*, IV, 27, 17 (murder of Acacius and Sittas; friend to Khosrow I).

elegant.[17] His career alternated between promotions and recalls, successes and disappointments. In 528 (or perhaps in 527) Belisarius, then Duke of Mesopotamia, suffered a setback, in a battle that was poorly located either in northern Mesopotamia at Thannuris in the desert (Tell Tunainir in Norhern Syria), or in Mindouos when he tried to erect a post there, and pitifully took refuge in Dara.

Despite his repeated misfortunes, Belisarius was appointed Master of the Soldiers to the East in 529 and continued the war against the Persians, defeating them at the Battle of Dara in June 530. But this victory was countered by his defeat on the Euphrates at Callinicum (or Kallinikion) on 19 April 531, followed by the fall of Abgerston fort to the Persians. These events led to him being dismissed and being replaced with Mundo a 'non-Roman'.[18] His first war as an army commander against the Persians did not suggest a great general, but to be fair he was then a novice at high-level command. No doubt as a result of his wife Antonina's friendship with the Empress, he regained his rank during the winter of 531–532.

In January 532, back from the Persian front, he distinguished himself by saving Justinian and his wife Theodora from the *Nika* (Win!) revolt thanks to the unrestricted ferocity of mercenaries Heruls and his own *bucellarii* (bodyguards). He killed around 30,000 rioters: a bloody massacre in a city strong of 300,000 to 400,000 inhabitants.[19]

His greatest feat of arms was the reconquest of North Africa from the Vandals. Here he demonstrated the ability of a great general. Between September and December 533, he fought two battles, Dekimon and Trikamaron, that destroyed Vandal power. Between these two dates, he restored the walls of Carthage. It took him just four months to achieve this strategic success, whereas it had taken him almost three months to make the sea voyage from Byzantium! Gelimer, driven into the mountains of Numidia, surrendered before March 534. During that month, or just after, Belisarius took the initiative of sending a corps to Sicily to seize the fortified port of Lilybaea (now Marsala) on the vague pretext that it was a city belonging to the Empire, because it had been given as a wedding present to a Vandal Prince. Belisarius tried to intimidate Amalasuntha the female regent of the Ostrogothic Kingdom, who replied, politely but firmly, that the decision must come from the Emperor, pointing out that he had exceeded his orders.[20] Belisarius left it at that. Recalled to Byzantium in the

---

17 Procopius, *BP*, I, 12, 21 (bodyguard); *BG*, VII, 1, 6 (description).
18 Procopius, *BP*, I, 13, 2–3 (Mindouos to the west of Nisibis); 4–8 (defeat); 9 (appointed master of the soldiers in Orient); 9–14, 1–55 (Dara); 18, 1–50 (Callinicum). (Pseudo-); Zachariah Rhetor, *HE*, IX, 2 (Thannuris or Tannuris in the desert); 3 (Dara); 4 (defeat on the Euphrates); 5 (Belisarius is recalled). John Malalas, *Chrgr.*, XVIII, 60 (Kallinikion); 61 (Abgerston then replaced by Mundo).
19 Procopius, *BP*, I, 24, 54 (30,000 civilians killed); M. Kaplan, *Byzance. Villes et campagnes* (Paris: Picard, Les médiévistes français, 2006), p.308 (estimated population in the sixth century, before the plague of 541).
20 Procopius, *BV*, IV, 11–19.

spring, he was given the wider task of retaking Italy the following year. One wonders whether Justinian did not want to shatter the glorious image of a possible rival by giving him orders that were impossible to carry out?

On 31 December 535, after completing the conquest of Sicily, Belisarius unusually allowed himself to celebrate his triumph when he entered Syracuse. During spring 536, he returned to Africa to restore the situation that had been compromised by a mutiny. In May, he returned to Sicily, landing at Rhegium (today Reggio Calabria) he advanced so far north that angry Ostrogothic rebels cut the royal throat of King Theodahad, and elected a more martial King – Vitiges. Belisarius occupied Rome on 9 December without a fight as the outnumbered and panic-stricken Ostrogoths preferred to withdraw from and not defend the huge city.

In Rome, between March 537 and March 538, Belisarius was besieged by the Ostrogoths for a year and nine days, according to Procopius, but held his positions.[21] As the situation of his troops had improved in 538, he gathered all resources ready to act. With a strong strategic intuition, he had Rimini occupied by recently landed reinforcements, which forced the Ostrogothic King Vitiges to lift the siege of Rome to protect his rear. Belisarius pushed his troops northwards, reconquered Tuscany where he had left three garrisons for over a year, and sent a troop to Milan. In July, he put his main effort on the Adriatic coast in Picenum and relieved Rimini, which had been besieged by Vitiges. The Ostrogoths were overwhelmed, and the road to their capital, Ravenna, was threatened. Belisarius conquered Picenum but suffered the jealousy of Narses the Eunuch, who abandoned him in December at the siege of Urbino and refused to send reinforcements to Milan, which was besieged jointly by the Ostrogoths and by the Burgundians. The fall of Milan in early 539 was a major defeat for Belisarius, although it was actually suffered by Mundilas, one of his lieutenants. This did not prevent him from entering Ravenna the following year and capturing Vitiges, who claimed to recognise him as Emperor of the West. Although refused by Belisarius, this proposal deliberately aroused the suspicions of Justinian, who recalled Belisarius to Byzantium in order to fight the Persians. Belisarius was once again placed at the head of the Eastern Army in the spring of 541. His failure there earned him a new recall in 542, and subsequently two years of imprisonment.

Then, he was sent back as *generalissimo* to Italy, where he found the manpower situation deteriorating once again and further undermined by the defection of troops to the Ostrogoths. Rome and its outer port of Pontus were held by the Patrician Bessas an experimented Imperial general of Gothic origin, but greedy and almost 70 years old. The harbours of Otranto in Apulia and Osimo were under siege by the Ostrogoths, Ravenna formed a bridgehead and Sicily remained a solid base. Belisarius could not work miracles, especially without financial aid, and his first task was to relieve the

---

21   Procopius, *BG*, VI, 10, 12.

two besieged ports. This is how Procopius summed up his second campaign in Italy during the so-called Gothic War:

> Belisarius returned to Byzantium without glory, having neither landed in Italy in five years nor succeeded in penetrating it, but having been forced all the time to hide and to flee, constantly sailing along the coasts, from one coastal fortress to another.[22]

The facts were more complex than that. With a reduced number of troops, which he further divided with John, the nephew of Vitalian who had been left behind in Apulia, Belisarius landed at Pontus and in December 546 lost Rome defended by the ageing Patrician and Master of the Soldiers Bessas. Nevertheless he had enough influence over the enemy to dissuade the new Ostrogothic King Totila from razing the Eternal City to the ground and then retook it without a fight in April 547. During 547, lacking resources, he was compelled to retreat to the south of the Italian peninsula. He garrisoned there, in Lucania, a holding force before moving on to Sicily and then Taranto, which he no doubt wanted to organise as his final strongholds. He withdrew hastily to Messina after Totila had forced his way through Lucania. The contingents that Belisarius sent to clear Rossano failed. Next he lost the city of Taranto and control of the Gulf of the Taranto around December. Only Sicily remained to him, and Belisarius ended his second Italian campaign where he had begun his Italian war.

Having failed, Belisarius was recalled to Byzantium in early 549, and thereafter, considered to be the first citizen of the Empire but was dismissed from his posts of Master of the Soldiers to the East and commander of the Imperial Guard. Narses the Eunuch was given the task of conquering Italy.[23] Ten years of being out of office followed for Belisarius, but in 559, at the age of 60, he nevertheless saved Byzantium from an invasion by the Huns Kutrigurs.[24] His last victory, although more of a big brawl than a pitched battle, was tarnished by the jealousy of leaders who slandered him. Belisarius was put into retirement very quickly by Justinian, so that the people would not give him a triumph: 'He did not even enjoy the honour due to what he had accomplished, but because of these people the fruit of the victory escaped him, eclipsed, left unrewarded and completely passed over in silence.'[25] He died in Byzantium in 565.

Time improved Belisarius's way of command. At Callinicum in 531, he pursued a smaller Persian Army retreating homeward along the Euphrates.

---

22 Procopius, *BG*, VII, 35, 1.
23 Procopius, *BG*, VII, 22, 7–17 (letter to Totila); 22, 18 (Ceraso); 24, 2 (reconquest of Rome); 24, 8–32 (Totila fails to retake Rome); 25, 14 (respected by Ostrogoths); 27, 16 (Sicily); 28, 1 (Taranto); 28, 18 (Messina); VIII, 21, 1–2 (loaded with honours).
24 Evans, J.A.S., *The Age of Justinian: The Circumstances of Imperial Power*, London, Routledge, 1996 repr. 2000, p.115–116.
25 Agathias, *Hist.*, V, 20, 6.

His men wanted to fight and he explained that, having won the campaign, there was no point in risking battle. He was insulted and called a coward by troops who displayed the usual arrogance of young soldiers. To avoid a undesirable outcome, he agreed to lead them into battle and hypocritically told them that he was not ignoring their ardent desire to fight and that he now trusted them. In fact, he was compelled to follow his men to maintain his authority and subsequently lost the battle.[26] His forethought was correct, for he had allowed an enemy that was withdrawing to go but which was likely to be spurred on by the courage of despair.

Belisarius's style of command resembled Wellington's, 'always being on the spot to see and do everything for myself,' as the Iron Duke put it. When the troops are outnumbered, Belisarius galloped in all directions to rally them and inveighed against them in terms that are easy to imagine but rude to report! When urgency dictated, he fought in the front line to impress his men. Besieged in Rome during the first Ostrogothic counter-offensive, as happened during the engagement at the Milvian Bridge in 537, he rode out as a cavalryman, a mistake that Procopius felt jeopardised the situation of the Imperial troops, especially as the deserters had recognised his horse and advised the Ostrogoths to kill him. But Belisarius killed those who tried to attack him and his bodyguards ended up surrounding him.[27] Two weeks later, to the admiration of his first-doubting men, he shot a Gothic leader in armour through the throat with an arrow, revealing his talents as a marksman with a bow.[28] Twenty-two years later, despite being in his sixties, he killed several Hun Kutrigurs and put the others to flight.[29] He was thus a physically courageous man and a skilful fighter. His hatred of deserters and the very act of desertion showed that he was demanding in terms of discipline. Simple in his dealings with the troops, according to Procopius, he treated them generously giving money to the wounded, gold bracelets and necklaces to the brave, and reimbursing the loss of a horse or piece of equipment in battle. Rarely did he mistreat the peasants of the countries he invaded.[30]

Belisarius tried to gauge the psychology of his immediate subordinates. During the landings in North Africa in late August or early September 533, he called together all those he called his 'fellow commanders' and let them express themselves freely on how to conduct the campaign in the manner of a *primus inter pares*. When all had spoken, he gave his own opinion, he

---

26 Procopius, *BP*, I, 18, 16–25.
27 Procopius, *BG*, V, 18, 4–6 (Belisarius fighting in the front row on horseback); 7 (deserters); 8–9 (the Goths set their sights on him); 11–13 (Belisarius killed his attackers, protected by his officers and his guard).
28 Procopius, *BG*, V, 22, 4–7.
29 Procopius, *BG*, V, 18, 4–12 (Milvian Bridge); 22, 5 (Rome). Agathias, *Hist.*, V, 19, 10 (Kutrigurs).
30 Procopius, *BG*, VII, 1, 7–8.

requested to be asked questions and gave answers, in a word, played more on persuasion than on the authority of rank.[31]

A similar episode occurred in Italy five years later. The situation was delicate and the atmosphere tense. John the nephew of Vitalian, had taken Rimini, where he found himself besieged by the Ostrogoths. Belisarius and his army were further south on the Adriatic coast at Fermo. Between the two towns, the Ostrogoths held Osimo, from where they could thwart any attempt to relieve Rimini. Most of the officers disliked John and suggested that he should be left to his fate, since he had disobeyed them. Narses the Eunuch came to his defence, pointing out that the Ostrogoth morale was broken but still had numerical superiority and that a Roman defeat would give them the upper hand. Belisarius allowed the dissensions to emerge, took note of a letter sent by John and then proposed a bold plan.[32] He apparently was to be seeking consensus, but these moments of free speech in staff conferences, allowed Belisarius to observe his officers and spot coteries or opposition. Some of them were jealous of him and had no hesitation in writing to the Emperor saying that he was preparing a plot. They even took the precaution of sending two messengers on two different ships. Belisarius, whose intelligence service intercepted one of the messengers, was informed of this manoeuvre and decided to go to explain it to the Emperor.[33] This painful incident also showed Belisarius' justified mistrust of his officers, whom he had discreetly guarded by his personal guard. His worst rival was Narses the Eunuch, who had joined him in mid-538 with reinforcements as strong as his own troops.[34] A new crisis erupted in Rimini, after it had been relieved. Belisarius, aware of this latent opposition, convened a council of war and urged caution, even if he did not convince Narses the Eunuch:

> Army commanders, I do not think I have the same view of this war as you do. I can see that you despise the enemy because they are suffering a total defeat. But I think that because of your arrogance we are going to fall into foreseeable danger, because, I know, the defeat we inflicted on the barbarians was not the result of their cowardice or their numerical inferiority. On the contrary, it was only our foresight and reflection that led them from defeat by force of arms to rout.[35]

This general principle of prudence did not convince Narses the Eunuch, who wanted to carry out more dynamic operations, and neither did the

---

31 Procopius, *BV*, III, 15, 1–30.
32 Procopius, *BG*, VI, 16, 1 sq.
33 Procopius, *BV*, IV, 8, 2–5.
34 Procopius, *BG*, VI, 18, 9, 10–11 (Narses and his officers).
35 Procopius, *BG*, VI, 18, 12–14.

letter from the Emperor that Belisarius brandished to make himself obey him.[36] He wanted Belisarius's job and finally got it.

From a tactical point of view, Belisarius had learned from his initial failures at Thannuris and Mindouos, where he had been outnumbered by the Persians. By June 530 under the walls of Dara, although he had an army of 25,000 men he was outnumbered by two to one! He gave an apparent indication of weakness to trap the overconfident Perozes the Mirranes, in command of the Sassanid troops, such as sending two letters to him the night before the battle humbly begging for peace, both letters received an arrogant answer from Perozes. Additionally, the fact Belisarius allowed the Persians to receive 10,000 men reinforcement the very morning of the battle shows he was encouraging the enemy to attack him. Very cautiously he offered battle in front of the fortress, close enough to be covered by missiles from the ramparts. He had a deep ditch built immediately in front of his left and right infantry wings, leaving an open space in the middle covered by a third further forward ditch in the center. The Persians attacked his apparently weak wings and were trapped and annihilated by counterattacks. It was a great disaster for Persians with more 8,000 killed in action although most of their army was further back and remained intact if demoralised.[37] Belisarius had mainly relied on his enemy's psychology.

At Callinicum in April 531, while facing a 15,000-strong cavalry army with 25,000 footmen he chose a much original tactic, with his infantry on the left flanking the Euphrates, his heavy cavalry in the centre and his Ghassanid allies on the right, who collapsed almost immediately letting his army be thrown into the river. It was not his best day.[38] Belisarius was by then more cautious in the conduct of his operations, particularly during the approach marches. He was preceded by a vanguard and secured on its flanks. These precautions prevented him from falling into the pincer movement that the Vandals were preparing for him in early September 533. Procopius, who accompanied him, paid tribute to the tactical acumen of his former commander: 'The fact is that, if Belisarius had not placed his army as we have said, ordering John and his men to form a vanguard and the Massagetae (Huns) to march on the army's left flank, we would never have been able to escape the Vandals.'[39] Both in North Africa and during his march from Reggio to Naples, he coordinated the movement between the fleet and the army, which moved parallel to each other, a measure that sheltered the fleet and allowed for rapid embarkation in the event of failure on land. Belisarius knew also how to combine security of forces with a bold manoeuvre.

---

36   Procopius, *BG*, VI, 18, 28–29.
37   Procopius, *BP*, I, 13, 19–22 (order of battle), 23 (numbers); 14, 1, 10,000 Persian reinforcements); 2–12 (letters exchange), 13–54 (battle).
38   Procopius, *BP*, I, 18, 26 (order of battle).
39   Procopius, *BV*, III, 18, 3.

His finest achievement was the relief of Rimini in August 538. The city was besieged by the Ostrogoths who further south held Osimo in order to cover the siege. But Belisarius launched an amphibious operation along several routes. Firstly, in order to ensure the security of the whole, he sent Aratius with 1,000 men to camp in front of Osimo in order to fix the enemy there. Secondly, Narses Kamsarakan, Aratius's brother both Persarmenian defectors (Persarmenians were Armenians who were under Persian rule), Uliaris and Herodian, under the command of Ildiger, moved by sea to Rimini with a considerable force. Thirdly, parallel to this naval force, Martin travelled along the coast with orders to multiply his number of campfires to give the impression of a large army. Quarto, himself and Narses the Eunuch made a detour inland via the town of Urbisaglia to arrive north of Rimini. The Ostrogoths, seeing themselves in a pincer from the north, south and the sea, fled without a fight, Rimini was relieved and the road to Ravenna was open. Belisarius calculations are explained by Procopius:

> As he was greatly outnumbered by the enemy, he did not want an open battle with them but, as he saw it, the barbarians were already exhausted as a result of events. On the contrary, he hoped that when they learned that his armies were approaching from all sides, they would no longer want to fight, but would rather think of withdrawing immediately.[40]

Sparing the lives of his soldiers, Belisarius, like Vegetius, believed that battle was too risky and should be avoided when possible.[41] He mastered long-distance manoeuvres. In March 538, after the Ostrogoths abandoned their first siege of Rome, Belisarius launched troops at Osimo and Milan, 450km apart, but he did not have the strength to support Milan, which fell at the beginning of 539, maybe a city too far. In the spring of this year, he sent troops to take Fiesole and Osimo, 288km apart. The very aim of all these manoeuvres was to cover his move to Ravenna, 265km away from Milan and 280km from Rome.[42] Even for a campaign area today, this would be a relatively wide area. Belisarius also handled amphibious operations well, but on these he was advised by experienced seamen.

Belisarius was quick to grasp the enemy's weaknesses. At Dekimon, and then three years later at Membressa in spring 536, he rushed into battle against an enemy in a bad position: either a disordered camp or a flanking march. He did not hesitate to provoke them in order to find weaknesses. At Trikamaron in December 533, he tested the enemy with three probing frontal attacks before launching a general assault. In March 537 when

---

40 Procopius, *BG*, VI, 17, 12–13.
41 Vegetius, *DRM*, III, 11.
42 Procopius, *BG*, VI, 18, 24 (Narses criticism of scattering along Osimo-Milan area); 23, 1 (Fiesole, Osimo).

defending Rome, cornered in front of the Salarian Gate, he routed a superior number of Goths by a counter-attack so aggressive that they believed that he had received reinforcements.[43] Belisarius possessed what Napoleon called 'coup d'oeil' - the glance. Belisarius's tactical genius also lay in playing quality against mediocrity. In Africa, he relied entirely on his cavalry and the role of his infantry was reduced to guarding the camp and the captured locations.

Belisarius had the self-confidence and activity necessary for a good general. When Solomon came to Syracuse to warn him of the mutiny in the army in Libya, he immediately went to Carthage with a single ship carrying 100 *doryphoroi* and *hypaspists*. By his name, he drove away the mutineers besieging the city and easily rallied the 2,000 men who had remained loyal. At Membressa, he had only 2,100 loyal soldiers against 8,000 mutineers, 1,000 Vandals and a large mass of slaves: at best a ratio of one to five with comparable weaponry.[44] This episode demonstrates that Belisarius believed in the value of command rather than superiority of numbers. In siege warfare, he did not develop the military know-how of the old Hellenistic or Roman generals, who built large earthworks and used complex machines. Perhaps he did not have the right military engineering tools. Nevertheless, in the early days of the conquest of Italy, Belisarius took Palermo and Naples with an economy of means and sustained a long defensive siege in Rome, despite the length of the area to be defended and the unreliability of the inhabitants.[45]

There are few faults that the analyst can impute to him. At the siege of Naples in 536, the ladders were too short to assault the ramparts. Procopius blamed the engineers who had built them without looking at the wall. It was up to Belisarius to check their height beforehand, but the soldiers' sense of improvisation remedied the situation by linking two ladders together to make a longer one.[46] His worst defeat was the loss of Milan around March 539, where he did not personally command. He had detached Mundilas with a contingent of 1,000 men, further reduced by outlying garrisons. It was undoubtedly a mistake to have sent such a small force commanded by a leader with little reputation into an area where the enemy remained powerful. Despite everything, Mundilas held out for several months against the enemy, who were content to maintain a blockade. Belisarius sent two generals to relieve the town instead of doing it himself. This was undoubtedly another mistake, as Martin and Uliaris hesitated to cross the Po for fear of the enemy's numbers. Their apparent hesitation may have had another

---

43 Procopius, *BV*, III, chap. 17–19. (Dekimon); IV, chap. 2–3 (Trikamaron); 15, 12–47 (Membressa); *BG*, 18, 27–28 (Salarian Gate).
44 Procopius, *BV*, IV, 15, 9–11 (Belisarius to Carthage); 15, 2–3 (numbers in Stotzas army).
45 Procopius, *BG*, V, 5 13–16 (Palermo); chap. 8 à 10 (Naples). Jordanes, *Getica*, LIX, 312 (14 months of siege in Rome).
46 Procopius, *BG*, V, 10, 22–23.

reason for exonerating Belisarius, as John the nephew of Vitalian and Justin refused to go any further without the agreement of Narses the Eunuch. The latter finally gave his consent, but John delayed and Milan fell just as winter was drawing to a close and while Belisarius was fighting in Picenum.[47] This defeat was due to a lack of personal involvement and absence of a good understanding between Belisarius and Narses the Eunuch. Following this setback, Belisarius abandoned all immediate projects on the Po plain and concentrated on the Adriatic coast. We may suspect than his strategic objective was to divert the enemy, and Narses, from his main goal.

While Procopius praised Belisarius in his *History of Wars*, he attacked him in the *Secret History*. He accused him of losing to the Persians in 541 through passivity or through fear. Procopius portrayed him as an unhappy cuckold, spineless and angry but consenting, with his wife Antonina, whom he loved blindly and who was said to be the daughter of a coachman and a prostitute – perhaps an ex-colleague of Theodora Empress...[48] Procopius reproached Belisarius for displaying a 'slave's fear' after his recall when, at odds with his wife and disgraced by the Empress, he feared assassination. Belisarius was said to be greedy and to have amassed a huge fortune during the Vandal and Gothic Wars, which the Empress Theodora ungratefully seized to benefit the Imperial Treasury. With more insight the Emperor gave Belisarius part of it back, but ordered him to finance his second Italian campaign out of his own funds.[49]

Between the cuckolded husband, the trembling greed and the great general, there was all the complexity of the human being.

Solomon, Between Tactics, Rigour and Nepotism

Solomon, who succeeded Belisarius in Africa in the spring of 534, did not have the aura of his predecessor. He was a competent man who learned the art of war by serving the most skilful general in Byzantium. Originally from Mesopotamia, he was secretary to the Duke Felicissimus and then to his successors like Belisarius around 526 or 527. When the latter left to conquer Italy, Solomon proved some skill in acting as Master of the Soldiers to Africa and Duke of Libya campaigning against the Moors in 534–535.[50] He faced enemies more numerous and more mobile than the Vandals. The Moors pillaged the country and fought two major battles, one at the plains at Mammes, south of present-day Ain Djeloula; the second the following

---

47   Procopius, *BG*, VI, 21, 1 *sq*. (fall of Milan); 22, 2 (Belisarius to Picenum).
48   Procopius, *Anecdota*, I, 11–42 (marital misfortune).
49   Procopius, *Anecdota*, I, 17–30 (Belisarius attitude as husband); III, 31 (idleness against the Persians); IV, 17 (confiscation and partial restitution of property); 22 (shy as a slave); 39 (promises not to ask the Emperor for anything to finance the Italian campaign); V, 4–5 (his greed in Italy).
50   A. H. M. Jones, J. R. Martindale, J. Morris, *PLRE*, 3b (1992) pp.1168–1177.

year at Mount Bourgaon (this may be Jebel Boukornine in modern central Tunisia). Before every battle, Solomon made a boastful speech to his men, who were at first troubled by the numbers of the enemy and by the novelty of the sight of a camp surrounded by camels at Mammes, then worried by the enemy's strong position on a slope at Mount Bourgaon. The Moors had already defeated the Vandals with the tactic of surrounding their camp with camels, the smell of which troubled the horses, and at the start of the battle of Mammes, they disorganised the Romans in this way and then launched a cavalry charge. Solomon, with great tactical intuition, dismounted and had his men fight in the same way, with sword and shield, disembowelling some of the camels to make their way into the heart of the camp. The Moors were routed, shamelessly abandoning their women, children and livestock. Another Moorish coalition refused to fight on the plains and waited on the steep slopes of Mount Bourgaon. Solomon camped at the foot of the mountain and, by night, led 1,000 infantrymen to the summit, crushing the Moors below in a pincer movement. To fool the enemy, he made them believe that his men were leaving to counter an outside attack. At daybreak, the Moorish encampment was attacked on foot from above and below.[51] The Moors fled without a fight. Unlike Belisarius, Solomon relied on infantry or dismounted cavalry.

He was not a brawler or a man-killer like John Troglita, but he fought bravely at the battle and gave his men courage through his inspiring speeches. He was a more tactical commander than Belisarius, who relied on the difference in quality between combatants. Moreover Solomon had some expertise in 'special ops' and knew the power of corruption, so he distributed wealth to his Moorish allies in the Aures Mountains to incite them into fighting the rebel leader Iaudas.[52] He was also intuitive and he knew the limit of their flawed loyalty and knew when they were leading him into a trap in the autumn of 535. His intuition stopped with the great mutiny of the African troops at Easter 536, which he did not foresee and which his eloquence and skill were unable to stop. Solomon showed his integrity or determination when he refused to grant his soldiers the land confiscated from the Vandals, on the pretext that it rightfully belonged to the Emperor. This was undoubtedly the main cause of the mutiny. Solomon escaped two assassination attempts that the mutineers did not dare carry out in the church where he had taken refuge. He fled Carthage by night on a longboat with five of his followers, including the historian Procopius. Later Solomon nearly lost control of the situation and called to Belisarius for help.[53]

---

51 Procopius, *BV*, IV, 11, 15–54 (Mammes); 12, 3–25 (Mount Bourgaon); P. Morizot, 'Recherches sur les campagnes de Solomon en Numidie méridionale', *CRAI*, (January-February (1993), pp.83–106.
52 Y. Modéran, 'Iaudas', *Encyclopédie Berbère*, 23 (Aix-en-Provence: 2000), pp.3565–3567.
53 Procopius, *BV*, IV, 13, 30 (Moors are bribed); 13, 36 (intuition); 14, 22–25

He seriously endangered Byzantine Africa, and from 536 to 539, he was effectively replaced with Germanus, the cousin of Justinian I, but once the situation had been re-established, Solomon returned to Africa. He sent the militarily unreliable elements and the Vandal women back to Byzantium. His last period in Libya was marked by the reorganisation of the province, the relative pacification of the Aures and nepotism.

Procopius, who served on his staff, saw him as a rigorous servant of the state, a good organiser and a methodical man: 'He surrounded each city with an 'enclosure' and, by being the meticulous guardian of the laws, ensured the security of the state as far as possible. Under his government, Libya became powerful thanks to its financial resources, and prosperity in general.'[54]

Solomon's actions against the Moors in the Aures Mountains were not limited to winning battles; he also fortified towns and borders. After a four-year hiatus, Solomon resumed the fight against Iaudas and the Moors of the Aures, forcing them to make peace. Solomon's nepotism was literal, as his nephews Sergios and Cyros were appointed Duke of Tripolitania and Duke of Pentapolis (present-day Cyrenaica). This favouritism can be explained by the mutiny of 536 and the need to rely on family members. However, his nephew Sergios proved incompetent and caused the Tripolitan Moors to revolt in 543. Solomon made another blunder in 544, when he suspended the allocation of wheat to Antalas, chief of the Frexes tribe, not without first having had the latter's brother executed for causing unrest in Byzacene. His last blunder proved fatal, because he had not shared the booty, some of his soldiers deserted him during the Battle of Theveste (now Tebessa). Fleeing, Solomon and his guard were massacred by the Moors of Antalas.[55] Solomon's rigorous accounting cost him his life. In the end, he was a better general than he was a governor. One more detail about him: he was an accidental eunuch but as with Narses, this condition in no way impeded his warrior character.

John Troglita, Natural Leader and Brawler

Helmet on his head, lance in hand, John Troglita, also known as John the Patrician, is the very archetype of the fighting general. He took his name, which was probably his origin, from a district of Macedonia.[56] His brother Pappos was one of the four commanders of Belisarius's cavalry during the war against the Vandals. In the same theatre and under the orders of Germanus, cousin of Justinian I, John Troglita commanded a cavalry wing

---

(Solomon escapes assassination).
54 Procopius, *BV*, IV, 19, 3–4.
55 Procopius, *BV*, IV, 21, 17 (Antalas deprived of its wheat allocation); 21, 25–27 (death of Solomon).
56 A. H. M. Jones, J. R. Martindale, J. Morris, *PLRE*, 3a (1992), pp.643–649.

against Stotzas and his deserters by 537 at the Battle of Skalai Beteres.[57] Sent as Duke of Mesopotamia in 538, four years later he relieved the cities of Theodosiopolis and Dara, which were under siege from Persian armies, capturing Memeroēs, a Persian general.[58] He had no doubt been raised to the patriciate for his deeds against Persia and was given the *Africae procuratio* (procuratoral governor of Africa). He went there with an expeditionary fleet to re-establish the province in 546.[59] From then on, the weight of the war fell on his shoulders. It was a difficult operation with an unclear chronology. John suffered a defeat in Tripolitania at Marta (today Mareth, Tunisia), but ended up defeating the Moors from the Aures, Byzacene and Tripolitania. His qualities were as much private as military. Piety, a traditional quality for the Roman general during Republican era, whether real or politically correct remained part of Romano-Byzantine Christian culture. Thus, when the storm scattered the fleet bound for Libya, John Troglita prayed to God, who answered his prayer.[60] Calmness, moderation and a certain form of clemency set John Troglita against the angry arrogance of the Moorish Ambassadors: the classic Greek pattern of self-control called *sôphrosynē*, against the angry madness or *hubris* that always characterises barbarians or tyrants.[61] Corippus concluded of him: 'This is how Roman virtue remains and always will.'[62]

When in camp, John Troglita was anxious to develop a strategy against the enemy:

> He bubbles over with worries and turns them over and over, wondering what he should do.... He gets up and prefers to confront his contrary thoughts in the middle of the camp, he makes and remakes the same paths, tiring his body and his mind. A man with the same worries accompanies him on his march [Ricinarius, Germanic officer].[63]

This account recalls the concern and solitude of the general, shared here by what we would call his chief of staff. The work of the staff reflects a wise man: '(John Troglita) awake all night, he distributed the duties in the middle of the camp. All around him, the commanders also took advice

---

57 Procopius, *BV*, IV, 28, 45 (brother of Pappos); IV, 17, 6 and 16 (cavalry officer); Corippus, *Joh.*, I, v. 380.
58 Evans J.A.S. (2000, p.166.
59 Corippus, *Joh*, I, v. 159–374. Procopius, *BV*, IV, 22, 3–4.
60 Corippus, *Joh*, I, v. 282–316.
61 J. E. Lendon, *Soldiers and Ghosts: A History of Battle in Classical Antiquity* (New Haven CT: Yale University Press, 2005), translated into French by G. Villeneuve as *Soldats et fantômes. Combattre pendant l'Antiquité* (Paris: Tallandier, 2009), pp.73–75.
62 Corippus, *Joh*, I, v. 504–508.
63 Corippus, *Joh*, II, v. 292–293 and v. 310–313.

on the most important subjects, and kept the night going with lively conversation.'[64] John Troglita's main quality is activity, close to Napoleon's principle of 'activity, speed'. From his arrival in Africa in the late summer or early autumn of 546 until the winter of 547, he was almost on continuous operations. He tracked down Antalas and the Moorish coalition in the winter and only returned to his quarters after defeating him. In the spring of 547, he had to face Carcasan and the Moors of Tripolitania, who were attacking southern Byzacene. He pursued them into the desert but suffered the perhaps deserved punishment for his impetuosity in a difficult retreat where he was, in his turn, pursued. Nevertheless, his activity enabled him to recover quickly by appealing to his Moorish allies and recruiting mercenaries. After a brief mutiny among his troops, he was able to defeat the Nasamons of Carcasan and the Moors of Antalas at the battle of Caton's Fields during the winter of 547.[65]

His value as a general was expressed not only as a strategist, but above all because he was a real leader of men. The severity of his discipline can be seen in a line in which the poet Corippus noted that the Romans were driven by 'love of country, their ardour and their fear of the general.'[66] If some doubt could be raised about the patriotism of Byzantine soldiers, the fear of their general was to them a more decisive stimulant. Corippus did not add an ounce of criticism to this remark and, because the fear inspired by the general is akin to the virtue of a good leader. However laudatory Corippus may be, he did not turn his hero into a marble statue of virtue alone. John Troglita is not a very easygoing leader, but can he be? As a good general, Troglita knew how to talk to his men. Before each battle, during it or when a retreat had to be conducted in an orderly fashion, he delivered a harangue. During an alarm, he speared the stragglers and insulted them.[67] This severity only existed in moments of combat, because it was dangerous to go too far with Byzantine soldiers who were quick to mutiny and quite capable of killing their general. In ordinary times, he knew how to negotiate his authority, because if supplies were lacking or the campaign was unsuccessful, he had to deal with desertion or mutiny. Bringing in supplies generally solved the problem of desertion, but the mutiny could be muzzled by a high spirited and convincing speech; in such a case John Troglita did not hesitate to threaten them with extermination by the Moorish allies who had remained loyal.[68]

Men as unreliable as Imperial soldiers would not accept the near-unhesitating obedience of the modern regular soldier, who does not see his general and is following instructions given by radio or computer. Early

---

64 Corippus, *Joh*, III, v. 4–7.
65 Corippus, *Joh*, VII, v. 76–77 (quick recovering); VIII, v. 47 (recruitment); v. 50–137 (mutiny); v. 166-*sq*. (Battle of Caton's Fields).
66 Corippus, *Joh*, II, v. 242.
67 Corippus, *Joh*, II, v. 246, 248.
68 Corippus, *Joh*, VIII, v. 131.

Byzantine combatants needed to be physically impressed by the courage of the general whose personal involvement legitimised his right to command. In other words, the general had to show himself. In battle, John Troglita commanded from the front, on horseback, and ranged himself in battle in front of his dukes or unit commanders.[69] He placed himself in a central position and could no longer give orders when battle opened: 'John placed his ensigns in the middle, directing everything with order and distributing the units through the columns, he [then] went right to the middle to fight with all of his weapons.'[70] He was an unstoppable killer, skilled with sword, javelin and lance, a hero worthy of the *Iliad* or the *Song of Roland*.[71] In a single battle against the Moors, he cut off the head of the Moorish Prince Mantisynan with a sword, leaving his dead body on the horse, split Laumasan's skull from temple to eyes, and shot a horse with a javelin that also pierced the right foot of its rider Guarsutia, who was crushed with the horse's falling, cut Manzerasen in half down by the middle, sliced off Iarti's right arm, deflected Mazana's shot with his shield, chasing and killing him, then pierced the shield and side of Gardius, the latter's brother. By the end he pursued the routed enemy, spear or javelin in hand.[72] Even Jack the Ripper could not have done better!

Contemporary readers may see in Corippus' martial poetry the hackneyed clichés of epic exaggeration and dismiss them as literature of no informational value. Nevertheless, there is one constant in war: a few combatants take the lion's share, while the masses form prey that barely defends itself. Even in the mechanical battles of the Second World War, some aces shot down several aircraft in the course of a sortie and some accumulated scores that made the exploits of an Achilles or a John Troglita seeming derisory. So, in the late-antique and early medieval context a fighter covered in armour, mounted on a sturdy horse, expert in the use of his weapons and animated by courage or bloodlust, can slaughter less well-equipped and less determined opponents.

The commander-in-chief of an expeditionary army was also a plenipotentiary diplomat, as it had been always the case in Roman wars ever since the Republic. John Troglita was no exception and proposed peace to the rebellious Moors through a messenger who conveyed the proposal orally.[73] John Troglita was undoubtedly the most skilful political general assigned to Libya. He succeeded in making solid allies of two Moorish Kings whom Solomon and then Belisarius had fought but not subdued, Cusina (or Koutzinas) and Iaudas. According to Procopius, it was thanks to Cusina that he managed to win the battle in 547, probably with more

---

[69] Corippus, *Joh*, II, v. 248.
[70] Corippus, *Joh*, IV, v. 565–566.
[71] Corippus, *Joh*, V, v. 104–140.
[72] Corippus, *Joh*, V, v. 104–140 and v. 147–151.
[73] Corippus, *Joh*, II, v. 359–414.

Moors in his army than Greeks or Latins.⁷⁴ Troglita was a more complex character than Corippus' epic poetry suggested. Justinian left him to govern Africa. In 551, when Totila seized Corsica and Sardinia, which depended on the Duke of Libya, John Troglita sent an expeditionary fleet that had to leave in a hurry after failing to reach Caranalis (a location that has not been identified).⁷⁵ The end of John Troglita's career is unclear.

Narses, Another Eunuch and Strategist

Embroidered and richly dressed, a small man inveighs in an acute but firm voice against several large men in scale armour. Narses (478–573) did not have the prestige that Belisarius left in the memory of men, but he was undoubtedly the best general of the period. He finally succeeded where Belisarius had failed: in puting an end to the Ostrogothic Kingdom of Italy. Why, then, has he been pushed into a relative and unfair oblivion? The first answer msut be that his military career was less rich and varied than that of Belisarius, who fought on all fronts. Narses was an Armenian from Persia who had originally had a civilian career as a cupbearer, treasurer maybe *sacellarius*, *spatharius* then head of the *spatharii*, and even as an adviser to the Emperor.⁷⁶ His face appears to have been identified on a mosaic in the Basilica of San Vitale in Ravenna, with a chubby face, a thin, drooping moustache and dark, medium-length, curly hair. Small in stature, his military training was not just booklearned, as he had fought on the Persian side with a command position. A genius at negotiation, Narses helped to end the *Nika* revolt of 532 by separating the Green Faction from the Blue. By this time, he was the head of the armed guard of the *spatharii* and of the *cubicularii* eunuchs. A few years later, he calmed a revolt in Alexandria.

Like Solomon, Narses was a eunuch, having undergone an operation as a child that was forbidden to Roman citizens but not to Armenians from outside the Empire, which he originally was and which led him to fighting Belisarius and Sittas before supporting the Empire. The Frankish Generals Buccellinus and Leutharis mocked his condition which was hardly in keeping with the military ideal: 'They said they were astonished that the Goths should have such a fear of a runt, of an effeminate and limp eunuch, deprived of a virile appearance.'⁷⁷ Agathias confirmed this physical aspect but said that Narses made up for it with moral strength: 'He was small in

---

74 Procopius, *BV*, IV, 28, 50 (Koutzinas). Corippus, *Joh*, VII, v. 277–278 (Iaudas is rallied). Y. Modéran, 'Koutzinas-Cusina. Recherche sur un Maure du VIᵉ siècle' in A. Mastino (ed.), *L'Africa romana 7. Atto del VII convegno di studio, Sassari, 1989* (Sassari: Edizioni Gallizzi, 1990), pp.393–407; Y. Modéran, 'Cusina', *Encyclopédie berbère*, 14 (1994), pp.2158–2159.
75 Procopius, *BG*, VIII, 24, 33–36.
76 A. H. M. Jones, J. R. Martindale, J. Morris, *PLRE*, 3b (1992), pp.912–928. Procopius, *BG*, VI, 13, 17 (guardian of the royal treasures, τῶν βασιλικῶν χρημάτων ταμίας).
77 Agathias, *Hist.*, I, 7, 8.

stature and very thin, but more than anything else he had courage and a taste for great undertakings. His generosity and nobility of spirit were such that they did not prevent him from being the best.'[78]

Narses's way of leading troops was not as a 'follow-me' general. He was not like Solomon who threw himself, sword in hand, into the brawl. He is not reported anywhere to have killed enemies with his bow or his lance, unlike Belisarius. If he commanded from the rear, Narses was no slouch however. Procopius said soberly that he was more energetic than one would expect from a eunuch.[79] Narses was a pious Christian, generous with the poor, he restored destroyed churches, founded a monastery in Bithynia and another in Rome. He attributed his victories more to God than to his weapons.[80]

His military career was upward but discontinuous. In the summer of 538, aged 52, he reinforced Belisarius with a new Illyrian and Herulic expeditionary corps.[81] Encouraged by his friends and his officers, he stirred up trouble in operations with the aim of undermining Belisarius and taking his place. He controlled the Illyrian General Justin and John the nephew of Vitalian, Narses Kamsarakan and his brother Aratius with the Heruls, a total force of almost 10,000 men. As Belisarius had dispersed his troops from Sicily to Picenum, he depended on reinforcements from Narses the Eunuch, who disobeyed him three times. Firstly, on the pretext of not dividing forces Narses refused to give Belisarius the troops to invade Liguria. During a stormy meeting with this unwilling subordinate, Belisarius showed a letter appointing him sole leader of the Army of Italy, but Narses hypocritically had the last words 'in the interests of the state' to persist in his refusal.[82] His second disobedience was more serious, as he abandoned Belisarius during the siege of Urbino, preferring to withdraw to Rimini and to conquer the Adriatic coastline opening the way to Ravenna. At the beginning of 539, when Belisarius ordered Justin and John, who were occupying Emilia, to join the troops of Martin and Uliaris south of the Po to relieve Milan, the two generals replied that they were only obeyed Narses. Belisarius then wrote to Narses, who agreed. But strangely enough, John fell ill and Procopius did not report on Justin's actions. Milan was taken by the Ostrogoths. Justinian blamed no one, but recalled Narses to Byzantium and confirmed Belisarius as commander-in-chief of Italy.[83]

---

78 Agathias, *Hist.*, I, 16, 2.
79 Procopius, *BG*, VI, 13, 16.
80 Paul the Deacon, *HL*, II, 3.
81 Procopius, *BG*, VI, 13, 16–17.
82 Procopius, *BG*, VI, 18, 29.
83 Procopius, *BG*, VI, 18, 4–11 (Narses breaks away from Belisarius); 18, 23–26 (first disobedience); 18, 28–29 (Narses misinterprets the Emperor's orders); 19, 10 (abandons Belisarius in front of Urbino); 21, 16 (refusal of Jean and de Justin); 21, 17–22 (request from Belisarius to Narses): 23 (Narses agreement); 21, 24 (John's illness); 22, 4–5 (recall of Narses).

THE TOUGH JOB OF BEING A GENERAL

The hour of Narses came 12 years later when, in 551, Justinian commissioned him to reconquer Italy, retaining the large pay and the bombastic civil title of *praepositus sacri cubiculi*. Despite his 74 years and his physical handicap, he showed astonishing energy. He came from Dalmatia with fresh troops gathered in Illyricum and raised the morale of the Italian Army, which had been discouraged by its initial setbacks.

Agathias portrayed him as a man of cool judgement: 'The general did everything in moderation and did not allow himself to be carried away by anger.'[84] On the whole, he painted a favourable picture of Narses the Eunuch: 'He was neither inclined to vulgar feelings, taking excessive pride in victory, nor – as another would have done – fell into indolence and sluggishness after his efforts.'[85] Narses practised too the 'activity-speed' principle praised by Napoleon. In 552, he dealt a decisive blow to the Ostrogoths, who were defeated and lost their King Totila at the Battle of Taginae (today Gualdo Tadino in Umbria or more precisely Busta Gallorum, modern Sassoferrato).[86] He then recaptured Rome around July 552, cleverly attacking an undefended part of the walls after launching several diversionary attacks. The following year, in October, Teias, Totila's successor, was compelled to retreat south and was defeated old eunuch by the old eunuch at the Battle of Mons Lactarius (today Monti Lattari), south of the Gulf of Naples and Mount Vesuvius. Some of the surviving Ostrogoths then agreed to become subjects of the Emperor, while the others were allowed to go north on a promise not to fight the Romans again. It can be hypothesised that they made an alliance with the Lombards but there is no confirmation of it.

In 553, the arrival of the Franks and the Alamanni, called in to help by the Ostrogoths, challenged Narses. He continued to clear the Tuscan towns in his rear, in particular Cumae where the Ostrogoths' treasury was located and which held out for a year. As the city resisted successfully, he left a blockade force there and set off to conquer the towns of Tuscany and moved against Lucca in the autumn.[87] While he personally remained in front of Lucca, he sent a detachment under the command of Fulcaris to the Emilia region as a delaying force to slow down the Franco-Alamanni advance. He therefore knew how to divide his forces, a difficult and perilous art, leaving a great deal of initiative to his great subordinates. This strategy of dividing forces succeeded, but not without damage: towards the autumn, Fulcaris, the Herulic general, died in a retreat and his detachment was routed in an

---

84   Agathias, *Hist.*, 12, 4.
85   Agathias, *Hist.*, I, 8, 2.
86   H. N. Roisl, 'Totila und die Schlacht bei den Busta Gallorum, Ende Juni/Anfang Juli 552', *Jahrbuch der Österreichischen Byzantinistk*, 30 (1981), pp.25–50; Ph. Rance, 'Narses and the Battle of Taginæ (Busta Gallorum) 552: Procopius and Sixth Century Warfare', *Historia*, 54 (2005), pp.424–472.
87   Procopius, *BG*, VIII, 33, 13–27 (capture of Rome); 34, 20–22 (Cumae, Centumcellae); 35, 15–32 (Lactarius). Agathias, *Hist.*, I, 1, 1 (submission of the Ostrogoths after the death of Teias); 8–11, (siege of Cumae); 12–13 (siege of Lucca).

ambush set up by the Franks in Parma. Narses was not impressed by this failure; still remaining at the siege of Lucca, he sent one of his relatives, Stephen, with an escort of 200 cavalry to restore the confidence of the detachment defeated at Parma. Calm, persuasive and methodical, Stephen carried out his mission and reported back. At the beginning of December, Lucca surrendered and Cumae fell shortly afterwards.[88] Narses then went to Ravenna and Rimini, the latter of which was soon attacked by 2,000 Franks. He defeated them by feigning retreat and then launching a swift counter-offensive.[89]

Like the best of the Byzantine generals, Narses knew how to address his troops, either to restore their obedience or to encourage them. Agathias reported his speeches after the defeat at Parma or after the victory of Volturnus or Casilinum.[90] Narses was not a general who favoured frontal attacks. He was sparing of the blood of his men. Instead of storming a city, he tried diplomacy or psychological warfare, preferring a long blockade to risky assaults. He retook Perugia in 552 by bribery as the city was held by Roman deserters. In this event the assassination of Uliphos, one of the two Ostrogothic commanders, was not planned by him but resulted from an internal dispute amongst the traitors. By late 553, Narses had achieved his main strategic objectives of gaining a foothold in the Parma region and controlling Tuscany.

At the beginning of the following summer, of 554, he gathered all his troops in Rome, where he had spent the winter, to train them intensively and prepare them for the campaign.[91] The 554 campaign, which completed the conquest, demonstrated Narses' tactical versatility. In the autumn, he destroyed the Frankish and Alemannic invading armies at Casilinum on the Volturnus River in a series of manoeuvres. Tactically, he used infantry to secure the area and then cavalry to encircle the enemy. During the winter of 554–555, he laid siege to Compsa, which was held by a powerful garrison of 7,000 Goths commanded by Ragnar.[92] Narses did not achieve the conquest of Italy because he was a better general than Belisarius, rather because he was a better administrator who knew how to make use of local resources and pay his troops. He was a generous benefactor to officers, soldiers and barbarians, particularly the Heruls, so many were happy to follow him in Italy. At the start of the Battle of Busta Gallorum he had gold bracelets, necklaces and bits hung from clearly visible poles to motivate his troops: gold for the brave![93]

---

88 Agathias, *Hist.*, 14, 1 (Roman retreat to Emilia); 2–15, 3 (defeat and death of Fulcaris in Parma); 17, 3–7 and 18, 1–2 (mission of Stephen).
89 Agathias, *Hist.*, 21–22 (victory at Rimini).
90 Agathias, *Hist.*, I, 16, 3–10 (Parme); II, 12, 1–10 (Capua).
91 Agathias, *Hist.*, II, 1, 1–2.
92 Agathias, *Hist.*, II, 13, 1–7.
93 Procopius, *BG*, VIII, 28, 15–17 (benefactor); 30, 21 (gold rewards).

THE TOUGH JOB OF BEING A GENERAL

Narses was also a better tax collector than governor. In 567, Italian nobles denounced him for his bad government and having amassed a huge fortune while Italy was impoverished after 30 years of war. Empress Sophia, Justin II's wife, threatened and humiliated him: 'she had him tell her, as he was a eunuch, that he would be sorted into bales of wool in the gynaecaeum, to which he replied that he would have her weave a sheet so tight that she would not be able to remove it for the rest of her life.' Narses had his pride. Ulcerated, he rebelled in Naples, and according to Isidore of Seville he invited the Lombards of Pannonia to settle in Italy.[94] However, this act of revenge is open to doubt, because in 573, Pope John III called Narses the Eunuch to defend Rome against the Lombard threat. It was after entering Rome that Narses lived out his days undefeated at the ripe old age of 95.

Sixth-Century Byzantine General
This character, freely inspired from Narses facedepiction on the San Vitale mosaic, is wearing an inverted scale armour well attested in later periods for depicting Saints and Emperors in full armour. A muscular cuirass could have been worn for parades. Leather *subarmalis* with *pteruges* is shown on the Barberini Ivory like the metal spaulders and the long sword. A decorated Baldenheim type segmented helmet in use amongst Germanic warlords is shown here because of its Byzantine origin. The black boots are also inspired by the Barberini Ivory. As purple was the reserved Imperial colour, red is used here as an indication of rank, and the gilded armour is well depicted in Byzantine icons.

---

94 Isidore of Seville, *Hist.*, 116. Paul the Deacon, *HL*, II, 5 (humiliating message from Sophie and sharp answer from Narses).

The General Appointed by Favour

Imperial favour has always been the 'open sesame' to obtain a high rank. During the pacification of Africa, Justinian I called on three of his relatives to replace Belisarius: first his cousin Germanus between 536 and 539, then his cousin by marriage Areobindus in 545 and by 563 his cousin Marcian.[95] Nepotism was an endemic blight on the regime, Emperors and generals alike were recruited from among nephews, cousins and close relatives considered trustworthy. The main beneficiary of the family favour under Justinian I was his cousin, and former nephew of Justin I, Germanus.[96]

Germanus began his career as Master of the Soldiers to the Thraces and repelled an invasion by the Antes tribe and another by the Sklavenes. Although disliked by Theodora, he rightly retained Justinian's confidence. Patrician in 536 and Duke of Libya until 539, replacing Solomon the Eunuch, it was he who ended the mutiny of Stotzas. Around 538, Maximinus, a *doryphoros* from the personal guard of Dorotheos of Cappadocia, organised another mutiny in Carthage, but his plot was skilfully foiled. Germanus, not showing that he was aware of the plot, tried to win Maximinus by flattery and forced him to swear loyalty to the Emperor. But this 'very ill-intentioned' Maximinus thought himself clever enough to continue his vicious game. When the conspiring soldiers went to the Carthage hippodrome, where the first mutiny had begun, Germanus had them attacked by loyal troops. He arrested Maximinus, and when mutineers who had been questioned said that Maximinus had indeed continued to plot, he had him executed.[97] Germanus only killed a perjurer and avoided a costly battle between the 'Romans'. However, assigned as Master of the Soldiers to the East in 540, he was unable to prevent the sacking of Antioch, the primary Romano-Byzantine city in the Middle East, and Belisarius replaced him. Nevertheless, Justinian believed his cousin Germanus was able enough to fight the Ostrogoths in Italy. In 549 he appointed him but then recalled him due to an obscure Palace intrigue, however the following year he again firmly entrusted him with the command. In addition to the Emperor's personal endowment, Germanus was wealthy enough to finance with his own funds a large army that he had hired in Dalmatia. While he found a way to pacify the Italian situation by marrying Queen Mathasuntha, heir to the Amal dynasty, he died suddenly of illness in late 550 when trying to fix the situation with the Sklavene raid in Illyricum. Germanus was a competent general. Procopius gives him as a fair man, a good administrator, pleasant and independent of character.[98] In this case cousinship was not synonymous with favouritism and incompetence. Germanus was one of Justinian's best generals.

---

95 V. Puech., 'Les officiers de l'armée d'Afrique sous Justinien', *RM2E – Revue de la Méditerranée, édition électronique*, t. II.2, (2015), pp.63–64.
96 A. H. M. Jones, J. R. Martindale, J. Morris, *PLRE*, 2 (1980), pp.505–507.
97 Procopius, *BV*, IV, 18, 1–18.
98 Procopius, *BG*, VII, 40, 4 (Sklavenes); 40, 6 (Antes): 39, 9 (commander-in-chief for

THE TOUGH JOB OF BEING A GENERAL

After the cousins, there were the nephews. They could be related to high officials. Sergios, appointed Duke of Tripolitania by his uncle Solomon, is without doubt the worst example of a general appointed through favour.[99] Some of Procopius' unflattering portrait of him says:

> Sergios was in fact a soft man and unfit for war, totally immature both in character and age, possessed to excess by jealousy and jesting towards all men, of effeminate morals and puffed up with vanity. But as he had become the fiancé of the daughter of Antonina, Belisarius' wife, the Empress had no intention of punishing him or relieving him of his command, even though she saw that Libya was continually and completely ruined.[100]

In 543, Sergios led Libya into one of its worst cycle of wars, which was ended by Troglita in 547. He treacherously achieved a surprise victory over the Levatha tribe during negotiations at Leptis Magna. But surviving Levathes sought revenge and Sergios, unable to face them, called his uncle to the rescue. Solomon could no longer even negotiate with the Levathes, as they no longer believed the Byzantine promises, even those pledged on the basis of Holy Scripture and which Sergios had nevertheless betrayed during the previous embassy.[101] After Solomon's death in battle in the summer of 544, Justinian sent Areobindos to Africa with the rank of general, 'a senator of noble origin, but who knew nothing of war.'[102] He was the son of Dagalaif and the grandson of another Areobindos, Consul in 506, and also the husband of Prejecta, Justinian's niece.[103] He shared his authority with Sergios limiting himself to Byzacene. As some of the army was not paid, a mutiny broke out led by the barbarian officer Guntharith, or Gontharis. In late 545 or early 546, Areobindos tried to defeat the mutiny by force, but during his first battle, paralysed by fear at the sight of the blood and the dead, he fled before being assassinated.[104] One of the last general officers appointed by Justinian was another of his nephews: Marcel. His only feat of arms was in 562 when he recaptured Obaisipolis/Odessos or Odyssus in Lower Moesia (now Varna in Bulgaria) from the Huns Kutrigurs.[105]

Nepotism was not related only to Justinian's reign and can be explained by the justified fear of a coup. In such cases, a brother could be better than a cousin or a nephew. Emperor Maurice appointed his brother Peter the Kouropalates to command the field Army of Thrace in 594, and again from

---

Italy); 39, 16 (Germanus partly finances the army); 40, 9 (personality and death).
99   A. H. M. Jones, J. R. Martindale, J. Morris, *PLRE*, 3b (1992), pp.1024–1028.
100 Procopius, *Anecdota*, V, 32–33.
101 Procopius, *BV*, IV, 21, 20–21.
102 Procopius, *BV*, IV, 24, 1.
103 A. H. M. Jones, J. R. Martindale, J. Morris, *PLRE*, 3b (1992), pp.107–108.
104 Procopius, *BV*, IV, 26, 16 (scare); 26, 33 (assassination).
105 Theophanes Confessor, *Chrgr.*, AM 6054, 237.

601 to 602.[106] On the first occasion, Peter was skilful enough to quell an army mutiny, but this did not protect Maurice from a second mutiny, which proved fatal to him and his brother. Two years later, the usurper Phocas appointed his nephew Domentziolus the Younger as Master of the Soldiers to the East, against a backdrop of incipient civil war and two successive defeats by the Persians.[107] Political caution outweighed military merit, but we must be wary of making hasty judgements for lack of evidence. Even Napoleon was defeated by larger armies commanded by experienced generals. Why would not Domentziolus have been so? His main quality was his loyalty, something more desirable than military genius because dynastic Emperors and usurpers all sit on a dangerous or deadly throne.

Theodore the Kouropalates, Heraclius' brother and unsuccessful general

Theodore the Kouropalates' most valuable asset was his status as the Emperor's brother, which guaranteed him political influence.[108] Following the deposition and assassination of Maurice and then Phocas, the Empire returned to an era of coups. Giving a high military rank to his brother was a way for Heraclius to ensure his own political safety. So Theodore was given the office of *curopalata*, in Greek *kouropalates* (the One who takes Care of the Palace), either at the start of his brother's reign or in 612: 'Heraclius placed in the (military) command held by Crispus his own brother Theodore, who held the second rank after the Emperor, a position present that common people called *kouropalatēs*, but also Philippicus who was the brother-in-law of the Emperor Maurice.'[109] This was a rank that was almost exclusively reserved for members of the Imperial family. The position first appeared in the fifth century and was held by the master of the offices. Emperor Maurice had previously bestowed this high function upon his brother, Peter, as a gilded path to further honours, such as the Patrician title.[110]

The other post entrusted to Theodore was to succeed Priscus as Master of the Soldiers to the East. An experienced commander Philippicus, who had just been recalled from his monastic retreat, was by his side. Philippicus was also the brother-in-law of the former Emperor Maurice. Theodore the Kouropalates' role was more political – to ensure the loyalty of the Eastern Army. His troubles began with the Persians, who defeated him twice, once near Antioch and once in Cilicia, around 613–614. However, it seemed more likely that he accompanied his brother Heraclius than that he took on

---

106 Theophylact Simocatta, *HU*, VIII, 4, 9–7 (594); 13, 1–2. (601–602).
107 Theophanes Confessor, *Chrgr.*, AM 6095, 282.
108 A. H. M. Jones, J. R. Martindale, J. Morris, *PLRE*, 3b (1992), pp.1277–1279.
109 Nikephoros of Constantinople, *Brev.*, 2, 55 (Κουροπαλάτης).
110 A. P. Kazhdan, A. M. Talbot, A. Cutler, T. E. Gregory, N. P. Ševčenko (eds), 'Kouropalates', vol. 2 (1991), pp.1157.

a real military command. Meanwhile, Philippicus led a separate campaign in Persarmenia, undoubtedly to repel Shahín, the bold Persian general who had ventured as far as Chalcedon on the Asian shore of the Sea of Marmara, opposite Byzantium.[111]

Philippicus died in 614, but the Persian war continued for another decade. Around 626, while Byzantium was under siege from the Avars and the war with the Persians was still raging, Heraclius entrusted him with a third of his army to fight Shahín. Theodore the Kouropalates enjoyed success in Armenia when an unexpected hailstorm decimated the enemy army while miraculously sparing his own – a military miracle.[112] By mid-August, Theodore had reached Byzantium, while the Khan had lifted the siege but was still ravaging the surrounding area. The Patrician Bonus warned the Avar ambassadors that they would have to deal with 'the brother of our most pious lord who has arrived with his army protected by God' and that he would pursue them up to their country'.[113] Stricken with panic the Avars fled in good order; however, it does not appear that Theodore the Kouropalates pursued them.

In 628, after the peace treaty was concluded, Theodore's Imperial brother sent him to organise the peaceful withdrawal of enemy troops from Osrhoene. However, at Edessa, the Persian garrison and the local Jewish population were firmly opposed to any such move. Theodore had to attack the town, which was a powerful fortress. The Persians finally agreed to leave, but Theodore was about to massacre the Jews when Heraclius ordered him to call off the attack.[114] In 634, Theodore confronted the Saracens, who had invaded Palestine and Syria, but he was defeated. He went too far by mocking his Imperial brother for marrying his niece, and he was dismissed from his military command and sent back to Byzantium, where he was publicly degraded by Heraclius' son, Constantine, before being imprisoned. His military command was given to Theodore Trithyrios the Sakellarios.[115] This marked the end of his career.

---

111 Sebeos, *Hist.*, 34, 1999, p.67 (Philippicus, Maurice's brother-in-law, converted and recalled to service, campaigns in Armenia); 68 (Antioch and Cilicia).
112 Theophanes Confessor, *Chrgr.*, AM 6095, 315. George Kedrenos, *Compendium Historiararum*, vol.1 (1838), pp.1727–1728.
113 *Chr. paschale*, a. 626.
114 Theophanes Confessor, *Chrgr.*, AM 6119, 328. George Kedrenos, *Compendium Historiarum*, vol. 1 (1838), p.735. Michael the Syrian, *HU*, XI, 3, t. 2 (1963), p.410.
115 Nikephoros of Constantinople, *Brev.*, 24, 4–10 (mockery and dismissal); 9–11 (transfer of command to Trythirios as 'strategist of Anatolia').

4

The Chain of Command of a Field Army

> The general is the guide and leader of the whole army and the sub-general is second in rank to him.
>
> Maurice, *Strategikon*, I, 4, 10–11

Early Byzantine perception of the hierarchical chain does not entirely correspond to ours. Where we see generals, officers, non-commissioned officers and enlisted men, Procopius or the *Strategikon* referred only to generals, sub-generals, commanders and soldiers, specialised or not.[1] The Roman Army is often praised for its tactical and logistical abilities. Behind these stood a strong chain of command, which remained in place in the early Byzantine military forces. As is the case today, a distinction must be made between function and rank. Sources are not always explicit about what seemed natural to their authors, and the polysemous term 'officer', which is used so widely today, could cause problems for historians in the future.

---

1 Maurice, *Strategikon*, I, 4, 5 (division of the army between 'leaders and soldiers', *archontes kaï stratiôtaï, ἄρχοντες καὶ στρατιῶται*).

THE CHAIN OF COMMAND OF A FIELD ARMY

Table 2 - The Chain of Command for a 9,000-man strong Army according to the *Strategikon*

MILITARY RANK	TYPE OF UNIT (Modern equivalent)	TOTAL EACH ARMY	NUMBER of subordinates
Commander-in-Chief			
Stratēgos	*Stratos* (Army) Division	1	9,000
Second-in-command general, Executive Officer			
Hypostratēgos	-	1	-
Senior officers			
Merarchs or stratēlatēs	*Meros* Brigade (former Legion)	3	3,000–7,000 (6,100 infantry, 730 cavalry)
Moirarchs, chiliarchs or dukes [*Taxiarch* in Agathias, *drongarios* in Leo VI]	*Moera/Moira Chiliarchia* Regiment	9	2,000 – 3,000
Junior officers			
Counts or tribunes, *tagmatarchs*	*Tagma/ bandon, arithmos* Squadron/ batallion	30	200–400
Hecatontarchs	*Hecatontarchia* Company	90	100
Non-commissioned officers			
Decarchs	*Decarchia* Squad	900	8–10 for *phoideratoi/ foederati, optimatoi* 7 for vexillations
Pentarchs, Tetrarchs (filecolsers)	*Pentarchia Tetrarchia*	1,800 2,250	5 4

From, F. Aussaresses, *L'Armée Byzantine à la fin du VIe siècle d'après le Strategicon de l'Empereur Maurice* (Bordeaux: Féret et Fils, Bibliothèque Universitaire du Midi, 14, 1909) completed by reference to Maurice, *Strategikon*, I, 4.

The General's Staff

The general's house is full of men. Some have massive faces, some are scarred, and some have thoughtful or dull features. Many seem to be busy; some even pretend to be. Scrolls of *papyri* are piled up on tables where scribes are hard at work writing down orders and statements. A campaign was being prepared. The staff of a Romano-Byzantine Army is chiefly known thanks to the writings of Procopius on the reconquest of Africa in 533. Belisarius was commander-in-chief. Solomon the Eunuch was mentioned as the second in command of the *foederati* and 'assisted Belisarius in his task as general'. He held the rank 'according to the Romans' of *domesticus*, *domestikos* in Greek. In the late Roman Army, the role was equivalent to that of an aide-de-camp, but by that time it had become equivalent to the rank of major general.

The commanders of *foederati* were Cyprian, Valerian, Martin, Althias and Marcellus. In this case, the *foederati* were a category of regular soldiers. They should not be confused with the two mercenary detachments: the Heruls of Pharas and the Huns of Sinnion and Balas. The commanders of the regular infantry were Theodore, Terentius, Zaidus, Marcian and Sarapis. They were all supervised by John of Epidamnos, who was equivalent to a general.

Belisarius had his own military *oikia* (house), a private army, in other words his *bucellarii*. Two of who were ranked as *doryphoroi* (senior officers), Rufinus the Thracian and Aigan the Hun, both in command of cavalry along with Barbatus and Pappus, officers who did not belong to Belisarius's military house. This makes a total of 22 senior officers, if we add the unmentioned chief of the Moorish auxiliaries.[2] Among them, the *bandophoros* carried the insignias of the army's command, the *bandon*, but he held a much higher rank than his counterparts in the common units. According to Procopius, Rufinus the Thracian, a man of great courage, was the standard-bearer of the general, 'whom the Romans call a *bandophoros*.'[3] During his march to the decisive battle against the Vandals in 533, Belisarius sent his *bandon* to the vanguard, presumably to mislead the enemy while he was absent.[4] The following year, Belisarius left Rufinus the Thracian, his personal *bandophoros*, in Africa under the command of Solomon. Together with Aigan the Hun, Rufinus led a patrol of 500 men who were wiped out by the Moors. Rufinus lost his life in the battle.[5] The commander-in-chief's *bandophoros* was a high-ranking senior officer and not a mere standard-bearer.

Belisarius was assisted in financial matters by a civilian, the Patrician Archelaos, ex-Praetorian Prefect, who had been appointed *tou stratopedou eparchos* (prefect of the army). Belisarius had his own military retinue, 'composed of numerous officers and soldiers, all valiant in war and well aware of its dangers.' The letter of mission given by the Emperor instructed him to take the best measures according to the circumstances and on his Imperial behalf.[6] At a time communications were lengthy and difficult,

---

2   Procopius, *BV*, III, 11, 5 (Dôrotheos); 6 (Solomon as δομέστικος; Cyprian, Valerian, Martin, Althias, Marcellus); 7 (Rufinus, Aigan, Barbatus, Pappus οἰκία; infantry commanders); 8 (John of Epidamnos); 9 (Hunnic origin of Aigan); 11 (Heruls of Pharas); 12 (Huns of Sinnion and Balas).
3   Procopius, *BV*, IV, 2, 1; 10, 4.
4   Procopius, *BV*, IV, 2, 1 (βανδοφόρος).
5   Procopius, *BV*, IV, 10, 4–10.
6   Procopius, *BV*, III, 11, 17–20 (τοῦ στρατοπέδου ἔπαρχος).

so Justinian I granted Belisarius the autonomy to take action as he needed. Contrary to the old Roman custom, Belisarius took his wife with him.[7] This was due to his position as head of the Libyan army, which also made him Governor of the province and meant he had to lead a life of representation. While Belisarius had remained only a half-year in Africa, later John Troglita stayed there for several years, his wife residing in Carthage, where every piece of bad news put her into a tizzy.[8] In Belisarius' retinue was the future historian Procopius, who was already *symboulos*, a jural adviser during the last Persian war and was then playing the role of liaison officer but was in fact a *paredros* – an intelligence officer.[9] Aides-de-camp or *hyperetountes*, were common before the time of Justinian I, but became rarer due to budget restrictions, 'squeezed by hunger and extreme poverty.'[10]

Administrative and Logistical Staff: Logisticians, *Scribones* and Delegators

One of Procopius's most scathing criticisms of Justinian I was his creation of the *logothetes*:

> Nor should his conduct towards the military be passed over in silence. He put the worst of all men in charge of them, instructing them to extract as much wealth as possible for themselves (they knew full well that a twelfth of what they obtained was theirs), and he gave them the name of *logothetes*.[11]

They had already existed by the time of Anastasius I. It is thought that they derived from the *scrinarii* of the praetorian prefecture, or perhaps the *rationales* or *procuratores*, who were originally responsible for the Emperor's private treasury or public funds. During the reign of Justinian I, the military *logothetes* corresponded to today's army comptrollers general, who are responsible for checking pay.[12] Their secondary role was to reduce expenditure in order to make savings. Procopius clearly accused them of prevarication. As a member of Belisarius' staff, he was undoubtedly very

---

7   Procopius, *BV*, III, 12, 2.
8   Corippus, *Joh*, VII, v. 155.
9   Procopius *BP*, I, 12, 23 (Belisarius's *xymboulos* or *symboulos*, σύμβουλος, since first Persian campaign); *BV*, III, 12, 3 (African campaign); III, 14, 3 (πάρεδρος).
10 Procopius, *Anecdota*, XXIV, 10 (ὑπηρέτης or servant, already has the meaning of aide-de-camp in Xenophon, *Cyrus*, II, 4, 4, VI, 2, 13; in Procopius the form under the plural: ὑπηρετοῦντες).
11 Procopius, *Anecdota*, XXIV, 1 (*logothethēs* plural *logothetai*, λογοθέτης plural λογοθέται).
12 R. Guilland, 'Les Logothètes: Études sur l'histoire administrative de l'Empire byzantin', *REB*, 29 (1971), pp.5–115.

familiar with their unfair practices. According to him, the *logothetes* pocketed the pay of the dead who were not removed from the strength lists, which were never updated. Consequently, there were too few soldiers in the army, and promotions for young recruits were blocked. The *logothetes* accused the soldiers of falsifying the Emperor's letters certifying their enlistment. They deprived the aides-de-camp of the very necessities of life and plunged them into poverty. This could have been the case with Procopius, who settled personal scores in his writings.[13] His attitude was very similar to that of Napoleon's Grande Armée officers when they wrote about the *commissaires aux guerres* in their memoirs. Agathias, Procopius' successor, was also highly critical of the *logothetes*.[14]

Was Procopius referring to the *scribones* when he spoke of 'Palace guards' who forced certain soldiers to beg on the pretext of their age or uselessness, and who took money from them under this threat?[15] In Latin, the *scribo* was an official responsible for registration of the recruits and not a mere scribe. In 584, when the Avars invaded the Adrianople region, just a few days' march from Byzantium, the *scribones* hurriedly recruited soldiers or extorted requisitions: 'They took children away from their parents and ruined the countries themselves. Everywhere they forced the inhabitants to pay tribute in the form of horses, oxen and even chickens.'[16] In the same year, Theophylact Simocatta observed that Comentiolus the Thracian, who would become a general, held the 'Latin rank of scribo' in the Imperial Guard. This fairly high position led to him being sent on an embassy with a former governor of Sicily to meet the Khan of the Avars. *Scribones* were increasingly entrusted with special missions and seemed to take precedence over *protectores domestici*.[17]

The creation of the positions of *logothetes* and scribones was undoubtedly intended to correct for the misdeeds of the *delegatores*, who were the army commissaries' equivalent. Their mission was to ensure the supply of troops and they received one-fifteenth of the price of the food and goods they bought for the army.[18] The vice of this method of remuneration was crystal clear – the more the *delegatores* bought, the higher was their salary. They were undoubtedly at the root of the deep malaise within the Romano-Byzantine Army during the sixth century, characterised by mutinies and frequent desertions. Procopius went even further: 'It was for this reason that the Roman possessions in Italy collapsed. Alexander the Logothete, sent there, had the nerve to unfairly criticise the soldiers without hesitation, and

---

13   Procopius, *Anecdota*, XXIV, 5 (*logothethai* prevent the dead from being removed from the roles); 6 (insufficient 6manpower and sharing of army funds between Justinian I and the *logothethai*); 10–11 (impoverishment of the aides-de-camp).
14   Agathias, *Hist.*, V, 14, 2–4.
15   Procopius, *Anecdota*, XXIV, 5, 8 (palace guards, *tôv ēn Palatiô philakôn tinēs, τῶν ἐν Παλατίῳ φυλάκων τίνες*).
16   Michael the Syrian, *HU*, X, 21, t. 2 (1963), p.362.
17   A. H. M. Jones, *The Later Roman Empire*, pp.658–659.
18   *Nov. J.*, 130, 1.

THE CHAIN OF COMMAND OF A FIELD ARMY

then demanded money from the Italians, declaring that he was punishing them for their favorable conduct towards Theodoric and the Goths.'[19] Then as now, management kills the mission…

Second in command generals

The *Strategikon* referred to the *hypostratēgos* (second in command general). Furthermore, it is the only source that mentions the rank of *merarch*.[20] Nevertheless this book leans more towards theory than practice and must be carefully interpreted. Neither *merarchs* nor *moirarchs* by name are to be found in Procopius or Agathias. A *merarch* was equivalent to a modern divisional or brigade general, or even to a Roman legion's legate. Maurice's *meros*, like Vegetius' classical legion, numbered around 6,000–7,000 men.[21] Ideally, to fight a battle the front line should be divided into three *meroi*: left, centre and right.[22] The role of the *merarchs*, three per army, was to lead the centre and the two wings. They should be 'prudent, practical, experienced and, if possible, able to read and write.' The *merarch* in the centre held the rank of *hypostratēgos*. Maurice also referred to the *merarch* as a *stratēlatēs*.[23] Before entering the ranks to fight, the *merarch* sat on horseback at the front of the battle line, surrounded by his command group.[24] Clearly, the *merarch* was more of a fighting and inspirational leader than an officer capable of writing reports or compiling logistical files.

In the army raised in 533 to invade Africa, an officer appeared to be the second in command, despite not being explicitly referred to as a *hypostratēgos*. His name was Dôrotheos and he was the first officer mentioned after Belisarius. He officially held the double function of count of the *foederati* and of general of the troops of Armenia. After him in the hierarchy came John of Epidamnos who commanded leaders of the regular infantry, excluding the *foederati*. This infantry amounted to a total of 5,000 men, a big of the army. John's real rank was perhaps as *magister peditum* (master of the infantry) and a survival from the late Roman Empire.[25] Dôrotheos and John of Epidamnos were the equivalent of *merarchs*. In 542, the expeditionary corps to Italy was commanded by the Patrician and Count of the Stable Constantianus with Alexander, as his *hypostratēgos* (second in command) who in turn had 10 commanders of units under in.[26] The dress of these second in command generals was designed to be recognisable from

---

19   Procopius, *Anecdota*, XXIV, 9.
20   Maurice, *Strategikon*, I, 3, 12 (*merarchēs*, μεράρχης).
21   Vegetius, *DRM*, III, 6. Maurice, *Strategikon*, I, 4, 25–26 (μέρος, plural μέροι).
22   Maurice, *Strategikon*, III, 6 (*meroi* lined up in battle order).
23   Maurice, *Strategikon*, I, 4, 14 (three); 16–17 (qualities of a *merarch*); 17 (*meros* in the centre); I, 4, 15; XII, B, 8, 26, 27, 28 (*stratēlatēs*, στρατηλάτης).
24   Maurice, *Strategikon*, XII, 11, 21; 17, 54.
25   Procopius, *BV*, III, 11, 5 (Dôrotheos); 8 (John).
26   Procopius, *BG*, VII, 3, 4.

afar because they were a rallying point amidst the turmoil of battle. During the Libyan War of 546–547, the *merarch* Fronimuth wore a polished iron helmet with a plume, and his horse was adorned with gold decorations.[27] Similarly, during a battle against the Persians in 586, the Duke and *Taxiarch* Vitalius put his helmet on a bodyguard so that this latter would be mistaken for him and thus draw the enemy's arrows.[28]

In the 580s, the *merarch's* command group consisted of two *mandatores*, two *kampidouktores*, one *stratôra*, one *spatharios*, and two *ornithobôres*.[29] *Mandatôres* and *kampidouktores* were junior officers who also existed in combat units. The *stratôr* was only mentioned in the specific context of escorting the *merarch*. During the classical Roman Empire, the person called in Latin a *strator* was a groom or even the footman of an Emperor, a praetorian prefect or of a proconsul. It also existed at lower ranks. A lintel on a temple at Dmer in Syria bears a dedication offered by a *strator* of the prefect of the Voconces cavalry *ala* during the reign of Septimius Severus (193–211). Another inscription found near Bonn in Germany mentions the *strator* of a tribune. The rank did not exist in the fleet. Ammianus Marcellinus gave to the *strator* the meaning of a squire, but in the Justinian Code it was used as a jailer. Throughout the sixth century, the *stratôr* was probably in charge of the *merarch's* mounts, a sort of steward or even a veterinary surgeon with a team under his command. Later, in the eighth and ninth centuries, the title of *stratôr* was used to designate a junior officer both in the army and in the civil service, and a golden whip or a baton of command symbolised his position.[30]

The *spatharius* in Latin or *spatharios* in Greek was literally a 'sword-bearer'. He escorted the merarch as to be part of his own staff. *Spatharioi* formed the general-in-chief's guard of honour in a marching army.[31] According to Leo VI the Tactician, they bore the arms of a commanding officer.[32] They were squires in the original sense of the word, bearing the shield, the helmet, the lance and, of course, the long sword or *spatha*. The presence of two escort *spatharioi* was perfectly justified: one was probably carrying the general's shield and lance, while the other had to bear the

---

27   Corippus, *Joh*, IV, v. 521 and 527–528.
28   Theophylact Simocatta, *HU*, II, 4, 3 (*taxiarchos*, ταξίαρχος). A. H. M. Jones, J. R. Martindale, J. Morris, *PLRE*, 3b (1992), pp.1381–1382 (Vitalis 4).
29   Maurice, *Strategikon*, XII, B, 11, 21; 17, 53 (*merarch* staff).
30   *IGRR*, III, 1094; *OGIS*, 628 (lintel of Dmer). *CIL*, XIII, 8089 (Bonn); Maurice, *Strategikon*, XII, B, 11, 20 (στράτωρ); 17, 53; Ammianus Marcellinus, *RG*, XXIX, 3, 5. *CJ*, IX, 4, 1; R. Cagnat, 'Strator' in Ch. Daremberg, E. Saglio, *Dictionnaire des Antiquités*, tome IV (Paris: Hachette, 1900), p.1530; A. P. Kazhdan, A. M. Talbot, A. Cutler, T. E. Gregory, N. P. Ševčenko (eds), 'Strator', vol. 3 (1991), p.1967; K. R. Dixon, P. Southern, *The Roman Cavalry* (London: Batsford, 1992), pp.157–158, 203; Y. Le Bohec, 'Écuyers et marins militaires sous le Haut-Empire romain', *Ktèma*, 21 (1996), pp.313–320.
31   Maurice, *Strategikon*, I, 9, 32 (σπαθάριος, plural σπαθάριοι).
32   Leo VI the Wise, *Taktika*, VII, 39.

helmet and sword. According to the *Strategikon* the merarch's staff had two *ornithobôres* (bird carriers). They were not to engage in combat as unarmed.[33] *Ornithobôr* was a Greek military slang expression referring to the former *aquilifer* (eagle-bearer) of the former Roman legion. By way of comparison, Napoleon's Grande Armée very similarly referred to the eagle on the Imperial flags as 'the Bird'. The suffix *bôr* is of Germanic origin: *bahre* in German as well bear in English both mean 'to carry'. Usefulness of two eagle carriers is something difficult to understand and, in addition, there is no evidence of carrier pigeons used for transmitting messages. *Ornithobôr* may unconvincingly have been taken as a misnomer for *ornibôr* (urn-bearers) an orderly holding orders or documents squeezed into an urn.[34] The duality of some ranks suggests a possible tactical organisation into two combat groups or redundancy in case of losses. Two centuries later, Leo VI the Tactician remained very close to the *Strategikon* about the combat staff of a *tourmarch*, rank synonymous with merarch: i.e. two *mandatôres*, two *kampidouktores*, a *stratôr* and a *spatharios*. Only the so-called 'bird carriers' were missing.[35]

Colonels, *moirarchs*, *chiliarchs* and *taxiarchs*

No source other than the *Strategikon* mentions the *moirarch*, equating this rank with the *taxiarch*.[36] A *meros*, or brigade, had three *moirata*, or regiments. Each *moira* was formed by several units called *tagma*, *arithmos* or *bandon*, equivalent to infantry battalions or cavalry squadrons.[37] Procopius barely mentioned the military ranks, but we can deduce from the numbers that the *moirarchs* commanded several units. Asbad demonstrates such a career profile: candidate in the Imperial Guard, then Justinian's *Doryphoros*, he became commander of several elite cavalry squadrons in Thrace in the fortress of Tzurullon (modern Çorlu in Turkey). He met a horrific end c. 550, when he clashed with a group of 1,200 to 1,800 Sklavenes. Captured, his back was cut into strips before he was burnt alive.[38] Constantine, Bessas

---

33 Maurice, *Strategikon*, XII, B, 7, 13–14 (two *ornithôbores* per *meros*; *ornithobôr*, ὀρνιϑόβωρ, plural ὀρνιϑόβωρες); 11, 21; 17, 54 (is standing along with the *merarch*), 24 (unarmed).
34 F. Aussaresses, *L'Armée Byzantine à la fin du VIe siècle d'après le Strategicon de l'empereur Maurice* (Bordeaux: Féret et Fils, Bibliothèque Universitaire du Midi, 14, 1909), p.49; Maurice (G. T. Dennis, ed. and translated into German by E. Gamillscheg) *Das Strategikon Des Maurikios*, (Vienna: Verlag der Österreichischen Akademie der Wissenschaften, 2021), p.425, n. 49.
35 Leo VI the Wise, *Taktika*, XIV, 72.
36 Maurice, *Strategikon*, I, 3, 13 (*moirarchēs*, μοιράρχης, *douks* δούξ); 23 (taxiarch, ταξίαρχος plural ταξίαρχοι).
37 Maurice, *Strategikon*, I, 3, 14 (three *moirata* in a *meros*, μοῖρα, plural μοῖρατα); 15 (*moira* is a gathering from different units).
38 Procopius, *BG*, VII, 38, 1–2 (2 Sklavene groups, one with 1,800 men out of 3,000); 4–6 and A. H. M. Jones, J. R. Martindale, J. Morris, *PRLE*, 3a (1992), p.133 (Asbadus

and Peranios had two to three units under their command, nearly 1,300 men, which corresponds to a *moirarch*. This rank equated to a nineteenth and twentieth century infantry colonel in terms of command, i.e. 2,000 to 3,000 men from the *Strategikon*. Their rank also equated with duke, *dux* in Latin, transcribed into Greek as *douks*, and *chiliarch* (a 1,000-man leader). They had to be 'prudent and disciplined.'[39]

Agathias ranked *taxiarchs* just after the *stratēgos* (general). These officers were more 'follow-me' leaders than subtle tacticians, mainly because tactics were the responsibility of the army commander and not them. They only need to know where to draw up their units and were themselves exposed to danger, like Palladios who was killed by an arrow at the siege of Cumae c. 552. Maxentios and Theodore were said to be 'good warriors and *taxiarchs*.'[40] However, when detached from the army, these officers had to show tactical initiative and were more or less successful. Cavalry officers were generally good, as they were used to improvising in reconnaissance missions. Thus, in the spring of 538, Ildiger and Martin at the head of 1,000 cavalry seized the Pertusa Petra Pass by taking advantage of the cliff overlooking the channel to crush the barbarian huts under rocks, forcing the Ostrogoths to surrender. Infantry officers used to simply obeying orders in battle had less tactical know-how. In 539, Conon, an infantry officer, defended Ancona with Isaurians and Thracians, using a tactic described by Procopius as 'madness'. Boldly leaving the fortifications without any garrison, he went out to face the enemy and lined up a thin phalanx of the type used in hunting. Outnumbered, Conon's soldiers fled as soon as they saw the enemy.[41] *Moirarch*, *chiliarch* and *taxiarch* seem to be some sort of temporary function entrusted to border dukes and unit commanders.

The *Strategikon* mentioned the *droungos*, a term quoted for the first time in Vegetius and meaning a 'cavalry unit', probably from military slang. Leo VI the Wise, c. 902, equated the *droungos* with *moira* and *chiliarchy* with 1,000 men each. There were four *droungoi* per *tourma*, from the Latin *turma* or cavalry regiment. But the *tourma* could be extended to a maximum of 3,000 men – a brigade.[42] The *droungarios* was a *droungos* commander.

---

1 killed by the Slavs, not to be confused with the Hercules officer Asbadus 2).

39 Maurice, *Strategikon*, I, 3, 13 (taxiarch assimilated to *douks* δούξ); 4, 13 (Duke assimilated to chiliarch, χιλιάρχης); 14 (qualities); 11–12 (numbers).

40 Agathias, *Hist.*, I, 9, 4 (Palladios); II, 20, 7 (Theodore of Tzane origin); III, 6, 9 and 21, 6 (Dabragezas of ante origin); III, 2, 4 (Rusticus was neither a general nor a taxiarch, but a disburser): IV, 13, 2 (Maxentios cited along with Theodore); 15, 1 (Elminsour of Hunnic origin).

41 Procopius, *BG*, VI, 11, 10–19 (Petra); 11, 5 (Isaurian footmen and Thracians of Conon); 13, 7–13. Vegetius, *DRM*, III, 15.

42 Vegetius, *DRM*, III, 16 and 19 (*drungus* synonym of *globus*); *Historia Augusta*, *Probus*, XIX, 2 (same meaning); Maurice, *Strategikon*, I, 3, 14; II, 1, 19; 2, 2; III, 10, 37, 48, 61; IX, 3, 104; XII, B, 20, 33, 36 (δροῦγγος, plural δροῦγγοι); Leo VI the Wise, *Taktika*, IV, 45 (assimilated to *moira*); 47 (3,000 men to the maximum), XVIII, 146 (4 *droungarioi* and 2 *tourmarchs* for 4,000 men); Ph. Rance, 'Drungus, Δροῦγγος and Δρουγγιστί – a Gallicism and Continuity in Roman Cavalry Tactics', *Phoenix*,

The rank was first mentioned on 25 March 628, during the war against the Persians, when the Master of the Soldiers Elias Barsoka and the *Droungarios* Theodotus were sent as reinforcements with recruits and 20 packhorses.[43] This rank was illustrated in 697 by the putsch of the African expeditionary army, when the Imperial title was usurped by the *droungarios* called *eis Kourikiôtas hyparchonta* (from the *Korykos* squadron), raised in the region of the *Kibyraiotes/Kibyrrheotes*, from *Kibyra* in Cilicia.[44] The rank is best known from later periods, such as eleventh century.

Unit Commanders or The Art of Commanding Forward

Procopius and Agathias were quite imprecise on military ranks. Procopius preferred a generic Greek term for commander, *archon*. Counts and tribunes corresponded to *archontes* (squadron or battalion leaders). They were in command of a unit variously called *tagma*, *arithmos* or *bandon*.[45] The latter term was not in use for infantry according to the *Strategikon*. Tagmatarch is only a historiographical form that did not exist in this treatise which used paraphrases such as *tou tagmatos ēgoumenos* (coach of a *tagma*), *tou bandou archontos/archonta* (commander/commanders of a *bandon*).[46] Throughout the fifth century a count, in Latin *comes*, was a general commanding elite troops or looking after a border region. By the sixth century, spelt in Greek *komēs*, he was demoted to head of a unit. The tribune retained his rank with the Greek name of *tribounos*. Justinian's edict of 13 April 534 on the Africa military organisation stipulated that each border duke had tribunes under his command.[47] A *papyrus* from Syene in Egypt, dated to the late sixth century, mentioned Menas who was *tribounos kai topotērētēs tou limitou* (tribune and defender of the frontier).[48] From the *Strategikon* each infantry *tagma* had its own tribune, who was requested to be 'respected, intelligent and skilled in close combat' and its own standard or *bandon*.[49] A tribune commanded from the front line, which means that he fought, leading troops by his example. In other words, he was a combat officer exposed to wounds and death. Therefore, Corippus often referred to the 'unfortunate tribunes' or the 'courageous tribunes.'[50]

---

58 (2004), pp.96–130. W. Treadgold, *Byzantium and its Army*, pp.104–105.
43 *Chr. Paschale*, a. 628 (δρουγγάριος).
44 Theophanes Confessor, *Chrgr.*, AM 6190, 371 (εἰς Κουρικιώτας ὑπάρχοντα).
45 Maurice, *Strategikon*, I, 3, 16 (*komēs*, κόμης; *tribounos*, τριβοῦνος; archôn, ἄρχων).
46 Maurice, *Strategikon*, I, 3, 16–17 (*tou tagmatos ègoménos*, τοῦ τάγματος ἡγούμενος); 5 (ἄρχων, plural ἄρχοντες); XII, 11, 4–5 (*archôn* of a *bandon*, *tou bandou archôn*, τοῦ βάνδου ἄρχων).
47 *CJ*, I, 27, 2.
48 *P. Monac*, 6, 10–11 (τριβοῦνος καὶ τοποτηρητὴς τοῦ λιμίτου).
49 Maurice, *Strategikon*, XII, B, 8, 20.
50 Corippus, *Joh*, IV, v. 43, 109.

Such senior officers wore rich equipment recognisable from a distance. During the 546–547 African War Putzintulus had a helmet with a high plume and a polished breastplate.[51] Gentius' horse was 'beautiful with its plumes and shining with gold'.[52] Marcentius also stood out for his remarkable weaponry and horse harness:

> A helmet of gold presses his tawny hair, reinforced with bronze and heavy with his plume, and a breastplate with glittering scales surrounds his fearsome shoulders, while his horse lays its hooves in proud steps, he carries on his back spears, a quiver and a sonorous bow with which he is girded, and bringing back bronze arrows for the wars.[53]

His colleague Geisirith was simply magnificent:

> His golden helmet is of flame, with iron mixed in; then a horse's mane makes up the aigrette and plumes. He encircles his gleaming belt with precious stones; a sword has adorned his side with an ivory scabbard. Then he had leggings on his calves, which a Parthian skin had attached to a lot of gold, and, skilfully, he put them on in red purple, skilfully adorned with gems.[54]

Their flashy, offensive weapons were also probably decorated, as was the case for another officer named Senator – or bearing that rank.[55] Archaeologists have found decorated belts and weapons from the later Roman Empire, covered with cabochons and made of silver or of gold-plated metal. Weapons gleaming with gold and purple were common to leaders of the middle ages and could be seen among the Franks and the Goths. It would be wrong to think this was only poetic exaggeration, because anyone who has seen the uniforms of the Napoleonic period knows perfectly well that the misery of the soldier in the field can be covered in shimmering colours or gold and even in the period of dull uniformology of the twentieth century, men from the *Wehrmacht* did not hesitate displaying their Iron Cross and medals on camouflaged outfits. However, the desire to be discreet to survive also existed in late antiquity. During a surprise sortie outside Rome against the Ostrogoths, Belisarius was not singled out by shiny luxurious armour, but by his grey horse with a white muzzle, which was identified by unashamed deserters.[56] Senior officers were armed like

---

51 Corippus, *Joh*, IV, v. 480 (plume) and 481 (cuirass).
52 Corippus, *Joh*, IV, v. 474.
53 Corippus, *Joh*, IV, v. 534–539.
54 Corippus, *Joh*, IV, v. 492–500.
55 Corippus, *Joh*, IV, v. 501.
56 Procopius, *BG*, V, 18, 6.

mounted *lanciarii*. Corippus praised them for their fighting qualities: 'Here, there was Liberatus, incomparable with his long spear; there, the handsome Ulitan, adorned with a variety of weapons, better with a spear and no worse with a curved bow. There was also Ifisdaias who knew how to twirl his horse around.'[57] Another senior officer, named Gregory, was carrying a lance, a light shield and a type of javelins known as 'Spanish'.[58]

Junior Officers, Non-Commissioned Officers and Specialists in a Legion *c.* 490

Pamphylia (today Aksu, in Turkey) was situated to the south of Anatolia on The city of Perge in the Mediterranean coast. Since the edict issued by Leo I in 472, this province was under a *comes rei militaris* (military count).[59] A legion was stationed there in the 490s as is mentioned in the Military Decree of Anastasius I. This almost complete text was found at Perge in Pamphylia. It contains 850 epigraphic fragments in Greek about the rank and file of a legion.[60] The Perge edict was fairly close to Vegetius's *De Re Militari*.

---

57 Corippus, *Joh*, IV, v. 541–544.
58 Corippus, *Joh*, IV, v. 486–487 (Senator); v. 541 (Liberatus); v. 542–543 (Ulitan).
59 *CJ*, XII, 59, 10.
60 F. Onur, 'The Anastasian Military Decree,' p.186. Text B, l.10, 12 and 30.

Table 3, The Chain of Command of a Legion according to Vegetius (390s) and the Military Decree from Perge of Anastasius I (490s)

Vegetius[61]	**Anastasius** (Latin transcription latine and original Greek text)[62]
Commanding Officers	
Tribunus maior (senior tribune): legion commander appointed 'by a sacred letter from the emperor.'	L. 3 Tribune commanding a unit, *tribunus numeri, tribounos tou arithmou*.
Minor tribune, *tribunus minor*: promoted "through hard work" on merit.	L. 4 *Tribunus minor, tribounos mikros*.
Junior Officers and Signals	
Ordinarii: officers at the head of the order of battle. In the past, these were the 5 centurions commanding the 10 centuries of the 1st cohort.[63]	L.5 *Ordinarii, ôrdinarioi*: 20 in number, equivalent to centurions.
Augustals, *augustales*: rank below the *ordinarii* created by Augustus.	L.7-8 *Augustales* and *augustales alii, augustalioi* and *augustalioi alloi* (other augustals): this refers to 120 non-commissioned officers who cannot therefore be equated with centurions or *centenarians* but rather with *decani*, or senior corporals.
Flavials, *Flauiales*: *ordinarii*, created by Flavius Vespasian, a rank lower than Augustals. It may be assumed that these ranks reflect less a tactical burden than the need to feed the promotion ladder.	L. 9-10 *Flaviales* and *flaviales alii, flabialoi* and *flabialoi alloi*: nearly 200 'corporals'.
Aquilifers, *aquiliferi*: eagle bearer; the eagle was the symbol of the legion	
Signifers, *signiferi*: Vegetius *DRM*, II, 20, estimates that there were 10 in the ancient legion, i.e. one per cohort, and that in his time they were called *draconarii*, II, 7.	L. 11 *Signiferi, signiphéroi*: 10 in number, reminiscent of the legion with 10 cohorts, which has very probably changed to 10 centuries. May be equivalent to *raconarii-draconarii*?

---

61 Vegetius, DRM, II, 7. Richardot Ph., 2005, p. 43-44 (late fourth-century military organization).

62 Onur F., 2017, p. 153-163. Text C gives the ranks in Greek (l.3-4 τριβοῦνος τοῦ ἀριθμοῦ, τριβ(οῦνος) μικρός, l.5 ὠρδ(ινάριοι), l. 7-10 αὐγ(ουστάλιοι), αὐγ(ουστάλιοι) ἄλλ(οι), φλαβ(ιάλιοι), φλαβ(ιάλιοι) ἄλλ(οι), l. 11 σιγνιφ(έροι/αι), l. 12 ὀπτιό(νες), l. 13-14 οὐερεδ(άριοι), οὐερεδ(άριοι) ἄλλ(οι), l. 15 β[η]ξιλ<λά>ρ(ιοι), l. 16 ἰμμαγνιφ(έραι), l. 17 λιβράρ(ιοι), l. 18 μήνσορ(ες), l. 19 τούβικ(ες), l. 20 κόρνικ(ες), l. 21 βουκινάτορ(ες), l. 22 πρέκωρ), l. 23 ἀρματοῦρ(οι) δουπλάρ(ιοι), l. 24 βενεφικ(ιάριοι), l. 25 τορκ(ουᾶτοι) σιμισ(σάλιοι), l. 26 βρακ(χιᾶτοι) σιμισ(σάλιοι), l. 27 ἀρματοῦρ(οι) σιμισ(σάλιοι), l. 28 μουνίφικ(ες), l. 29 κληρικοί κα[ὶ] δηπουτά[τοι]).

63 (Vegetius (*DRM*, II, 8, 6), who used sources such as the military Constitution of Augustus, the first cohort had ten cohorts led by five officers called *ordinarii*, unlike the modern scholars who are in favour of five large cohorts.

THE CHAIN OF COMMAND OF A FIELD ARMY

	L. 12 Optios, *optiones*, *optionès*, in Vegetius are below the imaginifers. In text A, l. 53-54 of the list from Perge, they are in charge of the distribution of the *annona* and are named *optionès tôv annônôn*. In Procopius, *BV*, IV, 20, 12, they distribute the military pay. John the Lydian makes them scribes, *grammateïs* (scribes).[64]
	L. 13-14 Messengers, *veredarii* and *veredarii alii-oueredarioi* or *ouredarioi alloi*. In Hyginus, *Munitionibus castrorum*, 30, the term *veredus* was originally attributed to fast post horses or to a corps of 800 Pannonian cavalrymen, but here it refers to legionary cavalry, i.e. around 275 men.
	L. 15 Vexillaries, *vexillarii*, *bèxillarioi*. John the Lydian gives them as *doryphoroi* (lance-bearers).[65]
Imaginifers, *imaginarii*: bear the 'images or effigies of the emperor., the common term is *imaginiferi*.	L. 16 *Imaginiferi*, *imaginiferaï*. John the Lydian gives them as *iconophoroi*, (image-bearers).[66]
Optios, *optiones* or *uicarii*: literally 'chosen' by their superiors, act as 'replacements' or vicars, i.e. lieutenants, second-in-command officers who, in the event of an illness or absence, replace their superiors.	
Draconaries, *draconarii* or *ex-signiferi*: dragon-standard-bearers.	
Tesseraries, *Tesserarii*: carry the instructions to the *contubernia*, the squads of 10 men.	
Campigenes or 'drill instructors', *campigeni*, who fight in front of the standards, *antesignani*: instructing officers who, with the tribunes or their vicars, ensured the smooth running of the army and, with the *principia*, allocated to each century the sector to be dug in entrenching the camp, Vegetius, *DRM*, III, 8. In battle, they were placed in front of the standards which they had to protect, they corresponded to the *campidoctores*. The term *campidoctor* was associated with fencing training, Vegetius, *DRM*, I, 13; II, 23; III, 8 and 26.	
NCO's and specialists	
Metators (those who delimit), *metatores*: pioneers who choose the location of the marching camp.	

---

64   Onur F., 2017, p. 146 (text A l. 53, ὀπτιόνες τῶν ἀννωνῶν). John the Lydian, De Magistratibus, I, 46, 4, 4 (γραμματεῖς).
65   John the Lydian, De magistratibus, I, 46, 4, 5 (βηξιλλάριοι, δορυφόροι).
66   John the Lydian, De magistratibus, I. 46, 5, 1 (ἰμαγινιφέροι, εἰκονοφόροι).

Beneficiaries, *beneficiarii*: non-commissioned officers promoted by the favour of the tribune.	
Caput contubernii (leader of Contubernium): this fourth century rank corresponds to the *decanus* of the ancient legion according to Vegetius. It refers to the 'corporal' commanding a squad or *contubernium* of 10 men, *DRM*, II, 8.	
Librarii (librarians): secretaries in charge of unit administration.	L. 17 *Librarii, librarioi*: are relatively important figures as there are only two of them, perhaps heads of archives and administration.
	L. 18 *Mensores, mènsores*: only three of them, perhaps showing their specific knowledge as surveyors.
Tubicines (trumpeters): musicians who play the tuba.	L. 19 *Tubicines, toubikes*. John the Lydian says that they are only infantry trumpeters.[67]
Cornicines (cornublowers): musicians who play the *cornu*, and give instructions for moving the *signa*, *DRM*, II, 22.	L. 20 *Cornicines, kornikes*: four *tubicines* and eight *cornicines* respectively, suggesting subordination or different uses.
Buccinators, *buccinatores*: musicians who play the *buccina* (similar to the *cornu*) used when the emperor is present in the army, during an execution and to transmit the general's orders, *DRM*, II, 22.	L. 21 *Buc(c)inatores, boukinatores*: the fact that there were two of them confirms their role as a means of transmitting important commands.
	L. 22 *Praeco, prékôr*, (crier). Restricted to one per legion
Armaturae duplares: soldiers probably skilled in swordfighting who received two rations or *annonae*.	L. 23 *Armaturae duplares, armatouroi duplarioi*: twenty in number. John the Lydian refers to the rank of *armatura prima*.[68]
Armaturae simplares: receive only one *annona*.	
Mensores (measurers): men who measure the spacing of tents and assign housing in towns.	
	L. 24 *Beneficiarii, benephikiarioi*: unlike Vegetius, John the Lydian calls them *benephikialioi* as orderlies in the service of veterans.[69] There are only four of them, perhaps in the service of the tribunes.

---

[67] John the Lydian, *De magistratibus*, I, 46, 4, 7 (τουβίκινες).
[68] John the Lydian, *De magistratibus*, I, 46, 5, 3 (ἀρματοῦρα πρῖμα).
[69] John the Lydian, De magistratibus, I, 46, 4, 17-18 (βενεφικιάλιοι).

THE CHAIN OF COMMAND OF A FIELD ARMY

Torquati duplares (double torcs): soldiers decorated with a golden torc and receiving a double ration.	L. 25 *Torquati semissales, torkouatoi simissalioi*: one and a half torcs numbering 136. John the Lydian says only that they wear 'necklaces'.[70] A Justinian guard is wearing one on the mosaic from the Basilica of San Vitale in Ravenna.
Torquati simplares (simple torcs): receive only one *annona*.	
Duplares (doubles): receive a double *annona*.	
	L. 26 *Bracchiati semissales, brachiatoi simissalioi*: the bracelet, *brachiale*, is another decoration. John the Lydian, who also calls them *armilligeroi* (from the Latin *armilla*), and says that they wear 'bracelets'.[71]
	L. 27 *Armaturae semissales, armaturoi simissalioi*: the *armaturae* 'one and a half' seem to be above the simple *armaturae* of Vegetius after the pay has been upgraded. 'Those who handle weapons best.' according to John the Lydian[72].
Sesquiplares (one and a halfs): receive one and a half *annona*.	
Candidati duplares (double candidates): receive double *annona*.	
Candidati simplares (simple candidates): receive a simple annona. With them ends the list of *milites principales* (principal soldiers) who have privileges.	
The Rank and File	
Munifices: ordinary soldiers who are responsible for carrying out *munera* (chores).	L. 28 *Munifices, mouniphikes*: John the Lydian calls them *mounérapioi*.[73]
	L. 29 *Clerici* and *deputati, klèrikoi kaï dèpoutatoi*: scribes and deputies (aides according to the *Strategikon*).

The Military Decree from Perge estimated a legion at nearly 1,000 men, a strength unchanged since the later Roman Empire.[74] It indicated the main ranks as *prinkipia*; for Vegetius *principia* was 'the correct term' to designate the officers.[75] In the 370s, a veteran like Ammianus Marcellinus referred

---

70 John the Lydian, *De magistratibus*, I, 46, 4,19-20 (τορκουᾶτοι)
71 John the Lydian, *De magistratibus*, I, 46, 4, 21 (βραχιᾶτοι ou *armilligéroi* ἀρμιλλίγεροι).
72 John the Lydian, *De magistratibus*, I, 46, 5, 4 (ἀρματοῦρα σημισσάλια).
73 John the Lydian, *De magistratibus*, I, 46, 4, 23 (μουνεράριοι).
74 Ph. Richardot, *La fin de l'Armée Romaine*, pp.63–64.
75 Vegetius, *DRM*, II, 7; F. Onur, 'The Anastasian Military Decree,' p.146 (text A, l. 55, πρινκιπία).

to *principales* and tribunes (first ones and tribunes) from the *Iovian* and *Herculian* legions.[76] Junior officers were also called *ordinarii* or in Greek *ôrdinarioi*. Since the third century, there had been the 20 centurions in a legion and increasingly the *primi ordines* i.e. the five centurions from first cohort.[77] 20 *ordinarii* centurions remained in Anastasius' decree. Amongst them persisted the old ranking as *flaviales*, in Greek *flabialoi*. A papyrus dated 530 ranked Flavius Ioannes as *flaouialos* 'from the unit of the very devoted Transtigritanians.[78] Until at least Justinian's reign, and probably after, the legionary ranks continued mostly unchanged.

Beneficiarii or *benephikiarioi* mentioned by Vegetius and by the Military Decree from Perge were soldiers freed from chores. During the second and third centuries, they were administrative personnel in the governors' offices as well as being present in all types of military units. They might have judicial, fiscal, customs, transportation, mining, state factory and/or public works functions. They were not exclusively bureaucrats, as 65 percent of their funeral inscriptions indicate that they had died in combat. They disappeared from epigraphy at the end of the fourth century and did not appear in the *Notitia Dignitatum*, but they remained in papyrology, no doubt because of a clearer separation between military and civil service.[79] In any case, it is difficult to know what their function was to be by the 490s, but four of them served in the Perge's legion. Another category called *veredarii* (messengers) was particularly numerous, some 275 in number, and may have been a legionary cavalry.

Table 4, Ranks and Personnel from Perge's Unit (490s)[80]

Rank	Number	Rank	Number
Tribunus Maior	1	*Librarii*	2
Tribunus Minor	1	*Mensores*	3
Ordinarii	20	*Tubicines*	4
Augustales	20	*Cornicines*	8
Augustales alii	30	*Buc(c)inatores*	2
Augustales alii	70	*Praeco*	1
Flaviales	60	*Armaturae Duplares*	20

---

76 Ammianus Marcellinus, *RG*, XII, 3, 2; XV, 8, 16.
77 E. Stein, 'Ordinarii et Campidoctores', *REB*, 8 (1933), p.379.
78 BGU, II, 369 (Φλ(αουίῳ) Ἰωάννῃ φλαουϊαλίῳ ἀριθμοῦ [τῶν καθοσιωμ(ένων) Τραν] στιγριτανῶν).
79 J. Nelis-Clément, *Les 'Beneficiarii': militaires et administrateurs au service de l'empire: Ier s. a.C.-VIe s. p.C.* (Bordeaux: Ausonius-De Boccard, 2000), pp.59–85 (duties); 89, n. 1 (killed in action) ; 233–243 (judiciary duties); 243–252 (tax collectors); 252–259 (customs, logistics); 259–264 (mining, industry); 264–268 (public works); 333–339 (relative disappearance in the fourth century).
80 F. Onur, 'The Anastasian Military Decree', p.186.

Flaviales alii	140	Beneficiarii	4
Signiferi	10	Torquati semissales	136
Optiones	10	Bracchiati semissales	256
Veredarii	50	Armaturae semissales	[20]
Veredarii alii	225	Munifices	[59 ?]
Vexillarii	10	Clerici and Deputati	73 ?
Imaginiferi	10	**TOTAL**	**1,245**

This list is incomplete and another part of the Military Decree from Perge adds the rank of *draconary* in connection with others: '*Drakonarioi, optiones, armatouroi, kornikes, toubikes, boukinatores*' (in Latin *draconarii, optiones, armaturae, cornicines, tubicines* and *buc(c)inatores*).[81] They were originally standard-bearers carrying the *draco* or dragon standard, a windsock with a gilded bronze head, the cohort's emblem in fourth century.[82] By this time, draconaries wore a torc collar according to Ammianus Marcellinus.[83] The Anastasian Military Decree from Perge and an inscription from Prusias, both mention in original Greek the *magisteros tôn drakônon/drakônariôn* (master of dragons or of *draconarii*) transcribed in Latin as *magister draconum/draconarium*.[84] The Anastasian decree specified that this charge was entrusted for two years, after which the holder had to give up his insignia of office.[85] He was the senior over common *draconarii*:

> Since any form of brigandage or corruption is out of the question, we decree that all men will be appointed according to their abilities and needs, so that *draconarii* are placed under the responsibility of the master of dragons; the *optiones* of *annonae*, which are distributed in categories, under the responsibility of the *principia*; *armaturae*, *cornicines*, *tubicines* and *bucinatores* under the responsibility of the *campidoctor* of any *schola*.[86]

Draconarii, or in plural *drakonarioi*, appeared later in 534 as a *schola* in the offices of the praetorian prefect of Africa. They may have been messengers, since in the fifth century Bishop Theodoret of Cyrus referred to the *drakonarioi* Patroinus and Theodotus, whom he had charged with

---

81 F. Onur, 'The Anastasian Military Decree,' p.177 (δρακωνάριοι, texte B, l. 46–50).
82 Vegetius, *DRM*, II, 13; Ph. Richardot, *La fin de l'Armée Romaine*, p.59.
83 Maurice, *Strategikon*, XII, B, 7, 5 (drakonarôs, δρακονάρως). Ammianus Marcellinus, *RG*, XX, 4, 18.
84 F. Onur, 'The Anastasian Military Decree,' p.146 (text A, l. 53 magister draconum, μα(γ)ίστερος τῶν δρακώνον; l. 57 τῶν δρακωναρ(ίων).
85 F. Onur, 'The Anastasian Military Decree,' p.146 (text A, l. 56–60), p.179.
86 *I Prusias*, 120; F. Onur, 'The Anastasian Military Decree,' p.146 (text A, l. 50–56) pp.178–179.

passing on his letters.[87] They were similar to eighteenth century ensigns or cornets, young second lieutenants who carried the standard of a regiment or a cavalry troop. The *Strategikon* mentions once a *drakonar(i)ôs* as an ensign bearer.[88] The museum of Cagliari in Sardinia has a sixth-century Latin funerary stele belonging to Gaudiosus who, after having been an *optio*, died as *draconarius* aged around 23.[89] An Egyptian *papyrus* dated 15 February 594 recorded in Greek the *drakonarioi* Flavios John Peter and Flavios Victor Menas from 'the unit of Syene'.[90] One of the sixth-century terracotta plaques found at Vinica, and now in the Museum of Macedonia in Skopje, shows St Theodore on horseback, wearing a scale cuirass and carrying a *draco* standard similar to the fourth-century model.[91] However, St Theodore was also reputed as a dragon-slayer and medieval iconography always depicted him on horseback impaling the dragon, which is not the case for the Vinica plaque, where the dragon, the size of a large fish, is brandished like a banner. Medieval artists may have been misled by representations of the dragon emblem, for which there is no other evidence of continuity for Romano-Byzantine Army. Nevertheless, the tenth-century *Book of Ceremonies* from Emperor Constantine VII Porphyrogenitus still referred to 'the clothing of *draconarii*'.[92]

Vegetius equated the *campidoctor* (drill instructor) with 'vicars or tribunes' in marches where seasoned officers hastened the stragglers and slowed down the faster ones.[93] This is an important rank that he cited five times.[94] Ammianus Marcellinus mentioned Marinus, ex-*campidoctor*

---

87 Theodoret of Cyrus, *Ep.* 59; 137 (Patroinus and Theodotus). *CJ*, I, XXVII, 1, 35 (*schola*).
88 Maurice, *Strategikon*, XII, B, 7, 5 (*drakonarôs*, δρακονάρως).
89 Museo Archeologico Nazionale di Cagliari, Epigrafe R20S09-2276 (inscription restored by the Museum as: *Gaudiosus (ir) d(evotus) optio / drac{c}onarius n(umer)o dr(aconariorum) S(ardorum)*. Uncertain inscription restored as *n(umero) dr(omaderiorum) S(ardorum)* in S. Cosentino, 'Gaudiosus Draconarius: la Sardegna bizantina attraverso un epitafio del secolo 6', *Quaderni della Rivista di bizantinistica*, 13 (1994), p.29; G. Ravegnani, 'Le unità dell'esercito Bizantino nel VI secolo tra continuità e innovazione' in S. Gaspari (ed.), *Alto Medioevo Mediterraneo* (Florence: Firenze University Press, 2005), p.194.
90 *P. Monac.*, 14, 105–106.
91 Dimitrova E., *The Ceramic Relief Plaques from Vinica.The most significant values of the cultural and natural heritage* (Skopje: Directorate for protection of cultural heritage, 2017), p.10–12; Ph. Richardot, *La fin de l'Armée Romaine*, pp.10, 43 (*draco*).
92 Constantine VII Porphyrogenitus, *De Ceremoniis*, I, 1 (*ta skeuē tôn drakonariôn*, τα σκευη των δρακοναρίων). M. Marciniak, *Draco – historia smoczego sztandaru – History of the Dragon standard, University of Varsaw*, Masters Degree in archaeology in the field of general anthropology n° 209 672 (Uniwersytet WarszawskiInstytut Archeologii, 2010), Polish text, p.136.
93 Vegetius, *DRM*, III, 6, 23 (*exercitatissimi campidoctores uicarii uel tribuni*).
94 Vegetius, *DRM*, I, 13, 1–3 (train recruits in the use of weapons); II, 23 (are in command of the *armaturae*); III, 6, 23 (with tribunes to speed up or slow down the march); 8, 10–11 (assign work for a stopover camp); 26, 36–37 (instructor for weaponry).

promoted to *tribunus vacans* (vacant tribune, i.e. without a specific command). *Campidoctor* was a rank below *principia* in the Military Decree from Perge and in Roman military tradition. An inscription from *Laodicea Combusta* (today Ladik in Turkey), mentions Paul '*ordinarius* after (having been) a *campidoctor*.'⁹⁵ Of course, *campidoctores* fought 'in front of the standards' and despite the fall of the Amida fortress in 359 their valour was such that Constantius II had statues erected of them in Edessa.⁹⁶ *Campidoctor* were known for their fighting spirit, to the extent that St Augustine of Hippo applied it to the apostle Paul, 'that great drill instructor', as a defender of the faith and the Bishop of Carthage Quotvultdeus even applied it to Christ.⁹⁷ This rank enjoyed a certain literary renown until the late middle ages.⁹⁸ Eucher Bishop of Lyon in the 440s praised the three martyrs of the Theban Legion executed under Emperor Maximian *c.* 285–286 at Agaune who included: *Primicerius* Maurice, *Campidoctor* Exsuperius and *Senator* Candidus.⁹⁹ A fifth-century collection of fables attributed to Romulus of Vienna gave the chain of command as counts, *primicerii*, *campidoctores* and common soldiers.¹⁰⁰ In these two fifth-century literary references, *campidoctor* came after *primicerius*, which is discussed below.

The Chain of Command of Units Smaller than the Legion

Besides existing legions, late Roman border troops, the so-called *limitanei* or *riparienses*, were organised into old-model cohorts for infantry, *alae* and the new model *cunei* for cavalry, while palatine elite troops were divided into *auxilia* and *scholae*. These wordings were no longer in use in sixth-century sources. Instead for standard units was the preferred term of *numerus* or *arithmos*. Nevertheless, ranks remained the same from the 380s to the 530s. *Primicerius* and *senator*, are attested from literary sources, epigraphy and papyrology from the late fifth century to Justinian's reign. The most famous *primicerius* was, of course, the one who suffered martyrdom for his faith

---

95 *MAMA*, I, 168 (*Paulou apo kampidouktorôn ôrdenariou*, Παύλου ἀπὸ καμπιδουκτόρων ὠρδεναρίου). Stein E. (1933, pp.379, 386–387. E. L. Wheeler, 'The legion as phalanx in the Late Empire, Part 2', *REMA*, 1 (2004), pp.168–169. Ph. Rance, 'Campidoctores Vicarii vel Tribuni', p.406; F. Onur, 'The Anastasian Military Decree,' p.179.
96 Ammianus Marcellinus, *RG*, XIX, 6, 11–12.
97 (St) Augustine of Hippo, *Serm*. 72, *PL* 39, col. 1885 (*ille maximus campi doctor*). Quotvultdeus, *De accedentibus ad gratiam*, I, IV, 1–2.
98 J. F. Domínguez Domínguez & R. Manchon Gomez, 'Recherches sur les mots campidoctor et campiductor: de l'Antiquité au Moyen Âge tardif', *Bulletin Du Cange*, 58 (2000), pp.5–44.
99 Eucher, *Passio Acaunensium martyrum*, 8, p.35.
100 Romulus de Vienna, *fab. Aesop*. IV, 8 (*comites, primicerii, campi doctores, milites*).

at Agaune, St Maurice.[101] Jerome of Stridon, now St Jerome in c. 386–387, spoke about soul levels using the example of the military hierarchy in a cavalry troop: at the top stood the tribune while the ranks below were *primicerius, senator, ducenarius, centenarius, biarchus, circitor*, cavalryman and recruit. Vegetius who wrote at the same time did not mention any *primicerius, senator* or *biarchus*. He alluded to the *ducenarius*, commander 'of two hundred' equivalent to two centuries (a maniple) and equating it with the centurion forward *hastatus*.[102] A law from Emperor Leo I, addressing to Master of the Offices Patricius, hinted at *ducenarii* among the ranking of the 1,248 Imperial messengers.[103] These were probably officers or non-commissioned officers from the regular army. In a law dated 13 April 534, that Justinian addressed to Belisarius, still Master of the Soldiers to the East, dealing with the pay of the staff of the border dukes in of Africa,[104] the ranking was very close to the text of Jerome of Stridon or the law of Leo I. The rank of *numerarius* could be that of a civil servant or the military equivalent of *senator*,[105] but, given the context and the hierarchical position, *numerarius* was perhaps the equivalent of a quartermaster. The ranks of *ducenarius* and *centenarius* were also those of senior financial civil servants and should not be confused with their military equivalents.

Table 5, The Chain of Command in a Border Troop or Staff, from Literary and Legal Sources

Jerome of Stridon, *Ep. 61, ad Pammachium* (c. 386-387)	*Justinian Code* (Leo I, 457-474) XII, 20, 3 *Schola* of messengers	*Justinian Code* (Anastasius I, 491-518), XII, 37, 19 Troop (*numerus*)	*Justinian Code* (13 April 534) I, 27, 2 Ducal staff
-	-	-	*Dux* (duke)
-	-	-	*Adsessor* (assessor)
Tribunus (tribune)	-	*Tribunus* (tribune)	-
-	-	*Vicarius* (vicar)	-
-		*Domesticus*	-
Primicerius	-	-	*Primicerius*
Senator	-	-	*Numerarius*
Ducenarius	48 *Ducenarii*	-	4 *Ducenarii*
Centenarius	200 *Centenarii*	-	6 *Centenarii*

---

101 H. Bellen, 'Der Primicerius Mauricius. Ein Beitrag zum Thebäerproblem', *Historia*, X, 2 (1961), pp.238–247.
102 Vegetius, *DRM*, II, 8.
103 *CJ*, XII, 23.
104 *CJ*, I, 27, 2.
105 A. H. M. Jones, (1964), p.194, n. 58.

THE CHAIN OF COMMAND OF A FIELD ARMY

-	-	*Actuarius*	-
Biarchus	250 *Biarchi*	-	8 *Biarchi*
Circitor	300 *Circitores*	-	9 *Circitores*
Eques (horseman)	450 *Equites*	-	11 *Semissales*
Tiro (recruit)	-	-	-

Italian or Egyptian papyrology gives something a little different. The tribune was seconded a *bikarios* (vicar from *vicarius*) a rank still existing late sixth century in the legion of Syene.[106] According to a law probably dated to Anastasius I, the tribune had under his command a *vicarius* or second in command, a *domesticus* and an *actuarius* (orderly or accountant)[107] *Domesticus* rank was found in combat units without any link to the *protectores domestici* from the Imperial Guard, as the Ravenna *papyri* shows.[108] Subordinate and non-commissioned officers, known as *principales* (the first ones) during the Classical Empire, are then called the *numeri principes* (first ones of the unit) in *Justinian Code*. The Greek *papyri* registered them quite accurately as *priores* or *prôtoi* and *prôteuontes tou arithmou*. They formed a *koinos* (community).[109] *Primicerius* is attested in its Greek form *primikērios* but rarely, such as for Theologios '*primikērios* among the other *priores* (first ranks)' acting in Thebaid during the second half of the sixth century. Below comes the rank of centurion with all its variants.[110]

By late sixth century, the legion of Syene included an *ordinarios*, in the person of Flavios Joseph Allamonos, evoking the legionary hierarchy mentioned by Vegetius and the Anastasian Edict of Perge from the 490s.[111] By this time, the rank of *augustalis* was mentioned several times. A document precisely dated to 15 February 594 mentions two officers of this rank using the Greek form *a(u)goustalios*.[112] Centurion itself is attested to five times in inscriptions from Syene in Egypt of the late sixth century, including to a Flavios Iohanes Abraamios who was *kentyriôn legeônos Syenēs*

---

106 *P. Monac.*, 8, 47 (ex-vicar, ἀπό βικαριανῶν).
107 *CJ* (from the time of Anastasius), XII, 37, 19.
108 *P. Ital.*, 18 (*domesticus numeri Dacorum*); 23 (*domesticus numeri Armeniorum*); 24 (two *domestici numeri Felicum Laetorum*). ChLA, XXII, 722 and XXIX, 877 (a single *domesticus numeri Inuicti*).
109 *CJ*, XII, 37, 19 (*numeri primi*). J. Maspéro, *Organisation militaire de l'Égypte Byzantine* (Paris: Champion, 1912), pp.104–105 (*priores tou arithmou*, πριόρες τοῦ ἀριθμοῦ; *prôtoi*, πρῶτοι; *prôteuontes*, πρωτεύοντες).
110 Red sandstone stele from Kom Ombo or Ombos, 2nd inscription, British Museum, 1196. J. Gascou, 'Deux inscriptions byzantines de Haute-Égypte (reed. from I. Thebes-Syène 196 r° and v°)', (Paris: Collège de France, Centre de recherche d'histoire et civilisation de Byzance, *Travaux et mémoires*, 12, 1994), p.340 (*prim(ikèriou) kaï lopois prôtôn*, πριμ(ικηρίου) καί λοποῖς πρώ(των)).
111 *P. Monac.*, 2, 18, 20, 22; 8, 15, 46; 16, 49 (ὀρδ(ινάριος).
112 *P. Monac.*, 2, 6; 8, 46; 13, 83–84; 14, 107–198 (15 February 594); 15, 25; 16, 50 (ἀγουστάλιος).

(centurion of the legion of Syene).[113] *Papyri* provide information on the administrative ranks, but not the tactical one, and gives a line of command as follows: *campidoctor* (instructor, second in command), centurion (in command of 100 or so), *actuarius* or *optio* (accountant who distributed food or military *annona*), *adiutor* (adjutant, secretary-scribe who recorded acts of enlistment), *drakonarios* (*draconarius*, standard-bearer), *biarchos* (commissary of food).[114] *Actuarius* and *optio* appear together in legal texts.[115] It has been conjectured that the rank of *optio* was inferior to that of *actuarius* but with the same function. Procopius explicitly designated the *optio* as the one who distributed the pay, and highlights the interesting case of Gezon who fought valiantly the Moors. The *optio* was not just a bureaucrat.[116] Some ranks are poorly documented, such as that of *circitor* described by Vegetius as an attendant on the watchtower and described in an edict by Anastasius as an inspector of *castra* (fortifications).[117]

Table 6, The Chain of Command in a Border Troop in Egypt according to the *Papyri*

Rank (Latin/Greek)	Function
Command	
Comes, tribunus/komēs, tribounos (Count, tribune)	Commanding Officer
Vicarius/bikarios (vicar)	Executive Officer
Domesticus/domestikos (domestic)	Aide-de-camp
Staff (*priores* or *prôtoi tou arithmou*, eventually *ordinarioi*)	
Primicerius/primikerios	First centurion
Centurio, centenaries/kentyriôn, kentenarios (centurion)	Centurion, captain
Draconarius/drakonarios or trakonarios [sic]	Standard-bearer (dragon ensign?)
Actuarius, optio/actuarios, optiôn	Accountant, treasurer
Biarchus/biarchos	Commissary of food
Campidoctor, campiductor/kampidouktôr	Drill instructor

---

113   *P. Monac.*, 8, 41 (κεντυρ(ίων) λεγ(εῶνος) Συήνης) and 45; 9, 105, 108–109; 16, 17. E. L. Wheeler, 'The legion as phalanx', p.168, n. 110.

114   J. Maspéro, (1912), p.105 (*domestikos*, δομεστικός; *kampidouktôr*, καμπιδούτωρ; *kentyriôn* or *kentenarios*, κεντυρίων or κεντηνάριος; *drakonarios* or *trakonarios*, δρακονάριος ου τρακονάριος; *biarchos*, βίαρχος, *actuarius* ἀκτουάριος; *optio*, ὀπτίων; *adioutôr*, ἀδιούτωρ; *benephikialoi*, βενεφικιάλοι).

115   *CTh*, VII, 4, 24 (year 398); VII, 7, 22. *CJ*, X, 22, 3; XII.49.9 (c. 470–473).

116   A. H. M. Jones, *The Later Roman Empire*, pp.626, 190, n. 38 (*actuarius* is over *optio* and according to him he is not a soldier). Procopius, *BV*, IV, 20, 12–16 (Gezon is described as a soldier enrolled as an *optio*: 'servant who delivers the pay', fighting at the front against the Moors).

117   Vegetius, *DRM*, III, 8. Ed. *Anas.*, 8.

THE CHAIN OF COMMAND OF A FIELD ARMY

Adiutor/adioutôr (adjutant)	Secretary dealing with unit administration
NCOs and Specialists	
Beneficiarii/benephikialoi	Soldiers promoted by the tribune's favour (in the fourth century)
Circitor	Soldier inspecting guard posts or a dispatch rider

According to a *papyrus* from 612, *bucellarii* who formed the latifondiary militia in Egypt had a different hierarchical chain, similar to that of the *Strategikon*.[118] The rank of *diatrechôn* or courier, and was found as such in the civil administration, but in the *papyrus* of 612, he can be found only as the officer of infantry, some equivalent of the *mandatôr* in cavalry.[119] Another *papyrus* from *Oxyrhynchus* speaks about a detail of *bucellarii* led by a tribune named Ouliôr.[120] A tribune of the *bucellarii* in commanded of 50 men was undoubtedly not on the same rank as a tribune from a regular unit in commanded of several hundred. The rank of *doryphoros*, often mentioned in Procopius, designated an officer, but did not appear in regular units and was only for *bucellarii*. John the Lydian, who wrote a little earlier, made the connection between the *vexillarii* from the ancient Roman legion and the term *doryphoros*.[121]

Table 7, The Chain of Command in a *Bucellarii* troop in Egypt according to a *papyrus* from 612

Rank (Latin/Greek)	**Function**
Command	
Tribunus/Tribounos (tribune)	Commanding Officer
Mandator/Mandatôr	Executive Officer and head of cavalrymen
NCOs and Specialists	
2 *Bucinatores/Boukinatôres* (trumpeters)	Transmit orders
Only in infantry part of the list	
Diatrechôn (courier)	Head of infantry
Toxopoios (bowyer)	Repairs or makes bows
Zabaros (armourer)	Repairs or makes coats of mail

---

118   *P. Oxy.*, XVI, 2045, 4 (*tribounos*, τριβοῦνος); 25 (*mandatôr*, μανδάτωρ); 28 and 34 (*boukinatôres*, βουκινάτωρες); 48 (*diatrechôn*, διατρέχων); (*toxopoios*, τοξοποιός); 53 (*zabaros*, ζάβαρος).
119   N. Gonis, 'Payments to Bucellarii in Seventh-Century Oxyrhynchus' in J. L. Fournet & A. Papaconstantinou, *Mélanges Jean Gascou*, Centre de recherche d'histoire et civilisation de Byzance, Travaux et Mémoires, 20/1, (Paris: Collège de France, 2016), p.189.
120   *P. Oxy.*, XVI, 2046, 1 –2, 5, 13, 27, 3. A. H. M. Jones, J. R. Martindale, J. Morris, *PLRE*, 3b (1992), p.959.
121   John the Lydian, *De magistratibus*, I, 46, 4, 5 (βηξιλλάριοι, δορυφόροι).

The Chain of Command for a 'Battalion-Sized' Unit c. 580s

The difficulty with Maurice's *Strategikon* is to know whether he was describing the situation from his time or the ideal army of his dreams. He differentiated the ranks between cavalry and infantry and half of them were a Greek transcription from Latin. Under the tribune or count, the second in command of a cavalry troop was known as the *ilarch* (squadron leader) from the Greek *ilēs* (squadron) and *archēs* (commander). He was a former veteran *hecacontarch* and had the same banner as the count or tribune of his *tagma*.[122] The *ilarch* had to be 'agile and bright' and each *tagma* had two of them, a requirement not found in the tactical formations recommended by Maurice. The *ilarch* was also part of the *merarch's* staff group.[123] In Maurice's treatise, cavalry ranks were given by the number of men commanded: *hecatontarch* (100), *decarch* (10), *pentarch* (5), *tetrarch* (4) also known as *phylax* (guard), and *ouragos* (file closer).[124] For infantry, *Strategikon* did not give ranks such as *hecatontarch* or *pentarch*. This does not mean that they did not exist. *Decarch* was the only infantry rank relating to a numbered strength.[125] Simplicity never was a Byzantine strength and a *decarchy* could be reduced to eight or even seven troopers in elite cavalry troops.[126] *Decarchs*, *pentarchs* and *tetrarchs* were equivalent to our corporals, lance corporals and sergeants. They made up almost half of the ranks. This high percentage of non-commissioned officers shows the importance of a solid tactical discipline, but also reveals the continuity of a career based on slow promotion, as in the army of the later Roman Empire. The next two cavalry ranks were *bandophoros* (standard-bearer) and *tēn kappam bastazon* (cape-bearer).[127] This so-called 'cape-bearer' was a mere position, probably in the service of the count or tribune.

The *Strategikon's* first specialised rank in an infantry *arithmos* was the *mandatôr*, a close Greek transcription from the Latin *mandator* (person who gives a mission). In the infantry, he had to be 'agile and bright with a loud and pleasant voice'. He was almost like the sergeant major of the old

---

122 Maurice, *Strategikon*, I, 3, 17 (second in command); II 20, 7 (has the same banner as the count or tribune); III, 1, 9; VII, B, 17, 33 (veteran *hecacontarch*); IX 3, 65 (*ilarchēs*, ἰλάρχης).

123 Maurice, *Strategikon*, I, 5, 16. (agile and bright, two per cavalry tagma); III 5, 2 (order-taker in a cavalry tagma); VII, B, 16, 20; 17, 21 (under the orders of the merarch).

124 Maurice, *Strategikon*, I, 3, 18 (*hekatontarchēs*, ἑκατοντάρχης); 19 (*dekarchēs*, δεκάρχης); 20 (*pentarchēs*, πεντάρχης; *tetrarchēs*, τετράρχης; *phylax*, φύλαξ); 21 (*ouragos*, οὐραγὸς).

125 Maurice, *Strategikon*, XII, B, 9, 6.

126 Maurice, *Strategikon*, II, 6, 20–26.

127 Maurice, *Strategikon*, I, 3, 21 (*bandophoros*, βανδοφόρος); 22 (*tēn kappam bastazon*, τὴν κάππαν βαστάζων).

THE CHAIN OF COMMAND OF A FIELD ARMY

British army. The fact that he was also required to speak Greek, Latin, and even Persian required a certain educational standard that set him apart from the ordinary soldier or mere dispatch rider. He was also a liaison officer. In the heavy infantry, he marched behind the unit commander, *archôn*, with the standard-bearer, the drill instructor and the trumpeter. His role was to repeat (loudly!) the orders of the commanding officer in combat and to hold his position alongside him and alongside the drill instructor during training. The *merach* was accompanied by two *mandatôres*, two masters-at-arms, a *stratôr*, a *spatharios* and two *ornithobôres*. Except when the drill instructor stood at the front during a reconnaissance, the *mandatôr* was always in second position which makes him the second in command.[128] *Bikarios* equated to *mandatôr*. After the *Strategikon* a tribune in command of an infantry *tagma* could be replaced by the *vicarius* in Latin, *bikarios* in Greek (vicar, substitute), or by the *campidoctor-kampidouktôr*. *Bikarios* occurs only once, so it was probably an outdated term and more of an acting commander than a rank.[129] This mission of acting commander was logically given to the *mandatôr* as a matter of priority and a later example confirms this. By the late ninth century, Leo VI the Wise (aka the Tactician) said that during an exercise the task of the *mandatôr* was giving the orders. In an encampment, each *tourmarch*, synonymous with the *merach*, should have his *mandatôr* near the general's tent and, conversely, the *drongarioi* and counts should have theirs near the *tourmarch*. During exercises or on the day of battle, the *mandatôr* had to advance in front of the army with a *kampidouktôr* in order to scout out the area and to pass on the orders.[130] All these made the *mandatôr* some sort of a signal officer.

The *kampidouktôr* (or drill instructor) came after the *mandatôr* in an infantry *arithmos*. He accompanied the commander of a heavy infantry company with the standard-bearer, the *mandatôr* and the trumpeter. As previously told, charged with reconnaissance duty, he remained in of front of the unit with the *mandatôr*. Additionally, in front of the battle line, two *kampidouktôres* escorted the *merach* with two *mandatôres*, a *stratôr*, a *spatharios*, two *ornithobôres* and a trumpeter. All returned to the ranks at the moment of combat. The *kampidouktôr*, by voice, hand signal or trumpet, gave the orders to go or stop but only during exercises.[131] Always

---

128 Maurice, *Strategikon*, XII, B, 7, 3 (acting in an infantry *arithmos*; agile, bright; loud voice and agreable), 4 (Latin, Greek and Persian speaking); 11, 5 (standing with the commanding officer, ἄρχων, the standard-bearer, the *campidoctor* and the trumpeter), 15 (transmitting orders), 18 (training), 20 (standing with the *merach*); 14, 2; 17, 52; 21, 12; 22, 29; 24, 4; D, 33, 37, 38, 39 (*mandatôr*, μανδάτωρ, plural *mandatôres*, μανδάτωρες).
129 Maurice, *Strategikon*, XII, B, 8, 2 (*bikarios*, βικάριος).
130 Leo VI the Wise, *Taktika*, VII, 38 (is accompanied by the *kampidouktôr* during militaryexercice) and 47 (training); XI, 18 (camp); XIV, 59 (before the battle).
131 Maurice, *Strategikon*, XII, B, 7, 4 (second in the list of specialised soldiers); 8, 20 (*bikarios*, βικάριος associated to *kampidouktôr*, καμπιδούκτωρ); 11, 6 (alongside with the commanding officer); 15 (reconnoissance); 18 (spearheading); 20

in the lead, he acted probably as bodyguard for the senior officer he was accompanying. He was also responsible for training the infantrymen.[132] Later, Leo VI the Wise described him as *tôn topôn odēgos* (guide to the places).[133] The oldest known Greek version of this very Roman rank can be found in a letter written by St John Chrysostom to Pope Innocent I in 404. He stated that hostile bishops had sent soldiers led by *kampidouktores* against him.[134] In a contract on *papyrus* dated 23 March 498 concerning the lease of a house to Arsinoe by Flavius Ploutammon, he is said to be one of the *kampidouktores* from the Transtigritanian unit, which suggests that there were several per unit.[135] They played a symbolically important role by the late fifth century and the beginning of the next. According to the *Book of Ceremonies*, two *kampidouktores* presented a torc to Leo I at his investiture in 457, as happened for Anastasius I in 491, who received it from a *kampidouktôr tôn Lankiariôn*, drill instructor of the *Lancarii*, a gesture expressing the army's support for the new Emperor.[136] Godilas, another *kampidouktôr tôn Lankiariôn*, presented a torc to Justin I at his investiture in 518. His career was boosted afterwards and 10 years later Godilas held the rank of *hypostratēgos* (sub-general) when, together with Baduarius, he drove the Huns out of the Bosphorus. Later the same year, after Baduarius and a Master of the Soldiers called Justin had been defeated in Moesia, Godilas defeated the Bulgars in a first battle but, in a second disastrous encounter, he was almost roped with a lasso while his two colleagues Constantiolus and Ascum were. By then his rank was probably *magister militum vacans*, a promotion that was undoubtedly exceptional.[137] A *papyrus* dating to the late sixth century alluded to a *kampidouktôr* from the Syene Legion.[138] A Latin inscription from Africa dating from the reign of Tiberius

---

(escorting the *meros* leader in front of the battle line; trumpeter quoted in 25); 21–22 (falling into line); 16, 4 (military exercices); 17, 53 (escorting the *meros* leader in front of the battle line). E. L. Wheeler, 'The legion as phalanx', p.168, n. 111 (epigraphy).

132 Ph. Rance, 'Campidoctores Vicarii vel Tribuni', pp.401–407.

133 Leo VI the Wise, *Taktika*, VII, 38 (ὁδηγός τῶν τόπων); XIV, 59 (ὁ μὲν ἐπὶ τοὺς τόπους ὁδηγῶν).

134 Jean Chrysostome, *Epist. ad Innoc. Papam*, 1, 3 (καμπιδούκτορας... προηγουμένους). J. F. Domínguez Domínguez & R. Manchon Gomez, 'Recherches sur les mots', pp.14–15.

135 British Library, Papyrus 113 (5) = Wessely C., 'Griechische Papyri des British Museum', *Wiener Studien. Zeitschrift für classische Philologie*, 9, 1887, p.262 (498), (Φλ(αονίῳ) Πλουτάμμωνι ἀπὸ καμπιδουκτόρων ἀριθμοῦ τῶν γενναιοτάτων Τρανστιγριτανῶν).

136 Constantine VII Porphyrogenitus, *De Ceremoniis*, I, 91 (Leo I); 92 (Anastasius I, καμπιδούκτωρ τῶν λαγκιαρίων). J. F. Domínguez Domínguez & R. Manchon Gomez, 'Recherches sur les mots', p.17.

137 Constantine VII Porphyrogenitus, *De Ceremoniis*, I, 93 (Justin I). A. H. M. Jones, J. R. Martindale, J. Morris, *PLRE*, 3a (1992), pp.539–540.

138 *P. Monac.*, 15, 17 (καμπιδούκτωρ ἀρ(ιθμοῦ) Σήυνης). J. F. Domínguez Domínguez & R. Manchon Gomez, 'Recherches sur les mots', p.15.

THE CHAIN OF COMMAND OF A FIELD ARMY

II Constantine (578–582), honouring the Master of the Soldiers Vita(lius?) mentioned two dedicatees *campiductores*. The u-letter appears in some manuscripts on Vegetius or Ammianus Marcellinus texts, but is common in African inscriptions.[139]

The standard-bearer was listed sixth place in a cavalry unit just after the *tetrarch*. His title came from the standard he carried: 'A *bandophoros* is a man who carries the *bandon*.'[140] When dealing with the transmission of orders in Latin, the *Strategikon* preferred to use the word *bandifer*, recalling the ancient Roman *signifer*.[141] The infantry standard-bearer was mentioned directly with the unit commander or came third among specialist soldiers. He was mounted on the march but fought on foot. He was also called a *bandophoros* but the *Strategikon* gave him as equivalent for the *drakonarôs*, another form for *drakonarios*.[142] *Bandophoros* seemed to be the function, *draconarius* was the military rank. Other specialist infantrymen according the *Strategikon* were the trumpeter, cape-bearer, armourer, bowyer, fletcher, 'and the rest according to the regulations.'[143] The problem is we do not know these regulations!

The weird rank of *tēn kappan bastazon* (cape-bearer) existed both in the infantry and the cavalry.[144] He was probably an orderly officer in charge of carrying the squadron leader's cape and other baggage. The trumpeter was the radio of the time in transmitting orders. Vegetius mentioned two names for the trumpeter: *buc(c)inator* and *tubicen*, which we find in *Strategikon* as *boukinatôr* and *toubatôr*. The *boukinatôr* stood with the *bandophoros* and cape-bearer close to the unit leader. Only the *merarch's* trumpeter or *buccinator* was allowed to sound the day of a battle to avoid confusion.[145] In charge of maintaining weapons *armator* and *samiator* (armourer and refurbisher) were Latin ranks transcribed into Greek as *armatouros* and *samiatôr*. Byzantine historians say little about 'non-commissioned officers' and enlisted men. However, specialists persisted or emerged later. John the Lydian, in his description of the ancient legion, gave sixth-century ranks:

---

139 *CIL*, III, 4354. A. H. M. Jones, J. R. Martindale, J. Morris, *PLRE*, 3b (1992), p.1382 (Vit(alius) the restoration of the name is probably erroneous). J. F. Domínguez Domínguez & R. Manchon Gomez, 'Recherches sur les mots', pp.13–14 (*campiductores*).
140 Maurice, *Strategikon*, I, 3, 21–22 (βανδοφόρος, τοῦ βάνδου βαστάζων).
141 Maurice, *Strategikon*, III, 5, 7 (βανδιφερ).
142 Maurice, *Strategikon*, XII, B, 7, 5 (*drakonarôs*, δρακονάρως); 8, 18 (each unit has a bandon); 17, 34–35 (travelled on horse but fought on foot).
143 Maurice, *Strategikon*, XII, B, 7, 5–7 (*boukinatôr*, βουκινάτωρ; *armatouros*, ἀρματούρος; *samiatôr*, σαμιάτωρ; *toxopoios*, τοξοποιός; *sagittapoios*, σαγιττοποιός).
144 Maurice, *Strategikon*, III 1, 7 (*tēn kappan bastazon*, τὴν κάππαν βαστάζων; ranked after the trumpeter in cavalry); XII, B, 11, 9 (ranked after *bandophoros* and before trumpeter in infantry).
145 Maurice, *Strategikon*, III 1, 7 (*boukinatôr* ranked before the cape-bearer in cavalry); XII, B, 7, 5 (ranked after *bandophoros* or *drakonarios*); 11, 6 (*tubatôr*, τουβάτωρ), 9–10 (ranked after bandophoros and cape-bearer under the name of bugle, *touba*, τούβα); 24–27 (buccin and tuba near the *merarch*). Vegetius, *DRM*, II, 7, 7.

'*primoscutarii*, soldiers charged with protecting others; these are what we now call *protectores*', '*flammularii*, those who have pieces of red cloth at the end of their lance.'[146] Obviously, the *protectores* he referred had nothing to do with the fourth-century *protectores domestici*.

The *Strategikon* also referred to medics called *deputati* in Latin, *dēpotatoî* in Greek. Each cavalry *tagma* had six to nine 'least qualified soldiers' for medical attendance to the wounded in battle. They carried a canteen filled with water, but nothing is said about bandages. Unarmed and positioned 30m behind the battle line, they also helped to look after the reserve horses during a battle, which says a lot about their medical skills. They could take loot from enemy bodies but had to give their booty to the *decarchs*. Nevertheless, a gold coin or *nomisma* was granted to them in addition to their pay.[147] It is likely that the infantry had their own medics. In a troop on the Egyptian border, a notarised document from the late sixth century mentioned a certain Joseph Victor, 'physician and soldier of the legion of Syene.'[148] Unlike today, physicians were not officers.

Table 8, The Chain of Command in an ordinary Troop (*tagma*, *bandon*, *arithmos*) according to the *Strategikon*

Rank (Latin or English translation-Greek)	Function
Command	
Komēs, tribounos (Count, tribune)	Commanding officer
Cavalry	
Ilarch, (squadron commander)	Executive officer
Infantry	
Bikarios (vicar)	Acting commander
All armed branches	
Mandator	Executive officer/ transmission officer
Infantry	
Kampidouktôr (drill instructor)	Third in command/instructor
Staff in all armed branches	
Bandophoros also *draconarius* (*drakonar(i)ôs*) in infantry	Standard-bearer

---

146 John the Lydian, *De Magistratibus*, I, 6 (*primoscutarii*); 7 (*flammularii*).
147 Maurice, *Strategikon*, P, 34; I, 3, 30 (are standing behind the front line); II, P, 13; 9, 3–4 (least qualified, 8 to 9 per *tagma*), 5 (unarmed), 6, (100 feet), 11 (*nomisma*), 12–16 (dépouilles), 19–21 (not allowed to loot), 29–30 (canteen); III, 7, 4; V, 2, 7 (are keeping the reserve horses); VII, B 17, 17 (least qualified, 6 à 8 per *tagma*; *dēpotatos/dēpotatoi*, δηποτάτος, plural δηποτάτοι).
148 P. Monac., 9, 107, (*iatros kaï stratiôtēs tôn legeônos Syēnēs*, ιατρός καί στρα(τιώτης λεγ(εῶνος) Συήνης).

Tēn kappam bastazon (cape-bearer)	Orderly
Bucinator (boukinatôr), tubator (toubatôr)	Tuba player and trumpeter
Officers and NCOs cavalry/infantry (?)	
Hecatontarch	Centurion, leader of 100 men
Decanus, decarch – recorded in the infantry	Leader of 10 men, 'sergeant'
Pentarch	Leader of 5 men, 'corporal'
Tetrarch also recorded as ouragos	File-closer
Soldiers from Commissariat (mainly attested in infantry units)	
Armatouros (armourer)	Repairs or makes chain mails
Samiatôr (refurbisher)	Refurbishes/repairs weapons
Toxopoios (bowyer)	Repairs or makes bows
Sagittapoios (fletcher)	Repairs or makes arrows
Deputatus	Medic (only recorded in cavalry units)
The rest according to the regulations	Not defined

Some ranks are difficult to explain. By the fourth century the rank of *adorator* was perhaps an alternative to *protector* for deserving soldiers. 'Adoring Purple' simply signified to be in the Emperor's entourage like *Protectores* or *Scholarii*.[149] According to John the Lydian: 'The Romans called demobilised soldiers *adoratores* (*adorea* in fact designates in their language military glory, according to the wheat and the marks of honour received by those they honoured), *ueterani* those who grew old under arms.'[150] Two *adoratores* are known from the late sixth century. The first is said *adorator* from the troop of *Theodosiaci* and was ranked between the tribune and the *optio*. A *papyrus* from 591 refers to John who held same rank in the Ravennates troop then was soldier in *Classis*.[151] The *adorator* was a sort of honorary rank/title for a first class soldier.

---

149 M. Emion, *Des soldats de l'armée Romaine tardive: les protectores (IIIe-VIe siècles ap. J.-C.)*, thèse de Doctorat en Histoire sous la direction de Pierre Cosme (Rouen: Université de Rouen-Normandie, École doctorale Histoire, Mémoire, Patrimoine, Langage ED 558, 2017). p.497.
150 John the Lydian, *De Magistratibus*, I, 46, 47 (*adôratôr*, ἀδωράτωρ).
151 *P. Ital.* I, 17 (*adorator numeri Theodosiaci*); II, 37 (*adorator numeri Felicum Rauennatium*, year 591, Classis).

BIRTH OF THE BYZANTINE ARMY 476-641 CE VOLUME 1: STILL LATE ROMAN?

Late Fifth-Century Foot Officer in Western Roman Dress
Aeneas dressed in full military array with scale armour, military cloak, brass helmet with a red feathered crest, round convex shield with pointed umbo, red boots. From a fifth-century manuscript of the *Aeneid* by Virgil. (MS Vat. lat. 3867 *Vergilius Romanus*, Biblioteca Apostolica Vaticana, f. 74v)

Sixth-Century Officer in Camp Dress
This officer wears a Phrygian cap as a 'service forage cap' instead of the *pileus pannonicus* and a ceremonial cloak as an indication of his higher rank. The silver or gold *maniakon* or torc was a tradition of Roman Army and persisted in the Byzantine tradition. Initially it was a *spolia opima* taken away a dead enemy, then a reward for gallant action and finally a rank marker. Embroidered silk tunics were common. (Photograph courtesy of the Numerus Invictorum)

Plate A. Emperor Justinian I
(Illustration by Renato Dalmaso © Helion & Company)
See Notes to colour plates for further information.

Plate B. Belisarius in parade armour
(Illustration by Renato Dalmaso © Helion & Company)
See Notes to colour plates for further information.

Plate C. *Bandophoros* or standard bearer
(Illustration by Renato Dalmaso © Helion & Company)
See Notes to colour plates for further information.

Plate D. The Emperor Justinian's bodyguard officer
(Illustration by Renato Dalmaso © Helion & Company)
See Notes to colour plates for further information.

Plate E. The Emperor Justinian's second bodyguard officer
(Illustration by Renato Dalmaso © Helion & Company)
See Notes to colour plates for further information.

Plate F. A Byzantine *Spatharius/Spatharios*
(Illustration by Renato Dalmaso © Helion & Company)
See Notes to colour plates for further information.

Plate G. A *Candidatus/Kandidatos*
(Illustration by Renato Dalmaso © Helion & Company)
See Notes to colour plates for further information.

Plate H. A late Roman infantry officer
(Illustration by Renato Dalmaso © Helion & Company)
See Notes to colour plates for further information.

Standards and Music

The poet Corippus mentioned 'victorious eagles'.[152] But to what extent was his poem singing the air of an eternal Rome real? What Vegetius called the *muta signa* (mute signs) or standards, still then existed, but *signum* was rendered by Procopius as *sēmeion*.[153] *Signa*, *vexilla* and *imagines* still existed in the 490s Perge Legion. The very first known flag in the West was painted during the fourth century BCE on a fresco adorning a tomb at Paestum in Lucania: a horseman is carrying two spears, one of which has a square banner. After the *Strategikon* general-in-chief and unit commanders were noted by 'the standard that the Romans call *bandon*.'[154] Simocatta said they were called *banda* 'according to the Roman pronunciation.'[155] This was a banner with several bands or literally *phlamoula* (flames) a term also in use to describe a lance's pennon.[156] A *bandon* is still visible on a sixth-century mosaic from the Mosaic of the Months now in the Archaeological Museum of Argos in Greece.[157] A soldier personifying the month of March and the God Mars (*Martios*) carries a lance with a small square, white flag with two flames possibly of a gold colour. It was the origin of the medieval oriflamme. The *Strategikon* proposed for each *meros* a banner with its own colour from which flames of different colours would emerge for each *moira*. The *tagmata* had to display distinctive flags. To deceive the enemy on one's strength, two banners per *tagma* were preferable; it was likely more a wish than a real practice. The *Strategikon* disapproved of the contemporaneous fashion of bulky banners and suggested that their size should be proportionate to the command. Some 15 to 20 elite fighters were to guard the standards.[158] *Mutare signa* (change the signs) meant in Latin to give a visual command by waving the standards. During the African War, in the event of danger, Hildimer's Vandals and Solomon's 'Romans' brought the standards back to protect them; but turned in the other direction, the standards also ordered a retreat. For Hildimer, this protective measure was misinterpreted, causing an unforeseen retreat: 'The standard-bearer, having dared to believe that the standard should change direction, pulled on his reins to turn back from

---

152 Corippus, *Joh*, I, v. 420 and v. 423 (trumpets); v. 519 (eagles).
153 Procopius, *BV*, IV, 10, 4 (σημεῖον).
154 Procopius, *BV*, IV, 2, 1. Maurice, *Strategikon*, I, 3; 4; II, 1; 4. 9; III, 5; 6; 7; 15; IV, 3; VII, B, 8; 16–17; XI, 4. Paul the Deacon, *HL*, I, 20, (*bandum*).
155 Theophylact Simocatta, *HU*, III, 4, 4.
156 *Phlamoulon*, Φλάμουλον, plural φλάμουλα.
157 R. Ginouvès, 'La mosaïque des mois à Argos', *Bulletin de Correspondance Hellénique*, 81 (1957), pp.216–268.
158 Maurice, *Strategikon*, I, 2, 75 (one specific colour per *meros*); 76 (distinctive *phlamoula* to indicate the *moira*); 77 (*tagma*); II, 14, 1–2 (ligther standards); 2–3 (cumbersome standards are criticised); 5 (*phlamoula*); 5–12 (banner size proportional to command); 15, 1–5 (guarding the banner); 20, 4–5 (2 *banda* per *tagma*); III, 5, 8–10 (banner size proportional to command according to *tagma*, *moirarchs* and *merarchs*).

the top of the mountain: a troop with close-knit weapons followed him.'[159] Waving the pennon of a lance ordered the unit to go forward.[160] Banners were, as today, symbols of military honour and not just tools for transmitting orders. A banner was used to present honours to a general, as happened in 593 with Peter the Kouropalates.[161] Losing the standard was of course a shame and to recover it a duty. Constantius, an officer in Scholasticus' army, lost his standard or *sēmeion* in a battle against the Sklavenes not far from Adrianople in 550. Shortly afterwards, he recovered it in an ambush, a fact of sufficient importance for Procopius to relate it.[162] It is likely that some standard, hand, cape or spear signals of the late Roman Army persisted.[163]

Vegetius did not describe the tuba or trumpet but briefly described the *bucina*: 'The buccina which is made of bronze is curved in a circular fashion.'[164] *Tubicines, cornicines* and *bu(c)cinatores* still existed in the Anastasian Edict of Perge. John the Lydian only considered *bukinatôres* as cavalry trumpeters.[165] The *Strategikon* envisaged two wind instruments for the infantry and cavalry, the *buccina* and the trumpet, *boukinon* and *touba*.[166] During the siege of Osimo in the summer of 539, Procopius pointed out to Belisarius that the ancient Roman practice of one trumpet blast for attack and another for rally had been lost. He advised him to re-establish this practice and to ensure that the signals used by infantry and cavalry were consistent. Belisarius agreed.[167] In 554, Narses the Eunuch during the drill had sounding the trumpet which accompany the battle cry.[168] The latter was intended to make and impression on the enemy and boost troop morale. The *Strategikon* alluded to a 'psyops' officer or herald called in Latin *cantator*, *kantatôr* in Greek (singer): 'The work of the *kantatôres* also seems useful to us in that they say an encouragement before the battle and remind the soldiers of previous victories; According to these words, every *tagma* must be formed and trained.'[169]

---

159 Corippus, *Joh*, III, v. 236–238.
160 Maurice, *Strategikon*, III, 5, 12 (the *phlamoula* give march order).
161 Theophylact Simocatta, *HU*, VII, 3, 1.
162 Procopius, *BG*, VII, 40, 41 (ensign loss); 45 (ensign recuperated).
163 Ammianus Marcellinus, *RG*, XIV, 2, 17; XV, 8, 15; XVI, 12, 13; XX, 5, 8; XXIII, 5, 24; XXIV, 3, 8; XXV, 3, 10; XXVII, 6, 10 (clashing spears and shields in order to express feelings of anger, impatience or approval); XXV, 6, 14 (raising hands and shaking capes as a sign of victory); XXVI, 7, 17 (lower the standards as a sign of submission); XXVI, 9, 7 (carry shields upside down as a sign of defection). M. Emion, *Des soldats de l'armée Romaine'*, p.397.
164 Vegetius, *DRM*, III, 5, 6 (*bucina*).
165 John the Lydian, *De magistratibus*, I, 46, 4, 8 (βουκινάτωρες).
166 Maurice, *Strategikon*, XII, B, 11, 25 (*Boukinon*, βούχινον and *tuba* τούβα for *merarch*); P, 42; II , P, 21; 17, 1–2, 5, 8; III, 5, 16; VII, A, 9, 3; B, 16, 13; 35, 49–50; 5, 102; XII B 11, 25; 16, 4; 90, 44. 91; 22, 45 (βούχινον); III, 5, 13; VII, B 10, 10; XII, B 11, 10, 25; 16, 5; 20, 45, 97; 22, 34 (τούβα).
167 Procopius, *BG*, VI, 23, 23–28.
168 Agathias, *Hist.*, II, 1, 2.
169 Maurice, *Strategikon*, II, 19 (καντάτωρ). Leo the Wise, *Taktika*, XII. 71, 72, 120.

THE CHAIN OF COMMAND OF A FIELD ARMY

Sixth to Twelfth Centuries Byzantine Standards
Upper left: the flag of the Senate, from the consular ivory diptych of Flavius Theodorus Philoxenus, domestic count, formerly military master to the Thracians, Consul in Constantinople in the year 525, (Bibliothèque Nationale de France, Paris, inventory 55298). Upper right: A *labarum* topped with a cross carried by St Julian or Mar-Elian, protector of Emesa (today Homs, Syria). (From a seventh-century silver dish, now in the Antaki Collection, London)
Bottom: Bandon-type flag as described in the late sixth-century *Strategikon* of Emperor Maurice. (After the twelfth century Madrid Skylitzes manuscript, in the Biblioteca Nacional de España, Madrid. Cod. Vitr. 26-2)

Sixth-Century Byzantine *Bandophoros* (Standard-Bearer)
The figure is carrying a *bandon*, a banner with two flames, the forerunner of the medieval oriflamme. The centre is white, the lining and flames are gold colour. The soldier's head is protected by an iron bandenhelm helmet with a mail neck guard. His body is protected by a gilded muscle-corselet. The chest belt and the three-pointed apron are yellow, and may be an indicator of rank. His tunic is red. The boots are black with white socks pulled down at the top. His legs are bare. The round shield and sword re suggestion added by the author. (After the mosaic depicting the month of March (*Martios*), from the Byzantine Mosaic of the Months found in Argos and now in Argos Archaeological Museum, Greece)

BIRTH OF THE BYZANTINE ARMY 476-641 CE VOLUME 1: STILL LATE ROMAN?

Sixth-Seventh Century St Phibamon With a Cross Standard
St Phibamon carrying a cross standard and dressed like an Emperor. (From a Coptic fresco in the monastery of Bawit, Egypt, Chapel XVII. After J. Clédat, (1904), pl. LIV)

Late Fifth-Century Romano-Byzantine Standard-Bearer
This figure is wearing an Intercisa-type helmet with a metal crest; the helmet could be silvered or gilded. The *skaplion* or shoulder-aventail and the body armour were made of gilded scales. This kind of armour was replaced by lamellar protection during the second half of sixth century. The long *spatha*-type sword was a characteristic of late Roman infantry but was initially manufactured for and used by cavalry and auxiliary units. The leg wraps are well attested on the late Roman Piazza Armerina mosaic. A sixth-century mosaic in the Archbishop's Chapel in Ravenna depicts Christ clad in Emperor's armour and carrying a cross-motif standard over his right shoulder. (Photograph courtesy of the Numerus Invictorum)

5

A Professional Army

> You came from the countryside, with only a sack and a small tunic; [the Emperor] gathered you together in Byzantium, then gave you so much importance that the Roman state now depends solely on you.
>
> Germanus cousin of Justinian I in Procopius, *Bellum Vandalum*, IV, 16, 13

For half a millennium, the Roman state has entrusted its security to a professional army. It gave up conscription towards the end of the Republic. Imperial Byzantium continued along the same path with its standing *Romaiôn Stratos* (Army of the Romans).[1] Of course, the situation was no longer the same and a number of questions have arisen, not least the source of military recruitment, the motivation but also discipline, mentality and the ethos of the troops. Despite constantly waging wars early Byzantine civil society was not on war footing as classical Athens had been.

Was Recruitment Easier Than in The Later Roman Empire?

Young men passed one after the other under the reproachful eye of a veteran to the table where an official in a coloured and embroidered tunic wrote their names on a roll of *papyrus* and asked to give them some coins. Under of Leo I's reign, in 472, the *Generalissimo* Zeno dismissed his rival the Patrician Aspar and reformed the army, changing certain rules that had been in force by the later Roman Empire. His law required that *probatoria* or 'enrolment list' should no longer be kept by the dukes and masters of the soldiers, but directly by the Emperor,[2] since, only the administration

---

[1] Procopius referred to the Ῥωμαίων στρατός as in *BP*, I, 15, 25.
[2] *CJ*, XII, 35, 17.

issued recruits with an enrolment certificate or *probatoria*. The aim of the law was to prevent what were known in the French *Ancien Régime* as *passe-volants*, fictitious recruits paid to the exclusive benefit of their corrupt officers. Since, only the administration issued recruits with an enrolment certificate or *probatoria*.

Who were those who enlisted in an essentially rural world if not landless peasants? That is to say 'yokels' who preferred fighting to scratching the ground or raising goats. Even Vegetius recommended recruiting peasants used to physical labour and being able to cope with the fatigue of war.[3] At the dawn of Byzantine Empire, the life of Justin I, born around 450, could still fit this model of a success story:

> At the time when Leo exercised Imperial power in Byzantium, three young peasants from Illyricum, Zimarchos, Ditybistos and Justin, who were constantly struggling with the evils of poverty and wanted to free themselves from it, set out to serve as soldiers. They travelled on foot to Byzantium, carrying on their shoulders bundles in which there was nothing when they arrived but the stale bread they had put there when they left. When they joined the ranks of the soldiers, the Emperor chose them for his guard, for they were all of tall stature.[4]

In 512, Anastasius I put an end to the practice of branding recruits with a red-hot iron, a brutal measure that had been in place since Diocletian to enable the tracking down the once numerous deserters. Its abandonment proved desertion was no longer a major problem.[5] Moreover, Imperial laws no longer cruelly punished deserters or those who harboured them. Serving was considered as an honour and a social promotion, as Germanus, cousin of Justinian I and then Duke of Libya from 536 to 539, told his soldiers.[6] Nevertheless when he took command of Carthage, he went through the rolls of the soldiers' names, and was able to discover the deserters names. This story shows a rigorous military administration that kept its enlistment registers up-to-date.[7] Unlike under his predecessors and successors, Justinian's reign saw recruitment shortages due to the continuous wars and the very irregular pay.[8] Despite some desertions and defections to the enemy, Imperial laws, unlike those of the fourth century, no longer obliged soldiers' sons to enlist. But enlistments were not entirely on a voluntary base, some compulsory enlistment remained. An episode dated summer

---

3 Vegetius, *DRM*, I, 3, 1.
4 Procopius, *Anecdota*, VI, 2–3.
5 S. Williams & G. Friell, *The Rome That Did Not Fall*, pp.114 (year 472), 116 (year 512).
6 Procopius, *BV*, IV, 21, 12.
7 Procopius, *BV*, IV, 16. 1.
8 A. Fotiou, 'Recruitment shortages in six Century Byzantium', *Byzantion*, 58 (1988), pp.65–77.

589 proves that enrolment from tax registers was still in use. Gregory, Bishop of Antioch entrusted by Maurice to enrol recruits for Eastern Army using the tax registers gathered 2,000 recruits at Litarba (now Terib in Syria). He welcomed them by handing out money, food and clothes, then he made a speech saying, 'Obey me since priesthood is mediating between Empire and army' and sent them to Philippicus Master of the Soldiers to the East whose headquarters was at Tarsus in Cilicia.[9]

As today, military tradition lived on some families. A *papyrus* dated 22 November 639 mentions Paulacis, a soldier enlisted in *Miles Numeri Arminiorum*, a unit of Armenians, was the son of Stephen, Primicerius from the *Veronenses* unit. There is no indication that the son was really Armenian, nor that the father was from Verona.[10] The designation of military units specified their original ethnicity or the place of their raising. The Christian conscientious objectors, who were a problem during the third century and even into the fourth century, no longer arose in the Romano-Byzantine Army. The first military saints were martyrs condemned to death for refusing conscription and therefore to fighting and shedding human blood such as St Maximilian of Carthage or St Martin of Tours. Others refused to persecute Christians because they were Christians themselves, such as St Maurice and his comrades from the Theban Legion, garrisoned in what is modern southern Switzerland.[11] When Byzantine history began in 476, the Emperor had been a Christian for over a century. The saints were now painted in military dress and in arms on the walls of churches. In an emergency, when Thrace was invaded by the Avars in 584, even some of the ecclesiastics were enlisted.[12] Until the reign of Heraclius I in the 610s, there were no recruitment problems.[13]

Count Marcellinus paid particular attention to the Illyrian troops, who had suffered several setbacks between 478 and 505. Their worst defeat was at the River Tzurta in 499, where 'the military flower of Illyricum' perished, along with a third of their field forces.[14] These Latin-speaking Balkan troops formed the most 'Roman' element of the Byzantine Army, and therefore the most likely to perpetuate military traditions. Thrace also provided a large

---

9   Evagrius Scholasticus, *HE*, VI, 11 (enrolment from the register); 12 (speech); 13 (2,000 recruits).
10 *Notitia Dignitatum*, OR.VI.31. *P. Ital.*, I, 22 (Paulacis, his father).
11 M. Hallot-Charmasson, 'Saints guerriers ou guerriers saints? Les saints militaires à Byzance des origines à 1204)' in M. (ed.), *Médiation, paix et guerre au Moyen Âge. Actes du 136ᵉ Congrès national des sociétés historiques et scientifiques, 'Faire la guerre, faire la paix', Perpignan, 2011* (Paris: Éditions du CTHS, Actes des congrès nationaux des sociétés historiques et scientifiques, 136-3, 2012), pp.51–62.
12 Michael the Syrian, *HU*, X, 21, t. 2 (1963), pp.361–362.
13 M. Whitby, 'Recruitment in Roman Armies from Justinian to Heraclius (*c.* 565–615)' in A. Cameron, L. I. Conrad (eds), *The Byzantine and Early Islamic Near East*, vol. 3, *States, Resources and Armies* (Princeton NJ: Darwin Press, 1995), pp.61–124.
14 Marcellinus Comes, *Chr.*, a. 499 (*Ibique Illyriciana virtus militum periit*).

pool of recruits. In the army led by Belisarius to Africa in 533, the majority of officers were of Thracian origin.[15] In fact, Procopius himself, a member of the expedition, noted the senior officers as 'almost all Thracians' with the exception of the Hun, Aigan, the Egyptian, Sarapis and Zaidus, probably an Arab.[16] By the beginning of the fifth century the Balkan provinces and the troops led by the first master of soldiers present accounted for just under half of the total number of units according to the *Notitia Dignitatum* – 235 units out of 491. The eastern regions such as Anatolia, Syria, Palestine and Egypt account for the majority, 256 units out of 491.

Epigraphy provides valuable clue to geographical origin. This is the case for the epitaph of a soldier of Thracian origin called Buraido, who died after 546 in Caesarian Mauritania when he was garrisoned at Rusguniae (now Tamenfoust) on the Bay of Algiers.[17] Buraido came from the *Numerus Hipponis Regii* or *Hipponenses Regii* to defend Romano-Byzantine Africa. This example shows that a frontier soldier was not necessarily drawn from the place he was defending. A long way from his homeland as Thracia, Buraido was either part of the field army brought to Africa by Belisarius or later by Troglita. Needs of the state, and perhaps Buraido's age, led him to this second-rate military status in a new-raised border unit. This unit was a creation of Justinian, its name indicating only the North African town where it was created, Hippo Regius (now Annaba in Eastern Algeria). Another unit with recruits from Thracian origin is known in Romano-Byzantine Africa thanks to a tribune named Flavius Ziper who left an epitaph at Tamenfoust around the middle of the sixth century. This senior officer belonged to the numerus *Primorum/Primi Felicium Iustinianorum*. Corippus mentioned in John Troglita's Army a Ziper who was an *armiger*, i.e. *doryphoros* or *bucellarius*, and later rose in rank in the regular army and was killed by the Moors between 546 and 548.[18] Another clue reveals that a soldier could move from one unit to another, by his own choice or under orders. A *papyrus* from 591 referred to a certain John 'who is now a soldier in the unit of the *Laeti*', then garrisoned at Classis whereas he previously held the rank of *adorator* in the Ravennates troop.[19]

Any Imperial Army is necessarily multinational as Roman, and then Byzantine, Armies were. As well as recruiting auxiliaries, it also practised 'press ganging', as the Royal Navy did during the eighteenth and early nineteenth century. This meant making up for losses by recruiting any suitable men, including POW's or enemy deserters. It is a common practice

---

15   V. Puech, (2015), p.59.
16   Procopis, *BV*, III, 11, 9–11.
17   D. Dana, 'Onomastique et recrutement de l'armée Byzantine d'Afrique, l'épitaphe du soldat Buraido révisée (ILAlg, I, 81)', *Antiquités Africaines*, 49 (2014), pp.151–160. CIL, VIII, 5229 = CLL, VIII, 17401 = ILCV, I, 549 = ILAlg, I, 81.
18   CIL, VIII, 9248 (=20849) = ILS, 2812 = ILCV, I, 442 (inscription). Corippus, *Joh*, IV, v. 395; VI, v. 535, 538, 638, 671 (Ziper). G. Ravegnani, 'Le unità dell'esercito Bizantino', pp.193–194; D. Dana, 'Onomastique et recrutement', p.157.
19   P. Ital., II, 37 ('Qui nunc milex numeri felicum Lectum', year 591, Classis).

A PROFESSIONAL ARMY

in all military history, right up to the Hispanic Legion made up of French deserters used by Wellington during the Peninsular campaign or by the *Wehrmacht*'s *Ostruppen* made up of Polish and Russian prisoners during the Second World War, and even present in the today Russo-Ukrainian War. In a more Romano-Byzantine context, wars in the East, Africa and Italy produced recruits from Persarmenians, Vandals, Moors and Ostrogoths. Goths and Persarmenians accounted for almost 10 percent of soldiers' names in Procopius.[20] Some individual fates resulted in international careers. Apollinarius was an Italian who, as a young man, moved to Africa to serve the Vandal King Ilderic. Transferring his allegiance to the Emperor, he distinguished himself at Tricamarum in 533, and the following year was given the mission of seizing the Balearic Islands. This was a man who had three allegiances in his life: Ostrogothic, Vandal and then Roman.[21] At Pertusa Petra, Urbino and Osimo in Italy, in c. 538–539, Belisarius and his lieutenants enlisted entire garrisons of captured Ostrogoths into their ranks. They treated these ex-enemies equally according to Procopius, but who did not specify whether they joined the *foederati* or the regular units. As an eyewitness to the Italian campaign, he liked to specify national identity for soldiers who were not subjects of the Empire.[22]

Contingents described by Procopius always included *foederati* and barbarian mercenaries, who made up a quarter of the total strengths. Eastern Roman Empire was still unable to find enough men on its own soil, and no doubt preferred to hire barbarians rather than to fight them.[23] A prosopographical study of some of Procopius' 238 military names shows that 61 percent were of 'Roman' origin, with Greek or Latin onomastics.[24] Barbarians or not, once enrolled in the Byzantine Army, the recruits were addressed by their leaders as *andres sustratiôtai* (comrades-soldiers).[25]

The Place of Latin in a Greek Empire

Torna. Torna. Fratre! (Turn back. Turn back. Brother!) On a stony road, an officer urges a muleteer to turn back, but his order is mistakenly passed on to the whole army. This happened during the 587 Danube campaign

---

20 D. A. Parnell, 'A Prosopographical Approach to Justinian's Army', p.13.
21 Procope, *BV*, II, 5, 7. A. H. M. Jones, J. R. Martindale, J. Morris, *PLRE*, 3a (1992), p.100 (Apollinarius I). V. Puech, (2012), p.61.
22 Procopius, *BG*, VI, 11, 19–20 (Pandra); 19, 3–17 (Urbino); 27, 33–34 (Osimo).
23 M. Rapport, *Nationality and Citizenship in Revolutionary France* (Oxford, Oxford University Press, 2000), p.15. S. Scott, *The Response of the Royal Army to the French Revolution: The Role and Development of the Line Army 1787-93* (Oxford: Clarendon Press, 1978), p.5.
24 D. A. Parnell, 'A Prosopographical Approach to Justinian's Army', p.11.
25 Procopius, *BV*, IV, 15, 54 (Stotzas to his troops); 16, 12 (Germanus to his troops; *andrēs sustratiôtaï*, ἄνδρες συστρατιῶται/ξυστρατιῶται).

against the Avars.²⁶ This simple injunction given in Vulgar Latin and understood by the whole army shows that Latin was still the working language for Illyrian and Thracian soldiers.²⁷ Another example occurred along the Danube campaign against the Sklavenes in 593, when Priscus harangued the army and Alexander ordered his cavalrymen to dismount 'in their ancestral [Roman] language.'²⁸ Even today, Romanian is still a Latin derivative although used north of the Danube and in the sixth century, what is now Bulgaria was a Latin-speaking region. Procopius even took offence when officers, no doubt Illyrian, were insulting some soldiers by calling them Greeks, 'as if it were not possible for any of those who came from Greece to be people of honour.'²⁹ Deeply hurt by this remark, Procopius, the historian born in Caesarea of Palestine, considered himself ethnically and culturally Greek, but patriotically he felt himself to be Roman, as Ammianus Marcellinus did two centuries earlier ending his *Res Gestae* by signing as 'Greek and former soldier'. Procopius's anecdote and anger shows that in the mid-sixth century, the Byzantine Empire was not yet fully considered as Greek. Procopius's communitarianism was also felt by Isaurians and Armenians, who spoke neither Latin nor Greek as their mother tongue, forming military and aristocratic clans. Furthermore, even under the classical Roman Empire, the administrative language in eastern provinces included Greek, as do the military archives from Egypt during the later Empire.³⁰ Procopius, who acted as intelligence officer, naturally understood Latin. By the same token, Maurice wrote in introducing his *Strategikon*: 'Many Roman terms and other common military expressions have been used to make the subject more comprehensible.'³¹ He insisted that each unit should have a herald, called by Latin name of *mandator*, and who should be 'able to speak Latin, if possible Persian and Greek.'³² Bilingualism was still common for Romano-Byzantine Army and Latin military vocabulary was transmitted to Byzantine Army, although in a Hellenised form.³³

In the *Strategikon* senior Roman officer ranks such as *komēs* and *tribounos* persisted. Count and tribune were likened to the Greek rank of *tagmatarch*

---

26 Theophanes Confessor, *Chrgr.*, AM 6079, 258.
27 G. Reichenkron, 'Zur romischen Kommando-sprache bei byzantinischen Schriftstellern', *BZ*, 54 (1961), pp.18–27. H. Mihaescu, '*Torna, torna, fratre*', *Byzantina*, 8 (1976), pp.21–35.
28 Theophylact Simocatta, *HU*, VI, 7, 9 (Priscus spoke to the Romans in their ancestral language); VII, 2, 6 (Alexander, Roman ancestral language).
29 Procopius, *Anecdota*, XXIV, 7.
30 Ph. Richardot, *La fin de l'Armée Romaine*, p.50.
31 Maurice, *Strategikon*, P, 29–31.
32 Maurice, *Strategikon*, XII, B, 7, 3–4 (*mandatôr*, μανδάτωρ).
33 F. Viscidi, *I prestiti latini nel greco antico e bizantino* (Padua: Olschki, Università di Padova. Pubblicazioni della Facoltà di lettere e filosofia, 22, 1944), p.11. H. J. Mason, *Greek Terms for Roman Institutions. A Lexicon and Analysis*, *American studies in papyrology*, 13 (Toronto: Hakkert, 1971), p.7. J. F. Domínguez Domínguez, R. Manchon Gomez, 'Recherches sur les mots campidoctor and campiductor: de l'Antiquité au Moyen Âge tardif', *Bulletin Du Cange*, 58 (2000), p.14.

but duke was equated to *moirarch*.³⁴ The *Strategikon* alluded only once to the *draconarius*, the bearer of the dragon-shaped standard.³⁵ According to Roman tradition, the wording for a specific standard-bearer gave first the standard's name (*aquila, vexillum, signum, imago*) followed by the suffix *fer* or 'bearer'. The mixed Latin/Greek word *bandifer*, banner-bearer was only referenced by the *Strategikon*.³⁶ Other Latin ranks transcribed into Greek were the drill instructor known as *kampidouktôr*.³⁷ The scout was not spelt in its complete Latin form of (*ex*)*sculcator* but only as *skoulkatôr*.³⁸ The squad, a 10 man's group sleeping under the same tent, kept his old name of *contubernium* but Hellenised as *kontoubernîn* or *kontoubernion*.³⁹ Of the four types of existing cavlry units in the *Strategikon*, three belonged to the late Roman Army: *vexillationes, Illyriciani, foederati*.⁴⁰ The Gallic term *drungus* for squadron is rarer and known for the first time in Vegetius.⁴¹ The most convincing evidence of Latin persistence was the transmission of orders in Latin transcribed into Greek letters.⁴² Weapons' names also came from Latin – the words for helmet, plume, lance, lancer, cavalryman, pennant, sword, shield and shield bearer all came from Latin: *cassis, tufa, contus, contarius, caballarius, flammula, spatha, scutum, scutatus/scutarius*. The first occurrences of *flammula* and *tufa* are in Vegetius, while *scutarius* emerged in Ammianus Marcellinus and the *Notitia Dignitatum*.⁴³ This

---

34 Maurice, *Strategikon*, I, 3, 16, 18; 4, 9; 6, 11; II, 20, 5 (*komēs, κόμης*); P, 220; I, 3, 16, 18; 4, 10; 6, 11; II, 20, 6; XII, P, 45; B, P, 35; 8 , 19; 22, 24, 30; 24, 2, 30 (*tribounos, τριβοῦνος*); 13, 13; 4, 13 (*doux, δούξ*) : B, 8, 2 (*bikarios, βικάριος*).

35 Maurice, *Strategikon*, XII, B, 7, 5 (*drakonarôs, δρακοωνάρως*). Ammianus Marcellinus, *RG*, XX, 4, 18.

36 Maurice, *Strategikon*, III, 5, 7 (*bandipher, βανδιφερ*).

37 Maurice, *Strategikon*, XII, B; 7, 4; 8, 20; 11, 6, 15, 18, 20; 16, 4; 17, 53 (*kampidouktôr, καμπιδούκτωρ*). Vegetius, *DRM*, I, 13; II, 23 (*campidoctor*). Ph. Rance, 'Campidoctores Vicarii vel Tribuni: The Senior Regimental Officers of the Late Roman Army and Rise of the Campidoctor' in A. S. Lewin, P. Pellegrini, Z. T. Fiema, S. Janniard (eds), *The Late Roman Army in Near East from Diocletian to the Arab Conquest: Proceedings of a colloquium held at Potenza, Acerenza and Matera, Italy, May 2005* (Oxford: *BAR* International Series, 1717, 2007), pp.395–409.

38 Maurice, *Strategikon*, P, 36; 13, 36; II, P, 15; 11, 1, 4; VII, B, 10, 6; 17, 20; IX 5, 55, 65, 66, 71; XII, D, 24.45.98 (*skoulkatôr, σκουλκάτωρ*).

39 Maurice, *Strategikon*, P 13, 32, 100; I, P, 9; 5, 3, 5, 18; 6, 3; II P, 11; 7, 1.2; VII P, 6; A 2, 1.2; B 17, 8; IX 5, 108.111; XII B 9, 25; D, 160 (*κοντουβέρνιον*).

40 Maurice, *Strategikon*, II, 6, 23; III, 8, 4 (*bixellationes, βιξελλατίονες*); II, 6, 34; III 8, 4; VI 3, 14 (*Illyrikianos, Ἰλλυρικιανός*, plural Ἰλλυρικιανόι); 12, 10; 11 6, 47; 11, 2; I, 6,7.8; 8, 4 (*φοιδεράτος*, plural *φοιδεράτοι*).

41 Vegetius, *DRM*, II, 16 (*drungus*). Maurice, *Strategikon*, I, 3, 14; II, 1, 19; 2, 2; III, 10, 37, 48, 61; IX, 3, 104; XII, B, 20, 33, 36 (*droungos, δροῦγγος*).

42 Maurice, *Strategikon*, Maurice, *Strategikon*, III, 4, 5 and 5, 2–8 (orders to put cavalry in combat formation); XII, B, 14 and 16 (orders to change infantry formation).

43 Maurice, *Strategikon*, I, 12 (*kassis, κασσίς*; *touphia, τουφίον*), 18 (*kontarion kaballarikon, κοντάριον καβαλλαρικὸν*), 19 (*phlamoulon, φλάμουλον*), 20 (*spathion, σπαθίον*); XII, B, 4, 1 (*skoutatos, σχουτάτος*); 2 (*skoutarion, σχουτάριον* as shield and not his bearer); Vegetius, *DRM*, II, 1 (*flammula*); III, 5 (*tufa*). Ammianus Marcellinus, *RG*, XIV, 7, 9; XX, 2, 5; 4, 3 (*scutarius*). CIL, 3, 4361

vocabulary was often hybrid, so the rider was said *kaballarios stratiôtēs* (soldier rider) a word derived from Latin *caballarius*, but he could also be simply referred as *kaballarēs*.[44] Nevertheless, the victory was sung in Greek, according to the tradition of the paean dating back to Homer. Procopius reported it at the Byzantine duellist's victory over two Persians in 530 at the Battle of Dara.[45]

Latin was used for giving orders until the 630s.[46] At that time, the Sklavenes colonised a large part of Illyricum, a situation leading to the disappearance of Latin from the Eastern Roman Empire and the reshaping for a log period of the ethnic and linguistic map of Europe. In Leo VI the Wise's treatise, written *c.* 895–908, orders were still transcribed from Latin into Greek.

Dressing the Romano-Byzantine soldier

A group of impecunious, fighting men, some scar faced, walks in the alleys of Byzantium. They wear the same boots and tunics, with big, martial looking belts. Dress always reveals the level of discipline of an army, as well as the military fashion of an era. It starts with the hairstyle. An officer such as the *bandophoros* Rufinus the Thracian was beheaded by the Moors and his head taken as curiosity because of the thickness of its long hair.[47] This example indicates that there were few Romano-Byzantine soldiers with long hair. As depicted on the mosaic of the Basilica of Ravenna, Belisarius had medium-length hair, moustache and beard. At the same time, in his Army of Africa, Romano-Byzantine soldiers were bearded, with the exception of eunuch generals such as Solomon and Narses the Eunuch who had only a fine and falling moustache.[48] Maurice' *Strategikon* prefers a short haircut for the infantry.[49]

The Byzantine soldier had a uniform making him recognisable, even when he was not carrying weapons. Procopius even wrote that some descendants of the Roman soldiers in Gaul in the service of the Franks preserved their former units and old military dress.[50] An episode during the rebellion of the Levathes of Tripolitania in 543 demonstrates this. A priest from the city of Hadrum (now Sousse) came to Carthage to ask Governor Sergios for help. He was given 80 soldiers, a large number

---

(*contarii* is a rare word); Ph. Richardot, *La fin de l'Armée Romaine*, pp.7, 61–66, 274, 305, 312, 325 (*scutarii* in late Roman Army).
44   Maurice, *Strategikon*, I, 2, 1 (καβαλλάριος στρατιώτης); III, 1, 15 (καβαλλάρης).
45   Procopius, *BP*, I, 38.
46   Ph. Rance, 'Drungus, Δροῦγγος and Δρουγγιστί', p.269.
47   Procopius, *BV*, IV, 10, 11.
48   Procopius, *BV*, IV, 8, 16–17.
49   Maurice, *Strategikon*, XII, B, 1.
50   Procopius, *BV*, V, 12, 17 (old standards preserved); 18 (*idem* for tactics and traditions); 19 (old Roman clothes and shoes).

A PROFESSIONAL ARMY

of sailors and Libyans 'dressed in the ordinary attire of Roman soldiers.' Paul anchored with this fictitious fleet near Hadrum and was then able to make believe that there was a landing of Imperial troops.[51] A *papyrus* found in Egypt and dated 350–450s gives Greek/Latin terms describing military clothes: *phailonion/paenula* (hooded cloak), *chlanidion/chlanis* for *chlamy* (large woollen coat), *ôrarion/orarium* (scarf). *brakion* for *brakai/bracae* (breeches), *tzankē* for *tzangē – tzanga* or *zanca* (a sort of popular shoe), *burrion* for *burros/byrrhus* (a waterproof cape). New words like *oloplak(inos)* (patchwork fabric), *stratiôti(?)* (fabric for soldier).[52]

The tunic, called *manicata*, which was worn from the later Roman Empire, had long sleeves. It was decorated with woven woollen round or square medallions on the thighs and upper arms, with two woven bands from the shoulders to the chest and on the back. Medallions and bands respectively were called *orbiculi* (singular *orbiculus*) and *claves* (*clavis*) until the fifth century. These ornaments were in bright colours, with vegetal, animal and human schematic and geometric figures. There are intact Coptic samples today on display in the Louvre Museum in Paris and in the Metropolitan Museum of Art in New York. During the sixth century this tunic was simplified, retaining one central band while the medallions disappeared.

In the late Roman Army, the *cingulum* (belt) had become emblematic of the military function but its fashion had spilled over into the public service. At the time of Justinian, removing his belt (*cingulum*) from a soldier was like driving him out of the army, following to the old Roman military tradition.[53] The *pileus pannonicus* (Pannonian pillbox) Vegetius was talking about and visible on mosaics in Sicily was certainly worn in the sixth-century army because this type of fur pillbox cap existed in the Balkans until the 1930s.[54] In 1896, the French archaeologists Albert Gayet and Émile Guimet discovered on the site of Antinoe in Egypt six Byzantine coats of caftan type with long sleeves – four of a carmine colour and two of turquoise; these are now in the Musée des Tissus, Lyon.[55] The Museum für Byzantinische Kunst in Berlin has a similar turquoise caftan-style coat with a red lining,

---

51 Procopius, *BV*, IV, 23, 22 (military dress); 23, 23 (successful stratagem).
52 A. Bataille, 'Un inventaire de vêtements inédit', *Eos*, 48, fasc. 2, 1956, pp.83–88; M. Hombert, 'Bulletin papyrologique, XXVIII, 1954 to 1959), 2ème partie', *REG*, t. 79, fasc. 374–375, January-June (1966), p.158, *papyrus* registered in the Bibliothèque de la Sorbonne, Paris, inv. 2142, Fonds Reinach : phaïlonion, φαιλόνι[ο]ν; chlanidion χλανιδι[ο]ν; ôrarion ὠράρι[ο]ν; brakion βράκι[ο]ν; tzankē, τξάγκη = τξάγγη, τξαγγίον; burrion, βύρρι[ο]ν = βύρρος, βίρρος; ὀλοπλακ() reconstituted ὀλοπλακιν[ο]ς; στρατωτι(?).
53 Procopius, *Anecdota*, XXIV, 8.
54 Vegetius, *DRM*, I, 20.
55 M. Durand, M. H. Guelton and *alii*, 'Les costumes des élégants d'Antinoé conservés au musée des Tissus de Lyon: approche historique, analyses techniques et analyses de colorants', *Techne*, 41 (2015), pp.32–45.

it is inventoried as a 'riding coat'.[56] This over coat was called a *kandys* and is probably of Sassanid origin. The long rigid and narrow sleeves were impractical and the *kandys* could worn be like a cloak as shown in a Sassanid embassy to Byzantine Empire depicted on a stone relief in Istanbul Archaeological Museums.[57] Gayet also found 15 tubular leggings, tapering towards the bottom and that could be slipped over the leg and going up to approximately mid-thigh. Some fabric gaiters protecting the leg between knee and ankle were also discovered.[58]

The carrying of weapons in a civilian setting followed strict rules. When soldiers escorted a leader into a city, they could carry only a sword.[59] For policing assignments they carried a spear and a shield. A sixth-century Coptic icon from the monastery of St Catherine shows a bearded and bareheaded St Theodore with a spear dressed in a short cloak, *manicata*, dark breeches and high boots. Colourful portrait of Romano-Byzantine soldiers are shown in a Syrian manuscript dated 586, known as the Rabula Gospels after the copyist from the monastery of St-Jean-de-Zagba.[60] On folio 13r, the frontispiece miniature has a crucifixion scene above one of the coming of the Holy Women to the Sepulchre. In the upper image, three soldiers play dice on the tunic while a fourth is piercing Christ's side with a spear. The latter wears a long pinkish-red tunic, but others are dressed in long grey, green or off-white tunics. All have black or tawny baldrics supporting a long sword on the left. In the lower image two soldiers are sleeping and a third is walking away from the Sepulchre. Two of them are carrying small, round, convex, grey or red shields but they all have black baldrics supporting a long sword. Their long tunics are ecru, pinkish-red or light grey. One has yellow breeches decorated with black dots. The soldiers are bearded with relatively long hair except two who are bald. So, there was no uniformity in colour of dress and the various colours probably related to personal taste. Green and blue were popular colours worn by circus charioteers and political factions, and were certainly in use among the army.

The Imperial soldier's outfit was also somewhat barbarised. John the Lydian, who wrote in about 550, noted: 'Today's soldiers imitate the barbarians who in return seek to imitate them themselves.'[61] Later, Paul the Deacon made the same remark about late sixth-century Lombards: 'They began to wear shoes over which, when riding, they wore wool gaiters,

---

56 Inv.-Nr. 9695.
57 Κάνδυς.
58 Fl. Calament, 'L'apport historique des découvertes d'Antinoé au costume dit de cavalier sassanide' in C. Flück, G. Vogelsang-Eastwood, *Riding Costume in Egypt. Origin and Appearance* (Leiden, Boston: Brill, 2004), p.45.
59 Procopius, *BV*, IV, 28, 8.
60 Biblioteca Medicea Laurenziana, Florence, inv. Plut. I.56. F. Boespflug, *La Crucifixion dans l'art: Un sujet planétaire* (Montrouge: Bayard Éditions, 2019), pp.77–78.
61 John the Lydian, *De Magistratibus*, I, 12, 5.

A PROFESSIONAL ARMY

Sixth-Century Hunter with Sword and Shield
This man is a wearing a long-sleeved red tunic of a common pattern with embroidery and probably linen or woollen gaiters. The long sword is of *spatha* type with an eagle head pommel. The scabbard is supported on a baldric. The shield is unusually large (artistic convention or a special hunting shield?). (Mosaic from the Kisuffim church, Neguev desert, Israel)

Sixth-Century Byzantine *Spatharios*
Spatharii or *spatharioi* (sword-bearers) were common as the escorting guard of a general. This man is on camp duty wearing only a long, white linen, T-shaped tunic with silk embroideries. He is carrying a short sword in its scabbard as the *spatharii* did during ceremonies. (Photograph courtesy of the Numerus Invictorum)

173

BIRTH OF THE BYZANTINE ARMY 476-641 CE VOLUME 1: STILL LATE ROMAN?

Sixth-Century Byzantine Light Infantryman
The man is equipped for *velitatio* (guerrilla warfare). He is wearing the *pileus pannonicus* cap mentioned by Vegetius and worn by both soldiers and civilians from the late third century to at least the fifth century and perhaps thereafter. He wears a dark blue *kandys* over a white linen shirt. Original samples found in Antinoe, Egypt, were turquoise blue, but may have discoloured. From Persian and Sassanid origin, the *kandys* is assumed to be a riding coat with overlong sleeves. It was an item of both male and female and even children's clothing. A hole at the elbow crease allowed the forearm to be able to move easier. (Photograph courtesy of the Numerus Invictorum)

Late Sixth- Century Romano-Byzantine Cavalryman Dismounted
This *scutarius* (shield bearer) is wearing a riding suit with a blue *kandys* and long boots in Hunnic-style. His weaponry is a round universal type of shield with an iron *umbo*, a long sword of *spathe* type and a spear. His protection consists with a Baldenheim type helmet with mail neck guard, a *petrichalion stroggylon* or padded scarf in the Avar-style, and a coat of mail. (Photograph courtesy of the Numerus Invictorum)

but this is a habit they had borrowed from the Romans.'[62] The *Strategikon* advised the infantry to wear Gothic shoes and Bulgar coats.[63] If Byzantine iconography tended to classicism and conservatism, reality was exotic and colourful.

Greeting a superior remains a ritual in modern armies and was also so in the Romano-Byzantine Army. Corippus alluded to a scout who, returning from a mission, kissed the feet of General John Troglita 'according to custom.'[64] It might be expected that this rather oriental practice was reserved for the Emperor, but it should be noted that a soldier also addressed it to his commanding general.

Irregular Pay Compensated for by Booty, Land or Begging

Military pay is a quite complex matter and historians try to compensate for the documentary void by the most ingenious of conjectures, even combining the sources from the 280s with those of the 840s. Historiography has assessed that the sixth-century Romano-Byzantine soldier would be paid each year an *annona*, or 5 *nomismata* – the *nomisma* being the Hellenic version of the *solidus* (gold coin) created by Constantine I *c.* 310. In 616, Heraclius I halved the pay then, later, the creation of *themes* would have made it possible to further reduce it in exchange for land to cultivate.[65] It is quite difficult to believe that military pay did not fluctuate over more than two centuries. Tax administration was finicky, as demonstrated for 525–526 by the *papyri* from the village of Aphrodito, near Thebes in southern Egypt.[66] Thanks to this cautious work military pay was partly given in cash, but the main part was delivered in *annona* and even in *capitum* or *capitus* (fodder). Conversion from one into the other was called *adaeratio*. The Anastasian Edict of Perge in the early 490s fixed the pay in a field army legion.

---

62 Paul the Deacon, *HL*, I, 22.
63 Maurice, *Strategikon*, XII, B, 1.
64 Corippus, *Joh*, IV, v. 310–311.
65 W. Treadgold, *Byzantium and its Army*, p.118 (issue of research).
66 C. Zuckerman, *Du village à l'Empire: autour du Registre fiscal d'Aphroditô (525/526)* (Paris: Association des Amis du Centre d'Histoire et de Civilisation de Byzance, Monographies, 16, 2004).

Table 9, Military Pay and Ranks of the Legion from Perge (490s)

Rank	Annual *annona* part (wheat ration) convertible into *solidi* (gold coins)	Rank	Annual annona part. convertible into *solidi*
Tribunus Maior	24	*Librarii*	1/1
Tribunus Minor	10	*Mensores*	1/1
Ordinarii	8	*Tubicines*	1/1
Augustales	5/1	*Cornicines*	1/1
Augustales alii	4/1	*Buc(c)inatores*	1/1
Augustales alii	3/1	*Praeco*	1/1
Flaviales	2.5/1.5	*Armaturae Duplares*	1/1
Flaviales alii	1.5/1.5	*Beneficiarii*	1/1
Signiferi	1.5/1.5	*Torquati semissales*	1/0.5
Optiones	1.5/1.5	*Bracchiati semissales*	1/0.5
Veredarii	1.5/1.5	*Armaturae semissales*	1/0.5
Veredarii alii	1/1	*Munifices*	1
Vexillarii	1/1	*Clerici and Deputati*	?
Imaginiferi	1/1	**TOTAL** (Convertible into *solidi*)	1,849 (1,054)

After F. Onur, 'The Anastasian Military Decree from Perge in Pamphylia: Revised 2nd Edition', *Gephyra*. 14. 2017, pp.187-188.

Around 495, Anastasius I forced landowners to pay their taxes in gold coin to remunerate soldiers with, so that the latter would not demand abusive donations in kind from them.[67] In 498, in order to make the service more attractive, he replaced the *annonae* with pay in coin. Anastasius also firmly reminded the master of the soldiers to Illyricum that he could not arbitrarily lower the soldiers' pay, a veiled accusation of fraud as the difference between pay received by soldiers and sums sent by the treasury would be embezzled by the officer.[68] Other proscriptions have been found in inscriptions at Perge in Pamphylia (Aksu, Turkey), at Qasr El-Hallabat and Bosra in Arabia, at Ptolemais in Upper Egypt and at Taucheira of Pentapolis in Cyrenaica.[69] Fraud was therefore obviuolsly widespread and well-known. The five-year *donativum* was still in use. Anastasius I offered his first in 496, then the second in 500 but reserved it for soldiers of Illyricum. After

---

67   John Malalas, *Chrgr.*, XVI, 3.
68   *CI*, 1, 29, 4.
69   F. Onur, 'The Anastasian Military Decree,' p.138.

511, he distributed an annual bonus instead of a real donativum.[70] The social condition of common soldiers improved under Anastasius I but deteriorated under Justinian. Until then pay in the army and in the civil service followed seniority according to Procopius:

> Those who stand guard or deal with dispatches or perform some service for the Emperor and the authorities of Byzantium are at first enrolled in the last rank, but in time they rise steadily to the place of those who have died or retired; all advance from the lowest rank until they reach the highest echelon and reach the pinnacle of their career. For those who reach this level, the salaries, fixed from ancient times, are so high that they reach 100 centenaria of gold per year.[71]

This system would have ensured decent treatment and retirement for civil servants and for the military if Justinian had respected it during the 32 years of his reign.[72] Procopius also accused Justinian of never distributing the donativum of five gold *staters* which the soldiers, by law, had to receive every five years.[73] The *scribones* drove out of the army those whom they considered useless or too old, without paying them a pension and forced them to beg on the streets.[74] Procopius accused the *logothetes* (paymasters) of not removing dead personnel from the rosters. This allowed them to retain the dead men's pay to their own benefit.[75] Agathias was also harsh on Justinian. He wrote that in his older age, after the conquest, the Emperor was indifferent and negligent of the soldiers. Fraudulent *logothetes* stole funds meant for the army. Deprived of food many soldiers deserted, which explains why Thrace and Byzantium's surroundings were left unprotected when the Kutrigurs attacked in 559.[76] Justinian, like Anastasius I before him, rightly feared fraud in the army's pay. In the 13 April 534 law creating the Diocese of Africa, he expressly reminded the dukes, their staff and the tribunes not to sell leave to soldiers or to cut their pay under penalty of being dismissed from their appointment.[77] Fraud over pay was thus a persistent and incurable illness. This law also makes it possible to know the pay for a border duke and his staff. An annona was worth 5 *solidi*, and the capitus, fodder, worth 4 *solidi*.

---

70   S. Williams, G. Friell, *The Rome That Did Not Fall*, p.116.
71   Procopius, *Anecdota*, XXIV, 30–31.
72   Procopius, *Anecdota*, XXIV, 32.
73   Procopius, *Anecdota*, XXIV, 27–29.
74   Procopius, *Anecdota*, XXIV, 8.
75   Procopius, *Anecdota*, XXIV, 5–6.
76   Agathias, *Hist.*, V, 14, 1–4.
77   CI, 1, 27, 2, 9a.

Table 10, Pay of a Duke and his Staff from the Province of Africa according to the Justinian Code, I, 27, 2 and 3 (13 April 534)

Ranks	Annual pay into *annonae*
Dux (duke) and his followers	190 *annonae*, 158 *capiti*
Cost	**1,582 *solidi***
Ducal Staff	
Assessor	8 *annonae*, 4 *capiti*
Primicerius	5 *annonae*, 2 *capiti*
Numerarius	4 *annonae*, 2 *capiti*
4 *Ducenarii*	3.5 *annonae*, 1.5 *capiti*
6 *Centenarii*	2.5 *annonae*, 1 *capitus*
8 *Biarchi*	2 *annonae*, 1 *capitus*
9 *Circitores*	2 *annonae*, 1 *capitus*
11 *Semissales*	1.5 *annona*, 1 *capitus*
Staff Cost	**674.5 *solidi***

According to a *papyrus* from 612, the Egyptian *bucellarii* were paid as follows: tribune 23 *solidi* ¼ *squiliqua* (carat) a year; *mandator*, trumpeters and horsemen 18 *solidi*; courier, bowyer, armourer and infantrymen 7½ *solidi* ¼ carats of gold (*squiliqua*) – each *solidus* was worth 24 *squiliquae*.[78] To make a crude comparison, *bucellarii* on foot were paid 30 percent more than the average 490s legionary. A merit bonus system existed, but it is poorly known. Thus, Agathias alluded *c.* 555 to a Rusticus who paid bonuses to the best fighters in the Army of Lazica.[79] This episode contradicts Procopius' comments on Justinian's avarice.

When were the soldiers paid? It occurred only once a year according to Simocatta. The example he gave took place in mid-spring 593, when the Army of Thrace was assembled for a review near Heraclea ahead of a campaign against the Sklavenes.[80] This field army probably gathered elite troops from Illyricum and Byzantium itself. The worst paid were the *limitanaioi*, the Greek form for *limitanei* (the border guards). According to Procopius, they were paid four to five years late, and their arrears were cancelled when peace came. At this point, no longer considered as soldiers they had to live on charity.[81] Was Procopius exaggerating again? Nothing in his time resembled the dereliction of *Noricum* in the late fifth century, when a handful of *limitanei* and inhabitants left to their own devices faced constant attacks and deserted some of the Danube cities to emigrate to

---

78 N. Gonis, 'Payments to Bucellarii', pp.184–185.
79 Agathias, *Hist.*, III, 2, 4.
80 Theophylact Simocatta, *HU*, VI, 6, 3–4.
81 Procopius, *Anecdota*, XXIV, 12–14 (λιμιτανάιος, plural λιμιτανάιοι).

Italy.⁸² Even poorly treated, the sixth-century *limitanei* continued to play their role.

In time of war, the spoils, the reward of the victorious army, restored the soldiers' morale.⁸³ During the hot summers of 534 and 535, after the battles of Mammes and Mount Bourgaon, Solomon's soldiers captured many women and children, who were sold as slaves: their abundance was such that a Moorish child was sold for the cost of a sheep.⁸⁴ Money, precious objects, cattle, slaves were all a 'nest egg' for the soldier's retirement. In addition, the women of a defeated army became those of the victorious soldiers. Nevertheless, as the soldiers were very poor according to Procopius, too much booty made them as uncontrollable. This is what happened after the victory of Trikamaron in 533, where Belisarius rushed round for the whole night, only managing to rally his troops early in the morning. Fortunately for him the Vandals counter-attack that he feared did not take place. The soldiers sent their booty with their slaves and their tent and table companions back to Carthage for safety .⁸⁵ The greatest disaster of the sixth century took place at Anglon in Persarmenia in 543. The cause was the lure of profit that prevailed over discipline and the military art even for the generals.⁸⁶ Although lands were not part of the normal spoils, in 536 Solomon provoked the mutiny of his soldiers by his refusal to redistribute to them the Vandals' estates.⁸⁷ Numerous desertions in Africa and Italy during Justinian's reign lend credence to the idea of irregular pay.

Stolen by their superiors, beggars, looters. Were Romano-Byzantine soldiers such a miserable, lumpen proletariat? Donations made by some of them to churches in Veneto and Ravenna in the late sixth and early seventh centuries prove that they were not quite destitute.⁸⁸

Avarice was a Dangerous Vice

If Justinian was accused by Procopius of being a poor paymaster, Maurice tended to sheer avarice. In 588 he reduced the pay of the Eastern Army, which had just fought a hard campaign against the Persians, by a quarter. The reaction was not long in coming. Priscus, the general who announced this to the troops gathered in Monokarton, saw his treasure and his magnificent personal effects looted and had to flee on a horse taken from a bodyguard,

---

82 Eugippius, *Vita Sancti Severini*, 44.
83 Corippus, *Joh*, VI, v. 7.
84 Procopius, *BV*, IV, 12, 27.
85 Procopius, *BV*, IV, 4, 3–7. Procopius does not expand on his meaning of 'tent and table companions'.
86 Procopius, *BP*, II, 25, 5–34.
87 Procopius, *BV*, IV, 14, 9.
88 *ILS*, II, 8883; *P. Ital.*, I, 24; 27 (*sc(h)ola armaturae*). G. Ravegnani, 'Le unità dell'esercito Bizantino', pp.197 and 200.

under the shouts, a hail of stones and brandished swords.[89] Maurice did it again in 594. He first dismissed Priscus and instructed his brother Peter to announce the reduction in pay to the Danube Army in Odessus. This time his decree divided the pay into three parts: the delivery of clothes, the supply of equipment and gold coin. In protest, the army abandoned the general and made camp at a distance. Peter, more appreciative of the situation and more skilful than Priscus, was able to appease the troops by letting them know retired soldiers living in the cities would be fed at the Emperor's expense and a soldier's orphans would be enlisted in the army, so the mutiny ended.[90] There is no confirmation that the announced social measures were ever applied, and some years later Maurice was beheaded by his soldiers.

The impoverished state is illustrated by a weird anecdote where Emperor Phocas was presented as a madman who threw the Imperial Treasury into the sea as a gift to Neptune. No wonder the Senate had his hands and feet cut off before throwing him into the sea and giving the crown to Heraclius in 610.[91] This stupid act attributed to Phocas was undoubtedly fake news to explain the lack of money. His successor Heraclius found an even more dishonest way by reducing the gold weight of the currency.[92] Even after his victory over Persians, the paymasters refused to pay 10 *milliaresia* of silver to the carters gathered at Ctesiphon, the Persian capital. St Anastasius the Persian helped the carters to send a delegation to Byzantium to collect their pay.[93] It is difficult to know whether the state had difficulty paying in gold, whether its officials embezzled part of its funds, or whether the Emperor was simply a bad payer.

The state of Imperial Treasury fluctuated. Some historians have speculated that, during the reign of Heraclius and his immediate predecessors, due to lack of money, tax-exempt lands were entrusted to border guards, like the Balkan lands threatened by barbarian raids.[94] However, at the very end of his reign, to face a desperate military situation, Heraclius found sufficient financial resources to re-establish the *donativum*, valued at 2,016,000 *nomismata*.[95] The ability to finance regular troops allowed the Eastern Roman Empire to survive. Romano-Byzantine soldiers were dedicated professionals who fought more for salary than for 'King and Country'.

---

89 Theophylact Simocatta, *HU*, III, 1, 1 (pay dropped by a quarter); 9–13 (mutiny). Evagrius Scholasticus, *HE*, VI, 4 (mutiny).
90 Theophylact Simocatta, *HU*, VII, 1, 2 (pay divided); 3–6 (mutiny); 7 (social measures).
91 Fredegar, *Chr*, IV, 63.
92 K. W. Harl, *Coinage in the Roman Economy, 300 B.C. to AD 700* (Baltimore, London: The John Hopkins University Press), p.201. W. V. Harris, *Roman Power: A Thousand Years of Empire* (Cambridge: Cambridge University Press, 2016), p.252.
93 *Miracula, Acta M. Anastasii Persae*, 3. W. Kaegi, (1992), p.91.
94 M. Whitby, 'Recruitment in Roman Armies', pp.111-114.
95 Nikephoros of Constantinople, *Brev.*, 29, 20–22.

Negotiated Discipline

From Julius Caesar to Aetius, the Roman Army had the paradoxical image of severe discipline and numerous mutinies. The Byzantine Army showed the same political discipline as in the previous 300 years. Some *pronunciamentos* occurred with Isaurian and Vitalian the Thracian's rebellions or the Stozas mutiny in the sixth century, plus the Maurice and Phocas executions in the seventh century. An anecdote reported by Procopius proved that the idea of the death penalty for indiscipline existed: during the war against the rebellious Isaurians (492–498), General John Gibbo 'the Hunchback' was tormented for three consecutive nights by a dream where a giant ordered him to remove to the death sentence of a soldier who, in the future would help when he was in trouble. Gibbo pardoned to the soldier who, 20 years later, became Emperor Justin I.[96] In 575 Justinian the son of Germanus took pains to correct the lack of discipline and training in the armies, but it was the nature of new troops to be inexperienced and undisciplined.[97]

The *Strategikon* approached the question of discipline from a theoretical angle. In its introductory Book I, three chapters described the sanctions concerning the troops, those concerning the officers and, finally, the punishments to be handed out.[98] According to this treatise, officers should have a written copy of the disciplinary code and explain it to soldiers. Disobeying a *pentarch* or *dekarch*, was punished, but disobeying a superior officer, tribune or count was punished with capital punishment, as was any conspiracy, abandonment of a garrison post or desertion. A soldier who found a stray animal or lost objects without reporting it to his superior, who harmed a taxpayer without giving him compensation or who neglected his weapons was punished and, in this case, his *dekarch* as well. The latter could be punished if he had not explicitly transmitted the orders. In all cases, the indicted soldier could appeal a wrongful accusation to his immediate superior or even beyond.[99] For unit commanders, disobedience was punished 'according to the law', harming a soldier or a civilian entailed financial compensation of double the damage, letting a soldier go on leave in wartime cost a fine of 30 *nomismata*, more than a year's pay for a tribune. Leaves of absence of two to three months were authorised only during winter quarters and, in peacetime, and within the limits of the province. Surrendering or evacuating a place without an order was punishable

---

96   Procopius, *Anecdota*, V, 6, 5–9.
97   Theophylact Simocatta, *HU*, III, 12, 7.
98   *Strategikon*, I, 6, 7 and 8.
99   *Strategikon*, I, 6, preamble (distribution of the regulations); rules: 1 (disobedience to a superior); 2 (disobedience to an officer); 3 (legal appeal); 5 (conspiracy, mutiny against an officer); 6 (abandonment of position); 7 (desertion); 8 (non-transmission of orders); 9 (marauding); 10 (harm to a taxpayer); 11 (bad maintenance of weapons).

by death.[100] In combat situation, the death penalty could be applied for: abandonment of post or his unit, charging or pursuing the enemy without instruction, looting while the fighting was not over. A retreating troop could be decimated from behind by other units. Degradation was required for standard-bearers that lost their standards. A punishment was to be given to a troop who fled without taking refuge in a nearby friendly camp. A soldier who gave up his weapons was to be regarded as arming the enemy.[101]

Patriotism was replaced with professional pride. Thus, in 478, while they had to face the rebellious Ostrogothic *foederati*, soldiers paid their superiors not to fight, but learning that Emperor Zeno himself would command them, they paid a second time to go to fight![102] The deep professional feeling introduced into the army a democratic, or rather a corporatist, mentality. Discipline was thus relegated from a dialogue not just between the general and the men but became internal to the troop.

Army debates during the campaign of 586 against the Avars were very similar to those of the 10,000 Greek mercenaries of Xenophon's *Anabasis*. Comentiolus the Thracian wanted to attack the Avars with just 4,000 men, but had beforehand to gain the confidence of his soldiers. He announced his decision in two stages: the first was to gather the officers in his tent to explain his plan; the next day he assembled the army to speak to it. At this point, the dialogue got out of hand. A tribune took the floor and bitterly contradicted Comentiolus, reproaching him for his incompetence, as having left a further 4,000 men behind, and mentioning his latest setback which had reduced the forces by a third. A veteran then called on his comrades to show courage and honour by asking a series of persuasive questions. This elderly soldier ignited the spirit of all and Comentiolus the Thracian was able to fight the battle he had asked for. The army functioned here like a union meeting deliberating on the continuation of a strike. We see the tribune contesting the general and a mere soldier having the last word over the tribune. The word equality comes to mind. After this *inter pares* discussion, the men were 'united like brothers' according to Simocatta.[103]

In another episode from this campaign, Theophanes reported that an order to turn around, given in Latin, included the word *frater* (brother)[104] – equating to 'brother in arms'. There was something democratic about this Romano-Byzantine Army. During the Easter mutiny of 588 at Monocarton, soldiers forced the haughty Priscus to flee, but they elected as their leader Germanus, the Duke of Phoenicia. The following year, the cut in pay imposed by the Emperor was cancelled and the mutiny lost its raison d'être.

---

100 *Strategikon*, I, 7, rules: 12 (disobedience); 13 (double compensation); 14 (leaves); 15 (surrendering a place).
101 *Strategikon*, I, 8, rules: 15 (death penalty); 17 (decimation); 18 (standard-bearers); 19 (flight); 20 (weapons).
102 Malchus, *Fragm.*, 18, 3.
103 Theophylact Simocatta, *HU*, II, 12, 10–15, 1.
104 Theophanes Confessor, *Chrgr.*, AM 6079.

A PROFESSIONAL ARMY

Then soldiers accepted Philippicus, appointed by the Emperor, as the new Master of the Soldiers to the East.

Above all, tactical discipline was generally strong. A specific example of this occurred during the Balkan campaign of 598. Comentiolus the Thracian, coming to relieve the besieged Tomi, drew the Avars to him. Suddenly panic-stricken, he abandoned his army, but which managed to force its way by fighting through the Shipka Pass while retreating southwards.[105] This episode shows that the men did not panic in the face of danger and that competent senior officers could lead them in the absence of a general who had abandoned them through cowardice. Imperial soldiers were not robots and knew how to manage in an unforeseen situation. While trapped under the too high walls of Naples in 536, they joined two ladders to make one longer one. Procopius did not mention any officer for this initiative and it probably originated with the men.[106] To prevent an imminent danger, the soldiers could even take the initiative of counter-attacking, as happened at Rhizaion against the Tzani by 559: 'The Romans judging that it would be shameful not to repel the enemies, but also not to kill many.'[107] This consensual union disappeared once the danger passed.

Imperial soldiers were violent, fickle people and difficult to keep out of combat. After his victory over Vandals at Dekimon in 533, Belisarius preferred to postpone his entry into Carthage for a day and forbade soldiers from entering at night to prevent any pillaging. He explained that the 'Libyans' were Romans oppressed by the Vandals and should be treated as friends. Procopius praised Belisarius's wise measures because the army behaved correctly, whereas usually even groups of 500 men acted like delinquents when in a town. On the other hand, these measures were foiled by the *navarch* Kalonymos who went to Carthage at night with a few ships and plundered both Carthaginian and foreign merchants. Belisarius, informed of this act by the complaints of the merchants, made Kalonymos agree to return his booty; Kalonymos promised to do so but did not return anything.[108]

The *Strategikon* recommended that the general show 'paternal affection' but intervene immediately at the slightest sign of indiscipline before problem escalated, be vigilant in his investigations and merciful in his punishments.[109] Nevertheless, camp and combat discipline could be brutal. When soldiers went foraging without authorisation, Belisarius inflicted corporal punishments 'not devoid of seriousness' on them according to

---

105 Theophylact Simocatta, *HU*, VII, 13, 8–14, 9.
106 Procopius, *BG*, V, 10, 22–23 (Naples).
107 Agathias, *Hist.*, V, 1, 8.
108 Procopius, *BV*, III, 20, 2 (delayed entry at Carthage); 16 (nighttime looting by Kalonymos); 17 (Belisarius remind to his troops that Libyans are Romans); 22–23 (Kalonymos did not surrender his booty); 21, 9 (good behaviour of Roman soldiers in Carthage contrary to usual).
109 Maurice, *Strategikon*, VIII, 3rd general instructions for the Commander; 96th maxim.

Procopius, these punishments are not otherwise described. Belisarius thought it necessary to explain such sanctions to the army: plundering the 'Libyans' Romanised populations of Africa, risked reconciling them with the Vandals and alienating their sympathy.[110] Strict discipline was frowned upon by barbarian mercenaries. Belisarius had two so-called Massagetae or Huns impaled on a hill for having killed one of their number who made fun of their drunkenness. The exposure on a hill for all to see and the cruelty of the treatment were to set an example at the start of the campaign. However, the Huns were utterly indignant and said that they did not have to be subject to Roman law; moreover, some regular soldiers supported their stance. So, Belisarius summoned the army to explain the moral and religious reasons for such a punishment – in short, he had to justify himself. With the Lombard mercenaries recruited in 552 by Narses the Eunuch, discipline just collapsed. They respected no rules, set fire to every building they could find and systematically raped women, even in churches. Narses paid them to leave and had them escorted out of Roman territory in Italy.[111] In combat situation, the general, like John Troglita, could insult and hit cowards because the context allowed it.

From Mutiny to Treason

Soldiers gather around the general's tent. Some have stones in hands, others have drawn their swords, their voices are threatening. Leaders want to be heard. The tendency towards mutiny and putsch, inherited from the Roman Army, persisted. The strangest and shortest-lived mutiny was led by a common soldier named John Cottistis at the Battle of Dara by 537. Nonetheless the would-be usurper was killed by some loyal soldiers with a valiant sausage seller who struck the first blow.[112] More seriously and more frequently, soldiers could go on strike for unpaid wages.

Desertion was a significant phenomenon within the army under Justinian. This was the case for the Army of Illyricum which deserted en masse from the Italian theatre in 544 to return to its lands. The soldiers sent a letter to Justinian to apologise for their conduct, but in which they explained by long arrears of pay and the fact the Huns had attacked Illyricum and threatened their wives and children. The Emperor forgave them because he did not have any alternative – and he was at fault.[113] Up to nine years away from their families and a long back pay justified their attitude.

Desertions could arise when food was short, as happened to John Troglita's army in summer 547 in Tripolitania. The ensuing retreat and the

---

110 Procopius, *BV*, III, 16, 1–8.
111 Procopius, *BG*, VIII, 33, 2–3.
112 Procopius, *BP*, I, 26, 5–12.
113 Procopius, *BG*, VII, 11, 14–16.

harshness of the campaign caused the start of a mutiny which John Troglita subdued by threats.[114] Treason blackmail was a method used by the troops to obtain their pay. During the summer of 548, the soldiers left in Rome killed their commander who had stolen the wheat ration owed to them. They also threatened to return the city to Ostrogoths if the arrears of pay remained unpaid and if pardon was not given for their mutiny. Justinian wisely granted everything.

Desertions to the enemy or even outright treason were frequent during African and Italian Wars, both by individuals and large groups. In 536, during the first siege of Rome by the Ostrogoths, some deserters even pointed out the horse of Belisarius who thus soon found himself in mortal danger. For money, the enemy could also buy the complicity of venal Romano-Byzantine soldiers. Two years later at Osimo, Bourkentios, a Thracian from the Bessi tribe, was paid by the besieged Ostrogoths to carry a message to Ravenna, three days distant. He brought them the answer; his betrayal was only known through the interrogation of a prisoner. For his trouble, Belisarius had him burnt alive. The Bourkentios episode also shows that the discipline of the Imperial Army had nothing to do with that of the modern era marked by daily appeals, because the person concerned passed off his absence of approximately six days as sick leave.[115]

Rome was twice taken by Totila through treachery. The first time in December 546 was due to two groups of four Isaurians who, at night, threw ropes over the walls or opened the gates to his troops. The second betrayal in January 550 was motivated by the memory that the first traitors had become rich thanks to Totila.[116]

In cases of mutiny, some did not hesitate to ally themselves with enemies of the Empire and engage in banditry, which was something new compared to earlier Roman periods. The worst case was in North Africa with the mutiny of Stotzas during the Easter celebrations of 536. A large part of the army, who had married Vandal captives, wanted to reclaim their wives' land, which had been confiscated by the state. Governor Solomon would have none of the idea. In the multinational army that was the Byzantine Army of Africa, more than 1,000 Herul mercenaries were of the Arian faith, a banned heresy. They were also incited to revolt by the Arian priests who remained in place after the defeat of the Vandals. In an aggravating fact, 400 Vandal prisoners, then enlisted in the cavalry, had hijacked the ships which brought them to the Orient and returned to Africa. The conspirators planned to launch their mutiny in March, around Easter; they hesitated, but then organised a meeting at the Carthage stadium where they insulted Solomon and their officers. They temporarily acclaimed Theodore of Cappadocia as Emperor then plundered the city, murdering those loyal to Solomon who took refuge in the church of the former royal palace. Solomon

---

114   Corippus, *Joh*, VI, v. 377–378 (desertions); VIII, v. 50–137 (mutiny).
115   Procopius, *BG*, V, 18, 7 (Rome); VI, 26, 5–15 (Bourkentios); 25–26 (punishment).
116   Procopius, *BG*, VII, 20, 4–16 (year 546); 36, 7–14 (549).

escaped during the night to rally the border troops. Next day, under Stotzas leadership the mutineers left Carthage, no doubt driven out by a resistance by the loyal troops. Their aim was nothing less than the seizure of Libya to form an independent state for their own. They initially numbered 8,000 men, but were joined by 1,000 Vandals, deserters and those who had escaped captivity, plus a large number of slaves. Stotzas had a 'touch of the Spartacus' about him. The mutineers planned to lay siege to Carthage, which Theodore of Cappadocia refused to hand over. Belisarius, then in Sicily, reacted swiftly: he disembarked with 100 men, rallied 2,000 loyal soldiers and defeated the mutineers at the Battle of Membressa, on what is now the Medjerda. but he had to halt the pursuit because his own troops that he had left in Syracuse had also mutinied. As the Duke of Numidia, Marcellus, had learned that Stotzas was in Gazophyla, a town located two days from Constantina (today in Eastern Algeria) he set out to capture him. But Stotzas' trade union-like speech: 'You are treated as slaves!' prevailed over Marcellus's men, who assassinated Marcellus.[117]

The new Governor of Libya, Germanus, a cousin of Justinian I, proved to be a shrewd man, making what could be described as a social speech to the deserters. He offered them understanding, forgiveness and payment for the months of desertion. He had simply noted from the registers that two-thirds of the Imperial Army of Libya had deserted. After the carrot, he used the stick when he thought he was on an equal footing with Stotzas and engaged in the difficult Battle of Skalai Beteres during the spring of 537. Vandal deserters were just massacred and Stotzas fled with the other mutineers to Mauritania.[118]

In Africa, Stotzas rebellion lasted almost nine years. From 543 to 545, he was allied to the Moorish King Antalas. Romano-Byzantine prisoners of war taken by the Moors rallied to him 'without hesitation' noted Procopius. Stotzas was killed at the Battle of Sikkabeneria or Sicca or Veneria or Thacia (modern Le Kef).[119] A Moor called John the Tyrant, who was sometimes nicknamed Stotzas the Younger, then led the deserters. He rallied to the usurper Guntharith Duke of Numidia who, in March 546, killed Areobindus, the Governor of Africa Proconsularis, in Carthage. Guntharith allied himself with the Moorish chiefs Antalas, Iaudas and Cusina with the intention of creating a Kingdom independent of Byzantium. After a short 36 days' reign, he was assassinated. At this point, John the Tyrant's force

---

117 Procopius, *BV*, IV, 14, 9 (Vandal women push for revolt); 14, 12–15 (Arianism of the Heruls); 14, 19 (desertion of the Vandal horsemen); 14, 22–25 (failed plot to kill Solomon); 14, 31–36 (mutiny in Carthage); 14, 38–42 (Solomon escape); 15, 1–4 (Stotzas leader of the mutineers); 15, 9–45 (Belisarius reaction); 15, 52–59 (Marcellus expedition). A. H. M. Jones, J. R. Martindale, J. Morris, *PLRE*, 3a (1992), pp.1199–1200 (Stotzas).

118 Procopius, *BV*, IV, 16, 3 (extent of desertions); 16, 4 (social-like speech); 16, 5 (return of some of the mutineers); 16, 7–35 (battle at *Skalaï Beteres*).

119 Procopius, *BV*, IV, 23, 1 (Stotzas allied with Antalas); 23, 17 (prisoners); 25, 6–11 (Stotzas death).

numbered 1,000 men: 500 Romans, 80 Huns, and the rest Vandals. After the death of Guntharith, Artabanes the Arsacid captured and sent him to Byzantium to be crucified.[120]

Having two-thirds of a field army being mutinied was exceptional and could be explained by the moral fatigue of veterans who had continuously fought Persians, Vandals and then Moors and who wished to settle down somewhere. A similar case occurred during the Italian War, at the beginning of 545. According to Belisarius most part of the troops there joined the Ostrogoths and he felt he had lost the right to command the remaining loyal soldiers who were still unpaid.[121] This demonstrated that the Ostrogoths maintained an efficient tax system and that the Romano-Byzantines were unable to establish themselves administratively.

Unpaid wages were not only a cause for desertion but, worse, also for defection. During the Persian War of 540, the garrison of Beroea of Syria (today Aleppo) resisted in the acropolis for a time, but ended up surrendering with the population when water ran out. After receiving a large ransom, Khosrow I generously let the population and soldiers leave but most of them went over to his side because of long arrears of wages after the Emperor had failed to pay them.[122] During the long Italian campaign, the soldiers who rallied to the Ostrogoths belonged to garrisons of the towns that had been taken. Totila cleverly promised life and free passage to those who wanted to return to the Empire, but confiscated their weapons, horses and possessions. He enlisted the others in his army. The majority of Romano-Byzantine soldiers joined Totila because of the prestige of the victor, the desire to keep wealth that was nothing less than their retirement insurance, and perhaps the desire to continue their military career although being paid by another employer. The figures speak for themselves: of the 400 men in the Rossano garrison in 548, only 80 returned to the Romano-Byzantine Army, while the others accepted service in the Ostrogothic cause. The following year, of the 400 cavalrymen captured in Hadrian's tomb (now Castel Sant'Angelo) the only two who refused to join Totila were their officers, to whom the Ostrogoths generously gave an escort and money to return to Byzantium. Long arrears of pay were the primary reason for the defection of the cavalrymen who were, after all, soldiers fighting for money.[123] Their mentality was not that of the citizen-soldiers who fight for a cause, but that of professionals. They changed armies as others might change companies today. Moreover, their loyalty to their new employers, the Ostrogoths, was not unalterable. At the beginning of 550, when they learned that Germanus, cousin of Justinian I, was coming to Italy with a

---

120 Procopius, *BG*, IV, 25, 3 (with Moorish rebelles Koutzinas, Iaudas and Antalas); 27, 7–8 (John joined Guntharith/Gontharis with 1,000 men); 27, 25 and 27 (John and Artabanes vs Antalas); 28, 39–40 (capture).
121 Procopius, *BG*, VII, 12, 6–8.
122 Procopius, *BP*, II, 7, 37.
123 Procopius, *BG*, VII, 30, 20–23 (Rossano); 36, 24–26 (Hadrian's tomb).

large army, they secretly sent him a letter to assure him of their support. The deserters who had been living off pillage in Emilia gathered together and went to wait for him in Istria. But the Patrician Germanus did not come. These defectors, commanded by a man named Coccas, were defeated with their new masters at the Battle of Taginae, or more exactly Busta Gallorum, in 552, captured in large numbers and duly executed.[124] The disloyalty of the troops to the Empire was matched only by that of the superior officers to their general. Thus Belisarius, after his easy and exemplary victory over the Vandals attracted jealousy if not hatred of his great subordinates. The cascade of betrayals had its source in the ingratitude of the Emperor who dismissed victorious generals and badly paid his soldiers.

The mutiny of November 602 led to the overthrow and death of Maurice because he granted nothing. The reason was that after a campaign in the Balkans, he ordered the army to winter north of the Danube among the Sklavenes. Not inclined to live in harsh condition and fearing for their loot, the soldiers claimed that their horses were tired and that the barbarians were gathering at the border. They first tried to negotiate with Peter the Kouropalates their general and brother of Emperor Maurice, but the latter would hear nothing of their complaints, ordering them to live on the country to spare the public treasury. As a result, the army mutinied and marched on Byzantium, after proclaiming an officer named Phocas as Emperor.[125]

When a general did not fairly share the spoils, he also had to expect trouble. This was why some of Solomon's troops refused to fight in his last, and fatal, battle.

An Army that Remained Christian

Since Constantine the Great's victory at the Milvian Bridge in 312, the Roman Army had officially become Christian, as demonstrated by the *chi rho* displayed on standards and shields, the military oath taken by recruits and the passwords invoking God, Christ and Holy Spirit.[126] However, in the fourth century, Christian references in military epigraphy were still rare and the *chi rho* on shields may have been more a matter of Imperial propaganda than general practice.[127] The *Notitia Dignitatum*, which depicted the shields of Roman units *c.* 400 does not mention any Christian symbols.

---

124 Procopius, *BG*, VII, 22–24 (letter to Germanus; Istria); VIII, 32, 20 (execution after the Battle of Taginae).
125 Theophylact Simocatta, *HU*, VIII, 6, 2 (order of Maurice; spoils; fatigue of horses; presence of barbarians); 3 (mutiny); 9 (delegation to Peter le Kouropalates); 10 (Maurice unwillingness); 7, 7 (Phocas Emperor).
126 Ph. Richardot, *La fin de l'Armée Romaine*, pp.9–12 (*Chi Rho* or *Chrismon*). Vegetius, *DRM*, II, 5 (*Deus nobiscum*).
127 M. Emion, '*Christum in scutis notat*: le bouclier au chrisme des gardes imPeri aux dans l'Antiquité tardive', *Journée des doctorants du GRHis*, Université de Rouen-Normandie, 7 mai 2014, http://grhis.univ-rouen.fr/grhis/?p=8903. Numerous

The late Roman Army used a war cry called *barritus* (the trumpeting of an elephant.) but 200 years earlier Tacitus had linked it to the Germanic tribes.[128] In the *Strategikon* this pagan battle cry was replaced with the then customary *Nobiscum* [God] with us! According to Maurice this was supposedly a dangerous habit petrifying timid soldiers, while the bolder ones got fierce and ran on the enemy breaking the line's cohesion. Recitations of the *Kyrie Eleison* (Lord, have mercy) seemed more appropriate to the author of *Strategikon*.[129] Christianisation of society and therefore of army was gradual. Christian discourse has been militarised since late fourth century.

St Ambrose of Milan developed the image of Christ as *bonus Imperator* (good Emperor). He compared the duties of a Christian to those of a soldier.[130] Justinian even went so far as to draw the parallel: 'The difference is slight between the priesthood and the Empire.'[131] As a consequence Byzantium's Army was a Christian army. An inscription from 446 found in Petra of Arabia mentioned a priest who consecrated a church with the presence of a troop of soldiers, which suggests a military chaplain.[132] Later, Bishops had administrative duties even in military matters. An edict from Anastasius I ordered the city bishops and city defenders, *defensores civitatis* (mayors) to ensure garrisoning soldiers were supplied in food by the farmers, who could not be forced to give cash instead.[133]

Military symbolism was Christianised. The *chi rho* was painted on the shields of Justinian's bodyguards in the Basilica of San Vitale in Ravenna. It is less common elsewhere. It seems to have been replaced with the cross, and Procopius claimed that it was the cross that won the Emperor victory.[134] On the Barberini Ivory, at the top, overlooking the Emperor on horseback stands a beardless Christ holding the cross in a medallion embossed with the sun, moon and star, with an angel on either side to carry it. In the centre, the winged victory holding the palm of victory is admittedly more pagan, but the old traditions were having a hard time dying out. However, the message is clear: only God gives victory. Professing the Christian religion

---

shields and labarum with chrisms on the Column of Arcadius drawings from manuscript O.17.2 in Trinity College Library, Dublin:
https://mss-cat.trin.cam.ac.uk/manuscripts/uv/view.php?n=O.17.2#?c=0&m=0&s=0&cv=9&xywh=-5051per cent2C-1 per cent2C15992per cent2C8603

128 Tacitus, *Germania*, 3. Ammianus Marcellinus, *RG*, XVI, 12, 34 (Germans); XXI, 13, 15; XXVI, 7, 17; XXXI, 7, 11. Vegetius, *DRM*, III, 18 and 24 (Romans).
129 Maurice, *Strategikon*, II, 18.
130 Ch. Pietri, 'Le serment du soldat chrétien. Les épisodes de la *Militia Christi* sur les sarcophages', *MEFR*, 74–2 (1962), pp.649–664.
131 C. Morrisson (ed.), *Le monde Byzantin*, pp.138–139 (head of the church; edicts; fixing religious holidays). *Nov J*.., VII, 2 (on priesthood and being an Emperor).
132 *IGLS*, XXI, *Inscriptions de la Jordanie. Tome 4. Petra et la Nabatène méridionale du Wadi al-Hasa au golfe de 'Aqaba*, 50.
133 *CJ*, I, 14, 8.
134 Procopius, *Aed.*, I, 2, 12.

was an obligation, but the soldiers still had to adhere to the Emperor's theological vision. Justin I in 519–520 and Justinian in 527 prohibited civilian and military positions to heretics.[135] The sixth-century army was employed to persecute heretical monks and bishops.[136] For a pagan and barbarian, baptism was a necessary path to high rank, as with Askum the Hun promoted in 528 as Master of the Soldiers to Illyricum soon after his conversion.[137] By doing so, Justinian displayed clearly an apostolic vision, but he did not repeat this kind of experiment after Askum' capture.

By the early seventh century, a general could be forced to become a monk. This happened first with Philippicus during the coup that overthrew Maurice. Instead of executing him, the usurper Phocas had him tonsured as a monk and sent to a monastery in Chrysopolis. Priscus suffered a similar fate after an unsuccessful campaign against the Persians in 611-612. He was removed from his post as Master of the Soldiers to the East, tonsured and sent to the Monastery of the Chora. This practice was probably borrowed from the Franks, where tonsure was an alternative to political assassination in cases of dynastic succession. By December 574, when Justin II appointed Tiberius as *Caesar*, he delivered a speech more likely to be found in a bishop's mouth than an Emperor:

> Listen it is God who magnifies you, it is God who gives you this dignity, not me, so that you may be honoured by him. Honour your mother who was your Empress [Sophie, wife of Justin II]. You know that you were first her slave, you are now her son. Do not rejoice in the shedding of blood, do not be an accomplice to murder, do not return evil for evil; do not resemble me for hatred because as a mere mortal I had the price, of course I was fallible, and I was paid in return for my sins. But I will plead my case before the Court of Christ against all those who have done wrong to me. Do not be tempted by this dignity as I was. Take care of others as you do for yourself. Measure what you have been and what you have become. Avoid arrogance and you will not be mistaken. You know what I was, what I became and what I am. All those around you are your children and your slaves. You know I honoured you at the expense of my own descendants. You, look at all these men around you, and you look at all those in our state. Take care of your army, do not interview informants. Do not let anyone tell you that your predecessor was

---

135 *CJ*, I, 4, 20 (law from 527). G. Greatrex, 'Moines, militaires et défense de la frontière orientale au VIᵉ s' in in A. S. Lewin, P. Pellegrini, Z. T. Fiema, S. Janniard (eds), *The Late Roman Army in Near East*, p.294, n. 72 (who sees in this law a survival of those from Justin I by 519–520).
136 G. Greatrex, 'Moines, militaires et défense', pp.285–297.
137 John Malalas, *Chrgr.*, XVIII, 21.

doing this or that; that made me suffer a lot. Let those who have goods benefit but give to those who have nothing.[138]

This speech was followed by a prayer from the Patriarch of Constantinople and then everyone said an Amen.

By the late sixth century the *Strategikon* was strict on liturgical duties and confirmed the presence of military chaplains. Any unit, *tagma* or *bandon*, alone or with the army, had to sing early in the morning and before anything else the triple Orthodox invocation, the *Trisagion*. The *Kyrië Eleison* had to be sung by priests, the general and the officers before leaving the camp, rather than shouting *Nobiscum*. The other war cry was also in Latin and was shouted three times: *Parati! Adiuta! Deus!* (Ready! Help us! God!). The treatise added that 'one or two days before the battles, the *merarchs* should have the standards blessed and given to the standard-bearers of the units.'[139] This blessing has not been confirmed by other sources, but it marked the deep Christianisation of spirit and its role on the morale of the soldiers. The *Strategikon* makes no less than 13 references to God in a treatise on tactics. Some of the late sixth-century *papyri* mentioned donations to churches made by soldiers of Ravenna – evidence for a vivid Christian faith.

When Heraclius chose to invade Persian Transcaucasia in September 626, he was first backed by Ziebel the Khan of the Khazars or Gokturks with 40,000 men, then deserted little by little by them. Adventured in enemy lands, he addressed his remaining troops as a Christian soldier to boost their morale. Byzantium and the Persians began religious wars before the arrival of Islam:

> Know, O brothers, that no one wishes to fight with us, except God and His Mother who bore Him without seed and this that He may show His might (since salvation does not lie in the abundance of soldiers and weapons, but to those who trust in His mercy) He sends down His aid.[140]

Heraclius was glorified to have retaken the True Cross from the Persians, but his soldiers were no less than him convinced Christians. The '60 martyrs of Gaza' story, massacred in 638 by Muslims, depicts Byzantine soldiers who bravely refused to apostatise their Christian faith. Their two units surrendered at Gaza, the *bandon* of the Scythians and the *bandon* of *Voluntarioi*. After a 16-month captivity, 10, including their leader

---

138 Theophylact Simocatta, *HU*, III, 11, 8–11. Speech repeated in shorter form by John of Ephesus, *HE*, III, 5; Evagrius Scholasticus, *HE*, V, 13.
139 Maurice, *Strategikon*, XII, 16 (three-stages order); VII, 1 (banner blessing).
140 Theophanes Confessor, *Chrgr.*, AM 6118, 317 (failed help from Turks and Heraclius'speech). Michael the Syrian, *HU*, XI, 3, t. 2 (1963), p.409 (40,000 Khazars sent by the Chagan or Khan, but no desertion).

Kallinikos, were brought to Jerusalem by the Arab general Amr ibn al-As, (in Greek Ammiras or Amrou), then beheaded as a warning to the others. Unwilling to become Muslim, the remaining prisoners were executed in Eleutheropolis the following month. Their names were predominantly and repetitively Christian: Himerios, Hērios, Theodore, Stephen, John, Paul, another John, another Paul, Phôtinos, Sitas, Eugene, Mouselios, a third John, Stephen, another Theodore, John, George, Theopemptos, another George, Sergios, a third un George, a third Theodore, Kyriakos, John, Sitas, a sixth John, Philoxenos, George, John again, George from the *bandon* of the Scythians; Peter, Paul, Theodore, John re-again, a ninth John, Theodore, Epiphane, John, Theodore, Sergios, George, Thomas, Stephen, Conon, Theodore, Paul, John, George, John, a 13th and last John, Paulinus, Kaioumas, Abraam, Mermēssos, Marinos and (other missing names) from the *bandon* of *Voluntarioi*.[141]

Contrary to what Edward Gibbon wrote in the late eighteenth century about the decline and fall of the Roman Empire, it is worthwhile noting that the more Christianised eastern part survived while the more pagan west collapsed. From the second half of the fourth century about 30 military saints were honoured as martyrs because they would not offer sacrifices to pagan idols or swear an oath to Emperors who persecuted Christians in the 280s–300s. The best known were Maurice of Agaune, George of Lydda (England's St George) and Theodore Tiro, from *tiro* (recruit). The latter had had a church in Byzantium since 452. Military holiness was particularly developed in the early Byzantine Empire.[142] Never before has a culture produced so many sacred figures in military attire.[143]

---

141 A. Guillou, 'Prise de Gaza par les Arabes au VIIe siècle', *BCH*, 81 (1957), pp.396–404. W. E. Kaegi, (1992), pp.95–97. D. Woods, 'The 60 Martyrs of Gaza and the Martyrdom of Bishop Sophronius of Jerusalem', *ARAM*, 15 (2003), pp.129–150.

142 H. Delehaye, Les légendes Grecques des Saints militaires (Paris: Picard et Fils, 1909).

143 P. L. Grotowski, *Arms and Armour of the Warrior Saints. Tradition and Innovation in Byzantine Iconography (843–1261)*, The Medieval Mediterranean, 87 (Leiden, Boston: Brill, 2010).

6

A Double Standard Regular Army

> The armies of the Romans were not as numerous as under the ancient Emperors, but only a very small part remained and that was no longer sufficient for such a vast Empire.
>
> Agathias, *Historiae*, V, 13, 7–8

An arc of circle going from the wooded Slovenian mountains to the sandy borders of Egypt through Syria – this is the territory that the Byzantine Empire had to defend in around 530: a space today uncontrollable by modern political and military means of a single state. How did the administrative heirs of the Romans achieve this with relatively few numbers on horseback or even just walking?

The Palace Guards – Parade Troops?

Well combed mid-length hair, brightly coloured tunics covered on the shoulders with purple embroidery highlighted with gold thread, a gold torc around the neck and white shoes with black espadrilles. If there were not their long swords hanging from a baldric, their green shields with a golden *chi rho* and the spears with coloured striped shafts one would have thought that these magnificent people were courtiers. At least, this is how the Imperial Guards are depicted by the mosaic in the basilica from San Vitale of Ravenna and by on older silver plate known as the Missorium of Theodosius, today in the collection of the Real Academia in Madrid.[1]

Scholae Palatinae, originally created under Diocletian or Constantine I as a real Imperial Guard and elite body, became over time parade troops.[2]

---

1. Z. Mrav, 'Maniakon. The Golden Torc in Late Roman and Early Byzantine Army' in T. Vida, Ph. Rance and *alii*, *The Frontier World. Roman, barbarians and Military Culture* (Budapest: Eötvös Lorand University, Martin Optiz Kiado, 2015), pp.287–303.
2. R. I. Frank, *Scholae Palatinae: The Palace Guards of the Later Roman Empire*

At the beginning of the fifth century, according to the *Notitia Dignitatum* eight *Scholae Palatinae* were in the Eastern Roman Empire under the master of the offices. In 479, during Zeno's reign, a *scholarios* named Spanikios was executed for attempting to assassinate the Patrician Illus; the name may reveal a recruitment of Hispanic origin.[3] According to Procopius, the number of *Scholarioi*, the Greek version of *Scholarii*, was then set at 3,500. Recruited on merit from the Armenians according to Procopius, they received high pay. But Zeno perverted the system by introducing cowards and the incompetent and even slaves, by bribery, could now enter it. When his uncle Justin was Emperor, Justinian I increased their number by 2,000 *supernumerarii*, a function he suppressed when he became the sole Emperor. To save money, he suggested that they either go to war, which Procopius said they were unfit for, or give up their pay for a certain period. The *Scholarioi* were then managed by a master of the offices named Peter, who stole from them of course.[4] Procopius' overcriticism must be questioned. A law from 542 mentioned *Scholarioi* who died in battle and the obligation made to *actuarii* for issuing a death certificate to their widows so that they could remarry. This contradicts the dark caricature made by Procopius.[5] However the bad reputation of *Scholarioi* persisted in historical sources, as the severe portrait made by Agathias about the siege of Byzantium in 559:

> They were not really combatants, or even people sufficiently trained in this field; they came from those units whose mission is to be present, day and night, at the Imperial Court, and who are called *scholae*. They are called soldiers and they are listed on the strength rolls, but most of them are city people who wear nice uniforms and only serve, I think, to enhance the pomp and the Imperial majesty when they show up in public. As there are no reviews, they are of course not obliged to the slightest exercise, having obtained this mark of honour and bought at a great price, a sinecure. Thus, such men, for lack of personnel experienced in wars, were stationed on the ramparts and seemed to stand guard there.[6]

During this siege, when the Huns Kutrigurs arrived before Byzantium, the walls were defended by *Scholarioi* and *Protiktores*, issued from *arithmoi*

(Rome: American Academy, Papers and Monographs of the American Academy in Rome, 23, 1969). A. P. Kazhdan, A. M. Talbot, A. Cutler, T. E. Gregory, N. P. Ševčenko (eds), 'Scholae palatinae', vol. 3 (1991), pp.1851–1852, (σακελλάριος).
3   Theophanes Confessor, *Chrgr.*, AM 5972, 128.
4   Procopius, *Anecdota*, XXIV, 15 (nombre des σχολάριοι); 16 (pay and origin); 17 (Zenon); 18–20 (Justinian I getting money from *scholarioi*); 21 (inability to campaign, renouncement to be paid); 22 (Peter).
5   *Nov. J.*, 117, 11; J. F. Haldon, *Byzantine Praetorians*, pp.126–128 (*scholares* in active duty).
6   Agathias, *Hist.*, V, 15, 2 and 3–5 (decadence since Zeno).

which is not otherwise defined, with the senators from the city.[7] Three years later, Justinian moved the seven *scholae* out of their garrisons at Nicomedia (present-day Izmit), Kios (Gemlik), Prusa (Bursa), Cyzicus (Bandirma), Koteaion (Kütahya) and Dorylaion (Eskişehir), where some had been since the fourth century, to redeploy them around Heraclea of Thrace. They mutinied and reproached their count for having suppressed certain gratuities. The Master of the Offices Theodore Kondocheres took them to discipline after some stern words.[8] In this mutiny, the *Scholarioi* did not turn against the Emperor, but against their commander. It was the prudent act of military unionists, who did not want to be considered as rebels. But they lost, subsequently, they gave up their Imperial Guard prerogatives to the *Excubitores* and were used as field troops, a change that proved they were fit for war.

A Byzantine Greek inscription from the late sixth century or early seventh century, found in a chapel in Lison di Portogruaro in Veneto, alludes to Stephen, *sinator scholes armatouron, senator* from the *Schola Armaturarum*. This unit was the continuation of the *Schola Armaturarum iuniorum* under the eastern master of the offices *c.* 400. By the mid-sixth century, the unit was mentioned at Ravenna under the name of *Sc(h)ola Armaturae* in a donation made by a soldier named Constantius to the city church. Another *schola*, is known from an anonymous donor, was in Ravenna by the mid-seventh century, the *Schola Gentilium* survivor of the *Gentiles Seniores* from the later Roman Empire. These examples show that after Justinian the *scholae* continued to be recruited, and acted again as combat troops.[9] Tiberius II, in *c.* 578, although under pressure from the Persians, at the request of the Senate of Rome could only send a small force to fight the Lombards. The *Scholae Palatinae* may have been involved. An episode dated 626 shows that the *Scholarioi* lost influence when John the Earthquake, a high-ranking official whose title is not otherwise known, wanted to divert their bread rations to regular soldiers. This unfair attempt was aborted when it was opposed by Leontius Count of the *Opsikion* (from the Latin *obsequium* or 'guard').[10]

John the Lydian declared that under Justinian the only troops that did not look like barbarians were the Palace guards: *Excubitores* in Latin,

---

[7] John Malalas, *Chrgr.*, XVIII, 129 (*scholae, protectores, arithmoi,* whole Senate). Agathias, *Hist.*, V, 15, 2–6 (*scholae*); 16, 2 (300 elite infantrymen and a mob); 3 (numerous peasants). Theophanes Confessor, *Chrgr.*, AM 6051, 233 (only source with Malalas quoting numeri and senators).

[8] Theophanes Confessor, *Chrgr.*, AM 6054, 236. Hoffmann D., *Das Spätrömische Bewegungsheer und die Notitia Dignitatum*, vol. 1 (Düsseldorf: Rheinland-Verlag, 1968), pp.279–303 (*scholae* in the fourth century).

[9] *ILS*, II, 8883 (Stephanus). *Notitia Dignitatum*, OR.XI.9 (*schola armaturarum iuniorum*); 6 (*schola gentilium seniorum*). *P. Ital.*, I, 24 (*schola Gentilium*); 27 (*scola armaturae*), G. Ravegnani, 'Le unità dell'esercito Bizantino', pp.197 (Stephen), 200 (Constantius).

[10] *Chr. paschale*, a.626, (2007), p.168.

Exkubitoi or *Exkubitoroi* in Greek, a term literally meaning 'those who come out of bed' or 'the awakened.'[11] Numbering some 300 and commanded by a count, they were created by Leon I (457–474) who wanted to recruit them from among the subjects of the Empire.[12] During the *Nika* revolt of 532, *Excubitores* and *Scholarii* sided with the people against Justinian. One party however was convinced to return to their duty by Narses the Eunuch.[13] *Excubitores* did not just have security functions or parade functions at the palace. During the pacification campaign against the Moors in 535, their leader Theodore was instructed with 1,000 infantrymen to take Mount Bourgaon at night in order to attack at dawn from the summit. Procopius on this occasion specifies that the Romans gave to the *Excubitores* the name of 'Guards.'[14] They were also called *Basilikoi Somatophilakes* (Royal Bodyguards).[15] In 583, Comentiolus the Thracian was still an *excubitor*.[16]

The Emperor also had some secret police of which little is known. In 563, police officers known as *commentarienses* went to arrest a certain Kaisarios of the Green Faction of hippodrome supporters, but they were massacred and mutilated. Then, for two days Justinian sent the *Excubitores* and soldiers who sustained many killed and wounded. The Blues, though traditional enemies of the Greens, also attacked the law enforcement forces in the same way as the city gangs of today. As the situation was getting uncontrollable the prefect of the City Zemarchos was dismissed. Julian, his successor, treated the Greens ruthlessly for 10 months with a display of terror: burning, impalement, castration, dismemberment. He managed to repress these coloured factions found guilty of theft, murder and piracy.[17] Over 20 years later, in 598, side by side with the factions the *Excubitores* were holding the Long Walls against the Avars.[18] A common threat could unite hippodrome hooligans and Palace guards. Nonetheless it was realised than slaughtering your own citizens in order to restore internal peace was not a good idea. To suppress a riot in Byzantium in 602 the Emperor's bodyguards, undoubtedly *Excubitores* and *Spatharii*, were specifically armed with maces, considered less lethal than swords, allowing them to break arms rather than disembowel the protesters.[19] After the death of Heraclius I, the *Excubitores* ceased to be a combat unit and their name, like for the *Scholarioi*, became an honorary title of administrative officer like that of *scribon*. It again became an elite cavalry troop, commanded by the

---

11   John the Lydian, *De Magistratibus*, I, 12, 5 (ἐξκουβίτορες ου ἐξκούβιτοι).
12   A. H. M. Jones, (1964), p.658.
13   *Chr. paschale*, a.532, 2007, p.124.
14   Procopius, *BV*, IV, 12, 17.
15   Procopius, *BG*, VIII, 21, 1 (βασιλικοί σωματοφυλάκες).
16   A. H. M. Jones, J. R. Martindale, J. Morris, *PLRE*, 3a (1992), p.321.
17   John Malalas, *Chrgr.*, XVIII, 151.
18   Theophylact Simocatta, *HU*, VII, 15, 7.
19   Theophylact Simocatta, *HU*, VIII, 4, 13.

domestikos ton exkoubitôn (servant of the awaken ones), during the reign of Constantine V (741–775) but it disappeared *c.* 1081.[20]

Since the third century, there had been many categories of *protectores*. Created under the Severan dynasty, this special rank was initially lower than that of centurion. Reserved to deserving junior officers, it was intended to qualify a military officer serving a governor or a praetorian prefect. Initially they were simply elite bodyguards, and *c.* 270–280, the *protectores* formed an escort for the Emperor or were entrusted with delegated missions, and were known as *Protectores Diuini Lateris Augusti*. In the following century, they escorted generals and were given the title *domesticus* (aide-de-camp) being a better description of their function than the literally 'servant'. From then on, they came from the privileged classes like the historian Ammianus Marcellinus, and it was a form of War College for future senior officers.[21]

Each part of the later Roman Empire had two *scholae*, servants on horseback and those on foot under the orders of a count. By the mid-sixth century, John the Lydian defined the *primoskoutarioi (primoscutarii)* or *yperaspistai*, as 'what we call *protectores*'. The dignity of *protector* was probably conferred on the *Schola Prima Scutariorum* under the master of the offices.[22] In Italy, the western *Protectores Domestici* continued even in the Ostrogothic Kingdom as a parade corps but disappeared after the Justinianic reconquest.[23] In Byzantium they formed the best paid corps and the apex of the Imperial Guard, because its members paid large sums to enter it. They were called *domestikoi tē kai protiktores*, in Latin *protectores domestici* (protectors and servants). Those who enlisted did so as rank and title. They were exempt from military action and based in Byzantium, Galatia and other places nearby. At a dark time when the state was short of money, Justinian gave them the choice between going on campaign and temporarily renouncing their pay.[24] The panegyric of Justin II by Corippus described a troop of *protectores, numerus protectorum,* forming a splendid guard of honour to the master of the offices during an embassy to the Avars, which seems to confine them to a parade role.[25] Menander Protector, who may

---

20 J. F. Haldon, *Byzantine Praetorians*, pp.136–137 (origin) (161 (decline by the end of seventh century); A. P. Kazhdan, A. M. Talbot, A. Cutler, T. E. Gregory, N. P. Ševčenko (eds), 'Domestikos ton exkoubiton', vol. 2 (1991), pp.646–647 (Constantine V). B. Croke, 'Leo I and the Palace Guard', *REB,* 75 (2005), pp.117–151, (ἐξκουβίτωρ/ἐξκούβιτος, plural ἐξκουβίτορες/ἐξκούβιτοι).
21 Ph. Richardot, *La fin de l'Armée Romaine*, pp.33–36.
22 John the Lydian, *De Mag.* I, 46, 6 (*πριμοσκουτάριοι, ὑπερασπισταί, οἱ νῦν λεγόμενοι προτίκτορες*). *Notitia Dignitatum*, OR.XI.4. M. Emion, *Des soldats de l'armée romaine tardive: les protectores (IIIe-VIe siècles ap. J.-C.)*, thèse Histoire, Rouen, Université de Rouen-Normandie, École doctorale Histoire, Mémoire, Patrimoine, Langage ED 558, (2017), p.464.
23 M. Emion, *Des soldats de l'armée Romaine*', pp.539–551, 565.
24 Procopius, *Anecdota*, XXIV, 24 (origin and venality of charges for *domestikoi tè kaï protiktores,* δομέστικοί τε καί προτίκτωρες; dispense with military duties); 25 (social status; garrison); 26 (Justinian).
25 Corippus, *In laud. Iust.*, III, 157–164. D.

have been from the *protectores domestici*, reported the duties performed by some sort of a *Protectores Domestici* during an embassy between Byzantines and Persians during the reign of Tiberius II around 579:

> He whom we call *methoniôn protiktor* (protector of the borders) which among the Romans indicates someone engaged in the Imperial Guard, prepared the tents under which the ambassadors of the two camps were to examine the proposals, a task which since the all beginnings had been entrusted to this protector.[26]

The body of *Protectores Domestici* did not survive beyond the sixth century, even if the title of *protector* itself persisted in watermarks until the medieval-Byzantine period.[27]

Armed cadets formed the corps of *Candidati* or *Kandidatoi* (candidates) so called because of their white tunics. Their uniform is depicted on folio 374v of a manuscript from the Bibliothèque Nationale de France, dated to around 880, on the *Commentaries* of Gregory of Nazianzus, the *Codex Parisinus Graecus*. Their dress is very similar in cut to those depicted on the sixth-century mosaic of San Vitale in Ravenna, but the colour has changed to white with gold embroidery on the shoulders, upper torso and lower tunic. The forearms are adorned with bracelets or similar embroidery. Like Justinian's bodyguards at San Vitale, the *candidatus* wears a *maniakion* (gold torc), and carries an oval red shield, with an *umbo*, and has a gold border. On folios 239r and 440r, two *candidati* carry golden swords adorned with pearls and jewels, on their shoulders. The necklaces are of a dark colour with two bows and pearls.[28] This ultra-privileged military corps had a controversial origin. It was said to be a creation of Gordian III in 243 and taken from the *Scholarioi*, 'men in the prime of life, able-bodied and of large size' according to a Byzantine source, but its first attestation dates only to 350.[29] Justinian was a member of it *c*. 518, and perhaps even from an earlier date. During his reign, belonging to the *Candidati* was the golden stepping stone to a career as a senior officer or general. This was the case for the ex-*candidatus*, Asbad, an officer of Germanic origin put at the head of elite cavalry units stationed at the fort of Tzurullon (Tzillarum or Tzoularon – now Corlu) in Thrace. Privileged candidates and *Scholarioi* were authorised to combine these two comparable functions in a law of 25 December 524 of the *Justinian Code*. Along with the *Spatharii* (sword-bearers) and

---

26 Menander Protector, *fr*. 26, 1 (τῶν μεθονίων προτίκτωρ). M. Emion, *Des soldats de l'armée Romaine*, p.505.
27 M. Emion, *Des soldats de l'armée Romaine*, p.566.
28 Two websites: https://gallica.bnf.fr/ark:/12148/btv1b84522082 and https://commons.wikimedia.org/wiki/Category:Bibliothper centC3per centA8que_Nationale_MS_Gr._510.
29 *Chr. paschale*, a.243 (1860), p.662. A. P. Kazhdan, A. M. Talbot, A. Cutler, T. E. Gregory, N. P. Ševčenko (eds), 'Spatharios', vol. 3 (1991), pp.1935–1936.

Cubicularii (chamberlains), they remained loyal to Justinian during the *Nika* revolt of 532 and arrested opponents. Then qualified as 'bearded', i.e. not eunuchs, they were commanded by Eulalios. The *Candidati* were probably drawn from the *Scholae Palatinae*, because their number seems small and was fixed at 40 members in the *Book of Ceremonies* written under Constantine VII (913–959). The unit disappeared around the middle of the eleventh century.[30]

The corps of *Spatharii* or *Spatharioi* was more exclusive. During the later Empire, the term was used to designate private or Imperial bodyguards. Under Julian, during the campaign against the Persians in 363, the Emperor's *Spatharii* were also known as 'chamberlains' and were eunuchs who, along with other troops, guarded the Imperial tent. When Marcian came to power in 430, he had the eunuch Chrysaphius, described as a *spatharius* but probably their leader, who had been very influential during the reign of Theodosius II, beheaded. In 479, the Patrician Illus was almost assassinated on the orders of the Empress, but a *spatharius* received the sword blow on his arm instead. By January 532, the Green Faction involved the otherwise unknown eunuch and *spatharocubicularius* Kalopodios in the hippodrome. This was the start of the *Nika* revolt, in which a part of the Imperial Guard sided with the rioters. Justinian, on the other hand, was able to rely on the armed guard of the *Spatharii* and *Cubicularii* as well as Belisarius and Mundo. Narses the Eunuch, then chief of *Spatharii* and *Cubicularii*, saved the day by slaughtering the rebels gathered at the hippodrome, killing no fewer than 35,000 people. The 'eunuch *Spatharii* and the bearded *Candidati*' imprisoned the main leaders of the insurrection. Belisarius put himself at the head of the *Spatharii* to place Hypatius under arrest. From then on, the *Spatharii* formed the Emperor's most trusted bodyguard. Their leader John was beheaded along with the leader of the *Candidati*, Tzittas (Sittas), in 605 for plotting against Emperor Phocas.

The importance of the corps was still perceptible in 626 when Patriarch Sergios, Praetorian Prefect Alexander with Count of the *Opsikion* and *Spatharios* Leontius obtained the resignation of John the Earthquake, who wanted to withdraw the *scholarioi's* bread ration in favour of the common soldiers. Later, *spatharios* rank became the stepping stone to higher office. Thus in 710, a *spatharios* named Elias was appointed Governor of Chersonese. Before he was Emperor, from 717 to 741, Leo III the Isaurian received the rank of *spatharios* from the Justinian II. By 717 a certain Sergios was *Strategos* of Sicily also held the honorary title of *protospatharios*. He rebelled and promoted a puppet Emperor when he learned that the Saracens were besieging Byzantium. In order to neutralise him, Leo III the Isaurian sent Paul the Chartularius and two *spatharioi*, who were tasked

---

30 Victor of Tunnuna, *Chr.*, a. 518 (candidate). *CJ*, XII, 33, 5, 4. Procopius, *BG*, VII, 28, 4–5 (Asbad 1 is not to be confused with Asbad 2). *Chr. paschale*, a.532, p.125 (bearded); Constantine VII Porphyrogenitus, *De Ceremoniis*, I, 86 (nombre); Ph. Richardot, *La fin de l'Armée Romaine*, pp.37, 317.

BIRTH OF THE BYZANTINE ARMY 476-641 CE VOLUME 1: STILL LATE ROMAN?

Justinian's Bodyguard
The shield with XP *Chi Rho* may be for an officer or a specific unit. After the sixth-century mosaic from the Basilica of San Vitale in Ravenna.

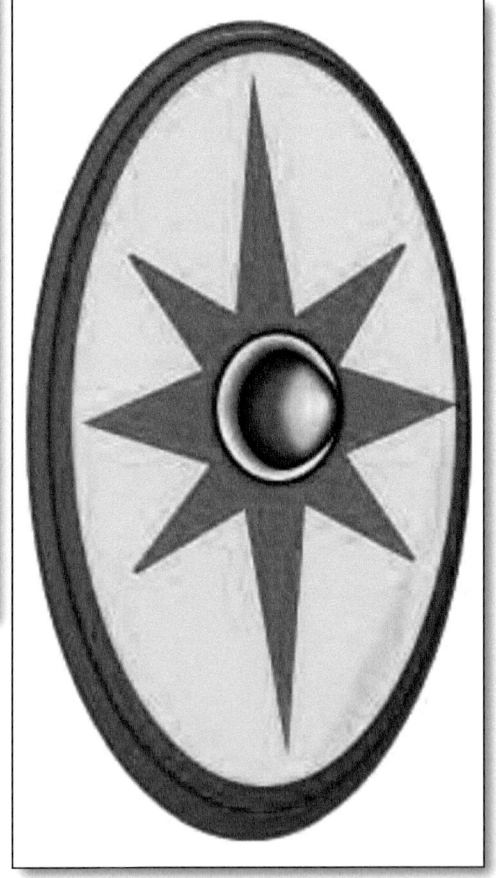

Justinian's Bodyguard Alternate Shield
Reconstructed version, it may be for another unit or a common soldier. After the sixth-century mosaic from the Basilica of San Vitale in Ravenna.

with carrying out dirty work such as decapitating Sergios and the usurper Basil Onomagoulos, and then preserving their heads in vinegar to bring them back. These *spatharioi* are to be distinguished from the aides-de-camp of the same name who escorted the ordinary generals. This honorific title disappeared after 1075.[31]

Intervention Troops

The later Roman Army was divided between intervention troops, called palatine, *palatinae*, when they were elite units stationed near Ravenna and Byzantium or field troops, *comitatenses* (accompanying) distinct from *limitanei* (border troops). Each border command had its own proper intervention troops, but only major commands under masters of the soldiers could raise field armies as did the masters of the soldiers present. But major field armies were ad hoc constructions from several major commands. This pattern was still observable under Anastasius I at the beginning of the campaign against the Persians in 503.

The troops used by the masters of Thrace and of the East or those who followed Belisarius in Africa and Italy were of course elite troops dedicated to intervention, but were they heirs of the old Roman units? This is difficult to prove because the first pitfall to detecting permanence is the transition to Greek terminology in the sixth century. The words legion, cohort, wing or auxiliary were no longer used. Moreover, unlike Ammianus Marcellinus, a career soldier who cited their names, the authors of the sixth century and their successors did so only exceptionally. Very fragmentary epigraphic and papyrological sources show the permanence of units of the later Roman Empire, at least in name.[32] The palatine troops who formed the elite of the elite in the later Roman Empire continued over the next two centuries. An inscription from Pylai in Byzantium around 531 still mentioned the *Deuteron Bandon Kônstantiniakon* (Second Band of the Constantinians); it aluded to the *Milites Secundi Constantini(aci)* (Soldiers from the Second

---

31 *Chr. paschale*, a.363, 2007, pp.41 (Julian); a. 450, p.80 (Chrysaphius); a.532, p.114 (*spatharios* Calopodius/kalopodios), p.123 (armed guard during *Nika* revolt), p.124 (Narses spathary and cubiculary), p.125 (arrest of the leaders of the revolt; so-called 'eunuchs'); a.605, p.145 (John); a.626, p.168 (Leontius). John Malalas, *Chrgr.*, XIV, 3 (Chysaphius liked by Theodosius II) and 6 (executed). Theophanes Confessor, *Chrgr.*, AM 5972, 127 and 128 (Illus); AM 6024, 181 (spathary Kalopodios; Nika revolt; 35,000 people killed), 185 (Mundo, Belisarius, Constantiolus, Narses the Cubiculary; cubicularies and spatharies backing the Emperor; Belisarius and spatharies arrested Hypatius; losses); AM 6203, 377 (Elias); AM 6210, 398 (Sergios and Basile). A. P. Kazhdan and alii (eds), 'Boukellarioi', 1991, vol. 3, p.1936.
32 G. Ravegnani, 'Le unità dell'esercito Bizantino', pp.185–205 (list of military units).

Constantinian), in 400 a palatine infantry auxiliary under the duke of Scythia on the Danube in the fortress of *Troesmis* (today Hui in Romania).[33]

Pope Gregory the Great in a letter dated July 592 spoke of *Theodosiaci* garrisoned in Rome and whose pay was slow to come. Around 600, it was in Ravenna under the name of *Numerus Felicium Theodosiacum*. It was probably a survival of the *auxilia palatina* known around 400 as the *Felices Theodosiaci* who depended on the second master of the soldiers present at Constantinople.[34] The *Daci* was an old palatine legion initially under the command of the first master of the soldiers present and subsequently they had a very mobile destiny. During the sixth century it was garrisoned at Arsinoe in Egypt, a form of 'downgrading'. At the beginning of the next century this unit was moved to Rome where it is mentioned in a donation made by the *Domesticus* John.[35] The oldest regular unit in a Byzantine historical source is that of the *Lanciarii* or *Lankiariôn* which, in 518, raised Justin I on a shield and decorated him with a torc and bracelets, traditional Roman insignia. A *campidoctor* named Godilas (a Hun?) crowned him. The *Lanciarii* was also known in the 400s to form two palatine legions at Constantinople: the *Seniores* under the command of the first master of the soldiers present and the *iuniores* under the second master. Another *legio comitatensis* of *Iuniores* existed with this name under the master of the soldiers to Illyricum.[36]

Procopius only mentioned a traditional unit by name once: the *Rhēges* that distinguished itself during the defence of Rome by Belisarius in 537, where it was commanded by an officer with the Latin name of Ursicinus (Little bear). Originally, it was known as the *Regii*, and had fought valiantly against the Alamanni at the Battle of Strasbourg in 357. The unit was later split into two during the division of the Empire between East and West. *C.* 400, the *Notitia Dignitatum* mentioned two *Regii* units, a *comitatensis legio* in Italy and an *auxilia palatina* in the East, which was the origin of Ursicinus' unit.[37] An epitaph from 547 in Florence for Macrobius *Primicerius*

---

33   *Notitia Dignitatum*, OR.XXXIX.23 (*Milites Secundi Constantini*). *AE*, 1995, 1427 (epitaph). C. Zuckerman, 'Le δευτερόν βάνδον Κωνσταντινιακῶν dans une épitaphe de Pylaï', *Tyche*, 10, 1995, pp.233–235.

34   Gregory the Great, *Registrum Epistolarum*, II, 45–46. *Notitia Dignitatum*, OR.VI.21 = 62. G. Ravegnani, 'Le unità dell'esercito Bizantino', p.201.

35   Wessely G. (ed.), *Studien zur Palaeographie und Papyruskunde*, Leipzig, 1921, XX, 139. *Notitia Dignitatum*, OR.VI.43. G. Ravegnani, 'Le unità dell'esercito Bizantino', p.192. *P. Ital.*, I, 18–19 = *ChLA*, 22 718, 1983 (*Iohannis, dom(esti)c(us) num(eri) diac(orum)*).

36   Constantine VII Porphyrogenitus, *De Ceremoniis*, I, 93 (καμπιδούκτωρ τῶν λαγκιαρίων). *Notitia Dignitatum*, OR.VI, 42 (*Lanciarii Seniores*); VI, 47 (*Lanciarii Iuniores*); IX.38 (*Lanciarii Iuniores* of master of the soldiers to Illyricum). G. Ravegnani, 'Le unità dell'esercito Bizantino', p.188.

37   Ammianus Marcellinus, *RG*, XVI, 12, 45 (Strasbourg). *Notitia Dignitatum*, OC.V.80 = 229 = VII.32; OR.VI. 8 = 49. Procopius, *BG*, V, 23, 3; Ph. Richardot, *La fin de l'Armée Romaine*, pp.86, 90, 119 (*Regii*). M. P. Speidel, 'Raising New Units for the Late Roman Army: *Auxilia Palatina*', *DOP*, 50 (1996), pp.163–164. Procopius,

of the *Primi Theodosiani* known by the *Notitia Dignitatum* as an *auxilium palatinum* in Constantinople and a *vexillatio comitatensis* in Thracia.³⁸ An inscription mentioning Paul, soldier of the Za unit, *milex (sic) of num(ero) Zal(iorum)* was found near *Aquileia* and is dated before this city was taken by the Lombards *c.* 568–569. This unit was identified with the *Salii*, a palatine auxiliary from the first master of the soldiers present at Constantinople.³⁹ Another *auxilium palatinum* survived in the Exarchate of Ravenna around 710 where a late source mentioned it as *Bandus Invictus* a possible survival of the *invicti iuniores* which *c.* 400 were under the command of the master of the soldiers to Illyricum.⁴⁰

The late Roman Army also included a particular category of intervention troops, the strangely called *legiones pseudocomitatenses*. They were border troops with the lower pay of the *limitanei* but used in intervention. Some of these units persisted into the sixth century, probably not in status but only in name. For example, the Isaurian unit, Isauri, present from 444 to 491 in the city of Alexandria, included in its ranks the father of St Sabas of Palestinian origin. This was probably the former *Prima Isaura Sagittaria* that was under the master of the soldiers to the East.⁴¹ However, the numerical importance of the Isaurians at the start of the Gothic War in Italy suggests the existence of new Isaurian units, undoubtedly formed for the campaign.

Garrisoned in Arsinoe, the *Transtigritani* also formed a *legiones pseudocomitatenses* under the orders of the second master of the soldiers present *c.* 400. As their name indicates, the *Transtigritani* were originally native or stationed beyond the River Tigris, perhaps a former detachment of the *II Legio Parthica*. This unit left papyrological traces from 498 to 531.⁴² A series of *papyri* show an *arithmos* of *Theodosiaci* active in the *castrum* or castle of Nessana, Palestine, between 504 and 596. This may be the former

---

    BG, V, 23, 3 (Πῆγες).

38 *Notitia Dignitatum*, OR.V.64 (*auxilium palatinum* from the master of the soldiers); VIII.27 (*vexillatio comitatensis* from the master of the soldiers to Thraces); *CIL*, XI, 1693 = *ILCV*, I, 486; *ILS*, 2806 (Macrobius *primicerius* of the *primi Theodosianorum Numeri* [*sic*]). G. Ravegnani, 'Le unità dell'esercito Bizantino', p.194.

39 *Notitia Dignitatum*, OR.VII.10 = 51; G. Ravegnani, 'Le unità dell'esercito Bizantino', p.195.

40 *Notitia Dignitatum*, OR.IX.28 (*Invicti iuniores*); Andreas Agnellus of Ravenna, *LPR*, 1985, p.140 (Invictus).

41 *Notitia Dignitatum*, OR.VII.56. Cyril of Scythopolis, *Cyrilli Vita S. Sabae*, ed. Schwartz E., Leipzig, J. C. Hinrich Verlag, 1939, I p.87; IX, p.92; XXV p.109; G. Ravegnani, 'Le unità dell'esercito Bizantino', P.191.

42 *Notitia Dignitatum*, OR.VII.22 = 58. British Library, Papyrus 113 (5) = Wessely C. (1887, p.262 (498). Wessely C. (ed.), (1921, XX, 131, (508); XX, 139 (531). A. H. M. Jones, vol. 3 (1964), p 355. G. Ravegnani, (2005), p.191. A. Benaissa, 'The Size of the Numerus Transtigritanorum in the Fifth Century', *Zeitschrift für Papyrologie und Epigraphik*, 175 (2010), pp.224–226, ANNONAE IN A PAPYRUS REFERENCED AS P.CTYBR, INV. 3912(A) IN YALE UNIVERSITY).

Balistarii Theodosiaci originally a *legio pseudocomitatensis* under the second master of the soldiers present then stationed for a time in Illyricum.[43]

During the classical Roman Empire period, *vexillatio* alluded to an operational detachment drawn from several units. In the *Notitia Dignitatum*, *vexillationes* were simply elite cavalry troops led by the two masters of the soldiers present in senior command in the Eastern Roman Empire. The first controlled five *palatinae* and seven *comitatenses* units while the second had six units of each category – a total of 24 units.[44] The regional master of the soldiers had 19 *vexillationes*, 10 accompanying 'to the East', three palatine and four accompanying 'to the Thraces', two accompanying 'to Illyricum'.[45] The total was 43 vexillations.

Late Roman cavalry units continued to survive in Romano-Byzantine Army. As late as 488, the *Armigeri* were stationed at Oxyrhynchus on the Nile, 160km south of Cairo. The *Armigeri Seniores Orientales* was a *vexillatio comitatensis* (field vexillation), a cavalry regiment under the command of the master of the soldiers to the East.[46] There were originally nine units of Dalmatian cavalry but, around 400, only five remained, then under Justinian there were only two. The first was a field vexillation from the master of the soldiers to the east called the *Equites Tertio Dalmatae*, present in *Notitia Dignitatum* and in a Justinian Edict dated 535–536.[47] An Egyptian *papyrus* from June 547 mentioned Maximus, soldier from 'the unit (*arithmos*) of the very valiant Sixth Dalmatians', a probable reference to the *Equites Sexto Dalmatae* vexillation under the second master of the soldiers present at Constantinople.[48]

Except for the Batavians and Germanic tribes not precisely defined, the men forming vexillations all came from the Eastern Roman Empire or from its borders. However, it must be remembered that the adjectives

---

43 *NOTITIA DIGNITATUM*, OR.VII.21 (BALISTARII THEODOSIACI)=57 (BAL. THEODOSIANI IUNIORES, LEGIO PSEUDOCOMITATENSIS IN ILLYRICUM). C. J. Kraemer (ed.), *Excavations at Nessana, III, Non-literary papyri*, Princeton NJ: Princeton University Press, 1958), NR. 14–30; G. Ravegnani, 'Le unità dell'esercito Bizantino', P.191.

44 *Notitia Dignitatum*, OR.V.27–32 (*vexillationes palatinae*) and 33–40 (*vexillationes comitatenses* of the master of the soldiers Present I); OR.VI.27–33 (*vexillationes palatinae*) and 34–40 (*vexillationes comitatenses* under une command of the master of soldiers Present II).

45 *Notitia Dignitatum*, OR.VII.24–34 (*vexillationes comitatenses* of the master of the soldiers to the East); VIII.24–27 (*vexillationes* of the master of the soldiers to Thraces); IX.18–20 (*vexillationes comitatenses* of the master of the soldiers to Illyricum).

46 *Notitia Dignitatum*, OR.VII.26. *P. Oxy.*, XVI, 1888; G. Ravegnani, 'Le unità dell'esercito Bizantino', P.191.

47 *Notitia Dignitatum*, OR.VII.27; G. Ravegnani, 'Le unità dell'esercito Bizantino', p.191.

48 *P. Cairo*, II, 67126, 7. *Notitia Dignitatum*, OR.VI.37 (*Equites Sexto Dalmatae*); G. Ravegnani, 'Le unità dell'esercito Bizantino', p.189.

Germanicus or *Persicus* in Roman tradition also designated a military leader or a unit that had defeated one of these peoples. At the tactical level, 13 vexillations were of ultra-heavy cavalry of the *cataphractii* or *clibanarii* type, six of heavy horsemen called *scutarii*, because they were equipped with shields, and six of mounted archers.[49] By the 570s–580s, the *Strategikon* spoke of *bixellationes*, a Greek deformation of the Latin *vexillationes*. These were only the horse units responsible for defending the first line left flank, but it cannot be determined whether this was reality or a mere wishful thinking of its author.[50] Some vexillations from the later Roman Empire still existed at the beginning of the seventh century, such as that of the *Comites Sagittarii Armeni*. Around 400, this cavalry unit was under the orders of the second master of the soldiers present. A *papyrus* dated 22 November 639 mentioned a certain Paulacis, *Miles Numeri Arminiorum*, (soldier of the Armenian troop) who donated to the church of Ravenna. He was the son of Stephen, *Primicerius* from the *Veronenses*. A later *papyrus* dated to 700 reported the presence in Ravenna of this *Numerus Armeniorum* (unit of the Armenians).[51]

In the *Notitia Dignitatum*, the ultra-heavy horsemen known as *clibanarii*, fully armoured on armoured horses, were also to be found in vexillations. However, while the *cataphractarii* and *clibanarii* were highlighted in fourth-century sources, nothing of the sort occurred afterwards. Only one unit continued under this name between 487 and 546, that of *Leones Clebanonarii*, also known as *Leontoclebanonarii*. This unit did not exist in the *Notitia Dignitatum* and so must have been raised later.[52] It was stationed at Arsinoe with the *Transtigritani* and the ex-palatine legion of the Dacians, with whom it seemed to form a strong intervention group.

A vexillation plus another intervention troop originating from late Roman Army still existed in 949 on a role from the *Thēma Thrakēsion* (theme of the Thraces). They were two squadrons, in Latin the *Theodosiaci* and *Victores*, or in Greek *Theodosiakoi* and *Biktores*. They were then under a squadron leader called *tourmachēs* (tourmarch).[53] The former unit was created by Emperor Theodosius I (379–395) and the *Notitia Dignitatum* mentioned two palatine vexillations of Theodosian Horsemen: The *Seniores* under the second master of the soldiers present, and the *Iuniores* bound to

---

49 Ph. Richardot, *La fin de l'Armée Romaine*, p.275 (types of late Roman cavalry units).
50 Maurice, *Strategikon*, II, 6, 23 ; III, 8, 4 (bixellationes, βιξελλατίονες).
51 *Notitia Dignitatum,* OR.VI.31 (*Comites Ssagittarii Armeni*). P. Ital., I, 22 (mention of Paulacis, his father and their respective units) and 23 (new mention about this very unit); G. Ravegnani, 'Le unità dell'esercito Bizantino', p.194.
52 J. M. Diethart, P. Dintsis, 'Die Leontoklibanarier. Versuch einer archäologisch-papyrologischen Zusammenschau', Βυζάντιος. Festschrift für Herbert Hunger zum 70. Geburtstag (Vienna: E. Becvar, 1984), pp.67–84; G. Ravegnani, 'Le unità dell'esercito Bizantino', p.191.
53 W. Treadgold, *Byzantium and its Army*, pp.97–100. (θέμα Θρακησίων, Θεοδόσιακοι, Βίκτορες τουρμάρχης).

the master of the soldiers to the Thraces. Only the *Iuniores* survived. The latter surviving unit was referred in the *Notitia Dignitatum* as the *Iuniores Victores*, an infantry *auxilium palatinum* under the first master of the soldiers present.[54] Both units were elite troops the reason for their survival across some five centuries.

During the later Roman Empire, only elite mobile forces, generally two to four units gathered in some sort of brigade, intervened in depth to block run-of-the-mill barbarian raids but, in 363, to confront the immense invading army of Persia, Julian mobilised a great part of the eastern border troops.[55] By the time of Justinian, intervention units of a duchy could assist another duchy. In 527 Kouzes and Bouzes 'leaders of the troops in Lebanon', in fact the Dukes of Phoenicia and of Syria, on the orders of the Emperor moved to reinforce Belisarius who, according to Procopius, was then 'commander of the troops of Dara' or Duke of Mesopotamia.[56] C. 400, some 15 units of *Illyriciani equites* (Illyrian horsemen) were stationed in the East: three each to the Dukes of Phoenicia and of Osrhoene, five to the Duke of Syria, four to those of Palestine and Mesopotamia. At the time, these Illyrians had no recognised tactical specificity, except those qualified as *scutarii*. Their name of Illyrians did not necessarily prove their ethnic origin since some of the units were also called 'Moors'. During the 570–580s, Maurice considered the *Illyrikianoi* as elite cavalry worthy of holding the right of the first line.[57] They held the most exposed position in the line, given only to the bravest. In the 630s, a cavalryman from the Illyrian Fifteenth *Bandon* was known to have spent his winter quarters in Caesarea of Palestine.[58] These examples argue in favour of the survival of some or all of the 15 Illyrian frontier squadrons inherited from the later Roman Empire.

It is difficult to pinpoint the origins of the *Optimatoi*, Greek version of the Latin *optimates*, literally 'the Best'. It was a Byzantine novelty but with a Latin name. These elite cavalrymen in *c.* 600 had a number of special privelges: their *moirarchs* were called *taxiarchs*, the *armatos symmachos* (armourer) of an *optimatos* was called *hypaspistēs* or *hypaspist* (squire), an honorific rank that was also found among the *bucellarii* and their *banda* could exceed 400 men, unlike the others. These were elite troops who fought in the second line just in front of the baggage and were grouped into *decarchies* of seven men, two of whom were squires.[59] It was up to them

---

54 *Notitia Dignitatum*, OR.V.63 (*Victores Iuniores*); VI.33 (*Equites Theodosiaci Seniores from the* master of the soldiers Present II); VIII.27 (*Equites Thodosiaci Iuniores* from the master of the soldiers to Thraces).

55 Ph. Richardot, *La fin de l'Armée Romaine*, pp.65–67, (brigades); 68–70 (invasion of Persia).

56 Procopius, *BP*, I, 12, 24 (Belisarius in command of Dara garrison); 13, 5 (Kouzes and Bouzes).

57 Maurice, *Strategikon*, II, 6: III, 8; VI, 3.

58 *Acta Sancti Anastasii Persae*, 26.

59 Maurice, *Strategikon*, I, 3, 23 (taxiarch, ταξίαρχος plural ταξίαρχοι); 24 (armatos

to deliver the final blow in a charge. Subsequently, they were sometimes confused with the Gothograikoi, or Gothogreeks, who mutinied in 715 with the soldiers of the *Opsikion* theme.[60] Their units persisted throughout the military history of Byzantium, but lost their prestige of the centuries.

Frontier Troops

'Those who once ruled over the Romans had stationed large numbers of soldiers to guard the borders of the Empire, particularly in the East, to contain the invasions of the Persians and Saracens. These soldiers were called border guards.'[61]

The border guards, also called *limitanei* in the *Justinian Code* and *limitanaioi* in Procopius, were inherited from the late Empire or even from older units. Justinian treated them with a great negligence, only paid their pay four or five years late and no longer paid them when peace returned, then removed from them the qualification of *strateia* (regular troops) and relegated them to begging.[62] Bitter words from Procopius, but in the end little is known about them, because there are few examples of units that have survived.

Several Greek *papyri* reported units in Egypt and Thebaid. *Sarapiôn stratiôtai arithmou* (Soldiers from the unit of Sarapiôn) were quoted in 507 during Anastasius' reign and garrisoned in the city of Antinoe/Antinoopolis. There were three places named *Serapeum* in Egypt, temples dedicated to the God of medicine Serapis, including two in Alexandria and one in Saqqara.[63]

A very incomplete document from late sixth century referred to the *Arithmos Ba(bylonios?)*. This unit was from Babylon of Egypt on the Nile Delta named *Babilona* in the *Notitia Dignitatum* and sheltering the *Legio Tertiadecima Gemina* under the count of the Egyptian frontier.[64] Other *papyri* dated mid-March 573, 7 September 577, 581 and 20 September 585 were concerning four soldiers of the unit from Syene in Thebaid (today Aswan). They probably came from the unit of miliary soldiers and the fifth cohort of Syenians garrisoning this locality c. 400. A late sixth-century *papyrus* mentioned two centurions, two soldiers, an ordinary, an ex-vicar and an *adiutôr* from the legion of Syene.[65] They were two different Flavios

---

symmachos, ἁρμάτος σύμμαχος, plural ἁρμάτοι σύμμαχοι); 25 (hypaspistes ὑπασπιστής plural ὑπασπιστές); 4, 24–25 (*bandon*); II, 6, 29 (2nd line); 30–31 (seven men per decarchy as following: 5 στρατιῶται and 2 ἁρμάτοι).

60   Theophanes Confessor, *Chrgr.*, AM 6027, 218.
61   Procopius, *Anecdota*, XXIV, 12 (λιμιτάναιοι).
62   Procopius, *Anecdota*, XXIV, 13–14.
63   *P. Brit.*, III, 992, 4 (Σαραπίων στρατιῶται ἀριθμοῦ).
64   *P. Brit.*, V, 1735, 23–24, 26–27 (ἀριθμός Βα[βυλώνιος?]). *Notitia Dignitatum*, OR.XXVIII.15.
65   *P. Brit.*, V, 1722, 59 (a. 573, Flavios Paeiôn son of Psachos); 1723, 27 (a. 577, Flavios

(Greek version of Flavius, 'sir') Paeiôn and two Flavios Pathermouthis only distinguished by the name of their father. This clearly suggests local and family recruitment, especially as the Patermouthis family had a strong presence in Thebaid. The soldier Flavius Patermouthis the son of Menas left numerous papyrological traces between 581 and 613. In 581, he belonged to the Syene Legion, but was later described as a 'soldier of the Elephantine unit' in Thebaid. This unit was a continuation of the 'First Happy Theodosian cohort' stationed at Elephantine.[66]

(H)ermopolis was the garrison of a Moorish unit from 340 to 538 under the Duke of Thebaid. The *Notitia Dignitatum* located at Lico/Lyco a *cuneus*, or wedge, of *Equites Mauri scutarii* but was also referring at Ermopolis to another frontier troop called the *Cuneus Equitum Schtariorum*.[67] These units seem to have continued service into the Byzantine period.

Some border troops took part in campaigns and even in major battles. During the Battle of Solachon against the Persians in 586, a border guard showed heroic courage when mortally wounded. He belonged to the *Quartoparthians* unit from the *legio quarta Parthica* created by Diocletian and stationed at Circesium around 400. Two centuries later, the *Kouartoparthoi* were garrisoned at Beroea of Syria (Aleppo) and became a part of the campaign army raised by Philippicus.[68] Theophanes mentioned the *Lykokranitai* stationed in Phrygia and accompanying Belisarius in May 529 to counter a Bedouin raid. According to Procopius these *Lykokranitai* were Pisidians and their name came from a mountain in their country called *Lykou Kranos* (Wolfhead). They were light mountain troops, capable of chasing the Isaurian bandits. A mosaic found at Mount Nebo in Jordan shows a foot spearman wearing a Phrygian cap, a reddish tunic and

---

Patermouthis son of John); 1726, 5–6 (a. 581, Flavios Pathermouthis son of Menas); 1731, 43–44 (a. 585, Flavios Paeiôn son of Dios soldier from the unit of Syene, qualified as στρατιώτης ἀριθμοῦ Συήνης). P. Monac., 8, 41 (κεντυρ(ίων) λεγ(εῶνος) Συήνης) and 45; 43–44 (soldier, στ(ρατιώτης); 46 (ordinarios, ὀρδ(ινάριος); 47 (ex-vicar, ἀπὸ βικαριανῶν); 50 (adiutôr, ἀδιούτ(ωρ). Notitia Dignitatum, OR.XXXI.35 (*milites Miliarenses*, Syene); 65 (*cohors quinta Suentium*); G. Ravegnani, 'Le unità dell'esercito Bizantino', p.193.

66   *P. Brit.*, V, 1724, 6, 31 (a. 578–582); 1727, 4, 62, 74 (a. 583–584); 1729, 7, 16 (12 March 584); 1730, 6, 31 (22 août 582); 1732, 1 (16 August 586); 1734, 32 (late sixth century); 1736, 4, 21, 35 (25 February 611); 1737, 4, 6, 28 (9 February 613, Flavios Patermouthis son of Menas, στρατιώτης ἀριθμοῦ Ἐλεφαντίνης). Notitia Dignitatum, OR.XXXI.64 (*Cohors Prima Felix Theodosiana apud Elephantinem*).

67   *Notitia Dignitatum*, OR.XXXI.23 (*Cuneus Equitum Maurorum Scutariorum*, Lico); 24 (*Cuneus Equitum Scutariorum, Hermupoli*). J. Maspéro, *Organisation militaire de l'Égypte Byzantine* (Paris: Champion, 1912), pp.142–143; G. Ravegnani, 'Le unità dell'esercito Bizantino', p.192.

68   *Notitia Dignitatum*, OR.XXXV.24 (duchy of Osr(h)oene, prefect of the *Parthica IV legio* at Circesium, *Praefectus legionis Quartae Parthicae, Circesio*).Theophylact Simocatta, *HU*, II, 6, 1–9 (heroic death) and 9 (Κουαρτοπάρθοί); G. Ravegnani, 'Le unità dell'esercito Bizantino', p.190.

Sixth-Century *Lykokranitai* Light Infantry
This hunter attacking a lion is sometimes associated with the *Lykokranitai* light infantry unit, but this is purely speculative. The tunic is reddish, the trousers are saffron yellow with beige stripes, the Phrygian cap is also saffron but with a blue cockade, the curved shield is carmine red while the interior is dark, the iron boss has a spike, the spear butt is an iron counterweight. After the mosaic from Diakonikon Baptistery, Mount Nebo, Jordan.

yellowish stripped trousers. Only the Phrygian cap presumably links it to *Lykokranitai*, and it may have be that the figure is simply a hunter.[69]

The eastern *limitanei* were able to resist locally but with the exception of the larger tows and cities where the population helped them, their garrisons were too small to stop a mass invasion. In 540, when Khosrow I invaded Osrhoene and then Syria, he delayed two days at the small stronghold of Sura. The garrison resisted for one day but its commander was killed by an arrow. The next day the bishop opened negotiations and the Persians took the opportunity to force the gate. The city was razed, not only because it was the first to resist but also because many Persian nobles had been killed in the action of the previous day. The garrison commanded by Arsace the Armenian was perhaps the heir of the *legio XVI Flavia Firma* which occupied the city around 400. This episode shows combative *limitanei* as long as their commander was alive but thet were quickly discouraged after his death.[70] Another episode demonstrates that the Persian invasion from

---

69 Procopius, *BG*, VII, 27, 20. Theophanes Confessor, *Chrgr.*, AM 6021 (Λυκοκρανιταί). Raffaele D'Amato, *Roman military Clothing (3): AD 400–640*, Men-At-Arms, 425 (Oxford: Osprey Publishing, 2005), pl. F2, p.46.

70 *Notitia Dignitatum*, OR.XXXIII.6 (*castellum*) and 24 (*Praefectus legionis Sextaedecimae Flaviae Firmae*). Procopius, Procopius, *BP*, II, 5, 8–33.

the 610s had not completely dislocated the network of late Roman border guards, this was that of the 60 martyrs of Gaza where *c.* 638 the *banda* of the *Scythians* and the *Voluntarioi Bandon* were based. In the late Roman Army, only two troops of *Scythici milites* existed but they were located on the Danube under the duke of Scythia, but they could have been afterwards reassigned to the East.[71] Like this Scythian unit, the border guards could therefore be transposed from one border to another if necessary. The cohorts of the so-called 'volunteers' had been created by Augustus in 6 from released or freed slaves. The *Notitia Dignitatum* mentioned only the *cohors VIII Voluntaria* stationed at Ualtha, a place identified by archaeology with the fort of Khirbat az-Zuna, less than 150 kilometres from Gaza and whose Byzantine occupation ended *c.* 640.[72] A 630-year existence is something to blow the mind. The system of border guards thus persisted in the East until the Arab conquest.

John Malalas reported an event *c.* 530, when Justinian garrisoned soldiers recruited from the Italians, but called *Hispani*, in the port of Bosporos on the Black Sea (ancient Panticapaea and present-day Kerch in Ukraine). The fact that a unit was called *Hispani* but was composed of Italians is not surprising in military history which shows many similar examples. Moreover, in Roman military history there are frequent cases of units stationed very far from their original recruitment area. The *Ala Secunda Hispanorum* at the beginning of the fifth century was under the orders of the duke of Thebaid and stationed in Poisariemetidos (probably Speos Artemidos - cave of Artemis – I the current Egyptian village of Istabl Antar). This unit was perhaps the Hispanics unit of which Malalas wrote and which was massacred by the Huns.[73] There remains, however, the objection: why and how recruiting Italians into this unit was possible when Italy had not yet been reconquered? But the answer is quite simple: even today, the French Foreign Legion recruits from all over the world without the need for France to conquer the other 147 countries. In the case of sixth-century Ostrogothic Italy, the profession of arms was reserved for the Ostrogoths themselves; an Italian who wanted to follow a military career had only the

---

71 J. Pargoire, 'Les LX soldats martyrs de Gaza', *REB*, 50 (1905), pp.40–43 (the source was a Latin text mistranslated from Greek from a list with the 60 martyrs' names: Sildevandus Citon = scilicet de vandu Sciton = ἐκ βάνδου Σκυθῶν; Devandus, Rolus, Tarisius = de vandu Voluntariorum = ἐκ βάνδου βολυνταρίων). *Notitia Dignitatum*, OR.XXIX.22 and 24 (duc de Scythie); XII, Maurice, *Strategikon*, XI, 2 (Chapter entitled 'Fight the Scythians. That is, Avars, Turks and other peoples whose way of life resembles that of the Huns').

72 *Notitia Dignitatum*, OR.XXXVII.33; C. Zuckermann, 'L'armée', p.163 (some thoughts about this unit). P. M. Michele Daviau, J. R. Chadwick, M. Steiner (eds), 'Excavation and Survey at Khirbat al-Mudayna and Its Surroundings: Preliminary Report of the 2001, 2004 and 2005 Seasons' in *Annual of the Department of Antiquities of Jordan* 50, (2006) pp.249–283 (about the Khirbet fort).

73 *Notitia Dignitatum*, OR.XXXI.43 (*Ala Secunda Hispanorum Poisariandemidos*, duchy of Thebaid). John Malalas, *Chrgr.*, XVIII, 14.

option of joining the Romano-Byzantine Army, whose working language he already spoke. When Italy became an Imperial possession again, the need to guard the reconquered lands prompted troops of border guards to leave their Danubian garrison. This may have been the case in 710 for the *Bandus Novus* stationed in Ravenna, which was probably the remnant of two border infantry units from Moesia, the *Milites Nouenses* and the *Auxiliares Nouenses*, which were raised in Nova (now Svichtov in Bulgaria).[74]

The relationship between these frontier troops and the local populations was nothing if not variable. In 528, the passage between Persian Iberia (Georgia) and Romano-Byzantine Lazica was guarded by natives living in two fortresses. When the Emperor had them replaced with soldiers, the local population stopped supplying the garrisons, who deserted, and the Persians took advantage of the situation to cross the border. This episode took place in a territory that was poorly Romanised, not to say hostile, but it demonstrated the dependence of the border guards on the natives for food in the absence of state supplies.[75] A law dated 9 April 542 ordered the count of Armenia Third to control the soldiers of his territory and to ensure that they did not oppress the subjects of the Empire. The Armenia Tertia was a part of Armenia Secunda renamed after Justinian I's provincial reorganization in 536 - its other name was Hexapolis (Εξάπολις). However, this brutal attitude was not common to all border guards. Indeed, an edict addressed to the prefect of the Eastern Court concerning the city of Alexandria and Egypt, dated about 538–539, reminded the military tribunes that if they did not force taxpayers to pay their tax, their property would be confiscated and the whole troop would be sent to guard the Danube border.[76] Such an edict clearly showed that Egypt was a quiet area compared with the Danube, which was presented as a sanction where, nevertheless, the links between the troops and the population could be strong.

Around 593, a fine-looking garrison was holding the town of Asemus on the Danube in Moesia, (now Osma Kalugerovo in northern Bulgaria). When Peter the Kouropalates, Master of the Soldiers to the Thraces, wanted to incorporate it into his field army, the garrison barricaded itself in the town church. Peter vainly asked the bishop to bring them out, and then just as vainly he sent the infantry general Gentzon to carry out this task. He then charged a *scribon* of the Imperial Guard with the same mission. The population roughly expelled this officer, closed the city gates, heaped insults on Peter the Kuropalates and, out of prudence, sang praises to the Emperor. Thus their insubordination did not appear to be a crime of lèse-majesté, but a legitimate protest against the arbitrariness of a general who was after all the brother of Emperor Maurice. Peter the Kuropalates did

---

74 *Notitia Dignitatum*, OR.IX.28 (Invicti iuniores); OR.XL.23 (milites Nouenses, Transmarica, Moesia II); XLI.23 (*auxiliares Nouenses, ad Nouas*, Moesia I). Andreas Agnellus of Ravenna, *LPR*, 1985, p.140 (Invictus, Novus).
75 Procopius, *BP*, I, 18–19.
76 *Edict.*, 13, 11, 1.

not insist and continued his journey towards the enemy. A threatened city in the heart of the Balkans had preferred to keep its garrison rather than remain unprotected. For its part, the garrison, already present in a local fortress by 400, had forged solid links with the population.[77]

After the northern Balkan invasion by Sklavenes and Avars (581–615), followed by the Arab conquest of southern Asia Minor (635–641), the old *liminatei* system collapsed. These lost provinces accounted for two-thirds of the units listed in the *Notitia Dignitatum*. The only parts of the Roman-style border troops that probably survived were in Thrace, Armenia and Africa.

The Justinianics and The New Border Guards, Units of The Later Empire Pattern

The reconquest of Africa and Italy extended the borders and required an increase the numbers of border guards. Justinian I created for Africa new units of border guards called *limitanei* following the title of the later Roman Empire. In 534 Justinian ordered Belisarius that: 'In addition to the *comitatenses* [field] troops, *limitanei* [border] troops were stationed in the forts to defend them and in the cities to cultivate the fields.' Justinian recommended that Belisarius recruit them from among capable provincials and those who had been soldiers there. It was necessary that: 'The dukes and the border guards can hold their positions themselves without the help of the field soldiers.'[78] Field troops were qualified as *milites* (soldiers) but the border guards were not, whom the state wanted to also make peasants in an obvious desire to save on their food. As Justinian planned to restore the Roman Empire to within its old borders, it was not surprising that border guard units were recreations of defunct units.

The epitaph of the Senator Maxentius, who died at Hippo aged 70 some time after the middle of the sixth century, revealed that he had served in the *Numerus bis Electorum*, perhaps a reference to the *Numerus Electorum* which had existed in Numidia and Caesarean Mauretania at the time of the Principate. Nevertheless, the *bis* attested to the creation of a second unit of this name. It has been transferred to Antaiapolis in Thebaid, where its full name was put on *papyri* dated between 539 and 552 as the *bis Electi Iustiniani,* in Greek *Biselektoi* or *Bisilektoi Ioustinianoi*.[79] Among the troops of the garrison of Oxyrhinchus in Egypt were the *Salonitae*, a military unit not otherwise known apart from the fact that it was created after 400 in

---

77 *Notitia Dignitatum,* OR.XII.19 (Asemus). Theophylact Simocatta, *HU*, VII, 3, 1–10.
78 *CJ,* I, 27, 2, 8.
79 D. Dana, 'Onomastique et recrutement', pp.156–157). *P. Stras.* K 283b (c. 539/540); *P. Caire,* II, 67139 V (c. 543–544); SB, XX, 14494 (C. 546/548); P. CAIRE, I, 67058 I (VERS 540/550); I 67057 I AND II (C. 551/552), (ΒΙΣΕΛΕΚΤΟΙ ΟΥ ΒΙΣΛΕΚΤΟΙ ΊΟΥΣΤΙΝΙΑΝΟΙ).

Salona, the capital of Dalmatia. As Dalmatia was outside of the Eastern Roman Empire between 481 and 536, the date of the Justinian reconquest, and since Salona was sacked by the Avars in 615, the creation of the unit of the *Salonitae* could fit into this interval, Justinian's reign being the most likely time.[80] A troop of this type, called the *Numerus Militum Sermisiani*, was stationed in Ravenna in the late sixth century as a *papyrus* about a soldier, Dominic, confirmed it. Towards the beginning of the following century, a *papyrus* concerning an *optio* called George enabled it to be located in Rome. The origin of this troop cannot be determined: Sirmium in Pannonia, Sermitium in Liguria?[81]

In Italy, where there were many cities, permanent garrisons were also necessary. In 540 the capture of Ravenna by Belisarius and that of Classis, its military and commercial port, led to the creation of a new troop, the *Ravennenses* mentioned in a *papyrus* from 568 which placed them very far from Italy under the orders of the Patrician Athanasius, Duke of Thebaid alongside, at the same time, Goths, probably ex-prisoners of war. It was an intervention unit that could be moved according to the strategic needs of the Empire, a detachment of which was dispatched to Thebaid. Indeed, an Italian *papyrus* from 10 March 591 revealed that the unit was still stationed in Ravenna. John, soldier of the unit of the *Numerus Felicum Ravennatum* [*sic* Felicium], bought land in the Ravenna region from another soldier (and his wife) called Tzittane, or Zittane (Zittas?) of the *Numerus Felicum Persoarminorum*. Another *papyrus* evoking a *Primicerius Num(eri) Rav(ennatis)* of *c.* 700 shows that the unit still existed in what had become the Exarchate of Ravenna.[82] Tarvisium, (present-day Treviso) also had a troop created for its protection, the *numerus Tarvianus*, or *Tarbisianus*. These 'Trevisans' are known thanks to the votive inscription of Zimarcus: *Primicirius Nomiri (sic* for *Primicerii Numeri) Tarbisiani votum solvit* (Zimarc [a Thracian name] *primicerius* from the unit of the Trevisans fulfilled his vow). This unit is attested as well by another inscription from Stephen, soldier, *milis* (*sic*). It was raised before the years 568–569, when Treviso was surrendered by its Bishop to Alboin, King of the Lombards. Grado, the town where the votive inscriptions of Zimarc and Stephen were found was probably their new garrison in the late seventh century.[83] Rimini,

---

80   G. Vitelli, M. Norsa and *alii, Papiri greci e latini,* III (Florence: Felice Le Monnier, 1914), p.247; G. Ravegnani, 'Le unità dell'esercito Bizantino', p.192.

81   *P. Ital.* I, 17 (*Dom(i)nicis*) (;27 (*Georgius*); G. Ravegnani, 'Le unità dell'esercito Bizantino', p.202.

82   *P. Ital.*, I, 23 (*primicerius*); II, 37 (John and Zittan). *Papiri greci e latini*, VIII, Florence, 1927, 953, 35. R. Rémondon, 'Soldats de Byzance d'après un papyrus trouvé à Edfou', *Recherches de Papyrologie*, I, (1961), pp.41–93; G. Ravegnani, 'Le unità dell'esercito Bizantino', p.198.

83   *CIL*, V, 1503 = *ILCV*, 1, 559 = I, *Aquileia*, II, 3344 (Zimarc, *n. Tarvianus*); *CIL*, V, 1614 = *ILCV*, 1, 488 A = *AÉ*, 1981, 33 (Stephen, *n. Tarbisianus*). Paul Diacre, *HL*, II, 12 (fall of Treviso); G. Ravegnani, 'Le unità dell'esercito Bizantino', pp.195–197; *Id.*, (2007), pp.527–529. G. Ravegnani, 'Soldati di Bisanzio in Italia nelle epigrafi

liberated by Belisarius, lost then reconquered by Narses the Eunuch in 549, was ruled by a Duke to whom Pope Gregory wrote in 591. Rimini had its garrison under the command of the *exarch* of Ravenna so that the city fell into the hands of the Lombards. A *Numerus Ariminensium* was mentioned in the garrison of Ravenna in the late seventh century.[84] Verona, taken from the Goths in 562, was taken by the Lombards in the 570s. An urban garrison was established there during this decade; the *Veronenses* was later mentioned in an act of donation on a *papyrus* dated 22 November 639 by its *primicerius* Stephen. The *Veronenses* became part of the Ravenna garrison, where the *papyrus* was written.[85]

A *papyrus* dated around the year 600 reported a donation of land by Adquisitus, *optio* of the troop of *Numerus Vict(ricium) Mediol(anensium)*. Milan was razed by the Goths in 539, taken over by Narses the Eunuch in 559, hence the name *victricium* (victors), and then fell to the Lombards in 569. Nevertheless, the Lombards seem to have allowed the Imperial soldiers to leave Milan for Ravenna.[86] When the Lombards took Padua in 601, they also allowed the Romano-Byzantine troops to go to Ravenna.[87] As capital of the exarchate in Italy, its garrison comprised elite and traditional units such as the troop of the Armenians and the troop the *Numerus Armeniorum* and the *Numerus Felicium Theodosiacum* whose presence was attested between the years 600 and 700. There also remained from late Roman period the so-called *laeti*. These were originally Germanic colonists settled in Roman territory, with the responsibility of cultivating it in exchange for military service. The *Notitia Dignitatum* located them in Gaul but the document we have today is quite incomplete and some *laeti* could have been installed in northern Italy, such as in the colony of Taivola. These *laeti* probably placed themselves in the service of the Ostrogoths, similar to those Roman units which, keeping their standards and their traditions, according to Procopius still fought for the Franks and the Armoricans.[88] The *Laeti* are known five times in the Romano-Byzantine Army. The first occurrence is from Genoa, the *Felices Laeti*, thanks to funerary inscription dated to 591 left by the soldier Magnus. They are also known thanks to *papyri*: one also dated 591 written in the harbor of Classis, and then by others from the second half of the seventh century which located them in Ravenna, after the loss of Liguria to the Lombards *c.* 641.[89] The *Laeti*, a former frontier troop formed initially

---

del VI secolo in G. Cresci Marrone', A. Pistellato, *Studi in ricordo di Fulviomario Broilo*, vol. 2 (Padova, S.A.R.G.O.N., 2007), pp.527-529.

84 Andreas Agnellus of Ravenna, *LPR*, 1985, nr 64. Gregory the Great, *Registrum Epistolarum*, I, 56; G. Ravegnani, 'Le unità dell'esercito Bizantino', p.201.

85 *Notitia Dignitatum*, OR.VI.31. *P. Ital.*, I, 22 (Paulacis, his father and their respective units) and 23 (new mention of this unit). Paul the Deacon, *HL*, II, 14 (Verona fell to the Lombards); G. Ravegnani, 'Le unità dell'esercito Bizantino', p.194.

86 *P. Ital.*, I, 20; G. Ravegnani, 'Le unità dell'esercito Bizantino', pp.198–199.

87 Paul the Deacon, *HL*, IV, 23.

88 Procopius, *BG*, V, 12, 16–18.

89 *CIL*, V, 2, 7771 (inscription *mil. nome. elicilando* falsely restitued as *miles numeri*

by barbarians, was now a regular garrison and an intervention troop on the new Byzantine model. Its members were no longer distinguished from other Romans.

Agnellus of Ravenna, who died in 846, drew up in his *Annals* a list which gave the order of battle of the garrison in 710, with the names of 11 units, most of which had existed since the late sixth century: 'Each soldier was distributed according to his weaponry and his unit, that is to say: Ravenna, First Band, Second Band, New Band, Invincible, Constantinopolitan, Those Standing Firmly, Happy Ones, Milanese, Veronese, from Classis.... and this order persists until today [ninth century].'[90] From this list, the Armenians, Theodosians and Sermisians have disappeared. This is also the case for a troop which was neither referenced in the *Notitia Dignitatum* nor with Agnellus, but which was garrisoned in Ravenna, the *Argentenses* whose *Primicerius* John donated to the church on 22 November 639. This unit may have been created after 400 in *Argentina* (today Srebrenica in Bosnia).[91] The early Byzantine Ravenna garrison was at first composed of intervention troops from the Eastern Roman Empire but new border units were created during the period of the conquest. After the loss of Milan and Verona their garrisons were withdrawn back to Ravenna.

Five units of Vandal cavalry, called *Vandali Iustiniani*, were sent to Byzantium and then distributed to the cities of the East.[92] The long war in Italy provided its share of Ostrogoths to Justinian's army. During the expedition, in *c.* 536/537, Narses the Eunuch campaigned against Philae in Egypt, he received three newly created units, the *Bis Electi Iustinani*, or *Bisilektoi*, with so-called Roman personnel, plus the *Numidae* and the *Scythae* all qualified as *Iustinianoi* recruited from Moorish and Ostrogothic former prisoners of war. The Justinianic *Numidae* were stationed in Egypt at Ermopolis, with a strength of 508 men according to a *papyrus*.[93] In the *Notitia Dignitatum*, the generic term 'Scythian', qualifying them as Goths, was attributed to units under the Duke of Scythia on the Danube.[94] The

---

Illyricianorum but corrected as *miles numeri felicium Landorum*) = ILS, I, 550 (Magnus, soldier in Genoa). *P. Ital.*, II, 37 (John was an *adorator* in the *Ravennates* unit, then in the *Felices Laeti*: qui *nunc milex (sic) numeri felicum Lectum*, year 591, Classe). *P. Ital.*, I, 21, (dom(esticus) num(eri) fel(icum) landon(um), mid-seventh century, Ravenna); 24, (dom(esticus) num(eri) fel(icum) land(orum), mid-seventh century, Ravenna); G. Ravegnani, 'Le unità dell'esercito Bizantino', p.200.

90 Andreas Agnellus of Ravenna, *LPR*, 1985, p.140 (*Unusquisque miles secundum suam militiam and numerum incedat, id est: Ravenna, Bandus Primus, Bandus Secundus, Bandus Novus, Invictus, Constantinopolitanus, Firmens, Laetus, Mediolanensi, Veronense, Classensis... And haec ordinatio permanans usque in praesentem diem*); G. Ravegnani, 'Le unità dell'esercito Bizantino', p.200.
91 *P. Ital.*, I, 22; G. Ravegnani, 'Le unità dell'esercito Bizantino', p.201.
92 Procopius, *BV*, IV, 14, 17–18 (*Justinianic Vandals*, Ἰουστινιανοὶ Βανδίλοι).
93 *P. Caire*, III, 67321 (strengths of the Νουμίδαι Ἰουστινιανοί). *P. Brit.*, V, 1663, 5, 18 (payment of *annona*, sixth century); G. Ravegnani, 'Le unità dell'esercito Bizantino', p.186; D. Dana, 'Onomastique et recrutement', p.157, (both units).
94 *Notitia Dignitatum*, OR.XXXIX.24 (*Milites Scythici* garrisoned at Dirigothia).

new 'Justinianic Scythians' garrisoned in Antaion or Antaiopolis (now Qaw el Kebir), probably after the diocese of Thebaid was reformed in 539. With the *Bisilektoi* they replaced a troop of Macedonians attested there before this date according to several *papyri*, probably a detachment from the V Legion Macedonia under the orders of the military count of Egypt and stationed in Memphis about 400. Additionally, in the late sixth century, several *papyri* alluded to 'the troop of Antaiopolis' not otherwise defined but probably related to the previous Macedonians.[95] The 7,000 strong Ostrogothic garrison of Compsa was sent complete to Byzantium after Compsa surrendered in 555.[96] They were probably split into various units to avoid any subsequent problems.

Only known by epigraphy, the *Numerus Devotus* was a testimony to this Romano-Byzantine habit of employing defeated troops in regular units. Indeed, a funeral inscription in Italy dated 561, at the very end of the Gothic War, bore the eminently Gothic name of Totila and was *milix (sic) de Numero Devote* (soldier of the devoted troop).[97] The Ostrogoths from Italy, whose Kings had done everything to maintain the Roman administration and monuments, were at that time a Latinised military elite and no longer the itinerant barbarians that they were a century before.

After Belisarius' victory over the Persians in 541 he enlisted a *Numerus Equitum Persoiustiniani* of Persians. Procopius mentioned them three times: the unit was 800 horsemen garrisoned at Sisauranon and commanded by Bleschames, after their surrender they were brought to Byzantium with their leader then transferred to Italy, finally the Armenian officer Artabazes took them back to Byzantium.[98] Traces of the unit have been found on a mosaic in the church of St Euphemia in ancient Gradum (now Grado) in Italy. The town, taken from the Ostrogoths in 540, was more firmly occupied from 550 onwards. A *Persoiustiniani* soldier made a dedication there in 579, at the time of the Lombard invasion. The same mosaic also identified the *Numerus Cadisianum*, the *Cadiseni/Kadiseni* were an eastern people and subject people of the Persians.[99] The same mosaic also cited the *Numerus Tarvianus*, or *Tarbisianus*, unit mentioned above. The presence

---

95 *Notitia Dignitatum*, OR.XXVIII.14 (*legio quinta Macedonica* at Memfi). *P. Caire*, I, 67 057, 8 (ἀριθμός Σκυθῶν); II, 67 002, 12 and 67 005, 23 (Macedonians garrisoned at Antaiopolis). *P. Brit.*, V, 1711, 69, 73, 86, 90, 91; 1844 (unit at Antaiopolis). J. Maspéro, (1912), pp.143–144; G. Ravegnani, 'Le unità dell'esercito Bizantino', p.192.

96 Agathias, Hist., II, 13, 4 (7,000 Gothic army at Compsa); 14, 7 (surrender).

97 *CIL*, VI, 2, 32967 = *ILS*, I, 529; G. Ravegnani, 'Le unità dell'esercito Bizantino', p.198.

98 Procopius, *BP*, II, 19, 3 (800 horsemen led by Bleschames in garrison at *Sisauranon*); 24–25 (sent from Byzantium to Italy); *BG*, VII, 3, 10–11 (Artabazes).

99 *CIL*, V, 1, 1591 = *ILCV*, I, 558 = *ILS*, I, 2810 (soldier from *Persoiustiniani*). *CIL*, V, 1, 1590 = *ILCV*, I, 546 = *ILS*, I, 2808 (*n. Cadisianus*). Procopius, *BP*, I, 14, 38–41 (Kadisenes); G. Ravegnani, 'Le unità dell'esercito Bizantino', pp.195–197; *id.*, (2007), pp.527–529.

of these three units in the same place shows that they were no longer ad hoc improvisations but regular troops. There is every reason to believe that more than 30 years after their creation, the *Persoiustiniani* and the *Cadiseni* no longer had anything Persian or Cadisenic about them. When Persarmenia was taken by the Romano-Byzantines in 571, it was probably an opportunity to create one or more new units. An Italian *papyrus* from 591 supports this hypothesis by attesting to the existence of a troop called, in the best Roman military tradition, *Numerus Felicum Persoarminiorum*. This was a contract between the Persoarmenian soldier Zitttan and a soldier from the Ravennate unit.[100]

The *Bucellarii* – the taste for Personal Guards

Richly dressed and armed, guards surround the general. A stroke of defiance and pride pierces under their eyes. Since the beginning of the fifth century, there were bodyguards called *bucellarii* in Latin, or in Greek *boukellarioi*; literally 'biscuit-eaters' as *buccellatum* was a twice baked military bread, a kind of biscuit. Olympiodorus recorded them twice during Honorius's reign (395–423): 'In the time of Honorius the name *bucellarius* was given not only to Roman soldiers but also to certain Goths.' The historian says that dry bread is called *bucellatum* and uses it as the scornful nickname for the soldiers, who are called from it *bucellarii*.[101] This nickname went to private military companies which reflected the privatisation of security and society.[102] In the West, they were probably a Roman copy of the Germanic retinues.[103] Early Byzantine *bucellarii* were chiefly recruited from among the warlike peoples of the Empire (Isaurians, Thracians, Besses, Dalmatians and Armenians) but also from among the barbarians. Two categories were known: the provincial watchmen and the personal guards for generals.

Bucellarii serving as watchmen existed in Egypt according to the *papyri*. They were raised by wealthy landowners to defend not only their lands but an entire district. A contract of sworn service or *sacramentum* linked the *bucellarius* to his employer. The Imperial state tirelessly fought this trend for more than a century. Laws of the *Theodosian Code,* repeated in the *Justinian Code*, prohibited private militias. From 394, the law punished with a fine of five pounds of gold anyone who employed a soldier as or in a *privatum*

---

100 *P. Ital.*, II, 37 (John and Zittan). Hoffmann D., Der 'numerus equitum Persoiustinianorum' auf einer Mosaikinschrift von Sant'Eufemia in Grado, *Aquileia Nostra*, 32/33, 1961–1962, pp.81–98; G. Ravegnani, 'Le unità dell'esercito Bizantino', p.198.
101 Olympiodorus, *Fragm.* 7.4 and 12 (Βουκελλάτον the biscuit; βουκελλάριος, plural βουκελλάριοι). J. Gascou, 'L'institution des bucellaires', *BIFAO*, 76, 1976, pp.143–156. A. P. Kazhdan et al (eds), 'Boukellarioi', 1991, vol. 1, p.316.
102 Ch. Lécrivain, 'Les soldats privés au Bas-Empire', *MEFR*, 10 (1890), pp.267–283.
103 H. H. Diesner, 'Das Bucellariertum von Stilicho und Sarus bis auf Ætius (454–455)', *Klio*, 54 (1972), pp.321–350.

obsequium (private guard). In 468, Leo I fined owners who maintained a militia composed of armed slaves, henchmen (or *satellites* in Latin) and Isaurians. The situation worsened, and in 542 Justinian had to punish with a fine those who employed deserters, both soldiers and *foederati* 'who fight for the freedom of *res publica* (public affairs)'.[104] Nevertheless, the *bucellarii* were not considered as such prohibited private militias. Because the state transformed this feudal tendency into an obligation for landowners or tax colleges to comply with the old law on the *hospitalitas* (hospitality of soldiers) imposed from fourth century. This law initially required the provision of fire, water and food to passing or garrison troops.[105] Around 400, the *Comites Catafractarii Bucellarii Iuniores* were under the authority of the master of the soldiers to the east.[106] This nearly regular unit was probably paid directly by a tax college.

In Egypt, a century later, provincial *bucellarii* were organised by 'tents', received state wheat rations or *annonae*, had wives, children and servants. Thus, they were not the property of those who paid and fed them, as their sponsors had to put them in the service of the state. *Bucellarii* were requisitioned to escort tax collectors, maintain public order or combat looters.[107] Competition could arise with the regular troops. By the 530s the *Transtigritani* unit stationed at Arsinoe in Egypt complained bitterly that the *bucellarii* of the powerful Apion family had stolen all of wheat rations from the village of Kerkē.[108] Their unit numbers in Egypt were small: 28, 29, 30, 35 and 50 men.[109] A *papyrus* from Oxyrhynchus in Egypt has revealed a pay list dated from 28 September to 27 October (the month of *Phaophi*) 612, with 32 cavalrymen and 26 infantrymen described as *bucellarii*. They were for the most part recruited locally from Upper or Lower Egypt but some were quite distant origins: 5 Romans (Latin speakers or inhabitants of Rome?), 2 Goths, 1 Cilician, 1 Ascalonian (from Ascalon in Palestine), 1 Armenian, 1 Persian, 1 'from the Oasis', 1 Saracen and 1 Slav very far from his homeland.[110] Small troops of provincial bodyguards did not have the same political significance as the vast retinues gathered around generals.

Having a personal guard was a mark of social status and a Roman tradition for generals and Emperors. Valerian Master of the Soldiers to Armenia joined Italy with a personal guard of more than 1,000 in 549, while

---

104 *C.Th.* VII, 1, 15 included in *CJ*, IX, 12, 10 (law of 468); XII, 35, 13 (law from December 398). *Nov. J.*, 116 (law from 9 April 542).
105 *C.Th.* VII, 8, 5.
106 *Notitia Dignitatum*, OR.VII.25. Ph. Richardot, *La fin de l'Armée Romaine*, p.120.
107 J. Maspéro, (1912), pp.68, 140.
108 J. Gascou, 1976, p.148 after the Berlin papyrus n°836 (Kerkē incident); 152 after *papyri*: *P. Oxy.* 2046 (organisation in tents); *P. Oxy.*, 1920, 2046, *PSI*, 953 (wifes, children and servants).
109 *P. Oxy.*, XVI, 2480, 3–4 (28 *bucellarii*); XVI, 2046 (29 *bucellarii*); XVI, 1903 and 2480, 85 (30 *bucellarii*); XXVII 2480, 68–9, 75 and 80 (35 *bucellarii*); XVIII, 2196r (50 *bucellarii*).
110 N. Gonis, 'Payments to Bucellarii', pp.175–192.

Belisarius had 7,000 horsemen in 540. It is not surprising that 21 percent of the military names cited by Procopius were *bucellarii*.[111] Furthermore, these elite troops played a considerable role in operations to the point that, during the first siege of their city by the Ostogoths in 537–538, the inhabitants of Rome had the impression that the victory was due only to Belisarius' personal guard. The following year, Belisarius had only 11,000 men to take Osimo, with the *bucellarii* certainly forming three-quarters of this force.[112] However, a general-in-chief did not have complete control over them, since this personal guard swore an oath not only to him but also to the Emperor.[113] Procopius reported: 'Now for a very long time it was the custom of all the Romans never to have any one appointed as an officer of the personal guard of any official, until they had first made him swear the most solemn oaths, and had obtained from him every assurance of his loyalty to that official, as to the Emperor of the Romans.'[114] Losing one's personal guard was therefore a clear sign of Imperial disgrace. This is what happened to Belisarius during his disgrace in 542. His personal guard was shared among the palace eunuchs by lot. He himself went about almost alone, 'like a simple individual.' A powerful man of this time was always protected by an armed escort. Senior officers also had their own *oikia* (house) a term understood militarily in the same way as the *Maison du Roy* during the French *Ancien Régime*, or the way that the British Horse and Foot Guards were 'Household Units' - an extended personal guard.

Bucellarii were considered as horsemen by the *Strategikon* who described how to equip them: 'It is not a bad idea for *bucellarii* squadrons to use iron gauntlets and small tassels on the straps that hold the caparison to the front and back of the horse, as well as small flames that hang on their shoulders over the mail.'[115] The iron gauntlets, literally *cheiromanika sidēra* (iron hand protection), are attested from archaeology and reveal a heavily armoured horseman. The *phlamoula mikra* (small flames) were the pennons attached to the lances and the strips of a banner. Four centuries later, they were called *phlamouliskia mikra* as ornaments covering the shoulders on the body armour or *zaba*.[116] They might have been shoulder ribbons, like the 'goose's feet' in civil and military fashion under Louis XIV. It could, perhaps more classically, be bands of coloured leather protecting the shoulders as on the breastplates from the Hellenistic and Roman eras. Another decoration,

---

111 Procopius, *BG*, VII, 1, 20 (7,000 horsemen); 27, 3, 1,000; D. A. Parnell, 'A Prosopographical Approach to Justinian's Army', p.14 (percentage).
112 Procopius, *BG*, VII, 1, 21 (inhabitants of Rome); VI, 23, 5 (army led by Belisarius at Osimo).
113 Procopius, *BV*, IV, 18,6.
114 *CJ*, IX, 12, 10 (Leon I); *NJ*, 30, 7 (Justinian); Procopius, *BV*, IV, 18, 6 (oath to the Emperor).
115 Maurice, *Strategikon*, I, 2, 22–26 (equipment); 23 (χειρομάνικα σιδηρᾶ); 23–24 (μικρὰ τουφία) 24–25 (φλάμουλα μικρά).
116 Leo VI the Wise, *Taktika*, VI, 3, 24 (φλάμουλα μικρά); 21, 123 (φλαμουλισκία μικρά).

this time reserved for *bucellarii*'s horses, was that their front and rear straps had to be trimmed with small tufts, *mikra touphia*, a term also used for the plume of the helmet. According to Maurice, this elegance was to give confidence to the soldiers instil fear in the enemy.[117] During the march of an army, he specified that the elite troops and the *bucellarii* were to form a guard of honour with the banners or *banda*, in front of the general. Just behind him followed the *spatharii*, and the troops of *bucellarii*.[118] In the various battles he fought, Belisarius assigned his personal guard the role of shock troops. This was particularly visible at the Battle of Trikamaron in 533, where he placed them in the centre with his banner and, under the command of John, had them lead the main assault without resorting to the infantry which had not even arrived on the field. Belisarius himself attended the battle with 500 cavalry as an escort.[119] He seemed to have more confidence in his *bucellarii*, whom he paid from his own money, than in the state troops, who were quick to mutiny as frequently they were unpaid – he was probably right.

The *bucellarii* had their own chain of command. Contemporary historiography translates as 'officer' and 'bodyguard' what Procopius called *doryphoros* (lance-bearer) and *hypaspist* (shield bearer). The context left no doubt that the *doryphoroi* were officers. During the Vandal War in 533, the *doryphoros* Diogenes was sent on reconnaissance with 22 *hypaspists* under his command while the *doryphoros* Uliaris led 800 *hypaspists* during the Battle of Dekimon.[120] The question arises of the origin of this terminology which had nothing Roman about it and was very anachronistic. In Homer's time, *hypaspists* were just servants at arms, squires in the medieval sense of the term. The meaning evolved and from 426 BCE it designated elite infantrymen. A century later, in the army of King Philip II of Macedonia they were just servants of the *phalangites*. Then they became armed servants and the best of them formed an elite royal troop who fought on the right under Alexander the Great. Around 326 BCE, the veterans were honoured by Alexander with the title of *argyraspides* (silver shields). Hellenistic Kings retained this large body of lighter infantry which formed the tactical link between the rigid phalanx and the mobile cavalry. By the second century BCE during the final battles when Macedonia was subjugated by Rome, some 3,000 to 5,000 *hypaspists* formed the elite of the army of King Philip

---

117 Maurice, *Strategikon*, I, 2, 25–27.
118 Maurice, *Strategikon*, I, 9, 29–33 (dispositions of a marching army). 31 (*banda*); 32 (*spatharioi*); 32–33 (rest of the *bucellarii*).
119 Procopius, *BV*, IV, 3, 5 (at centre with general's standard); 6 (500 horsemen); 10 and 12 (1st and 2nd attacks with few Belisarius' *hypastpists*; 13 (third attack with almost all the *doryopohoroi* and *hypaspists* of Belisarius, ξὺν πᾶσι σχεδὸν τοῖς Βελισαρίου τε δορυφόροις καὶ ὑπασπισταῖς).
120 (*Doryphoros*, δορυφόρος, plural δορυφόροι. *Hypaspistēs*, Ὑπασπιστής, plural ὑπασπισταί). *P. Oxy.* 1888 (papyrus). Procopius, *BV*, III, 23, 5 (Diogenes); 19, 23 (Uliaris).

V.¹²¹ Afterwards, during the Roman period the word *hypaspist* disappeared except in the books of Hellenic-speaking tacticians, coming back in the sixth century – some sort of Greek revenge on Roman culture. Tactically, Byzantine *hypaspists* were mounted spearmen. The use of this ancient word was a trait of Greek culture, heroic and backward-looking, just as the diffusion of the peltast in the classical age was a Homeric reminder.¹²² The term *hypaspist* therefore conferred a heroic companionship to one who had the privilege of being surrounded by a private guard.

Doryphoroi and *hypaspists* deserved these classic words because in difficult times they remained alongside with their general to the bitter end. During a cavalry encounter at the Milvian Bridge in 537, Belisarius, known for his white-fronted grey horse, was the target of the Ostrogoths:

> He himself turning from one side to the other, slaughtering all those who approached him, had great benefit from the loyalty of his *doryphoroi* and his *hypaspists* in this moment of peril. For they were all around him, and they were so valiant, I believe, that to this day they have never been. Holding their shields high to protect the general and his mount, they not only received all the missiles but repelled all the attackers.¹²³

The same year at Skalai Beteres, the Patrician Germanus fell after his horse was killed and his *doryphoroi* surrounded him, giving him another horse. A similar fate befell Solomon near Thebestē (modern Tebessa) in 544, but probably suffering from a broken limb he could not hold his reins, falling again he was killed by the Moors with many of his *doryphoroi*. The same tragedy occurred when the Herul General Fulcaris was trapped in Parma by the Franks in 553; only his bodyguards remained and all of them died with him, while the remainder of the army fled. Making a barrier of his body was not just an image. In 539, Unigast stopped an arrow aimed at Belisarius' abdomen by stopping it with his right hand, which remained permanently crippled. The bodyguards also proved to be exceptional combatants. Thus, during the defence of Ancona, around July 538, Ulimuth and Gubulgudu, respectively *doryphoroi* of Belisarius and of Valerian armed with swords repelled a mass of Ostrogoths, although they were seriously wounded.¹²⁴

From this manly behaviour we can deduce that a code of honour existed among these *doryphoroi*, who were not only devoted bodyguards but also leaders in battle. In 533, during a reconnaissance mission against the

---

121 E. M. Anson, 'Alexander's Hypaspists and the Argyraspids', *Historia*, 30 (1981), pp.117–120. E. Foulon, 'Hypaspistes, peltastes, chrysaspides, argyraspides, chalcaspides', *REA*, 98 (1996), pp.53–63.
122 J. E. Lendon, *Soldiers and Ghosts*, pp.103–110.
123 Procopius, *BG*, V, 18, 11–13.
124 Procopius, *BV*, IV, 17, 23 (Germanus); 21, 27–28 (Solomon); VI, 27, 13–15 (Ounigast); 13, 14–15 (Ancona). Agathias, *Hist.*, I, 15, 1–2 (Fulcaris).

Vandals, the *doryphoros* Diogenes commanded from the front, arms in hand and fought to free himself from encirclement and despite his shield, he was wounded three times in the face, in the left hand and almost fatally in the neck. The following year another *doryphoros*, Aigan the Hun, had to carry out a similar mission where, surrounded, he fought to the last arrow and then with his sword before succumbing to enemy blows. These dangerous reconnaissance missions corresponded to a modern rank of lieutenant or captain, but the *doryphoroi* could rise to more important commands, as was the case with Sittas and Belisarius. They could also be given temporary commands; when two, the Pisidian Principios and the Isaurian Tarnuntos, asked to command the infantry in place of the ordinary officers, whom they considered as cowards, Belisarius granted their request. They died covering the army's retreat during the Battle of the Field of Nero in 537.[125] Nevertheless, exceptions are needed to confirm the rules. The *doryphoros* Indulf otherwise named Gundulf, left behind in Italy after the departure of his master Belisarius, joined Totila, who made him a general and sent him to conquer Dalmatia. There he defeated an Imperial force at Laureate in 549. Abandoned on the spot, Indulf simply found another employer to earn his living.[126]

Their ability to serve a former enemy shows what the *doryphoroi* were: professional officers exercising tactical commands which correspond to a large variety of missions that in modern terms would be undertaken by a range of officers from lieutenant to general. Favour or experience rather than a formal hierarchy seemed to make the distinction. *Doryphoroi* recruited for Belisarius and his officers were from quite cosmopolitan origins: the most cited like Aigan, Aischmanos (Eichmann?), Bochas, Chorsomanos, Chorsamantis, Gubulgudu, Zarter and Oldagan were Huns, Artasires was Persian, Kutilas and Ulimuth were called Thracians but were probably Thracian Goths like Mundilas. Indulf and Uliaris had some Germanic origin, Paucaris was Isaurian, Trajan, Maxentius and Maxentiolus were certainly Illyrians.[127] The *bucellarii*, by their hybrid status of private troops taking an oath to the Emperor, are very likely close to today's *Blackwater* or *Wagner* PMCs which intervene alongside regular troops.

---

125 Procopius, *BV*, III, 23, 17 (Diogenes); IV, 10, 4 (Aigan); *BG*, V, 28, 23–29 (Principios and Tarnuntos); 40–43 (killed in action).
126 Procopius, *BG*, VII, 35, 23–27.
127 Procopius, *BP*, I, 16, 1; II, 26, 25–26; *BV*, III, 11, 7–9; *BG*, VI, 1, 21–34; 2, 9–10 and 20–24; 13, 12–15; VII, 30, 5–6 and 19–21. S. Janniard, 'Procope, les Huns et les transformations tactiques de la cavalerie romaine au VIe siècle' in G. Greatrex & S. Janniard (eds), *Le monde de Procope/ The World of Procopius* (Paris: O&M, 28, 2018), p.208.

The Strength of the Imperial Army

Nothing can be said for the 500–510s, but under Justinian, the army's strength was clearly insufficient.[128] Agathias gave a pessimistic report for the year 559:

> The armies of the Romans were no longer as numerous as under the ancient Emperors, and only a very small part remained which was no longer sufficient for such a vast Empire. When the total force would have had to reach 645,000 men, there were then barely 150,000. and among these, some were stationed in Italy, others in Libya, others in Spain, others among the Colchians, others in Alexandria and Thebes of Egypt; some on the eastern borders with Persia, where no more was needed, because the clauses of the treaties were rigorously respected. Thus, today their number had been reduced to a very small part and had declined due to the negligence of the rulers.[129]

This text corroborates the law of 566 in which Justin II accused his predecessor Justinian of having reduced the total strength of the army to 150,000 men.[130] On the other hand, historiography assumes a total strength of 379,300 men guesstimated for the year 565 after too much skilful equations.[131] As sources are insufficient, only comparative military history gives a shady approach to the total strength. In March 1815, the King Louis XVIII of France's army had an establishment of 149,000 men, but only 98,000 were in active service as a result of periodical leave, disease and desertion in a country of 20,000,000 inhabitants.[132] In January 2023, for a country of 67,000,000 people there were 190,170 service personnel in the UK forces while the full-time, trained strength of the army was 75,710.[133] But of this number only 25,000 might be real combat soldiers and not administrative or logistics personnel. Ruling over some 30–50 million subjects Justinian could have an army probably of around 150,000 soldiers with a comparable number of servants for them. Most of the troops were confined to garrison duties, hence the difficulty of forming an expeditionary force.

The distribution of the strength across the regions leaves only room for speculation and guesstimation. The few coastal pockets reconquered in Spain could not accommodate large garrisons. Italy by the time of Agathias

---

128 Procopius, *Anecdota*, XXIV, 6.
129 Agathias, *Hist.*, V, 13, 7–8.
130 Nov. J., 148. C. Zuckermann, 'L'armée', pp.162–163.
131 W. Treadgold, *Byzantium and its Army*, p.162.
132 A. Zeller, *Soldats perdus. Des armées de Napoléon aux garnisons de Louis XVIII* (Paris: Perrin, 1977), p.102.
133 https://lordslibrary.parliament.uk/size-of-the-army-numbers-tech-and-the-latest-on-the-integrated-review/

absorbed the bulk of the field army. In its geographical survey, Agathias has, strangely, omitted the Balkans, the most attacked sector and the shield of the city of Byzantium. The Near East was probably the biggest sector with 40,000 men. Others were 10,000–20,000 strong. However, these numbers have to be seen through the eyes of Byzantium' enemies. Before his victory at Dâthín and al-Araba in 634, Amir ibn al-As found the Imperial troops numerous and requested reinforcements from the Caliph Abu Bakr.[134] When Syria and Egypt fell, between 636 and 646, the Empire lost two large recruitment pools, the territorial base for about 200 Roman units according to the *Notitia Dignitatum*, or 40 percent of the seventh-century army. During his brief reign between 11 February and 23 April 641, Constantine III granted the army 2,016,000 *nomismata* as the traditional gift of advent, the *donativum*.[135] Historiography assigns conjecturally 5 *nomismata* per head plus pay which roughly fits with Agathias' estimate of the army's strength.[136]

Byzantium's core army relied on permanent units. The *Strategikon* refers to the usual combat unit by three terms, *tagma*, *arithmos* or *bandon*, led by a count or a tribune.[137] *Tagma*, plural *tagmata*, comes from the Greek verb *tassein* which means 'tidying up' or putting a troop in combat formation. This term was used for both cavalry and infantry.[138] Cavalry *tagma* was supposed to have 310 men according to the Maurice's *Strategikon*.[139] The Roman generic word for a military unit was *numerus* and its Greek equivalent was *arithmos* (number). Procopius also used the term *katalogos* (list).[140] The *Strategikon* clearly stated that the *arithmoi*, infantry units were not equal in number and that it was difficult to distribute them into subdivisions or *tagmata*.[141] This statement contradicts the equivalence between *arithmos* and *tagma* that had been established above, an ambiguity that still exists in modern military language when we speak of units. A standard military unit was called a *bandon*, plural *banda*, a name derived from the flag that guided it.[142] *Bandon* was exclusively used by Maurice for cavalry, but the infantry standard-bearer was described as '*bandophoros* or *drakonarios*'.[143] Modern French and English keep the meaning of 'band' but

---

134 Al-Baladhuri, *Kitab*, II, 1 (1916), p.167.
135 Nikephoros of Constantinople, *Brev.*, 29, 20–22.
136 R. P. Duncan-Jones, 'Pay and Numbers in Diocletian's Army', *Chiron*, 8, (1978), pp.544–545. W. Treadgold, *Byzantium and its Army*, pp.145–146 (estimation up to170 366 men after complex equalisation).
137 Maurice, *Strategikon*, I, 3, 15 (hierarchical equivalence of the three terms).
138 (Verbe τάσσειν, τάγμα, plural τάγματα). Maurice, *Strategikon*, XII, B, 4, 1 (equivalence for infantry of *tagma*, *arithmos*).
139 Maurice, *Strategikon*, III, 2, 1.
140 (*Arithmos*, plural *arithmoi* ἀριθμός, plural ἀριθμοί). Procopius, *BG*, VI, 23, 2 (κατάλογος, plural κατάλογοι).
141 Maurice, *Strategikon*, XII B, 8, 12–13.
142 Procopius, *BV*, IV, 2, 1 (βάνδον, plural βάνδα). A. P. Kazhdan, A. M. Talbot, A. Cutler, T. E. Gregory, N. P. Ševčenko (eds), 'Bandon', vol. 1 (1991), p.250.
143 Maurice, *Strategikon*, XII B, 7, 5. Assimilating *Bandon* solely to the cavalry for

in Spanish *bandera* retains the dual military meaning of flag and troop. An inscription found at *Pylai* in Byzantium, *c.* 531, quoted the *deuteron bandon Kônstantiniakon* who were known as *Milites Secundi Constantini(aci)* in the *Notitia Dignitatum*.[144] A *bandon* roughly equalled a cavalry regiment or an infantry battalion for both field and border troops. The episode of the 'Sixty Martyrs of Gaza' around 638 featured two *banda* of border infantry, Scythians and Volunteers descended from old Roman troops.[145] By the tenth century, five to seven *banda* formed a cavalry regiment called *tourma* since *turma* in Latin means 'squadron'.[146]

What was the size of these units? By the 490s, the Perge Legion numbered 1,245 officers and men.[147] The *Transtigritani* in 498 received some 1,335 *annonae* in wheat rations, which was consistent with 1,100 to 1,200 officers and men.[148] Procopius was realistic when dealing with military numbers and some examples permit assess to unit size.[149] The best known but not the clearest instance was Belisarius' army for Africa in 533. It comprised 15,000 soldiers and *foederati* distributed into 17 units, an average of 882 soldiers per unit.[150] In 542, during the Italian campaign, a 12,000-strong army was led by 11 *archontes* including two generals, a ratio of one senior officer for 1,000 men,[151] but some units had only half as many. The expeditionary force to Italy in 535 numbered 4,000 regular soldiers and *foederati* led by three cavalry and four infantry commanders, an average of 571 men per unit.[152] During the year 539, to take Fiesole Belisarius sent some Isaurians and 500 infantrymen from a regular unit called *ek katalogou*, led by Demetrios.[153]

---

    lack of other sources is a mistake made by Ph. Rance, 'Campidoctores Vicarii vel Tribuni', p.395 and n. 4.

144 OR.XXXIX.23 (*Milites Secundi Constantini*). (*AE*, 1995, 1427 (epitaph). C. Zuckerman (1995, pp.233–235.

145 J. Pargoire, 'Les LX soldats martyrs de Gaza', pp.40–43. A. P. Kazhdan, A. M. Talbot, A. Cutler, T. E. Gregory, N. P. Ševčenko (eds), 'Bandon' vol. 1 (1991), p.250.

146 A. P. Kazhdan, A. M. Talbot, A. Cutler, T. E. Gregory, N. P. Ševčenko (eds), 'Tourma' vol. 3 (1991), p.2100 (τούρμα).

147 F. Onur, 'The Anastasian Military Decree,' p.186.

148 NOTITIA DIGNITATUM, OR.VII.22 = 58. WESSELY G. (ED.), STUDIEN ZUR PALAEOGRAPHIE UND PAPYRUSKUNDE, LEIPZIG, 1921, XX, 131, (508); XX, 139 (531). A. H. M. JONES, VOL. 3 (1964), P 355; G. Ravegnani, 'Le unità dell'esercito Bizantino,'), P.191. A. Benaissa, 'The Size of the Numerus Transtigritanorum', PP.224–226 (ANNONAE IN A PAPYRUS QUOTED AS P.CTYBR, INV. 3912(A), YALE UNIVERSITY).

149 C. Whately, 'Some Observations on Procopius' Use of Numbers in Descriptions of Combat in Wars Books 1–7', *Phoenix*, 69, 3/4, (2015), pp.394–411.

150 Procopius, *BV*, III, 11, 2 (soldiers and *foederati*, *ek té stratiôtôn kaï phoidératôn*, ἐκ τε στρατιωτῶν καὶ φοιδεράτων); 6 (seven leaders for the *foederati*); 7 (four cavalry leaders, six for infantry).

151 Procopius, *BG*, VII, 3, 4.

152 Procopius, *BG*, V, 5, 2 (regular troops, *ek katalogôn* plural ἐκ καταλόγων; *foederati*); 3 (officers).

153 Procopius, *BG*, VI, 23, 2 (500 infantrymen form a regular unit, πεντακόσιοι πεζοὶ

This was very close to the fourth-century practice of taking 300 or 500 men from a unit to make special detachments.[154] Such a detachment was called vexillation in the Roman period. C. 548–550, the *Numidae Iustiniani* stationed in Ermopolis, Egypt, had, according to a *papyrus*, 508 men almost the equivalent of a cohort.[155] As numbers were generally lower for cavalry, the *Strategikon* advised: 'Make sure that each *bandon* has no fewer than 200 men and no more than 400.'[156] The pattern was close to the late Roman Army with 500 to 1,200 strong units.

Whatever its numbers were, the Imperial Army of Byzantium had a reputation of being a military superpower as stated by the Georgian Prince and historian Juansher Juansheriani (died *c.* 790) about the late fifth century. Vakhtang I Gorgasali is supposed to have said to other Kings: 'You know the great numbers in the Greek army and their menacing nature in battle and the swiftness of their ships. They invaded Persia, a country of knights and Goliaths, and the Persians were unable to withstand them.'[157]

ἐκ καταλόγου).
154 Ammianus Marcellinus, *RG*, XX, 4, 2; XXXI, 10, 13; 11, 12; Ph. Rance, 'Campidoctores Vicarii vel Tribuni', p.395.
155 *P. Caire*, III, 67 321.
156 Maurice, *Strategikon*, II, 20, 18–19.
157 Juansher Juansheriani (translated into English by D. Gamq'relidze), 'The Life of Vakhtang Gorgasali' in *Kartlis Tskhovreba. A History of Georgia*, Oxford Oriental Monographs (Tbilissi: Artanuji Publishing, 2014), p.90.

7

Mercenaries and Barbarian *Foederati*

> Do not believe that Huns, Lombards, Heruls who have put themselves in the service of the Romans for I do not know what pay will expose themselves to dangers to the point of death.
>
> Totila, King of the Ostrogoths, to his warriors, Procopius, *Bellum Vandalum*, VIII, 30, 18.

It was an old tradition from late Roman Republic to employ barbarian mercenaries with unique tactical abilities. Julius Caesar conquered Gaul with Balearic slingers, Numidian light cavalry and Germanic heavy cavalry. During the Principate this principle was standardised with the use of auxiliary units. At the time of Trajan, legionaries specialised in the assault of fortified places, while auxiliaries took on a large part of the pitched battle. This trend grew in the Western late Roman Army which recruited its best troops among the Germans, grouped in the *auxilia palatina*. On the other hand, the Eastern Roman Empire's troops cultivated a distrust of the barbarian auxiliaries from late fourth century, refusing to use them as a primary force but still using them. How did the Romano-Byzantines managed to reconcile this distrust with the utter need of barbarian mercenaries when the Western Roman Empire vanished for not having been able to do so?

The Mercenaries of the Empire: a New Concept of *Foederati*

In 542, to impress the new Persian Ambassadors, Belisarius had a tent pitched in the middle of a plain. He deployed Thracians and Illyrians on one side, and on the other barbarian mercenaries of Goths, Heruls and Moors. All were only dressed in linen tunics and armed either with a riding crop, a sword, an axe or even a bow without a quiver, as if they were hunting. The Persian emissaries were impressed by the handsome appearance of all these men and their very relaxed manner of behaviour in enemy territory.[1] The late Roman, then Romano-Byzantine Army no longer had permanent auxiliary units but preferred *foederati*, *phoideratoi* in Greek. The latter were originally barbarians from a people who had sworn a military agreement or *foedus* with the Empire and received land or tribute in exchange for service. They were, as Malchus of Philadelphia said, among 'those whom the Romans call *foederati*'.[2] Such was the original concept throughout the fourth and fifth centuries. According to Olympiodorus the meaning changed by the reign of Honorius: 'similarly the name of *phoideratoi* was given to a diverse and mixed body of men.'[3] Unlike the situation for other soldiers, according to a law dated 527 Goths could serve as *foederati* without professing the Orthodox faith, the only true faith as stated by the Council of Chalcedon. This notable exception was granted to them because 'by nature and by their history they have no spirit.'[4] It was true that as Arians the Goths were just heretics. Like Olympiodorus, Procopius explained the term's evolution:

> In the past, in fact, only barbarians were enlisted as *foederati*; even then, they were not men reduced to slavery – because they had not suffered defeat at the hands of the Romans – but people who were integrated into the Empire on a completely equal footing. The Romans called *foedera* the treaties they concluded with their enemies. Nowadays, however, anyone can claim to be a federate, and there's no reason why they should not, because time absolutely refuses to keep things as they are, and everything is constantly evolving at the whim of men, who disregard previous designations.[5]

The prosopographical study of soldiers shows that 39 percent of them bore names of barbarian origin.[6] Some of them adopted Roman names, as formerly auxiliaries had done. In Belisarius' army in 533, *foederati* leaders were either Greeks or had Greek or Latin names: Dôrotheos, general of the Armenian troops and Belisarius' second in command, Solomon, Cyprian, Martin, John, Marcel and Cyril. The Hun Althias was the only exception.[7] On the Heruls Procopius noted: 'some of them have even become Roman soldiers and serve among the *phoideratoi* as they are called.'[8] They were foreign troops belonging to the regular army, much like the Gurkhas of the

---

1 Procopius, *BV*, II, 21, 3–14.
2 Malchus, *Fragm.*, 15 (φοιδεράτοι).
3 Olympiodorus, *Fragm.* 7.4.
4 *CJ*, I, 5, 17.
5 Procopius, *BV*, III, 11, 3–4.
6 D. A. Parnell, 'A Prosopographical Approach to Justinian's Army', p.11.
7 Procopius, *BV*, III, 11, 5–6.
8 Procopius, *BG*, VII, 33, 13.

British and Indian Armies today. Procopius estimated the barbarians housed in Byzantium at 70,000, pointing out they caused much inconvenience to the civilians who had to host them.[9] This large force most probably included women, children and servants; for Byzantium was never able to send such a large body of barbarians into the field, and in the second half of Justinian's reign the city garrison was almost nil. Another figure that should be taken with caution, is that in 574, the Emperor sent 15,000 men to the East led by the Count of the *Foederati* Maurice, the future Emperor, supported by another general.[10] It would be wrong to assume from this episode the creation of the new cavalry corps identified with the *foederati* quoted in the *Strategikon*. This questionable hypothesis ignores the fact that Procopius stated these troops already existed in Justinian time.[11]

Barbarians were also hired from far outside the Empire as mercenaries paid only for a campaign. Thus in 535 when he was opening the Gothic War in Italy, Justinian ordered Constantine, Constable, *Comes Stabuli*, and head of Imperial security, to occupy Salona, the capital of Dalmatia but the latter recruited mercenaries from Illyricum because no troops were allowed to him.[12] The Huns fit into this category of extra-Imperial mercenaries.

The Huns

The Huns, coming from the Pontic steppes and the Caucasus were barbarians among the barbarians and restless enemies of the Empire but also its most efficient mercenaries. Huns, more probably proto-Bulgars to whom Procopius gave the archaic name of Massagetae were as frequently enemies as allies. The Huns did not form a single political entity but were divided into tribes, and the Byzantines could exploit that. In 551, to drive out the Huns Kutrigurs who were devastating the dioceses of Moesia and Thrace, Justinian paid the Utigurs to attack their territory, a ploy that succeeded too well, because driven from their land by the Utigurs, 2,000 Kutrigurs led by Sinnion, a former leader in the service of Belisarius, asked Justinian for land on which to settle as *foederati* with their wives and children. Justinian granted this to them.[13]

During the reign of Justin I, Probus was sent with money to the city of Bosporus on the Black Sea to recruit an army of Huns to fight in Caucasian Iberia. The prosopographical study of Procopius reveals that 19 percent of military names were Hunnic, forming the largest foreign contingent.[14]

---

9   Procopius, *Anecdota*, XXIII, 24.
10 Theophanes Confessor, *Chrgr.*, AM 6074, 252.
11 J. F. Haldon, *The Byzantine Wars*, pp.17, 61 (in favour of a new type of unit created in 577), 70 (use in 578).
12 Procopius, *BG*, V, 7 (26–29).
13 Procopius, *BG*, VIII, 18, 19–25. 19, 5–7 (lands granted to Sinnion Kutrigurs). Janniard S. (2018, p.207.
14 D. A. Parnell, 'A Prosopographical Approach to Justinian's Army', p.13.

More than their numerical weight, this proportion reveals their tactical effectiveness, which led Procopius to mention them more frequently than other foreign mercenary troops. They took part in most of the wars under Justin and Justinian, those of Lazica in 527, Mesopotamia in 530 against the Persians, the reconquest of Africa from the Vandals and Italy from the Ostrogoths.[15] The use of Hun officers and mercenaries in various theatres of war showed their military effectiveness. However, the generals of Byzantium did not like having strong single-nation contingents and preferred to bring together several barbarian nations. At the Battle of Dara in 530, 1,200 Hun horsemen were present, split into two forces led by Sunicas and Aigan, Simmas and Ascan along with the 300 Herul horsemen of Pharas. Three years later in Africa, a 'brigade' combined the 400 Heruls of Pharas with 600 Huns 'all horse archers' led by Sinnion and Balas.

In 535, only 200 Huns and 300 Moors were with Belisarius' army for Italy, the rest either remained in Africa or returned home. In 537 Martin and Valerian landed in Italy with a reinforcement of 1,600 horsemen mainly Huns, Antes and Sklavenes.[16] The size of a Hun contingent corresponded to a small or medium-sized cavalry regiment from between 200 and 600 men, and they fought in 70 to 80 man squadrons.[17] Getting military discipline from Huns was a difficult task for a Romano-Byzantine general. After the execution of two of their own people, the Hun mercenaries made it clear to Belisarius that they did not want to be subjected to Roman discipline.[18] Such friction at the start of a campaign was exceptional. The Huns influenced the late Roman cavalry with archery and the tactic of simulated flight, the joint use of one assault group with another one covering. This tactic of the defender and the runner was masterfully used in 537 during an ambush set by the Romano-Byzantines besieged in Rome against the Ostrogoths. The cavalry was split into two tactical groups of *cursores* and *defensores*, which literally translates as 'runners' and 'defenders'. The defenders were in a, more or less, static formation while the runners attacked and harassed the enemy then took refuge behind the defenders. One evening, an officer called Constantius went out of the city and put the Huns on foot along a street in the suburb known as Field of Nero to wait for the enemy:

> As the Massagetae [Huns] were excellent archers and they hit a compact crowd, they hit an enemy fighter with almost every shot.

---

15   Procopius, *BP*, I, 12, 6–9 and *BG*, IV, 11, 22–34 (Lazica); *BP*, I, 13, 19–21; 14, 37–50; 18, 35–42. John Malalas *Chrgr.*, XVIII, 50 and 60. (Pseudo-)Zachariah Rhetor, *HE*, IX, 3 (Mesopotamia); Procopius, *BV*, I, 11, 2–12; 12, 6–10; 17, 1–4; 18, 3 and 12–19; II, 1, 5–6 and 9–10; 2, 3; 3, 7 and 16 (Africa). *BG*, I, 5, 2–4; 27, 1–2 and 21–29; II, 1, 4–10; 2, 8 and 19–24; 4, 11–12 and 16–18; III, 6, 10; IV, 26, 13; 30, 18; 31 (Italy).

16   Procopius, *BP*, I, 13, 19 (300 Heruls)–20 (600 Huns); *BV*, III, 11 (400 Heruls and 600 Huns), 12 (Sinnion and Balas); *BG*, V, 5, 4 (200 Huns); 22, 27 (1,600 horsemen).

17   Procopius, *BV*, IV, 13, 2–3, IV, 27, 8.

18   Procopius, *BV*, III, 12, 10.

MERCENARIES AND BARBARIAN *FOEDERATI*

When the Goths realised they had lost half their strength and the sun was already setting, they fled in disarray. This led to the loss of many of them, for the Massagetae pursued them, and as they knew how to handle the bow at full gallop, they shot their enemies from the back.[19]

Huns had their warrior customs. Before going into contact with the enemy, by ancestral privilege, they allowed a young warrior to attack first. In 533 such a youngster approached to demand a single combat from the

Fourth to Sixth Century Hun Horse Archer
This horse archer is wearing a round cap, goat-hair trousers and loose boots, his face is scarified as Ammianus Marcellinus described the Huns in Book XXXI, 2, 2-6. The round cap is also attested by a fifth-century Bactrian statuette of an Alxon Hun rider from the Pritzker Family Collection, Chicago; which also shows the long sword and horse fittings. Shoulder decorations, earrings, necklace, and maybe the tunic's upper attachment are shown on Alxon or Alchon Hun coinage with the cranial deformation typical of the Huns from fourth to the sixth centuries. The haircut is from Procopius, long but with the temples clear. The non-symmetric composite bow typical of steppe and mongoloid peoples is found in Hunnic graves. Hunnic mercenaries of Byzantium may have looked like this.

---

19   Procopius, *BG*, VI, 5, 9–10.

Fifth to Seventh Century Hunnic Heads

Left, Scythian cap from a sixth or seventh-century funerary terracotta statuette (*mingqi*) of a Xiongnu rider, in the Karakorum Museum, Mongolia. The Latin expression *galeris incurvis*, from Ammianus Marcellinus, could designate a round (fur) cap or a shaped one. Right, cranial deformations are found on fifth to sixth-century skulls from Hun and Burgundian graves.

stunned Vandals. As the Vandals did not move, he returned to his people proudly announcing 'that a ready-made meal awaits them'. Like voracious hawks, the Huns dashed on the enemy who was utterly beaten.[20]

The Other Barbarians

The exotic side of barbarian mercenaries allowed chroniclers to describe them in more detail, as Agathias did for the siege of Phasis by the Persians in 556:

> In the middle, Angilas with Moors armed with shields and spears, Theodore with Tzani infantrymen, Philomathios with slingers and throwers with Isaurian javelins. A short distance from them, a detachment of Lombards and Heruls stood guard under the command of Gibros.[21]

The Lombards and the Moors were outside the Empire. Ildigisal was a Lombard from noble lineage who was garrisoned in Thrace with a personal retinue of 300 warriors from his own people and Justinian gave him the command of a *Schola Palatina*.[22] Some Lombards served as mercenaries in Italy with Narses the Eunuch who judged them undisciplined plunderers. He finally preferred to send them back under escort after defeating Totila in 552. Three years later they nevertheless provided small units in distant geographical areas, such as Phasis in Lazica, present-day Poti in Georgia.[23]

---

20   Procopius, *BV*, III, 18, 13–14.
21   Agathias, *Hist.*, III, 20, 9–10.
22   Procopius, *BG*, VIII, 27, 2 (*schola*); 3 (retinue).
23   Procopius, *BG*, VIII, 33, 2 (dismissed by Narses). Agathias, *Hist.*, III, 20, 10 (service in Eastern provinces).

MERCENARIES AND BARBARIAN FOEDERATI

The Moors, recently encountered and on the borders of the Empire, first served in Belisarius' army in Italy. Procopius noticed their efficiency at night sorties during the first siege of Rome in 537:

> Wherever the Moors found the enemies sleeping or moving in small detachments as often happens in an army in the necessities of service (for grazing horses, mules or cattle), they killed them and quickly stripped them. Then they withdrew at full speed before the enemy came running in greater numbers to attack them; because the Moors, lively by nature and lightly equipped, can outpace all of their pursuers.[24]

Peoples who submitted could also join the army. By 554 Goth defectors in Italy, such as Aligern, fought alongside Narses, and the remnants of the Vandals formed five cavalry units at the Battle of the Volturnus (or Casilinum).[25] Lazians were a vassal people who helped the Romano-Byzantines to halt the Persian invasion on their own land, Lazica. They were well-trained soldiers and their cavalry could dismount and fight in a phalanx formation alongside Imperial soldiers, as at the River Hippis in 550.[26]

Isaurians were rebellious Imperial subjects to whom Ammianus Marcellinus gave a reputation for banditry. They were barbarians within the Empire's borders, carried their native weaponry and a national (bad) temper. Isauria was a poor mountainous country on the southern coast of Asia Minor within the Mount Taurus region of present-day Turkey, and to its warlike people the Imperial Army was a resource. Throughout the third to fifth centuries, taking advantage of a rugged coast and the mountainous territory, they looted the surrounding areas. The regular army even had to intervene in 367 while the local 'police' forces had failed against them. In the following century they provided light troops to the Imperial Army, and the Emperors Zeno and Leo III were both Isaurians.[27] However, the Isaurians never lost their clan spirit, so during an urban revolt against Zeno, Isaurian soldiers built up a stock of torches and threatened to set fire to Byzantium if they were attacked.[28]

Losing influence after Zeno's death threw the Isaurians into a rebellion that lasted from 492 to 497.[29] Anastasius I then decided to use powerful

---

24 Procopius, *BG*, V, 25, 9.
25 Procopius, *BV*, IV, 14, 17 (Vandals). Agathias, *Hist.*, II, 9, 13 (Aligern).
26 N. Khoperia, 'The Byzantine Lazic Phalanx at the Battle of the Hippis River (550 CE)', *The Journal of Politics and Democratization-Online Publication*, 4/2, January (2020), p.18.
27 Ammianus Marcellinus, *RG*, XXVII, 9, 7; Ph. Richardot, *La fin de l'Armée Romaine*, pp.218 (367 campaign), 325 (enlistment).
28 Malchus, *Fragm.*, 22.
29 Marcellinus Comes, *Chr.*, a. 492.

resources against them: an entire army with Huns, Goths and Besses (actual Vlachs) under the Master of the Soldiers Present John Gibbo 'the Hunchback', supported by John the Scythian and the Patrician Diogenes. In 492, the rebels were crushed at the Battle of Cottiaeus, or Kotyaion, in Phrygia but took refuge in their mountains. Imperial troops ravaged the land, destroyed the cities and burnt the fortresses. In 497, Longinus of Cardala was the first Isaurian leader to be captured. Other rebel leaders were taken the following year. Among them was Conon, former Bishop of Apamea, Indes and Longinus of Selinus. The prisoners were sent to Byzantium to be exhibited at Anastasius' triumph, tortured and finally beheaded to the great enjoyment of a public audience – according to Marcellinus the rebel leaders' heads were displayed at a gate of the city of Niceae. After Theophanes Confessor only the rebel leaders' heads were sent to Byzantium and then paraded on stakes with Isaurian prisoners in chains.[30] No Isaurian unrest was subsequently reported. Like other tribal peoples on the edge of empires, Isaurians were poor, proud, bad tempered and with a strong identity. It was better paying them as soldiers than to leave them unemployed and have to fight them. Justinian understood that well, and Isaurians were among his best 'shock troops'.

Procopius always distinguished Isaurians from what he called 'Roman' troops. Isaurians were 2,000-strong in the Belisarius's 20,000 man Army of the East at the Battle of Callinicum in 531.[31] Four years later, they provided 3,000 men to Belisarius's expedition to Sicily out of a total of 7,500, or 40 percent of the Imperial troops, and 20 percent of the total if Belisarius's personal *bucellarii* are included. Two years later, among the reinforcements sent to Belisarius, the Isaurians numbered 3,000 men, more than half of the force, the other troops numbered only 2,600 regular cavalry. Procopius pointedly stated that in 541 Naples was defended by Romans and Isaurians.[32] The Gothic War was a period of full employment for Isaurians and they remained loyal as they were regularly paid. Already mentioned as slingers and javelin throwers, an episode from the Battle of the Field of Nero in 537 showed a man named Tarmout, who fought on foot, holding his two *akontia isaurika* (Isaurian javelins) one in each hand to pierce the enemy on one side or the other.[33] All this clarifies the Isaurians as light troops but, like the Moors, they were undisciplined if brave. During the siege of Phasis in 556, 200 Isaurians and Moors commanded by Angilas and Philomathios attempted a sortie against the orders of General Martin, but they were soon surrounded by Dilimnites, tribal warriors employed by the Persians, and

---

30 S. Williams & G. Friell, *The Rome That Did Not Fall*, p.114; Marcellinus Comes, *Chr.*, a. 498. Evagrius Scholasticus, *HE*, III, 35. Theophanes Confessor, *Chrgr.*, AM 5988, 140.
31 Procopius, *BP*, I, 18, 5.
32 Procopius, *BP*, I, 12, 5; *BG*, IV, 5, 2 (3,000 Isaurians, 4,000 Romans and foederati); V, 5, 4 (3,000 Isaurians and 2,600 horsemen); VII, 6, 1 (Naples).
33 Procopius, *BG*, V, 29, 42 (ἀκόντια Ἰσαυρικὰ).

they formed a defensive circle and managed to return to the city.³⁴ As a consequence, the Isaurians were indispensable but really could not be used as regular troops. Procopius criticised the military valour of Lycaonians, and of whom Malalas, who called them Phrygians, noted that they fled to Callinicum after the death of their leader and the capture of his banner by the Persians. They were followed, according to Procopius, by 'Roman Saracens', i.e. Saracens in Roman service from the Ghassanid tribe.³⁵

Procopius considered Armenians the way that he did Isaurians. During the Italian campaign he mentioned a certain Gilakios, in command of a group of his Armenian fellow countrymen, 'who did not speak Greek, neither Latin nor Gothic and no other language but Armenian.'³⁶ Nonetheless, Armenians could reach the peak of command and military fame – as Narses the Eunuch did. Their total number in the Imperial Army is quite difficult to assess. They were probably the main component among the 26 units, which numbered between 12,000 an 25,000 men, defending Armenia minor in the year 400. They were certainly involved in any war against Persians. Nevertheless, some Armenians participated in operations in other theatres, and they were present in Italy during the Gothic War.³⁷ A few Armenians deserters from the Persian Army served with the Romano-Byzantines and led by Artabanes and John, sons of John the Arsacids, were sent to Africa in 545 with Aerobindus the newly-appointed Master of the Soldiers to Africa. Artabanes and his men joined the usurper Guntharith but killed him. Artabanes was then appointed the new commander-in-chief to Africa.³⁸ In 547, an 800-strong Armenian contingent under Varazes command was committed to Italy with Valerian the Master of the Soldiers to Armenia and his 1,000 *bucellarii* probably from various origins.³⁹ In the 626 siege of Byzantium, Armenian soldiers played an important role in defending the north-eastern gate, but no numbers are available.⁴⁰

After being enemies of Byzantium, the Slavic Antes, from the 540s onwards became its mercenaries. In 547, around 300 Antes were fighting the Ostrogoths in Lucania in Italy. Procopius even praised their ability to fight in rugged terrain.⁴¹ Around 555, an Ante named Dabragezas was taxiarch, sharing with Usigardos the command of 600 'Roman' cavalrymen in Lazica.⁴² If all sources depicted the Huns as horsemen, this was not the case of the Antes and Sklavenes who are presented as light infantry armed

---

34 Agathias, *Hist.*, III, 22, 3–8.
35 Procopius, *BP*, I, 18, 36. John Malalas, *Chrgr.*, XVIII, 60.
36 Procopius, *BG*, V, 26, 24.
37 Procopius, *BG*, VII, 6, 10; 26, 24; 27, 3, 10 and 16.
38 Procopius, *BV*, IV, 24, 2 (sent as reinforcements); 27, 9 (rallied to Guntharith); 28, 6–30 (murder of Guntharith).
39 Procopius, *BG*, VII, 27, 3.
40 *Chr. paschale*, a.626, (2007), p.178.
41 Procopius, *BG*, VII, 22, 3.
42 Agathias, *Hist.*, III, 6, 9; 7, 2; 21, 6 (taxiarch). A. H. M. Jones, J. R. Martindale, J. Morris, *PLRE*, 3a, 1992, pp.378–379.

with javelins, bows and small shields but never with armour. Nevertheless, they seem to have had some sort of mounted infantry, moving on horseback but fighting as light infantry.[43] Seventh-century Anglo-Saxon graves, such as those on display in the British Museum may be evidence for mercenary service to the Byzantine Empire, but this is a hypothesis and is yet to be confirmed.

The Heruls in the Service of Byzantium

The Heruls were the most common *foederati* throughout the sixth century. In 509, after having temporarily subjugated the Lombards, they waged one war too many which resulted in them being almost exterminated and driven from their land.[44] They found refuge in Rugiland, then in the neighbourhood of the Gepids before being pillaged by them.[45] In 512 Anastasius I generously settled a group of Heruls in Pannonia, near Singidunum.[46] Their military strength was 4,500 warriors out of a population estimated to between 20,000 and 25,000.[47] These inconvenient migrants mistreated the Roman populations and Anastasius brought them to a peaceful attitude with the sword but, instead of exterminating them, offered the survivors the opportunity to serve him. Under Justinian, they received good land, became Christianised and mostly served with the Romano-Byzantines in their wars. The Heruls were not established outside the Empire but integrated within its border, and therefore strongly subject to its influence and culture, becoming provincials. Their morals, however, remained depraved according to Procopius.[48]

---

43 Procopius, *BG*, VII, 14, 25 (infantrymen without cuirass, with small shields and short javelins); Maurice, *Strategikon*, II, 11, 4; John of Ephesus, *HE*, III, 6, 25 (light infantry). John of Ephesus, *HE*, III, 6, 25. Theophylact Simocatta, *HU*, VII, 4, 11 (Slavic horsemen). Procopius, *BG*, V, 27, 1–2 (mercenaries in Byzantine service). M. Kazanski, 'La cavalerie slave à l'époque de Justinien', *Archaeologia Baltica*, 11, (2009), pp.229–239, Russian version, 'О раннеславянской коннице', *Stratum Plus*, 5, (2009), pp.457–471, study on Martin and Valerian's Slavic horsemen, archaeological evidence of horsemen in the sixth-century Slavs).

44 A. Sarantis, 'The Justinianic Heruli: from allied barbarians to Roman provincials' in Curta F. (ed.) *Neglected barbarians* (Turnhout: Brepols, 2011), pp.361–402.

45 Procopius, *BG*, VI, 14, 10–21 (war against Lombards); 24–26 (installation in Rugiland, Gepids).

46 Marcellinus Comes, *Chr.*, a. 512.

47 Procopius, *BG*, VII, 34, 42–43 (military strength). V. Ivanišević, M. Kazanski, 'Illyricum du Nord et les Barbares à l'époque des Grandes Migrations (V^e-VIe siècles)', *Starinar*, 64, (2014), p.147, installation in Singidunum and nearby fortresses and population).

48 Procopius, *BG*, VI, 14, 28 (welcomed by Anastasius); 29 (looting Romans); 30 (defeated by Anastasius); 31–32 (service offer, opinion of Procopius on Heruls); 33 (Justinian); 34 (christianisation and military help); 35 (national customs).

The Emperor also gave the Heruls Dacia and the city of, Singidunum in Northern Illyricum. From there, forgetting their oaths, some plundered Thrace and Illyricum and others, loyal, served as *foederati*.[49] On the two banks of the Danube between Singidunum and Viminacium, graves with weapon grave-goods testify to their presence: lenticular or laurel spearheads, arrowheads, ombons, shield handles, *spatha* swords, seaxes, more rarely Baldenheim type helmets or fragments of lamellar armour.[50] They provided bodies of 300 to 3,000 men to Justinian's army. After the Huns, they were the second most cited foreign contingent by Procopius in the armies, accounting for nearly 13 percent of military names.[51] Their Kings had a sense of propriety; c. 528, Grepes came to Constantinople to pledge his allegiance to Justinian and asked to be baptised. This was a reminder that he was there, ready to serve in a very feudal way.[52] One of their leaders, Pharas, wrote to the Vandal King Gelimer: 'We also come from noble families, and we are now proud to be in the service of the Emperor.'[53] Procopius did not think much of the Heruls, whom he thought were homosexuals, disloyal and drunkards, but he did justice to individuals. He even gave the desire of one Herul officer to be acquainted with Roman way of life:

> Aruth from the nation of Heruls, who since childhood admired Roman ways and had married the daughter of Maurice the son of Moundos, himself became a valiant warrior and brought with him a large number of Heruls who had distinguished themselves in the perils of war.[54]

At the Battle of Dara in 530 against the Persians, the Heruls, commanded by Pharas, held the extreme left position, hidden behind a hill.[55] It was not the position of honour, but their surprise attack on the Persians right wing was decisive. They thus played an important role in the field armies. Jordanes used them as lightly armed fighters during the Battle of Nedao.[56] Procopius confirmed this, even specifying that they suffered heavy losses from the Persian arrows:

> The Heruls have no helmets or breastplates and no armour of any kind, except a shield and a thick tunic, which they don before battle.

---

49 Procopius, *BG*, VII, 33, 13 (Singidunum); 14 (foederati).
50 I. Bugarski, V. Ivanišević, 'Sixth Century *Foederati* from the Upper Moesian Limes: Weapons in a Social Context' in S. Golubović, N. Mrđić (ed.), *Vivere militare est*, I (Belgrade: Institute of Archaelogy, Monographies, 68/1, 2018), pp.291–332.
51 D. A. Parnell, 'A Prosopographical Approach to Justinian's Army', p.13.
52 John Malalas, *Chrgr.*, XVIII, 6.
53 Procopius, *BV*, IV, 6, 15–34.
54 Procopius, *BV*, IV, 4, 29–30 (Pharas); *BG*, VIII, 26, 13 (Aruth).
55 Procopius, *BP*, I, 14, 33.
56 Jordanes, *Getica*, I, 261.

> The Heruls' slaves go into battle without even a shield and, when they prove their worth in war, their masters allow them to cover themselves with a shield. This is the way of the Heruls.[57]

Part of the Herul contingent sent to Africa with Belisarius was made of Arians, and therefore heretics in the eyes of Byzantium.[58] Paul the Deacon referring to an earlier period gave the following military portrait of them:

> It must be said that the Heruls were then experienced in military exercises and very well known for the bloody defeats they had already inflicted on numerous enemies. Either to lighten themselves, or out of contempt for the wounds they might receive from their adversaries, they fought naked, covering only their genitals. However, their slaves go into battle without even a shield, but when they have shown themselves valiant in battle, then their masters allow them to carry one in battle.[59]

Heruls fought on all fronts, in Persia, Italy, Africa and Thrace. The most unexpected front was that of the interior, where they helped to put down the bloody *Nika* revolt in 532. Narses the Eunuch won their confidence by leading them in a charge against the Persians. By spring of 539, when he lost the Imperial favour and left his command in Italy, they withdrew from the war, made an agreement with the Ostrogoths to sell their prisoners and have free passage further north. They even went so far as to swear never to fight them again, although they regretted the wrong done to the Emperor once they were back, and some went to Byzantium to apologise.[60]

Under the command of the Master of the Soldiers to Illyricum Vitalius the Heruls paid a heavy toll during the Battle of Treviso in 541. They sallied out the city of Treviso and were defeated by the ephemeral Ostrogothic King Ildibad. Visandus, the Herul leader and a trusted officer, was killed during this action while Vitalius fled.[61] In 547, the Heruls were divided into two camps: those loyal to the Empire with Suartuas and the vassals of the Gepids. The former provided 1,500 men to help an Imperial expeditionary force against the rebels who fielded 3,000 men. The two sides faced off in a pitched battle when Romano-Byzantine troops attacked the rebel Heruls with the Gepids inflicting heavy losses on them, including Aordus, brother of their King.[62] After this ordeal, the Heruls all returned to their allegiance

---

57 Procopius, *BP*, II, 25, 27.
58 Procopius, *BV*, IV, 14, 12.
59 Paul the Deacon, *HL*, I, 27–28.
60 Procopius, *BP*, II, 25, 20–26 (Narses the Persamenian in Persia); *BV*, VI, 22, 6–8 (Italy).
61 Procopius, *BG*, VII, 1, 34–35.
62 Procopius, *BG*, VII, 34, 41–45.

with Byzantium. In 552, they were again in Italy under the command of Narses the Eunuch, and were well disposed to him because he treated them well. Two years later, just before the Battle of the Volturnus, or Casilinum, Narses the Eunuch had one of their nobles executed for murder. As a result, they avoided the battle and their leader Sindual had to convince them to fight. They arrived late, but not too late, seeking to distinguish themselves by their courage and actions.[63] Subsequently, in the period 570–600, the historian Theophylact Simocatta, although prolific on the Balkan wars, no longer spoke of the Heruls, undoubtedly they had been annihilated by the Lombards and the Avars during the war of 567 which had also broken the Gepids. In Svetinja, in a fort located northwest of the Roman town of Viminacium, traces of occupation by a Germanic tribe *c.* 570–580 were found, probably from the last of the Heruls.[64]

Table 11 - Heruls in the Service of Justinian

Theatre Of Operations	Numbers/Leaders (underlined when Heruls)	Source
Persia 530	300 cavalrymen/<u>Pharas</u>	Procopius, *BP*, I, 13, 19; 14, 33 and 39
543	<u>Philemuth</u> and <u>Beros</u>	Procopius, *BP*, II, 24, 14 and 18
	Narses Kamsarakan	Procopius, *BP*, II, 25, 20
Byzantium, repression of *Nika* revolt 532 Byzantium 551	General of Illyricum Mundo	Procopius, *BP*, I, 24, 41
	<u>Suartuas,</u> military Governor of Byzantium	Procopius, *BG*, VIII, 25, 11
Africa 533-534	400/ <u>Pharas</u>	Procopius, *BV*, III, 11, 11
537	<u>Pharas</u>	Procopius, *BV*, IV, 4, 28-30; 6, 15
	Mutined with Stotzas	Procopius, *BV*, III, 17, 14-15
Italy 537	<u>Gontharis/Guntharith</u>	Procopius, *BG*, VI, 4, 8
538	2,000/ <u>Visandus, Aluith</u> and <u>Phanitheus.</u>	Procopius, *BG*, VI, 13, 18
	Army of Narses the eunuch	Procopius, *BG*, VI, 18, 6
	<u>Phanitheus</u>	Procopius, *BG*, VI, 19, 20
539	<u>Visandus, Aluith, Philemuth</u> and <u>Phanitheus</u>	Procopius, *BG*, VI, 22, 5-6
541	<u>Visandus</u> killed in action near Treviso	Procopius, *BG*, VII, 1, 34-35

---

63 Procopius, *BG*, VIII, 26, 17 (Narses). Agathias, *Hist.*, II, 2–7; 8, 6; 9, 7 (Capua).
64 V. Ivanišević, M. Kazanski, 'Illyricum du Nord', pp.147–148.

545	Army of Narses the eunuch Philemuth	Procopius, *BG*, VII, 13, 21-26
548	Arulf	Procopius, *BG*, VII, 26, 24
549	300 Verus Verus killed in action	Procopius, *BG*, VII, 27, 3; 37, 28
	1,500 Philemuth (3,000 with Gepids as foe)	Procopius, *BG*, VII, 34, 42 Procopius, *BG*, VII, 34, 43
550	Philemuth	Procopius, *BG*, VII, 39, 10
552	3,000 cavalrymen Philemuth and others including Aruth	Procopius, *BG*, VIII, 26, 13
	Army of Narses the Eunuch	Procopius, *BG*, VIII, 28, 10
	Battle of Taginae/Busta Gallorum dismounted as infantry with Lombards and unspecified barbarians in central position	Procopius, *BG*, VIII, 31, 5
	Besieged Rome under Philemuth	Procopius, *BG*, VIII, 33, 19
553	Philimuth/Philemuth killed replaced with Fulcaris Fulcaris killed at Parma	Agathias, *Historiae*, I, 11, 13; 14, 3-7 and 15, 1-5
	Aruth and Sindual candidates to their command	Agathias, *Historiae*, I, 20, 8
	At Volturnus/Casilinum shun the battle before being drawn back into it by Sindual	Agathias, *Historiae*, II, 7, 2-7; 8, 5-6; 9, 7
Persarmenia 543	Philemuth and Verus Battle of Anglon, right wing under Narses Kamsarakan	Procopius, *BP*, II, 24, 14 and 18 Procopius, *BP*, II, 25, 20-28
Gepids lands around Sirmium 548	1 500 Philemuth	Procopius, *BG*, VII, 34, 42
Lazica 550	Uligang fighting around Archeopolis	Procopius, *BG*, VIII, 9, 5; 13, 9
555 556	Uligang	Agathias, *Historiae*, III, 6, 5
	Defence of Phasis	Agathias, *Historiae*, III, 20, 10

MERCENARIES AND BARBARIAN *FOEDERATI*

Sixth-Century Herul *Foederatus*
This Herul warrior, like most Germanic infantry, is unarmoured, armed with a spear a round shield plus a *scramasax*-type sword. (After items in the Hungary National Museum for History, Art and Archaeology, Budapest)

The Purple was not fit for The Semi-Barbarian

Vitalian the Thracian was the great-grandson of Aspar the *Generalissimo*, Patrician and Consul. Flavius Ardabur Aspar, like Ricimer in the West, was an 'Emperor-maker', but unlike Ricimer, he was unable to control his puppet Leo I who had assassinated him in 471. His assassination may have saved the Eastern Roman Empire. According to Count Marcellinus, Vitalian was nicknamed Scytha, 'the Scythian', a catch-all term for the Goths. He was clearly a Gothic man for Zachariah Rhetor. Vitalian would also have had some Thracian ancestry after Evagrius Scholasticus who also believed him to be the leader of a number of Hunnic tribes, as did John Malalas who added the Bulgars and the Goths.[65] Vitalian, Count of the *Foederati* in Thrace, rose in 515 after the payment of subsidies had ended. Against a backdrop of religious revolt in Byzantium against the Monophysite reforms of Anastasius I, Vitalian cleverly forgot his barbarian origins and prudently positioned himself as a defender of orthodoxy and avoided presenting himself as a candidate for the Empire. Regular troops and peasants joined him. Theophanes declared that Vitalian had rebelled at the request of the Patriarch of Scythia and Moesia, while Michael the Syrian made him the nephew of Patriarch Makedonios.[66] His direct superior Hypatius, Master of the Soldiers to the Thracians, had to flee. Vitalian's army camped in front of Byzantium for the first time in 513. Anastasius gave in, dismissed Hypatius, whom he replaced with Cyril, and promised to have the theological dispute arbitrated by the Pope in Rome. Vitalian returned to Moesia. The following year, the truce was broken: after a local success Cyril was beaten and killed by Vitalian at Odyssus. In a night attack at Acris, or Acres, on the Black Sea, he defeated and captured Hypatius who was held to ransom. In 514, he launched a fleet of 200 ships from the Black Sea to intimidate Anastasius as he faced further riots in Byzantium. The Emperor had no choice but to treat, promise a council, and grant a pardon to Vitalian, who was appointed for the occasion Master of the Soldiers to the Thracians.

In 515 Anastasius broke his promise and declared Vitalian 'a public enemy'. The latter came again to camp with his army at Sycae, on the outskirts of Byzantium. The Praetorian Prefect Marinus of Syria defeated Vitalian's fleet at Bytharia at the mouth of the Golden Horn but Vitalian's improvised fleet was manned by Bulgars, Huns, and Scythians (Goths) according to Malalas.[67] Defeated but not destroyed, Vitalian took refuge in Thrace. The ascent of Justin in 518 brought about a turnaround. The new Emperor, ex-chief of the guard or Comes Excubitorum, needed Vitalian and promoted him successively Master of the Soldiers Present, honorary

---

[65] Evagrius Scholasticus, *HE*, III, 43. John Malalas, *Chrgr.*, XVI, 16. (Pseudo-)Zachariah Rhetor, *HE*, VII, 13; VIII, 2.

[66] Theophanes Confessor, *Chrgr.*, AM 6005, 157–158. Michael the Syrian, *HU*, IX, 9, t. 2 (1963), p.164.

[67] John Malalas, *Chrgr.*, XVI, 16.

Consul, and then Patrician. Vitalian's career seemed to make him a new Aspar. The year 520 marked the peak and the end of his career when, having been appointed Consul, he was lured to Byzantium and then, in July, assassinated in the middle of the palace by members of the Blue Faction, probably under Justin's indirect control. His fate did not affect his family: his three sons Bouzes, Coutzes, Venilos and his nephew John became active generals under Justinian.[68] Nevertheless, in Byzantium, the Imperial Purple was not for barbarians, even Romanised ones. They could, however, help the Emperor to recover his throne, as the Bulgar or Khazar *foederati* did for Justinian II in 705.[69]

The Barbarian Disloyalty

The old Greek xenophobia may have saved the eastern part of the Roman Empire from a fate comparable to that of the more open West, which had ended up drowning its field army in a Germanic ocean. The Romano-Byzantines' mistrust of their barbarian *foederati* is perceptible in the arrangements for battle. 'Long before the battle, troops of the same race as the enemy must be separated from the army and sent elsewhere to prevent them from joining him at a critical moment.'[70] At Taginae in 552, Narses the Eunuch not only placed the Lombard and Herulic *foederati* in the centre, asking them to fight on foot so that they would not flee, but also flanked them with 8,000 archers.[71] The question arises, was this mistrust justified? For the Huns, there is no doubt whatsoever. During the Vandal War of 533, their behaviour was ambiguous. They wiped out the Vandal vanguard at the Battle of Dekimon, and then, once in Carthage, they allowed themselves to be corrupted by Gelimer to betray Belisarius in battle. Knowing it, Belisarius tried to restore their loyalty with gifts and daily flattery. Selling themselves to the highest bidder, they appraised Belisarius of the manoeuvres of Gelimer and expressed their fear of not being brought back to the country of their ancestors and of being left languishing in Libya, they also declared their dissatisfaction following the ban on pillaging. Furthermore, they claimed to have been deceived by the Master of the Soldiers Peter who had recruited them and then brought them here in defiance of the oaths sworn. Peter, who had suffered a defeat in Lazica around 527, had brought this Hunnic contingent back to Byzantium. Belisarius promised to repatriate them with their loot. The Huns therefore decided for the last part of the Vandal War not to fight again, but only to pursue the defeated after the final battle.[72]

---

68   A. H. M. Jones, J. R. Martindale, J. Morris, *PLRE*, 2 (1980), pp.1171–1176; S. Williams & G. Friell, *The Rome That Did Not Fall*, pp.216–218.
69   *Chr.754*, 49.
70   Maurice, *Strategikon*, VII, A, 15.
71   Procopius, *BG*, VIII, 31, 5.
72   Procopius, *BV*, IV, 1, 8–10 (the Huns bribed by Gelimer then by Belisarius); 2, 3

During the African War in 536, the Heruls mutinied, as did some of the Vandals who had been defeated and then integrated into the Roman Army.[73] When Narses the Eunuch, was recalled from Italy and was replaced with Belisarius, the Heruls asked to leave. They packed their bags, set off for Liguria and made an agreement with Uuraias, the head of the Ostrogoth army. They sold all the cattle and slaves they had captured and obtained free passage to the Empire against an oath not to fight the Goths again. When they reached Veneto, they relented and divided themselves: Visandus and his troops remained there with a Roman contingent, Phaniteus was killed by his men, Aluith and Philemuth went to Byzantium to ask forgiveness.[74] Cyprian, a valiant senior officer of Belisarius was entrusted with holding Perusia in 545. As he refused to surrender the city, Totila bribed one of his bodyguards, a man named Uliphos, to assassinate him. The crime committed, Uliphos took refuge with Totila who later entrusted him, and another Roman deserter named Meligedios, with holding Perugia which had been taken at the beginning of 549 after a tight blockade. By 552 in order to retake Perugia, Narses the Eunuch bribed Meligedius but Uliphus and his supporters tried to oppose it and were massacred.[75] Treason is a double-edged weapon, but for the Hunnic *bucellarius* Uliphus it was a lethal boomerang.

Sklavene mercenaries were particularly disloyal, but examples of their treachery dated from the second half of the seventh century. In 663, according to Theophanes, when Abd al-Rahman ibn Khalid invaded Cappadocia, 5,000 Sklavene *foederati* joined him and settled in Syria in the region of *Apamea* at the village of *Seleukoboulos* (today Selûqiye). In 683, 7,000 Sklavene *foederati* joined Muhammad, Emir of Dzezireh, who invaded Cappadocia and were settled in Antioch and Cyrrhus/Kyrrhos,14 kilometres from Kilis in Syria, where they received women and a share of the tribute.[76] A similar incident occurred again in 692 unless the sources have confused the same event. Four years previously, Justinian II had captured a large number of Sklavenes from Thrace and deported them to Asia Minor in the area of Opsikion, which bordered the Sea of Marmara. In preparation for war against the Arabs, he armed 30,000 under the command of a Slavic nobleman called Neboulos. They served as a 'strike force' in the war to liberate Armenia but, bought by Arab gold, they turned against the Romano-Byzantines during the Battle of Sebastopolis and as a reward were installed in Antioch and Kyrrhos by their new masters. Furious, Justinian

---

(Huns duplicity).
73 Procopius, *BV*, IV, 14, 12–15 (Heruls); 14, 19 (Vandals).
74 Procopius, *BV*, VI, 22, 5–8.
75 Procopius, *BG*, VII, 12, 19–20 (Cyprian assassination); VIII, 33, 10–12 (Uliphus assassination).
76 Theophanes Confessor, *Chrgr.*, AM 6156, 348. Michael the Syrian, *HU*, XI, 15, t. 2 (1963), p.470.

II massacred their families who had remained in the garrison of Leuketē (today Yelkenkayaburnu in Turkey) in the Gulf of Nicomedia.[77]

These numerous examples of treachery justified a necessary mistrust of barbarian mercenaries whose interests were not the same as those of the Empire. However, it should be added immediately that the 'Roman' soldiers were just as disloyal as the barbarian mercenaries. The most disloyal of the ethnic contingents employed by Byzantium were not strictly speaking barbarians, even if Procopius considered them as such. This was the Isaurians. On 17 December 546, four of them allowed Totila to take Rome in exchange for gold. In January 550, it was the entire Isaurian contingent which again allowed the Ostrogoths to retake the city. Nevertheless, suspicious Romano-Byzantine authorities could not do without barbarian mercenaries and generals. At the beginning of the reconquest of Italy, Belisarius recognised that the barbarians were a majority in his army.[78] The *Strategikon* even advised that they should be treated fairly.[79] The biggest peddler of anti-barbarian clichés, Procopius himself, honestly reported the heroic death of many barbarian officers.

Reciprocal Influence

Barbarian *foederati* modified the culture of Imperial Army and introduced specific vocabulary: such as the standards known as *tufa* and *bandum*, in Greek *toupha* or *touphion* and *bandon*. The *tufa* of which Vegetius already spoke seemed to be an aigrette, a tuft of feathers or rather of horsehair as on Turkish and Mongolian banners.[80] *Bandum* was a sixth-century word, frequently used as *bandon* in Maurice's *Strategikon* for a combat unit or the banner guiding it.[81] This term could be from the Gothic *bandwo*, and is the origin of the later 'band'. The *carrago*, originally used to designate a barbarian defensive circle of waggons in the fourth century, came to refer

---

77 Theophanes Confessor, *Chrgr.*, AM 6180, 364 (30,000 Slavs captured in 688; led by Neboulos); AM 6184 (30,000 Slavs captured; led by Neboulos: 20,000 Slavic defectors at *Sebastopolis*). Elias of Nisibis, *Op.Chr.*, 73. Nikephoros of Constantinople, *Brev.*, 38, 1–28 (did not locate the battle and does not evoke the revenge of de Justinian II).
78 Procopius, *BG*, V, 9, 27.
79 Maurice, *Strategikon*, VIII, 2, 50.
80 Vegetius, *DRM*, III, 5 John the Lydian, *De Magistratibus*, I, 8. Maurice, *Strategikon*, I, 2, 12, 24, 44; XII B 4, 3 (τουφίον).
81 Maurice, *Strategikon*, P 39, 40, 45, 99; I, 2, 75–78.81; 3, 15–16, 22; 4, 25, 33; 5, 23; 8, 5, 20, 22; 9, 31; II P, 18, 19, 24; 1, 40; 4, 4–5, 12, 16, 20; 5, 3; 9, 4; 14, 1–2, 8; 15, 1–2; 16, 10; 20, 1, 3–4, 7, 10, 12, 15–16, 19; III 1, 5; 5, 1, 53, 55, 62, 77, 86, 88, 100, 106, 115; 6, 5. 6; 7, 10; 8, 5; 14, 7; 15, 24, 27; IV, 3, 79–81, 89; 5, 24; V, 3, 8; 4, 9; VII, P,5; A, 1, 1–2; B, 5, 6; 8, 3; 9, 5, 13; 16, 8, 16, 25, 26, 29, 31–32, 34; 17, 4, 26–27, 31, 44, 57; IX, 3, 65; XI, 4, 177, 198, 201–202,209; XII, A 1, 10–11; B, 8, 18, 35; 11, 4, 23; 17, 21; 21, 9; 24, 5 (*bandon*, βάνδον). Paul the Deacon, *HL*, I, 20, (*bandum*).

to the impedimenta in the *Strategikon* under the form *karagos*.⁸² *Drungus*, in Greek *droungos* (a cavalry unit) has a Gallic origin, coming from a word which became in old Irish *drong* or in old Breton *drogn* or *drog* (a band, gathering or crowd).⁸³

Some pieces of barbarian equipment were recommended for soldiers by the *Strategikon*, as 'gothic tunics that come down to the knees', 'Avar-style cavalry lances with a loop at the centre of the staff and a pennon', 'the Avar-style gorget', 'the Avar-style broad cloak', 'Avar-style tents that are beautiful and practical', the Herulic sword and the Sklavene javelin.⁸⁴

The barbarians from the steppes brought two technological revolutions to the Romano-Byzantine Army: the composite bow, already adopted in the fourth century and iron stirrups, probably a contribution of the Avars, mentioned for the first time in the *Strategikon* under the term *skala* with other materials of Avar origin. This treatise recommended having on the left of the saddle at the back an additional stirrup to recover wounded or fallen riders.⁸⁵ The single-edged sword or *seax* had a long variant which bore the names of *scramasax*, *langsax* with a width of 3cm or 4cm and a length of 30cm to 60cm. This variant was found across the Carpathian Basin throughout the second half of the fifth century in Hunnic tombs, then it was in use by Gepids in the following century and in territories that covered present-day Serbia or Bulgaria. Some examples are associated in some fortifications of the Balkans with Baldenheim type helmets. This typically Germanic weapon was used by *foederati* in the service of the Empire but does not seem to have been of Byzantine production.⁸⁶ The appearance of a Romano-Byzantine Army was thus barbarised, not only by the presence of *foederati* but also by the equipment. While the *Strategikon* has mentioned the influence of the barbarians, especially the Avars and other nomads, on Romano-Byzantine armament, clothing and tactics in the 590s,

---

82   *Scriptores Historiae Augustae*, *Gall.*, XIII, 9; *Claud.*, VIII, 2 and 5; *Aurel.*, XI, 6. Ammianus Marcellinus, *RG*, XXXI, 2, 18 and 7, 7. Vegetius, *DRM*, III, 10. Zosime, *Historia Nova*, I, 45, 1. Procopius, *BG*, VI, 5, 3. Maurice, *Strategikon*, XII, B, 7, 10; 18, 2; 22, 99 and 122; 23, 4; C, 2 (*carrago*/*karagos*). After Ph. Rance (2004), pp.307–308. G. T. Dennis, 'Byzantine Battle Flags', *Byzantinische Forschungen*, 8 (1982), pp.51–59.

83   Ph. Rance, 'Drungus, Δροῦγγος and Δρουγγιστί', p.101.

84   Maurice, Strategikon, I, 2, 18–19 (Avar-style cavalry lances), 20 (round neck pieces), 46–48 (broad coat), 60–61 (tents); XII, B, 1, 1 (tunics); 4, 1–2 (sword); 5, 6 (javeline). F. Curta, 'Chronology: what is the date of the earliest stirrups in Europe?' in F. Curta, R. Kovalev (eds), The Other Europe in the Middle Ages. Avars, Bulgars, Khazars and Cumans, East Central and Eastern Europe in the Middle Ages, 450–1450, vol. 2 (Leiden, Boston: Brill, 2009), pp.302–303.

85   Maurice, *Strategikon*, I, 2, 41 (two stirrups attached to the saddle); II, 9, 23 (an additional stirrup for recovering casualties); X, 1, 52 (siege ladders). A. P. Kazhdan, A. M. Talbot, A. Cutler, T. E. Gregory, N. P. Ševčenko (eds), 'Stirrup', vol. 3 (1991), p.1958 (σκάλα).

86   P. A. Kiss, 'Huns, Germans, Byzantines? The origins of the narrow bladed long seaxes', *Acta Archaeologica Carpathica*, 49, (2014), pp.131–164.

archaeologists believe that the weapons found in the barbarian tombs show in return the Roman influence on the barbarians. The Romano-Byzantines practised mimicry to learn from their adversaries.[87]

Barbarian Officers Integrated into the Regular Army

Riding on his horse, wearing an officer's coat, a rough man with a blond beard lectures the Emperor's soldiers in a strong Germanic accent. How could a barbarian become an officer in the regular army at the time of Justinian? Some barbarian officers, such as the sons of chiefs sent as hostages to the Emperor from childhood to ensure good relations between the two peoples, had received a Roman education. Attila had once experienced this kind of education. Bilingual and acquainted with the customs of their masters, these Romanised barbarian officers were the most acceptable intermediaries in relations with their fellows: 'Among the taxiarchs there was a most remarkable man, called Theodore; he was Tzan by birth, but had been brought up among the Romans, stripped of his native barbarian ways, and transformed into a perfectly civilised man.'[88] Early Byzantine chroniclers believed in the value and superiority of Greco-Roman education which, more than lineage, made the man. Other barbarian officers were, more prosaically, former warband leaders who had left their people to enjoy the advantages of Greco-Roman civilisation, economic migrants in a way. The Hun Sinnion is only known on two occasions during Justinian reign, 20 years apart: in 533, he commanded 600 Hun horsearchers during the African expedition and in 550 he asked Justinian to be welcomed into Thrace with 2,000 Kutrigur Huns who had fought the Empire.[89] Sinnion was a dissident since Zabergan remained the King of the Kutrigurs who invaded Thrace and attacked Byzantium in 559.

These officers possessed all the military qualities and flaws of the barbarians. Fourth-century historian Ammianus Marcellinus, an Oriental Greek and ex-officer, always pointed out the barbarian origin of officers and went there with his ethnic commentary, sometimes accompanied by a compliment to deserving individuals. Procopius did the same. According to him, Uliaris one of Belisarius' *doryphoros*, was a strong and brave soldier but was not professional and loved wine and partying too much.[90] Of Pharas, an officer charged by late December 533 to reduce the Vandal leader Gelimer who had taken refuge in a mountain of Kroumirie, Procopius declared: 'This Pharas was an energetic man, extremely serious and very brave in spite of his Herulic origin. It is because, for a Herul, it is difficult,

---

87 G. Dagron, 'Modèles de combattants et technologie militaire dans le *Strategikon* de Maurice' in *ARB-AFAM* (1990), pp.279–280.
88 Agathias, *Hist.*, II, 20, 7.
89 Procopius, *BV*, III, 11, 12; *BG*, VIII, 19, 6–7.
90 Procopius, *BV*, IV, 4, 16.

and therefore very commendable, to renounce disloyalty and drunkenness, in order to show, on the contrary, bravery. Pharas was not the only Herul to love discipline: all those who accompanied him did the same.'[91] Procopius nevertheless liked to show that barbarian mercenaries, in particular the Huns, such as Askan, commander of cavalry, Kutilas Bucellarius and Chorsamantis, officer of Belisarius' bodyguard, fought with blinded ferocity and often to the death.[92] During the battle of Callinicum in 531, Askan targeted the Persian notables and killed many before he himself succumbed to their numbers.[93] During the first siege of Rome by the Ostrogoths in 537, Kutilas continued to fight fiercely even with a javelin stuck in his head. He later died when it was removed.[94] During the same fight, Chorsamantis participated in the sorties led by small groups of horsemen through the Field of Nero. Although already wounded and convalescent, he decided 'in drunkenness, for he was usually drunk at lunchtime, to go to fight the enemy alone to avenge the wound inflicted on the lower leg.' After several individual exploits, he perished under the mass of the enemy to the sadness of Belisarius and the army.[95] The regrets noted by Procopius showed the existence of camaraderie links between the Hunnic *bucellarii* and their Roman counterparts.

Bonds of esteem and camaraderie could also have linked the barbarians to their Romano-Byzantine employers. Narses the Eunuch was much appreciated by the Herul and by barbarian *foederati*.[96] Despite distrustful or derogatory remarks over barbarians, Byzantine sources also showed a genuine consideration for those who served the Emperor with loyalty and dignity.[97] Procopius and Agathias always pointed out when barbarians were commanding so-called Romans. Barbarian officers were mostly infantry tribunes or *taxiarchs*. In 504, during the siege of Amida, a Goth tribune named Ald was the second to emerge from a tunnel; he then killed three Persians before being wounded.[98] During the African expedition of 533, of the 22 officers named by Procopius, only one was identified as a 'Massageta', aka Hun, Aigan, one of the four cavalry chiefs in the regular army.[99] An Ante called Dabragezas rose to the rank of *taxiarch* and fought in the Roman cavalry c. 555–556 in Lazica. He often had a shared command with Huns of the same rank, as with Usigard. Both were leading 600 horsemen, with whom they opposed the arrival of the Persians. Then Dabragezas

---

91 Procopius, *BV*, IV, 4, 29–31.
92 D. A. Parnell, 'Procopius on Romans, non-Romans, and battle casualties' in G. Greatrex & S. Janniard (eds), *Le monde de Procope*, pp.249–262.
93 Procopius, *BP*, I, 18, 38.
94 Procopius, *BG*, VI, 2, 14–15 and 30–31.
95 Procopius, *BG*, VI, 1, 27–26 (drunk); 33–34 (death; regrets).
96 Procopius, *BG*, VIII, 26, 17.
97 D. A. Parnell, 'Barbarians and Brothers-in-Arms. Byzantines on barbarian Soldiers in the Sixth Century', *BZ*, 108, 2 (2015), pp.809–826.
98 Joshua the Stylite, *Chron.*, 74.
99 Procopius, *BV*, III, 11, 7.

MERCENARIES AND BARBARIAN *FOEDERATI*

and Elmigeiros carried out a dangerous patrol.[100] Another example was the Hunnic *taxiarch* Elminsur who with 2,000 horsemen was ordered to retake the Lazic city of Rhodopolis from the Persians in 557, a mission of some trust.[101]

Barbarian officers also gave their opinion at staff meetings, like any other officer. During the Lazic War in 555, when a Persian Army on its way to relieve a fortress under Imperial siege, Uligang, leader of the Herulic contingent supported General Bouzes' advice to attack it rather than continue the siege, quoting a barbarian proverb: 'Chase the bees to get the honey'. But Rusticus, the general in charge, imposed his ill-fated point of view.[102] Some barbarians rose to the highest ranks as master of the soldiers; they were high-ranking defectors or nobles serving as *foederati* but of recognised value.

Cut off from their original people, these generals had a good career without representing an ethnic threat like Ricimer or Odoacer had once. Bessas was one of those Goths of Thrace who refused to follow Theodoric the Amal in 488 – according to Jordanes, he came from a colony of Sarmatians, Cemanders and Huns settled in Castra Martena (now Kula, Bulgaria). In 503, he fought the Persians as officer and then rose to the rank of general. Procopius called him a *stratēgos* and spoke highly of him: 'He was an energetic man and a competent warrior. He was both a very good general and a gifted man of action.' In 535, he served under Mundo during the invasion of Dalmatia. The following year, under Belisarius, he participated in the attack from Sicily and then commanded a contingent during the siege of Naples. He took the city of Narni in Tuscany, played an important role in the battle for Rome and twice faced the Goths in pitched battle. He held the rank of *magister militum vacans*. He saved Belisarius' life during an bitter dispute with Constantine, another *magister militum vacans*. He obtained the supreme dignity of Patrician in 540 and remained in Italy after the departure of Belisarius. Beaten and wounded by the Ostrogoths in 542, two years later he became military governor of Rome which he defended, alongside Conon, in 545–546 against Totila. Then he made a lot of money by selling the grain to the Roman population at unfair prices. The bitter result was starvation and a lack of cooperation from the inhabitants. Additionally, he refused to sally from the city to join up with Belisarius's forces when they landed at Portus Romanus (today Porto), south of Rome. When the city fell due to treachery on 17 December, he lost his ill-gained fortune but was able to escape and the Emperor kept him in Italy. Returning to Byzantium in 550, he was appointed master of the soldiers to Armenia and Lazica until 554. There he had to deal with a rebellion among the Abasgians, a restless tribe north of Lazica. Although in his seventies, eager to redeem himself he showed courage and activity in Lazic War against the Persians

---

100 Agathias, *Hist.*, III, 6, 9 (Dabragezas and Usigard); 21, 6 (Dabragezas, Elmigeiros).
101 Agathias, *Hist.*, IV, 15, 1.
102 Agathias, *Hist.*, III, 6, 5 (Uligang).

and retook the fortress of Petra. But subsequently, he failed to stabilise the situation and, accused of cowardliness, and maybe corruption, by Gubazes the King of Lazians, Bessas was exiled to the Abasgian people.[103] An old Gothic Byzantine Scrooge in arms is the infamous memory left by Bessas, Patrician of the Eastern Roman Empire.

A Persian with the Greek name of Petros, Peter, was originally a slave captured as a child in 504 in Arzanene by Justin, who sent him to study and then made him his secretary when he became Emperor. Out of favour, Peter of Arzanene was promoted to vacant master of the soldiers in 526, leading a small expeditionary force in 526–527 in Lazica to help Iberians against the Persians and suffered a defeat causing him to be recalled to Byzantium. A year later he returned to Lazica to replace three masters of the soldiers with whom the Emperor was displeased. According to historians, Peter of Arzanene either defeated the Persians or forced them to retreat. He was greedy and stupid according to Procopius and Jean Tzibos replaced him. He took part in the war against the Persians in 541. His slander led to the recall of Belisarius, accused of plotting the following year. In 543, although under the orders of Martin, a veteran of Africa and Italy and now Master of the Soldiers to the East and without informing his colleagues, Peter of Arzanene crossed the Persian frontier. The army joined him and was beaten in front of the fortified village of Anglon. He kept the position of Master of the Soldiers until 544, when he was besieged at Edessa by Khosrow I.[104]

The most obvious case of a defector won over to the Byzantine cause was that of the Gepid Mundo (or Mundus or Mundovers or Moundos), the son of King Giesmos, the nephew of Thrapsila killed when fighting Theodoric the Amal in 488. Exiled from the Gepids, Mundo crossed the Danube and seized the tower of Herta, probably an abandoned Roman watchtower. From there he gathered a band of cattle thieves and raided Roman territory. In 505, Sabinian the Younger, Master of the Soldiers to Illyricum, was hunting him with the Bulgar *foederati*. But Mundo received help from the Ostrogoth Count Ptizia causing the Army of Illyricum to be destroyed at Margoplanum, or Horreum Margi. In gratitude Mundo went into the service of King Theodoric the Great. But after the latter's death in 526, in

---

103 Procopius, *BP*, I, 8, 3 (officer); *BG*, V, 5, 3 (Dalmatia); 10, 2, 5, 10, 11–12 and 20 (Naples); 16, 2–3 (Goth from Thrace); 16, 2–3 (Narnia); 17, 4–5 (1st battle with Goths); 17, 35 and 19, 15 (defence of Rome); 27, 18 (2nd battle with Goths); VI, 8, 15 (protecting Belisarius); VII, 5, 5–18 (wounded); 11, 37 (Governor of Rome); 18, 8 (defence of Rome); VIII, 9, 4 (Armenia); 11, 40 (70 years old); 11, 11–62 (Lazica). Agathias, *Hist.*, III, 2, 3–7. Jordanes, *Getica*, L, 265 (*Castra Martena*); A. H. M. Jones, J. R. Martindale, J. Morris, *PLRE*, 2 (1980), pp.226–228 (Bessas).

104 Procopius, *BP*, I, 12, 9 and 14 (Lazica, defeat); II, 15, 7–8 (Justin's origin and greed) and 9 (recall); 24, 18 (invasion); 25, 5–34 (Anglon); 26, 25 (Edessa). Procopius, *Anecdota*, IV, 4 (slander). John Malalas, *Chrgr.*, XVIII, 4 (three generals ousted and retreat). *Chron. Pasch.*, a. 528 (victory over Persians). Theophanes Confessor, *Chrgr.*, AM 6020, 174 (victory over Persians). Martindale J. R., Morris J., *PLRE*, 2 (1980), pp.870–871 (Petrus 27).

529 or 530 Mundo offered his services to Justinian. At the time the Bulgars had invaded Thrace and were holding the Master of the Soldiers Terentiolus for ransom. Justinian had real no choice but to hire Mundo, who defeated the Bulgars and was, exceptionally, allowed to drag the prisoners he made in a sort of triumph celebrated at Byzantium's hippodrome. In 531, at the express will of Justinian, Mundo temporarily replaced Belisarius as Master of the Soldiers to the East after the fall of Abgersaton Fort in Osrhoene that followed the defeat at Callinicum. The next year appointed Master of the Soldiers to Illyricum, he and Belisarius they crushed in blood the Nika revolt along the street and the hippodrome of Constantinople. Three years later, he began the great offensive against the Ostrogoths in Italy by attacking Dalmatia and the city of Salona. His son bore the Latin name of Maurice as a sign of integration and was killed in 536 in a reconnaissance fight near Salona. In revenge and blinded by anger, Mundo fought an open battle that he won but was killed as he pursued the fleeing enemy. Procopius said, in praise of him, 'Though Moundos was a barbarian by birth, he was very loyal to the Emperor's cause and competent in matters of war.'[105]

A Gepid officer called Asbadus or Asbad in 552 brought a retinue of 400 men from his nation to Narses the Eunuch. After the Battle of Taginae, Asbad killed with his spear the Ostrogothic King Totila, and thus he was promoted master of the soldiers and put in charge with an army corps north of the Po, while Narses was commanding the southern zone with the bulk of the forces. Asbad's promotion is known only thanks to an epitaph copied during the Lombard period in a supplement to the *Chronicle* of Prosper of Aquitaine, written *c.* 623 for Queen Theodelinda. The Latin epitaph, inscribed in the basilica of St Nazario e Celso in Pavia, formerly Ticinum and the last Gothic capital, revealed the military and civil role of Asbad: chasing the Goths from the Alps and recovering the cities of Liguria. Asbad probably died of illness *c.* 555–560.[106]

The Khan of the Avars was severely beaten during summer 586 by a General named Drokton (after Simocatta), in fact named Droctulf, second

---

[105] John Malalas, *Chrgr.*, XVIII, 46 (Mundo as the son of a Gothic King, with his uncle Thraustila in Sirmium, at Theodoric service then Justinian as Master of the Soldiers to Illyricum destroying a Hunnic-led army); 61 (replaced Belisarius as Master of the Soldiers to the East). Jordanes, *Getica*, LVIII, 300–301 (Mundovers or Mundo, Gepid origin, linked to Attila dynasty, cattle thief's leader, Sabinian, at Ostrogothic service). Theophanes Confessor, *Chrgr.*, AM 6032, 219 (Mundo as the son of a Gepid King). Procopius, *BG*, V, 5, 2 (mission in Dalmatia and portrait); 7, 2–5 (death of Maurice and Mundo). A. H. M. Jones, J. R. Martindale, J. Morris, *PLRE*, 3a (1992), pp.903–905 (Mundus is not the Mundo Hunnic warlord in Ostrogoths service).

[106] Procopius, *BG*, VIII, 32, 22–24 and A. H. M. Jones, J. R. Martindale, J. Morris, *PLRE*, 3a (1992), p.133, (Asbadus 2 killed Totila). Ch. Badel, 'Un chef germain entre Byzance et l'Italie. L'épitaphe d'Asbadus à Pavie (Suppl. It. 9, 15)' in M. Ghilardi, Chr. J. Goddard and P. Porena (eds), *Les cités de l'Italie tardo-antique (IVe-VIe siècle). Institutions, économie, société, culture et religion* (Rome: CEFR, 2006), pp.91–100.

in command of the Balkan Army: 'This man was of Lombard race, a very brave and powerful fighter in the war.' He then fought his fellow Avars in Italy where he died. An epitaph to San Vitale of Ravenna given by Paul the Deacon described him as 'exterminator of his own people.'[107]

Another German, Goudoues, whose real name was probably Godwin, liberated Singidunum from the Avars in 595 by launching an amphibious operation on the Danube then wiped out 2,000 Avars in an ambush recovering their booty. He was the very type of trusted officer, charged with delicate missions and capable of initiative.[108]

Expelled by his people, the Heruls, who considered him too subservient to the Empire, in 551 Suartuas was appointed Master of the Soldiers Present in Byzantium and fought Gepids next year.[109]

The proportion of barbarian officers in the army was given for the expeditionary force sent to Sicily in 535. Among the commanders of units, 8 out of 14 were 'Romans': Constantian, originally from Thrace, Valentin, Magnus and Innocent as cavalry officers, Herodian, Paul, Demetrios and Ursicin as infantry officers. Bessas was a Goth from Thrace, Media (of royal blood) and Peranios were Iberians, perhaps Lazians, while the Isaurians were commanded by one of their own people named Ennes, the Hunnic and Moorish troops also had commanders from their own people. Barbarians formed almost 42 percent of the senior officers. The era of a *generalissimo* like Aspar was over, Byzantium ensured that the regular army did not fall into their hands but continued to spawn with the essential barbarian mercenaries.

---

107 Theophylact Simocatta, *HU*, VII, 16, 8 (promoted second in command); 9 (description); 10–13 (victory). Paul the Deacon, *HL*, III, 18–19. Christie N., *The Lombards. The Ancient Langobards* (Oxford, Cambridge MA:, Blackwell), 1995, pp.84–86.

108 Theophylact Simocatta, *HU*, VII, 11, 6–9 (Singidunum taken by Godwin); 12, 2–9 (ambush). Theophanes Confessor, *Chrgr.*, AM 6091, 278. A. H. M. Jones, J. R. Martindale, J. Morris, *PLRE*, 3a (1992), pp.561–562.

109 Procopius, *BG*, VI, 15, 32–36 (Herulic King); VIII, 25, 11 (*stratēgos* of Byzantium garrison); 13 (expedition against Gepids). A. H. M. Jones, J. R. Martindale, J. Morris, *PLRE*, 3b (1992), p.1205 (Suartuas).

Notes to colour plates

Plate A.

Triumphant Emperor Justinian I wearing the *toupha*. The mounted Emperor is from the Barberini ivory, in the Louvre Museum, Paris. The portrait of Justinian is from the San Vitale Basilica mosaic in Ravenna. The Byzantine Imperial *toupha* seems to have been a crested ornament put on a diadem for a triumph, after the Gunthertuch of Bishop Gunther's (d. 1065) tomb from Bamberg, Germany, showing an allegory of Byzantine officer offering a *toupha* to either the Emperor John I Tzimiskes (971–976) or Basil II (976–1025). The horse harness is also depicted after the same so-called Bamberger Gunthertuch, in fact a Byzantine silk tapestry. The complex fibula is after the San Vitale mosaic, a model close to a late Roman-inspired Frankish looped fibulae of the mid-sixth century in the Musée des Antiquités Nationales, Saint-Germain-en-Laye. Cf plate 4.

Plate B.

Belisarius in parade armour. His head is drawn after the mosaic depicting him on the Basilica of San Vitale in Ravenna. The body is after the officer standing left of the Emperor from the Barberini Ivory in the Musée du Louvre, Paris. The boots are white according the manuscript *Vaticanus Vergilius*, f. 73v, depicting the Trojan Council, and the pteruges/pteryges are according to the mosaics depicting Herodes on the fifth-century mosaics from the Basilica Santa Maria Maggiore in Rome.

Plate C.

Sixth-century *Bandophoros* or standard bearer. The figure is carrying a *bandon*, a banner with two flames and the origin of the medieval *oriflamme*. After the mosaic depicting the month of March (Martios), from the Byzantine Mosaic of the Months found in Argos, now in Argos Archaeological Museum, Greece. This kind of banner stood near an officer ranked as *tribunus/tribounos*. After Maurice, *Strategikon*, XII, B, 8, 20. He supposedly belongs to the *Felices Theodosiaci* a unit of the *auxilium palatinum*, which, *c.* 400, was under the command of the *magister militum praesentalis II*. This unit still existed later and in 592 was garrisoned to Rome then in Ravenna in 600. The sun emblem is probably a remembrance of the pagan *Sol Invictus*. *Notitia Dignitatum*, OR.XXXIX.23 (*milites secundi Constantini*). Cf Plate 9.

Plate D.

Justinian's bodyguard officer. He may be from the *Scholarii/Scholarioi* or from the *Excubitores/Exkoubitoroi*, literally 'Those out of bed' or 'the Awakened'. Depicted close to the Emperor he is possibly a count. After the sixth-century mosaic from the Basilica San Vitale in Ravenna. Spears are gilded and decorated. Most of the time in late Roman and Byzantine iconography, the spear shafts are shown monochrome in a colour suggesting wood.

Plate E:

Justinian's bodyguard officer second in rank to the officer depicted in plate 4. After the sixth-century mosaic from the Basilica of San Vitale in Ravenna.

Plate F.

A Byzantine *Spatharius/Spatharios*. This honorific function is first mentioned during the reign of Theodosius II (408–450) had continued until the middle of the eleventh century or the early twelfth century. A *spatharios* is literally a '*spatha* bearer'. Men from this corps were court eunuchs with no real military duties. After f. 239r of a manuscript in the Bibliothèque Nationale de France, *Commentaries of Gregory of Nazianzus*, the *Codex Parisinus Graecus*, and dated *c.* 880.

Plate G.

A *Candidatus/Kandidatos*, called a 'white-dressed'. Created by 243, this was a corps of cadets, picked promising officers, and bodyguards linked to the Emperor, and Justinian I had been one of them during his youth. No sword is depicted, but there could have been one. *Kandidatoi* are not mentioned again after the middle of the eleventh century. After ff. 215v and 374v of a manuscript in the Bibliothèque Nationale de France, *Commentaries of Gregory of Nazianzus*, the *Codex Parisinus Graecus*, and dated *c.* 880.

Plate H.

Aeneas depicted as a late Roman infantry officer from the Western Empire After *Vergilius Romanus*, Biblioteca Apostolica Vaticana, f. 74v; counterparts from the Eastern Empire during Emperor Anastasius' reign

NOTES TO COLOUR PLATES

were probably very similar. Purple was the Imperial colour and wearing it was a *lèse-majesté* offence punishable by death during the fourth century, in a military context it was perhaps a distinctive sign for senior officers. The shield pattern is from the *Lanciarii Seniores* a palatine legion which was under the command of the first master of the soldiers in the Imperial Presence. After *Notitia Dignitatum*, OR.VI, 42. The unit still existed in 518 during Emperor Justin I's investiture. See Plate 6.

Bibliography

Abbreviations

AE	*Année épigraphie*
Aed.	*Aedificiis* from Procopius
AFAM	*Association française d'Archéologie Mérovingienne*
AH	*Hijri* year (*Anno Hegirae*) which begins on 16 July 622 in the Gregorian calendar and is based on lunar months
AG	Year of the Greeks (*Annum Graecorum*) instituted by the Seleucids (1 October 312 BC)
AJA	*American Journal of Archaeology*
AM	Year of the World (*Annum Mundi*) since the creation of the World according to the Bible
Ant tard	*L'Antiquité tardive*
ARB-AFAM	M. Kazanski, F. Vallet F. (eds), *L'armée romaine et les Barbares du IIIe siècle au VIe siècle*, Colloque international organisé à Saint-Germain-en-Laye, 1990 (Association française d'Archéologie Mérovingienne et Société des Amis du Musée des Antiquités Nationales, t. 5 des Mémoires publiés par l'Association française d'Archéologie Mérovingienne: 1993)
BAR	British Archaeological Reports
BCH	Bulletin de Correspondance Hellénique
BG	*Bellum Gothicum* from Procopius of Caesarea, Books V to VIII of *The History of the Wars*
BGU	*Ægyptische Urkunden aus den königlichen Museen zu Berlin, Griesche Urkunden*, I-IV (Berlin: 1895-)
BIFAO	*Bulletin de l'Institut français d'archéologie orientale*
Brev.	*Breviarium* from Nikephoros of Constantinople
BP	*Bellum Persicum* from Procopius of Caesarea, Books I to II of *The History of the Wars*
BV	*Bellum Vandalum* from Procopius of Caesarea, Books III to IV of *The History of the Wars*
BZ	*Byzantinische Zeitschrift*
CCSL	*Corpus Christianorum Series Latina* (Turnhout: Brepols, 1945-)

BIBLIOGRAPHY

ChLA	*Chartae Latinae antiquiores* A. Bruckner, R. Marichal (eds), papyrus and parchments before 800, 49 vols
Chr.	*Chronicle from* Fredegar, Joshua the Stylite, Count Marcellinus (Marcellinus Comes)
Chr. 754	Mozarabic Chronicle from 754
Chr.VT	*Chr. continuans Victorem Tunnunensem* from John of Biclaro.
Chrgr.	*Chronographia* from John Malalas or Theophanes Confessor.
CEFR	Collection de l'École Française de Rome
CFHB	*Corpus Fontium Historiae Byzantinae* (1967-)
CIG	*Corpus Inscriptionum Graecorum* (Berlin, 1828–1877)
CIL	*Corpus Inscriptionum Latinarum* (Berlin: 1863-)
CJ	*Codex Iustinianus* in *Corpus Iuris Civilis*, P. Krüger, Th. Mommsen (eds), (Berlin: Weidmann, repr. 1970–1973, 2 vols)
CNRS	Centre National de la Recherche Scientifique
CQ	Classical Quarterly
CR	Classical Review
CRAI	Comptes rendus des séances de l'année. Académie des Inscriptions et Belles-Lettres
CSEL	*Corpus Scriptorum Ecclesiasticorum Latinorum* (Vienna: 1866-)
CSCO	*Corpus Scriptorum Christianorum Orientalium* (Paris: 1903-)
CSHB	*Corpus Scriptorum Historiae Byzantinae*
CSM	*Corpus Scriptorum Muzarabicorum*, Insituto Antonio de Nebrija, Madrid
CTh	*Codex Theodosianus*, Th. Mommsen (ed.), (Berlin: 1904–1905).
CUF	*Collection des Universités de France*, associated to *LBL*
DBG	*De Bello Gallico* from Julius Caesar
DOP	*Dumbarton Oaks Papers*
DRM	*De Re Militari* from Vegetius
Ed. Anast.	Emperor Anastasius (edict on Libya Pentapolis), *Die vom Kaiser Anastasius fur Libya Pentapolis erlassenen Formae*, K. E. Zakariä von Lingenthal (ed.), (Berlin: *Monatsberichte der k. Akademie der Wissenschaften zu Berlin*, 1879), pp.134–158
EFR	*École Française de Rome*
EH	Hispanic era (38 years longer than the Julian Calendar).
Ep.H	*Epitome Historiarum* from Zonaras
Ep.	*Epistulae* (Letters) from Sidonius Apollinaris or Gregory the Great
Exc.	*Excerpta Valesiana*, extracts from Anonymus Valesianus, *pars posterior*
Fragm.	*Fragmenta* (fragments)
FHG	*Fragmenta Historicorum Graecorum*, 4, K. Müller (ed.), (Paris: Firmin Didot, 1848–1870)
GRBS	*Greek, Roman and Byzantine Studies*
HE	*Historia Ecclesiastica* from Evagrius Scholasticus, John of Ephesus, (Pseudo-)Zachariah Rhetor
HF	*Historia Francorum from* Gregory of Tours
Hist.	*Historiae* from Agathias, Isidore of Seville, Sebeos

HL	*Historia Langobardorum* from Paul the Deacon
HU	*Historia Universalis* from Theophylact Simocatta
IBLA	*Institut des Belles Lettres Arabes*
IGLS	*Inscriptions grecques et latines de la Syrie*, Paris, Librairie Orientaliste Paul Geuthner, Bibliothèque archéologique et historique, 1929–2009
I Prusias	Inscriptions from Prusias
Joh	*Johannis* (*Johannide* in French) *from* Corippus
JRS	*Journal of Roman Studies*
Kitab	*Futuh al-Bouldan* from al-Baladhur
LBL	*Les Belles Lettres*, Paris
LPR	*Liber Pontificalis sive vitae Pontificum Ravennatum* from Andreas Agnellus of Ravenna (also known as *Breviarium Ecclesiae Ravennatis*).
MAMA	*Monumenta Asiae Minoris Antiqua* (Oxford: 1928–2014, 11 vols)
MEFR	*Mélanges de l'École Française de Rome*
MGH	*Monumenta Germaniae Historica*, G. H. Pertz and *alii* (eds), (Berlin/Munich/ Hanover: 1823–1874)
	Online version in digitalen *Monumenta Germaniae Historica* (dMGH): https://www.dmgh.de
MIFAO	*Mémoire de l'Institut Français d'archéologie orientale*
Nov. J.	*Novellae Justiniani* in *Corpus Iuris Civilis*, t. 3, R. Schoell, G. Kroll (eds), (Berlin: 1895)
Op.Chr.	Elias of Nisibis, *Opus Chronologicum*
O&M	*Orient & Méditerranée*
P. Brit.	*Greek papyri in the British Museum*, F. G. Kenyon (ed.), (London: British Museum, Dept. of Manuscripts, 1893)
P. Caire	*Papyrus grecs d'époque Byzantine*, J. Maspéro (ed.), I and II (Cairo: Catalogue général des antiquités égyptiennes du Musée du Caire, n°67 001–67 187, 1910–1912)
P. Ital.	*Die nichtliterarischen lateinischen Papyri Italiens aus der Zeit 445–700*, J. O. Tjäder (ed.), (Lund: *Papyri* 1–28, 1955, tome I; Stokholm: *Papyri* 29–59, 1982, tome II)
P. Monac	*Byzantinische Papyri in der Königlichen Hof und Staatsbibliothek zu München*, A. Heisenberg., L. Wenger (eds), (Leipzig-Berlin: 1914)
PL	*Patrologia Latina*, J. P. Migne (ed.), (Paris: Jacques-Paul Migne Imprimerie catholique, 1841–1865, 221 vols)
	Online version in *Documenta Catholica Omnia*: http://www.documentacatholicaomnia.eu/25_10_MPL.html
PEFR	*Publications de l'École Française de Rome.*
PG	*Patrologia graeca*, J. P. Migne (ed.), (Paris: Jacques-Paul Migne Imprimerie catholique, 1857–1866, 161 vols)
	Online version in *Patrologia Graeca*: https://patrologia.graeca.org/phd/apix/jsasync/pg_https.html http://patristica.net/graeca/

PLRE	A. H. M. Jones, J. R. Martindale, J. Morris, *The Prosopography of the Later Roman Empire* (Cambridge: Cambridge University Press (years 260–395) tome 1, 1971, tome 2 (395–527) 1980, tome 3 (526–641) 1992)
	Online version in Internet Archive archive.org:
	Vol. 1 https://archive.org/details/prosopography-later-roman-empire/PLRE-I/.
	Vol. 2 https://archive.org/details/prosopography-later-roman-empire/PLRE-II/.
	Vol. 3 a https://archive.org/details/prosopography-later-roman-empire/PLRE-III-A/.
	Vol. 3 b https://archive.org/details/prosopography-later-roman-empire/PLRE-III-B/.
PO	*Patrologia Orientalis*, R., Graffin, F. Nau (eds), (Paris: Firmin Didot; Turnhout: Brepols, 1899-)
	Online version in Tertullian.org:
	https://www.tertullian.org/fathers/patrologia_orientalis_toc.htm.
P. Oxy.	*The Oxyrhynchus Papyri* published by the Egypt Exploration Society in *Graeco-Roman Memoirs* (London: 1898–2020, 85 vols. The vol. quoted in this book is B. P. Grenfell, A. S. Hunt, H. I. Bell (eds), *The Oxyrhynchus papyri*, XVI, 1924)
REA	Revue des Études Anciennes
REB	Revue des Études Byzantines
REG	Revue des Études grecques
REL	Revue des Études Latines
REMA	Revue des Études militaires anciennes
RG	*Res Gestae* from Ammianus Marcellinus.
RH	*Revue Historique*
SC	*Sources Chrétiennes*, Le Cerf
Tarikh	*Tarikh al-Rusul wa al-Muluk* from Tabari
TTH	*Translated Texts for Historians* (Liverpool University Press).
VE	*Variae Epistulae from* Cassiodorus

Note regarding Sources

Most ancient authors have digital original versions or translations available in the public domain: Internet Archive, archive.org, Academia.edu, Dokumen, The Online Books Page, Perseus Digital Library, The Internet Classic Archive, The Project Gutenberg eBook, The Latin Library, Corpus Scriptorum Latinorum forumromanorum.org, Digital Fragmenta Historicarum Graecorum.

1, Latin and Greek sources

Acta Sancti Anastasii Persae in *Saint Anastase le Perse et l'histoire de la Palestine au début du VIIe siècle*, B. Flusin (ed.) *Le texte*, vol. 1, (Paris: édition du *CNRS*, 1992).

Agathias, *Agathiæ Myrinæi Historiarum libri quinque*, R. Keydell (ed.), (Berlin: De Gruyter, *CFHB*, 2, 1967)

Agathias, *Agathiæ Myrinæi Historiarum libri quinque*, S. Costanza (ed.), (Messina: Biblioteca di Helikon, Testi e Studi, 7, Università degli Studi, 1969)

Agathias, *The Histories*, translated into English by J. D. C. Frendo (Berlin, New York: De Gruyter, 1975)

Agathias, *Histoires. Guerres et malheurs du temps de Justinien*, translated into French by P. Maraval (Paris: *LBL*, La Roue à Livres, 2007)

Andreas Agnellus of Ravenna, *Breviarium Ecclesiae Ravennatis (Codice Bavaro) secoli 7–10*, G. Rabotti, C. Curradi, A. Vasina (eds), (Rome: Istituto Storico Italiano per il Medioevo, Nella sede dell'Istituto, 1985)

Andreas Agnellus of Ravenna, *The Book of Pontiffs of the Church of Ravenna*, translated into English by D. Mauskopf Deliyannis (Washington: Catholic University of America Press, 2004)

Anonymus Valesianus, *Origo Constantini imperatoris sive Anonymi Valesiani pars prior; Anonymi Valesiani pars posterior*, Th. Mommsen (ed.), (Berlin: Weidmann, *MGH*, 9.1, Auctores Antiquissimi, Chronica minora Sæc. IV.V.VI.VII*, 1961), *pars prior*, pp.7–11, *pars posterior*, pp.306–328

Anonymus Valesianus, *The Excerpts of Valesius*, in *Ammianus Marcellinus*, 3rd edition translated into English by J. C. Rolfe (London: Heinemann, Loeb Classical Library; Cambridge (Massachusetts): Harvard University Press, 1986), pp.506–569

Anonymus Valesianus (*pars posterior*), *Aus der Zeit Theoderichs der Grossen. Einleitung, Text, Übersetzung und Kommentar einer anonymen Quelle*, I. König (ed.), (Darmstadt: Wissenschaftliche Buchgesellschaft, 1997)

Arrian, *Arriani Nicomediensis Scripta Minora*, R. Hercher, A. Eberhard (eds), (Leipzig: Teubner, 2008)

Athenaeus Mechanicus, *Griechische Poliorketiker*, vol. III, R. Schneider (ed.), (Berlin: Weidmann, 1912)

Athenaeus Mechanicus, *Traduction du traité des machines*, translated into French by M. de Rochas d'Aiglun (Paris: Ernest Thorin, 1884)

Athenaeus Mechanicus (translated into English by D. Whitehead & P. H. Blyth), *On Machines*, (Stuttgart: Franz Steiner Verlag *Historia-Einzelschrift*, 182, 2004).

(Saint) Augustine of Hippo, *Opera omnia*, J. P. Migne (ed.), (Paris: Jacques-Paul Migne Imprimerie catholique, *PL*, 32–47, 1841–1849).

(Saint) Augustine of Hippo, *Oeuvres complètes de Saint Augustin*, translated into French by J. B. F. Poujoulat and Abbot Raulx (Bar-le-Duc:1864–1872)

Cassiodorus, *Cassiodori Senatoris Variæ*, Th. Mommsen, L. Traube (eds), (Berlin: Weidmann, *MGH* 12, Auctores Antiquissimi, 1898)

BIBLIOGRAPHY

Cassiodorus, *Cassiodori Senatoris Chronica*, Mommsen Th., (ed.) (Berlin: Weidmann, *MGH*, 11, *Auctores Antiquissimi, Chronica minora sæcula* IV, V, VI, VII, 1961), pp.109–161

Cassiodorus, *Magni Aurelii Cassiodori Variarum Libri XII*, A. J., Fridh (ed.), (Turnhout: Brepols, *CCSL*, 96, 1973)

Cassiodorus, *The Variæ of Magnus Aurelius Cassiodorus Senator*, S. J. B. Barnish (ed.), (Liverpool: Liverpool University Press, *TTH*, 12, 1992)

Caesar, *La guerre des Gaules*, translated into French and commented by L. A. Constans, (Paris: *LBL, CUF*, 1967)

Caesar, *Caesar: The Gallic War*, translated into English by C. Hammond (Oxford: Oxford University Press, 1996)

Chronicle of 452 and *Chronique of 511* [Anonymous Latin chronicle written in Gaule *c*. 452 and 511], *Chronica Gallica a. CCCCLII et DXI*, Th. Mommsen (ed.), (Berlin: Weidmann, *MGH*, 9.1, *Auctores Antiquissimi, Chronica minora sæcula IV, V, VI, VII*, 1961), pp.615–666

Chronicle of 452 [Anonymous Latin chronicle written in Gaul from 379 to 452], *The Gallic Chronicle of 452* [R. W. Burgess, ed.] *A New Critical Edition with a Brief Introduction*, R.W. Mathisen, D. Shanzer (eds), *Society and Culture in Late Antique Gaul. Revisiting the Sources* (Aldershot: Ahsgate, 2001), pp.52 seq

Chronicle of 511 [Anonymous Latin chronicle written in Gaul *c*. 452 and 511], *The Gallic Chronicle of 511: A New Critical Edition with a Brief Introduction*, R. Burgess in Mathisen R.W., Shantzer D. (eds), *Society and Culture in Late Antique Gaul: Revisiting the Sources*, (Aldershot: Ahsgate, 2001), pp.85–100

Chronicle of 741, Continuatio Byzantina-Arabica a DDCXLI, Th. Mommsen (ed.), (Berlin: Weidmann, *MGH, Auctores Antiquissimi*, 11.2, 1981), pp.323–359

J. J. Batista Rodríguez, R. Blanco Silva, 'Un cronica mozarabe a la que se dado en llamar Arabigo-bizantina y una traduccion', (*Rivista de Filología de la Universidad de la Laguna* 17, 1999), pp.153–167

Chronicle of 754 [Anonymous Mozarabic Latin chronicle from 610 to 754], *Continuatio Isidoriana Hispana a. DCCLIV*, Mommsen Th. (ed.), (Munich: Weidmann, *MGH, Auctores Antiquissimi*, 11.2, 1981), pp.323–368

Chronicle of 754, Chronica Muzarabica, J. Gil (ed.), (Madrid: Instituto Antonio de Nebrija, *CSM*, 1, 1973)

Chronicle of 754, Cronica mozarabe de 754: edicion crítica y traduccion, J. E. Lopez Pereira (ed.), (Zaragoza: Anúbar, 1980)

Chronicle of 754, in *Conquerors and Chroniclers of Early Medieval Spain*, translated into English by K. B. Wolf, (Liverpool, Liverpool University Press, *TTH*, 9, 1999), pp.111–160

Chronicon Paschale, translated into Latin by J. P. Migne (Paris: Jacques-Paul Migne Imprimerie catholique, *PG*, 92, 1860)

Chronicon Paschale. 284–628 AD, translated into English by M. Whitby (Liverpool: Liverpool University Press, *TTH*, 7, 2007)

Claudius Ptolemy, *Klaudios Ptolémaios Handbuch der Geographie*, translated into German by Stückelberger A. and *alii* (Basel: Schwabe Verlag, 2006), 2 vols

Constantine VII Porphyrogenitus, *Livre des cérémonies*, Books 1–2, translated into French by A. Vogt (Paris: *LBL*, Collection Byzantine, 2006)

Constantine VII Porphyrogenitus, *The Book of Ceremonies in 2 volumes*, from *CSHB*, J. J. Reiske Bonn, Weber, 1829–1830 edition and translated into English by A. Moffatt, M. Tall, (Canberra: Australian Association for Byzantine Studies, *Byzantina Australiensia*, 18, 2012).

Corippus, Flavii Cresconi Corippi Iohannidos seu de bellis libycis libri VIII, I. Diggle, F. R. D. Goodyear (eds), (Cambridge: Cambridge, University Press, 1970)

Corippus, *In laudem Iustini Augusti minoris libri IV*, translated into English by A. Cameron (London: University of London, The Athlone Press, 1976)

Corippus, *Éloge de l'empereur Justin II*, translated into French by S. Antès (Paris: *LBL, CUF*, 2002)

Corippus, *Panégyrique d'Anastasius. Éloge de Justin II*, translated into French by S. Antès (Paris: *LBL, CUF*, 1981)

Corippus, *Flavii Cresconi Corippi Iohannidos liber primus*, M. A. Vinchesi (ed.), (Naples: M. d'Auria editore, 1983)

Corippus, *La Johannide ou sur les guerres de Libye*, translated into French by J. C. Didderen (Paris: Errances, 2007)

Cyril of Scythopolis, *Cyrilli Vita S. Sabae*, E. Schwartz (ed.), (Leipzig: J. C. Hinrich Verlag, 1939)

(Delehaye, H., ed.), Synaxarium Ecclesiae Constantinopolitanae (Brussels: Propylaeum ad Acta Sanctorum, 1902)

Diocletian (Emperor), *An English Translation of the Edict on Maximum Prices, also known as the Price Edict of Diocletian (Edictum de pretiis rerum venalium)* translated into English A. Kropff (Published at Academia.edu April 27, 2016)

Elias of Nisibis, *Eliæ Metropolitæ Nisibeni Opus Chronologicum, pars prior*, translated into Latin by E.W. Brooks (Rome, Paris, Leipzig: *CSCO, Scriptores Syri*, 3, 7, 1910)

Ennodius of Pavia, *Opera Omnia*, W. A. Hartel (ed.), (Vienna: C. Gerold, 1882)

Eugippius, *Vie de Saint Séverin*, Ph. Régérat (ed.), (Paris: Le Cerf, *SC*, 374, 1991)

Evagrius Scholasticus (J. Bidez & L. Parmentier, eds), *The Ecclesiastical History of Evagrius*, (London: Methuen, 1898)

Evagrius Scholasticus (translated into French by A. J. Festugière), (*Byzantium*, 45, 1975), *Histoire ecclésiastique*, pp.187–488

Fredegar, *Fredegarii Scholastici libri IV cum Continuationibus*, B. Krusch (ed.), (Berlin: Weidmann, *MGH, Scriptores Rerum Merovingicarum, Fredegarii et aliorum Chronica. Vitæ Sanctorum*, 2, 1888), pp.1–193

Fredegar, *The Fourth Book of the Chronicle of Fredegar with its Continuations*, translated into English by J. M. Wallace-Hadrill (London: Greenwood Press, 1981)

Fredegar, *Fredegaire, Chronique des temps mérovingiens*, translated into French by O. Devillers, J. Meyers (Turnhout: Brepols, 2001)

George Kedrenos/Cedrenus (Becker ed.) *Compendium Historiarum*, vol. 1, (Bonn: Weber, *CSHB*, 4, 1838–1839), 2 vols

George of Pisidia (translated into Latin by J. P. Migne, ed.), *Georgius Pisida, Diaconus Constantinopolitanus, opera omnia*, (Paris: Jacques-Paul Migne Imprimerie catholique, *PG*, 92, 1860), *De Heraclii Expeditione Persica*, col. 1198–1262, *Bellum Avaricum*, col. 1263–1297, *Heraclias*, col. 1298–1334

George of Pisidia (A. Pertusi, ed.), *Giorgio di Pisidia. Poemi. I. Panegirici epici* (Ettal: Buch-Kunst-Verlag, *Studia Patristica et Byzantina*, 7, 1959)

Gregory I the Great (L. M. Hartmann, ed.), *Gregorii I Papæ Registrum Epistolarum* (Berlin: Weidmann, *MGH*, *Epistolæ*, 2.34, 1899)

Gregory I the Great (translated into French by P. Minard), *Registre des lettres (livres I et II)* (Paris: Le Cerf, 1991)

Gregory of Tours, *Gregori Turonensis Opera. Teil 1. Libri Historiarum X*, 3 t., B. Krusch, W. Levison (ed.), (Hanover: Hahn, *MGH*, *Scriptores rerum Merovingicarum* 1.1, 1993)

Gregory of Tours (translated into French by H. Latouche), *Histoire des Francs* (Paris: *LBL*, Les Classiques de l'Histoire de France au Moyen Âge, 1995)

Gregory of Tours (translated into French by F. Guizot, Dom Bouquet, ed.), *Histoire des Francs, Œuvres complètes*, tome 1, Livres I à V, tome 2, Livres VI à X (Clermont-Ferrand: Paléo, L'Encyclopédie médiévale, 2001)

Gregory of Tours (translated into French by J. J. E. Roy), *L'Histoire des rois Francs par Gregory of Tours*, Paris: (Gallimard, *NRF*, L'Aube des peuples, 2006)

Hierocles (E. Honigmann, ed.), *Le Synecdèmos d'Hiéroclès et l'opuscule géographique de George de Cyprus* (Brussells: Éditions de l'Institut de Philologie et d'Histoire orientales et Slaves, 1939)

Hydatius (translated into English by R. Burgess), *The Chronicle of Hydatius and the Chronica Constantinopolitana: Two Contemporary Accounts of the Final Years of the Roman Empire* (Oxford: Oxford University Press, 1999)

Isidore of Seville (translated into English by St. A. Barney, W. J. Lewis, J. A. Beach and O. Berghof), *The Etymologies of Isidore of Seville*, (Cambridge: Cambridge University Press, 2006).

Isidore of Seville (translated into Spanish by J. Oroz Reta, M. A. Marcos Casquero), *Etimologías*, (Madrid: Biblioteca de Autores Cristianos, 2009)

Isidore of Seville (J. P. Migne ed.), *Historia de regibus Gothorum, Wandalorum et Suevorum* (Paris: Jacques-Paul Migne Imprimerie catholique, *PL*, 83, 1862), col. 1057–1082

Isidore of Seville, *Historia Gothorum, Wandalorum et Sueborum*, (Berlin: Weidmann, *MGH*, Auctores Antiquissimi, Chronica minora sæc. IV. V. VI. VII., 11, 1894), pp.241–390

Isidore of Seville, *Chronique Universelle. Histoire de l'Espagne wisigothique*, tome 1 and 2, translated into French by N. Desgrugillers (Clermont-Ferrand: Paléo, L'Encyclopédie médiévale, 2009)

Isidore of Seville, *Le Livre des Hommes Illustres. Histoire de l'Espagne wisigothique*, tome 3, translated into French by N. Desgrugillers (Clermont-Ferrand: Paléo, L'Encyclopédie médiévale, 2009)

Jean de Joinville, *Vie de Saint Louis*, J. Martin (ed.), (Paris: Le Livre de Poche, Lettres Gothiques, 1995)

(Saint) Jerome of Stridon, *Correspondance*, translated into French by J. Labourt (Paris: *LBL*, *CUF*, 2002), 8 vols.

John of Antioch, *Fragmenta*, K. Müller (ed.), (Paris: Firmin Didot, *FHG*, 4, 1851), pp.535–662; 5, (1870), pp.27–38

John of Antioch, *Ioannis Antiocheni fragmenta quae supersunt omnia*, translated into English by S. Mariev (ed.), (Berlin, New York: De Gruyter, *CFHB – Series Berolinensis*, 47, 2008)

John of Biclaro, *Chr. continuans Victorem Tunnunensem*, Th. Mommsen (ed.), (Berlin: Weidmann, *MGH*, Auctores Antiquissimi, 11.1, 1961), pp.211–220

John of Biclaro, *Conquerors and Chroniclers of Early Medieval Spain*, translated into English by K. B. Wolf (ed.), (Liverpool: Liverpool University Press, *TTH*, 9, 1991)

John of Epiphania, *Fragmenta*, C. Müller (ed.), (Paris: Firmin Didot, *FHG*, 4, 1851), pp.272–276

John the Lydian, *De Magistratibus*, R. Wünsch (ed.), (Leipzig: Teubner, 1963)

John the Lydian, *John the Lydian. On the Magistracies of the Roman Constitution (De Magistratibus)*, translated into English by T. F. Carney (Sydney: Coronado Press, 1971)

John the Lydian, *Joannes Lydus. On Powers or The Magistracies of the Roman State*, translated into English by A.C. Bandy (Philadelphia: American Philosophical Society, 1983)

John Malalas (L. Dindorf, ed.), *Ioannis Malalae Chronographia* (Bonn: Weber, *CSHB*, 32, 1831)

John Malalas (E. Jeffreys, R. Scott, eds), *The Chronicle of John Malalas* (Melbourne: Australian Association for Byzantine Studies, *Byzantina Australiensa*, 4, 1986)

Jordanes (Th. Mommsen, ed.), *Iordanis Romana et Getica* (Berlin: Weidmann, *MGH*, Auctores Antiquissimi, 5.1, 1882)

Jordanes (translated into French by O. Devillers), *Histoire des Goths* (Paris: *LBL*, La Roue à Livres, 1995)

(Kenyon, F. G., ed.), *Greek papyri in the British Museum* (London: British Museum, Dept. of Manuscripts, 1893)

(Kraemer, G. J., ed.), *Excavations at Nessana, III, Non-literary papyri* (Princeton: Princeton University Press, 2016)

(Krueger, P. ed.), *Justinian Code, Codex Justinianus* (Berlin: Weidmann, 1877)

Leo VI the Wise, the Tactician (translated into Latin by J. P. Migne) *Taktika* (Paris: Jacques-Paul Migne Imprimerie catholique, *PG*, 107, 1863), col. 669–1116

Leo VI the Wise (translated into English by G. T. Dennis), *The Taktika of Leo VI, Text, Translation and Commentary*, *CFHB*, 49 (Washington: John Duffy, 2010)

Liudprand of Cremona (E. Dümmler, ed.), *Relatio de legatione constantinopolitana* (Hanover: Hahn, *MGH*, *Scriptores rerum germanicarum*, 41, 1877), pp.124–136.

Liudprand of Cremona (translated into English by J. J. Norwich), *Liudprand of Cremona: The Embassy to Constantinople and Other Writings* (London: Rutland, 1993), pp.177–210.

Malchus of Philadelphia (K. Müller, ed.), *Fragmenta* (Paris: Firmin Didot, *FHG*, 4, 1851), pp.111–132

Malchus of Philadelphia (translated into English by R. C. Blockley), *The Fragmentary Classicising Historians of the Later Roman Empire: Eunapius, Olympiodorus, Priscus and Malchus*, 2, translated into English by R.C. Blockley (Cambridge: Francis Cairns Publications, ARCA Classical and Medieval Texts, Papers and Monographs, 10, 2007)

Marcellinus Comes (Th. Mommsen, ed.), *Chr.* (Berlin: Weidmann, *MGH*, *Auctores Antiquissimi*, 11.2, 1961), pp.37–108

Marcellinus Comes (translated into English by B. Croke, Th. Mommsen, ed.), *The Chronicle of Marcellinus: A Translation and Commentary (with a reproduction of Mommsen's edition of the Text) by Comes Marcellinus* (Sydney: Australian Association for Byzantine Studies, 1995)

Marius Aventicensis (translated into French by N. Desgrugillers), *Chronique 455–581 suivie de sa Continuation jusqu'à l'année 615*, (Clermont-Ferrand: Paléo, L'Encyclopédie médiévale, 2007)

(Maspéro, J., ed.), *Papyrus grecs d'époque Byzantine*, I and II, (Cairo: Catalogue général des antiquités égyptiennes du Musée du Caire, no. 67 001–67 187, 1910–1912)

Maurice (translated into English by G. T. Dennis), *Maurice's Strategikon* (Philadelphia: University of Pennsylvania Press, 1984)

Maurice (G. T. Dennis, ed. Translated into German by E. Gamillscheg), *Das Strategikon Des Maurikios* (Vienna: Verlag der Österreichischen Akademie der Wissenschaften, 2021)

Menander Protector (translated into English by R.C. Blockley), *The History of Menander the Guardsman* (Liverpool: Francis Cains, ARCA, Classical and Medieval Texts, Papers and Monographs, 17, 2006)

(Lemerle, P., ed.), *Miracula Sancti Demetrii*, Les *plus anciens recueils des miracles de Saint Démétrius et la pénétration des Slaves dans les Balkans, I – Le texte, II – Commentaire* (Paris: Éditions du *CNRS*, 1979–1981)

Nikephoros (translated into English by C. Mango), *Nikephoros, Patriarch of Constantinople. Short History* (Dumbarton Oaks: Trustees for Harvard University, *CFHB*, 13, 1990)

Olympiodorus (translated into English by R. C. Blockley), *The Fragmentary Classicising Historians of the Later Roman Empire: Eunapius, Olympiodorus, Priscus and Malchus* (Cambridge: Francis Cairns Publications, ARCA Classical and Medieval Texts, Papers and Monographs, 10, 2007)

Paul the Deacon (translated into English by W. D. Foulke), *History of Langobards* (Philadelphia: Department of History, University of Pennsylvania; New York: Longmann, Green and Co, 1907)

Paul the Deacon (L. Bethmann, G. Waitz, eds), *Pauli Historia Langobardorum* (Hanover: Hahn, *MGH, Scriptores rerum Langobardicarum et Italicarum sæc. VI-IX*, 1964), pp.12–188

Paul the Deacon translated into French by F. Bougard) *Histoire des Lombards* (Turnhout: Brepols, Miroir du Moyen Âge, 1994)

Paul the Deacon (H. Droysen, ed.), *Historia Romana*, (Berlin: Weidmann, *MGH, Auctores Antiquissimi*, 2, 1882)

Peri Strategikes (translated into English by G. T. Dennis), *Three Byzantine Military Treatises*, *CFHB*, 25, (Dumbarton Oaks: Trustees for Harvard University, 1985), pp.1–136

Polybius (translated into English by William R. Paton), *Polybius: The Histories* (London: Heinemann, Loeb Classical Library, 1922–1927)

Polybius (translated into French by D. Roussel), *Histoire*, (Paris: Éditions Gallimard, coll. Quarto, 2003)

Pomponius Mela (translated into French by A. Silbermann), *Pomponius Mela. Chorographie* (Paris: *LBL, CUF*, 1988)

Priscus of Panium (Priscos Panita) (K. Müller, ed.), *Fragmenta* (Paris: Firmin Didot, *FHG*, 4, 1851), pp.69–110

Priscus of Panium (Priscos Panita) (translated into English by R. C. Blockley), *The Fragmentary Classicising Historians of the Later Roman Empire: Eunapius, Olympiodorus, Priscus and Malchus*, 2 (Cambridge: Francis Cairns Publications, ARCA Classical and Medieval Texts, Papers and Monographs, 10, 2007)

Procopius of Caesarea (Procopius) (translated into English by H. B. Dewing et al), *History of the Wars*, 6 volumes (London: Heinemann, Loeb Classical Library, 1979)

Procopius of Caesarea (Procopius) (translated into English by H. B. Dewing, revised and modernized, with an introduction and notes by A. Kaldellis, maps and genealogies by I. Mladjov), *Prokopios. The Wars of Justinian*, (Indianapolis: Hackett Publishing Company, Inc., 2014)

Procopius of Caesarea (translated into English by E. H. Warmington), *The Anecdota* (London: Heinemann, Loeb Classical Library, 1979)

Procopius of Caesarea (translated into English by H. B. Dewing), *Buildings* (London: Heinemann, Loeb Classical Library,1979)

Procopius of Caesarea (translated into French by D. Roques), *La guerre contre les Vandales* (Paris: *LBL*, La Roue à Livre, 1990)

Procopius of Caesarea (translated into French by P. Maraval), *Histoire secrete* (Paris: *LBL*, La Roue à Livres, 2004)

Procopius of Caesarea (translated into French by D. Roques), *Constructions de Justinien Ier* (Alexandria: Edizioni dell'Orso, 2011)

Procopius of Caesarea (translated into French by D. Roques), *Histoire des Goths*, translated into French by D. Roques, J. Auberger (Paris: *LBL*, La Roue à livres, 2015)

Procopius of Gaza (J. P. Migne, ed.), *Panegyric of the Emperor. Anastasius I* (Paris: Jacques-Paul Migne Imprimerie catholique, *PG*, 87, 1865)

Prosper of Aquitaine and his continuor (Th. Mommsen, ed.), *Prosperi Tironis Epitoma Chr. ed. primum a. CCCCXXXIII* (433), *continuata ad a. CCCCLV* (455) (Berlin: Weidmann, *MGH, Auctores Antiquissimi, Chronica minora sæcula IV, V, VI, VII*, 9, 1961), pp.341–501

Sidonius Apollinaris (translated into French by A. Loyen), *Tome II: Correspondance. Livres I-V, Tome III: Correspondance. Livres VI-IX* (Paris: *LBL, CUF*, 1970)

Socrates of Constantinople (Scholasticus) (translated into English by A. C. Zenos), *The Ecclesiastical History of Socrates Scholasticus*, in Ph. Schaff and H. Wallace (eds), *Nicene and Post-Nicene Fathers*, Second Series, vol. 2 (New York: Christian Literature Publishing Co., 1890), pp.1–178

Socrates of Constantinople (G. Hansen, ed., translated into French by P. Maraval), *Histoire ecclésiastique* (Paris: Le Cerf, *SC*, 477, 493, 505, 506, 2004–2007)

Synesius of Cyrene (translated into English by A. Fitzgerald), The letters of Synesius of Cyrene (London: A., Oxford University Press, 1926)

Synesius of Cyrene (A. Garzya, ed., translated into French by D. Roques), *Lettres*, 2 vols (Paris: *LBL, CUF*, 2003)

Theodore Synkellos (translated into French by F. Makk), *Traduction et Commentaire de l'homélie écrite probablement par Théodore le Syncelle sur le siège de Constantinople en 626* (Szeged: Acta Universitatis de Attila Jozsef Nominatae, *Acta antiqua et archaeologica*, 19, 1975)

Theodore Synkellos (S. Szadeczky-Kardoss and Th. Olejos, eds), Breviarium homiliae Theodorei Syncelli de obsidione avarica Constantinopolis (Turnhout: Brepols, Analecta Bollandiana, Revue critique d'hagiographie, 108, 1, 1990)

Theodoret of Cyrus (Y. Azéma, ed.), Correspondance (Paris: Le Cerf, 1964)

Theophanes Confessor (I. P. Migne, ed.), Theophanis Abbatis Agri et Confessoris Chronographia (Paris: Jacques-Paul Migne Imprimerie catholique, PG, 108, 1863), col. 55–1009

Theophanes Confessor (C. de Boor, ed.), *Theophanis Chronographia*, 2 volumes (Leipzig: Teubner, 1883)

Theophanes Confessor (translated into English by C. Mango & R. Scott), *The Chronicle of Theophanes Confessor. Byzantine and Near Eastern History AD 284–813* (Oxford: Clarendon Press, 1997)

Theophylact Simocatta (Simokatès), *Histoire de Constantinople depuis le règne de Justin jusqu'à la fin de l'Empire traduite sur les originaux grecs par Mr Cousin* (Paris: Damien Foucault, 1685)

Theophylact Simocatta (C. de Boor, ed.), *Theophylacti Simocattæ Historiæ* (Leipzig: Nabu Press, 2014)

Theophylact Simocatta (translated into German by P. Schreiner), *Theopylaktes Simokates: Geschichte* (Stuttgart: Hiersemann, 1985)

Theophylact Simocatta (translated into English by M. and M. Whitby), *The History of Theophylact Simocatta: An English Translation with Introduction*, translated into English by M. and M. Whitby (Oxford: Oxford University Press, 1986)

Vegetius (Flavius Vegetius Renatus) (K. Lang, ed.), *Flavii Vegetii Renati Epitoma Rei Militaris* (Leipzig: Teubner, 1967)

Vegetius (translated into English by N. P. Milner), *Vegetius: Epitome of Military Science* (Liverpool: Liverpool University Press, TTH, 16, 1993)

Vegetius (Translated by M. D. Reeve), Epitoma Rei Militaris (Oxford: Clarendon Press, 2017)

Virgil, Vergilius Vaticanus facsimile edition (Graz: Akademische Druck-u. Verlagsanstalt (ADEVA), 1980)

Virgil, Vergilius Romanus facsimile edition (Zurich: Belser Verlag, 1985)

Victor of Tunnuna (Tonnena) (C. Cardelle de Hartmann, ed.), Victor Tunnunensis, Iohannes Biclarensis. Chronicon cum reliquiis ex Consularibus Caesaraugustanis (Turnhout: Brepols, CCSL, 173 A, 2001)

Victor of Tunnuna (translated into English by J. R. C. Martin), *Arians and Vandals of the 4th–6th Centuries: Annotated translations of the historical works by Bishops Victor of Vita (Historia Persecutionis Africanae Provinciae) and Victor of Tonnena (Chronicon), and of the religious works by Bishop Victor of Cartenna* (Newcastle: Cambridge Scholars Publishing, 2008)

Vitelli, G., Norsa M., et al (eds), *Papiri greci e latini*, III (Florence: Felice Le Monnier, 1914)

Wessely, C., 'Griechische Papyri des British Museum' (Vienna: Universität Wien, *Wiener Studien. Zeitschrift für classische Philologie*, 9, 1887), pp.235–278

(Wessely C., ed.), *Studien zur Palaeographie und Papyruskunde*, XX (Leipzig: Verlag von E. Avenarius, 1921)

Xenophon (translated into English by C. L. Brownson), Anabasis. Books I-VII (London: Heinemann, Loeb Classical Library, 1989)

(Pseudo-)Zachariah Rhetor (translated into English by G. Greatrex), *The Chronicle of Pseudo-Zachariah Rhetor: Church and War in Late Antiquity* (Liverpool: Liverpool University Press, 2011)

(John) Zonaras (L. Dindorf, ed.), *Epitome Historiarum Ioannis Zonarae Epitome Historiarum*, 6 volumes (Leipzig: 1868–1875)

(John) Zonaras (translated into English by T. Banchich & E. Lane), *The History of Zonaras: from Alexander Severus to the Death of Theodosius the Great* (London: Routledge, Routledge Classical Translations, 2009).

Zosimus, *Histoire Nouvelle* (edited and translated into French by F. Paschoud), *Histoire Nouvelle*, 5 volumes (Paris: LBL, CUF, 1971–1989)

Zosimus (translated into English and ed. by J. J. Buchanan & H. T. Davis), *Historia Nova; the Decline of Rome* (San Antonio: Trinity University Press, 1967)

2, Middle-Eastern Sources

Agapius of Hierapolis (Agapios Manbidj or Maḥbūb ibn Qusṭanṭīn) (translated into French by A. A. Vasiliev), *Kitāb al-'Unvan*, 2nd part (Paris: Firmin Didot, *PO*, 8, 1912), pp.399–554

Al-Azdi (translated into English by H. Hamada & J. Scheiner), *The Early Muslim Conquest of Syria: An English Translation of al-Azdi's Futüh al-Sham*, (London: Routledge, 2019)

Al-Baladhuri (translated into English by Ph. Hitti), *The Origins of the Islamic State*, Studies in History, Economics and Public Law 163 (London: P. S. King and Son, 1916)

Al-Hakam (Ch. C. Torrey ed.), *The History of the Conquest of Egypt, North Africa and Spain: known as Futuh Misr by Ibn Abd al-akam* (New York: Cosimo Classics, 2010)

Al-Hakam (translated into English by Y. Hilloowla), *The History of the Conquest of Egypt, being a partial Translation of Ibn'Abd al-Hakam Futuh Misr and an Analysis of this Translation. A Dissertation Submitted to the Faculty of the Department Near Eastern Studies*, (Tucson: The University of Arizona Press, 1998)

Al-Mo'izz Mohammad ibn Mohammad (*Futuh al-Bahnasâ*) (translated into French by É. Galtier). *Foutouh al-Bahnasâ* (Cairo: Imprimerie de l'Institut français d'archéologie orientale, *MIFAO*, 22, 1909)

Bar Hebraeus (translated into English by E. A. Wallis Budge), *The Chronography of Gregory Abû'l Faraj, commonly known as Bar Hebraeus*, (London: Oxford University Press, 1932)

Bar Hebraeus, (translated into French by Ph. Talon), *La Chronographie de Bar Hebraeus* (Brussels: EME éditions, Nouvelles Études Orientales, 3 volumes, 2013)

(Chabot, J. B. ed.), *Chronicle of 1234* [Anonymous Syrian chronicle of 1203–1204], *Anonymi auctoris chronicon ad annum 1234 pertinens* (Paris: *CSCO*, 14–15, *Scriptores syri*, 3, t. 1, 1937), pp.118–126

(Chabot J. B., ed.), *Zuqnin Chronicle* (also known as *Chronicle of Pseudo-Denys of Tell-Mahré*), *Incerti auctoris chronicon Pseudo-Dionysianum vulgo dictum*, II, Scriptores Syri 53, (Leuven: and CSCO, 104, 1933)

Eutychius of Alexandria (translated into German by M. Breydy), *Das Annalenwerk des Eutychios von Alexandrien* (Leuven: Peeters, 1985) 471–472

(Harrak, A., translated into English by), *Zuqnin Chronicle, The Chronicle of Zuqnîn, parts III and IV (A.D. 488–775)*, Scriptores Syri 213 (Toronto: Pontifical Institute of Medieval Studies, *CSCO*, 507, 1999)

(Hespel, R., translated into French by), *Zuqnin Chronicle* (also known as *Chronicle of Pseudo-Denys of Tell-Mahré*) (Leuven: Durbecq, 1989).

Ibn Khaldun (translated by F. Rosenthal), *The Muqaddimah: An introduction to History*, 3 volumes (New York: Pantheon Books, Bollingen Series, 1958)

Ibn Khaldun (extracts translated into French by A. Cheddadi), *Peuples et nations du monde. Extraits des Ibar*, 2 volumes (Paris: Sinbad, La Bibliothèque arabe, 1995)

John of Nikiu (translated into French by H. Zotenberg), *Chronique de Jean, évêque de Nikiou* (Paris: Imprimerie nationale, 1883), Notices et extraits des manuscrits de la bibliothèque Nationale, 24

John of Nikiu (translated into English by R. H. Charles), *The Chronicle of John Bishop of Nikiu* (London: Text and Translation Society, 1916)

John of Ephesus (translated into English by E. W. Brooks), *Ecclesiastical History*, CSCO, 106, Scriptores Syri, 55 (Leuven: Secrétariat du CSCO, 1952).

Joshua the Stylite (translated into English by F. R. Trombley and J. W. Wat), *The Chronicle of Pseudo-Joshua the Stylite* (Liverpool: Liverpool University Press, 2000)

Juansher Juansheriani (translated into English by D. Gamq'relidze), 'The Life of Vakhtang Gorgasali' in *Kartlis Tskhovreba. A History of Georgia*, Oxford Oriental Monographs, (Tbilissi: Artanuji Publishing, 2014), pp.77–134

Michael the Syrian (translated into French by J. B. Chabot), *Chronique de Michel le Syrien*, vol. 2 (Brussels: Culture et civilisation, 1963)

Michael the Syrian (Michael the Great) (G. Yuhanna Ibrahim, ed.), *Text and Translations of the Chronicle of Michæl the Great, The Edessa-Aleppo Syriac Codex of the Chronicle of Michæl the Great*, vol. 1, (Piscataway: Gorgias Press, 2009)

Movses Dasxuranci (transmated into English by C. F. J. Dowsett), *The History of the Caucasian Albanians by Movses Dasxuranci*, London Oriental Series 8 (London: Oxford University Press, 1961)

Strategius (Antiochus Strategos) (F. C. Conybeare, ed.), The Capture of Jerusalem by the Persians in 614,' *English Historical Review*, 25, 1910, pp.502–517

Strategius (translated into French by G. Garitte). *La prise de Jerusalem par les Perses en* 614, CSCO, 202–203, Scriptores Iberici 11–12 (Leuven: Peeters, 1960)

Tabari, (translated into French by H. Zotenberg), *Chronique de Abou-Djafar-Mo' hammed-Ben-Djarir-Ben-Yezid-Tabari, traduite sur la version persane d'Abou-'Ali Mo' hammed Bel'Ami d'après les manuscrits de Paris, de Gotha, de Londres et de Canterbury*, 4 volumes (Paris: Librairie G. P. Maisonneuve, Éditions Besson et Chantemerle, 1958)

Tabari (translated into English by F. Rosenthal), *The History of al-Tabari*, 5 volumes (Albany: State University of New York, 1989)

Thomas the Presbyter (translated into Latin by J. B. Chabot), *Chronicon miscellaneum ad annum Domini 724 pertinens* or *Liber Calipharum*, (Paris: CSCO, Scriptores Syri, vol. 4, 1904), pp.61–119

Al-Waqidi (translated into English by W. N. Lees), *The Conquest of Syria, commonly Acribed to Aboo Abdallah Mohammad B. Omar Al-Waqidi*, Bibliotheca Indica 66 (Calcutta: F.Carbery, 1854).

Al-Waqidi (translated into English by Mawlana Sulayman al-Kindi), *The Islamic Conquest of Syria. A Translation of Futuhusham by al-Imam al-Waqidi*, (London: Ta-Ha Publishers, 2012)

3, Scholarly Works

Abadie-Reynal, C., 'Séleucie-Zeugma et Apamée sur l'Euphrate: étude d'un cas de villes jumelles dans l'Antiquité' *Histoire urbaine*, 1/3, (2001), pp.7–24

Ager, B., 'West Wight, Isle of Wight: Anglo-Saxon Grave Assemblages (2004 T187)' in *Treasure Annual Report 2004* (London: Department for Culture, Media and Sport, 2006), pp.68–71

Akram, A. I., *The Sword of Allah: Khalid bin al-Waleed – His Life and Campaigns* (Oxford: Oxford University Press, 2004)

Al-Shbib, Sh., 'La défense des villes à l'époque Byzantine: alternance entre les tours et les bastions, tradition ou innovation?' *Syria*, 95 (2018), pp.413–430

Anson, E. M., 'Alexander's Hypaspists and the Argyraspids', *Historia*, 30 (1981), pp.117–120

Arce, I., Feissel, D., Weber-Karyotaki, Th. M., 'The Anastasius Edict Project: A Preliminary Report. Part 1 – The Epigraphic Evidence' in C. Sebastian Sommer & S. Matešic (eds), *Limes*, XXIII, Sonderband 4 / II, *Proceedings of the 23rd International Congress of Roman Frontier Studies, Ingolstadt, 2015, Akten des 23. Internationalen Limeskongresses in Ingolstadt 2015* (Mainz: Nünnerich-Asmus Verlag, 2018), pp.673–681

Aussaresses, F., *L'Armée Byzantine à la fin du VIe siècle d'après le Strategicon de l'empereur Maurice* (Bordeaux: Féret et Fils, Bibliothèque Universitaire du Midi, 1909)

Asufay-Effenberger, N., *Die Landmauer von Konstantinopel-Istanbul: Historisch-topographische und baugeschichtliche Untersuchungen* (Berlin: De Gruyter, 2007)

Bachrach, B. S., 'On Roman Ramparts 300–1300' in G. Parker (ed.), *The Cambridge illustrated History of Warfare: The Triumph of the West* (Cambridge, Cambridge University Press, 1995), pp.64–91

Badel, Ch., 'Un chef germain entre Byzance et l'Italie. L'épitaphe d'Asbadus à Pavie (*Suppl. It.* 9, 15)' in M. Ghilardi, Chr. J. Goddard and P. Porena (eds), *Les cités de l'Italie tardo-antique (IVe-VIe siècle). Institutions, économie, société, culture et religion* (Rome, CEFR, 2006), pp.91–100.

Baldwin, B., 'The Career of Corippus' *CQ*, 28 (1978), pp.195–212.

Barnea, I., 'Dinogetia – ville Byzantine du Bas-Danube, sec. IV-XII', *Byzantina*, 10 (1980), pp.237–287

Bass, G. F. & Doorninck, F. H. van Jr., *Yassi Ada I: a Seventh Century Byzantine Shipwreck* (College Station: Texas A & M University Press, 1982)

Bataille, A., 'Un inventaire de vêtements inédit', *Eos*, 48, fasc. 2 (1956), pp.83–88

Bavant, B., 'Le duché Byzantin de Rome. Origine, durée et extension géographique', *MEFR, Moyen Âge, Temps modernes*, 91, n° 91-1(1979), pp.41–88

Bavant, B., 'La ville dans le Nord de l'Illyricum (Pannonie, Mésie I, Dacie et Dardanie)', *PEFR*, 77 (1984), pp.245–288

Baynes, N. H., 'The Supranatural Defenders of Constantinople' in *Byzantine Studies and Other Essays* (London: The University of London, Athlone Press, 1955), pp.248–260

Bellen, H., 'Der Primicerius Mauricius. Ein Beitrag zum Thebäerproblem', *Historia*, X, 2 (1961), pp.238–247

Benaissa, A., 'The Size of the Numerus Transtigritanorum in the Fifth Century', *Zeitschrift für Papyrologie und Epigraphik*, 175 (2010), p 224–226

Bénazeth, D., 'Calques de Baouit archivés à l'Ifao', *BIFAO*, 105 (2005), pp.1–12

Boespflug, F., *La Crucifixion dans l'art: Un sujet planétaire* (Montrouge, Bayard Éditions, 2019)

Bohlendorf-Arslan, B. & Ricci, A. (eds), 'Early Byzantine Iron Helmets from Novae (the Diocese of Thrace)', *BYZAS*, 15, *Byzantine Small Finds in Archaeological Contexts*, DAI Istanbul (2012), pp.91–104

Boozer, A. L., 'Frontiers and Borderlands in Imperial Perspectives: Exploring Rome's Egyptian Frontier', *AJA*, 117/2 (2013), pp.275–292

Borel, C., 'Spangenhelm' in M. Martiniani-Reber (ed.), *Byzance en Suisse, catalogue d'exposition* (Genève: Musées d'art et d'Histoire, 2015), pp.400–405

Börm, H., *Westrom. Von Honorius bis Justinian* (Stuttgart: Kohlhammer, 2013)

Bréhier, L., *Les institutions de l'Empire Byzantin*, L'Évolution de l'humanité (Paris, Albin Michel, 1970)

Brodka, D., *Die Geschichtesphilosophie in der spätantiken Historiographie. Studien zu Prokopios, Agathias von Myrina und Theophylaktos Simokates*, Studien un Texte zur Byzantinistik 5, (Frankfurt am Main: Peter Lang, 2004)

Brown, T. S., *Gentlemen and Officers: Imperial Administration and Aristocratic Power in Byzantine Italy, AD 554-800* (London: British School at Rome, 1984)

Bugarski, I., 'A Contribution to the Study of Lamellar Armours', *Starinar*, 55 (2005), pp.161–180

Bugarski, I. & Ivanišević, V., 'Sixth century Foederati from the Upper Moesian Limes: Weapons in a Social Context' in S. Golubović, N. Mrđić (eds), Vivere militare est, vol. I (Belgrade: Institute of Archaelogy, Monographies, 68/1, 2018), pp.291–332.

Burck, E., 'The Die Iohannis des Corippus' in E. Burck (ed.), *Das römische Epos* (Darmstadt: Buchgesellschaft, 1979), pp.379–399

Bury, J. B., A History of the Later Roman Empire from the Death of Theodosius I to the Death of Justinian (AD 395 to AD 565), (New York: Dover Publications, 1958), 2 vols

Butler, A., *The Arab Conquest of Egypt and the Last Thirty Years of the Roman Dominion* (Oxford: Clarendon Press, 1902)

Caetani, L., *Annali dell'Islam* (Hildesheim: G. Olms, 1972), 10 vols.

Cagnat, R., 'strator' in Ch. Daremberg, E. Saglio, *Dictionnaire des Antiquités*, tome IV (Paris: Hachette, 1900), p.1530.

Calament, Fl., 'L'apport historique des découvertes d'Antinoé au costume dit de cavalier sassanide' in C. Flück, G. Vogelsang-Eastwood, *Riding Costume in Egypt: Origin and Appearance* (Leiden, Boston: Brill, 2004), pp.37–72

Cambeda, A. Ceccherelli, *Le Mura di Aureliano, itinerari d'arte e di cultura* (Rome: Fratelli Palombi Editor, 1990)

Cameron, A., *Agathias* (Oxford: Oxford University Press, 1970)

Cameron, A., 'Agathias on Sassanians', *DOP*, 23, 1969–1970), pp.78–176

Cameron, A., *Circus Factions. Blues and Greens at Rome and Byzantium* (Oxford: Oxford University Press, 1976)

Cameron, A., 'The Virgin's Robe: An Episode in the History of Seventh Century Constantinople', *REB*, 49 (1979), pp.42–56

Cameron, A. & Conrad, L. I. (eds), *The Byzantine and Early Islamic Near East*, vol. 1, *Problems in the Literary Source Materials* (Princeton NJ: The Darwin Press, 1992)

Cameron, A., *The Mediterranean World in Late Antiquity AD 395–600* (London: Routledge, 1993)

Cameron, A. & Conrad, L. I. (eds), *The Byzantine and Early Islamic Near East*, vol. 3, *States, Resources and Armies* (Princeton NJ: Darwin Press, 1995).

Cameron, A., Ward-Perkins, B., Whitby, M. (eds), *Late Antiquity: Empire and Successors, AD 425–600*, The Cambridge Ancient History, 14 (Cambridge, Cambridge University Press, 2008).

Canard, M., 'The Arab Expansion: The Military Problem' in F. M. Donner, *The Expansion of the Early Islamic State* (London: Routledge, 2007) pp.63–80

Caprioli, M., '… a parte Romanonum octo milia numerus. Considerazioni sulla batalla dello Scultenna (643) e sull' esercito esarcale (VI-VIII secolo)', *Nueva Antologia Militare*, 3, fasc. 9, Storia Militare Medievale (2022), pp.7–19

Casson, L., *Ships and Seafaring in ancient Times* (London: British Museum Press, 1994)

Chabot, G., 'La vitesse des navires anciens', *Annales de Géographie*, 288 (1942), pp.284

Chadburn, C., 'Les guerriers berbères dans l'Antiquité', *Prétorien*, 15 (2010), pp.21–28

Chagnon, L., *La conquête musulmane de l'Égypte* (Paris: Economica, 2008)

Chamoux, F., 'Une nouvelle copie de l'édit d'Anastasius Ier sur la Cyrénaïque', *Comptes rendus des séances de l'Académie des Inscriptions et Belles-Lettres*, 99-3 (1955), pp.333–334

Charles, M. B., 'Vegetius on Liburnae: Naval Terminology in the Late Roman', *Scripta classica Israelica*, 24 (2005), pp.181–194

Chatzidakis, M., *Byzantine Art in Greece, Mosaics – Wall Paintings. Hosios Loukas* (Athens: Melissa, 1997)

Chauvot, A., 'Figure du cercle et représentation des Goths chez Ammien Marcellin', *Ktèma*, 35 (2010), pp.231–241

Chevedden, P. E., 'Artillery in Late Antiquity: Prelude to the Middle Ages' in J. F. Haldon (ed.), *Byzantine Warfare* (Aldershot: Ashgate Publishing, 2007), pp.453–496

Christie, N., *The Lombards. The Ancient Langobards* (Oxford: Blackwell, 1995)

A. Claridge, *Rome: An Oxford Archaeological Guide* (Oxford: Oxford University Press, 1998)

Clédat, J., *Le monastère et la nécropole de Baouît*, MIFAO 12, 1 and 2 (Cairo: Imprimerie de l'Institut français d'archéologie orientale, 1904)

Colin, F., *Les peuples libyens de la Cyrénaïque à l'Égypte d'après les sources de l'Antiquité* (Brussels: Académie Royale de Belgique, 2000)

Comfort, A. M., 'Roman Bridges of South-East Anatolia' in H. Bru, G. Labarre, *L'Anatolie des peuples, des cités et des cultures (IIe millénaire av. J.-C.-Ve siècle ap. J.-C.). Colloque international de Besançon – 26–27 novembre 2010*, vol. 2 (Besançon: Institut des Sciences et Techniques de l'Antiquité (ISTA), 1277-2, 2013), pp.315–342.

Conant, J., *Staying Roman. Conquest and Identity in Africa and the Mediterranean, 439–700* (Cambridge: Cambridge University Press, 2012)

Cosentino, S., 'Gaudiosus Draconarius: la Sardegna bizantina attraverso un epitafio del secolo 6', *Quaderni della Rivista di bizantinistica*, 13 (1994)

Courtois, C., *Les Vandales et l'Afrique* (Paris: Arts et Métiers Graphiques, 1955)

Croke, B., 'Two Early Byzantine Earthquakes and Their Liturgical Commemoration', *Byzantion*, 51 (1981), pp.122–147

Croke, B., 'The Date of the 'Anastasian Long Wall' of Thrace'', *GRBS*, 23 (1982), pp.59–78

Croke, B., *Count Marcellinus and His Chronicle* (Oxford: Oxford University Press, 2001)

Croke, B., 'Leo I and the Palace Guard', *REB,* 75 (2005), pp.117–151

Crow, J. & Ricci, A., 'Investigating the Hinterland of Constantinople: Interim Report on the Anastasian Long Wall,' *Journal of Roman Archaeology*, 10 (1997), pp.235–262

Curta, F., *The Making of the Slavs. History and Archælogy of the Lower Danube c.500–700* (Cambridge: Cambridge University Press, 2001)

Curta, F. & Kovalev, R., (eds), *The Other Europe in the Middle Ages. Avars, Bulgars, Khazars and Cumans, East Central and Eastern Europe in the Middle Ages, 450–1450*, vol. 2 (Leiden: Brill, 2009)

Curta, F., 'Chronology: what is the date of the earliest stirrups in Europe?' in F. Curta & R. Kovalev (eds), *The Other Europe in the Middle Ages. Avars, Bulgars, Khazars and Cumans* (Leiden: Brill, 2009), pp.297–326

Curta F., (ed.) *Neglected barbarians* (Turnhout: Brepols, 2011)

Dagron, G., 'Modèles de combattants et technologie militaire dans le *Strategikon* de Maurice' in *ARB-AFAM* (1990), pp.279–284

Dain, A., 'Les stratégistes byzantins', Collège de France, Centre de recherche d'histoire et civilisation de Byzance, *Travaux et Mémoires*, 2 (1967), pp.317–392

Dain, A., 'Urbicius ou Maurice', *REB*, 26 (1968), pp.123–136

D'Amato, Raffaele, *Roman military Clothing (3): AD 400–640* (Oxford: Osprey Publishing, 2005) Men-At-Arms series 425

D'Amato, Raffaele, 'A Sixth or Early Seventh Century AD. Iconography of Roman Military Equipment in Egypt: The Deir Abou Hennis Frescoes' in G. Theotokis, A. Yıldız, *A Military History of the Mediterranean Sea* (Leiden: Brill, *History of Warfare*, 118, 2018), pp.105–152

D'Amato, Raffaele & Pflaum, V., 'Two Suites of Lamellar Armour from Kranj (Carnium), Slovenia, in the light of Archaelogical Analogies, Written Sources and Contemporary Iconography', *Acta Militaria Medievalia*, 15 (2019), pp.7–50

D'Amato, Raffaele *Roman Heavy Cavalry (2) AD 500–1450* (Oxford: Osprey Publishing, 2019) Elite series 235

Dana, D., 'Onomastique et recrutement de l'armée Byzantine d'Afrique, l'épitaphe du soldat Buraido révisée (ILAlg, I, 81)', *Antiquités Africaines*, 49 (2014), pp.151–160

Delehaye, H., *Les légendes grecques des Saints militaires* (Paris: Picard et Fils, 1909)

Dennis, G. T., 'Flies, Mice, and the Byzantine Crossbow', *Byzantine and Modern Greek Studies* 7 (1981), pp.1–5

Dennis, G. T., 'Byzantine Battle Flags', *Byzantinische Forschungen*, 8 (1982), pp.51–59

Dey, H., 'Verso una storia edilizia delle Mura Aureliane, da Aureliano a Onorio (271–403 d.C.)' in R. Rita Volpe, R. Santangeli Valenzani, D. Esposito et al (eds), *Le Mura Aureliane nella storia di Roma, 1, Da Aureliano a Onorio, Atti Primo Convegno, 25 Marzo 2015* (Rome: TrE-Press, 2017), pp.13–28

Diehl, Ch., *Études sur l'administration Byzantine dans l'exarchat de Ravenne (568–751)*, Bibliothèque des Écoles Françaises d'Athènes et de Rome 53 (Paris: Ernest Thorin, 1888).

Diehl, Ch., *L'Afrique Byzantine. Histoire de la domination Byzantine en Afrique (533–709)* (Paris: Ernest Leroux, 1896)

Diesner, H. H. 'Das Bucellariertum von Stilicho und Sarus bis auf Ætius (454–455)', *Klio*, 54 (1972), pp.321–350.

Diethart, J. M. & Dintsis, P., 'Die Leontoklibanarier. Versuch einer archäologisch-papyrologischen Zusammenschau', Βυζάντιος. *Festschrift für Herbert Hunger zum 70. Geburtstag* (Vienna: E. Becvar, 1984), pp.67–84

Dillemann, L. *Haute Mésopotamie et pays adjacents: contribution à la géographie historique de la région du Ve s. avant l'ère chrétienne au VIe s. de cette ère*, Bibliothèque archéologique et historique 72 (Paris: Geuthner, 1962)

Dimitrova, E., *The Ceramic Relief Plaques from Vinica. The most significant values of the cultural and natural heritage* (Skopje: Directorate for protection of cultural heritage, 2017)

Dixon, K. R. & Southern P., *The Roman Cavalry* (London: Batsford, 1992)

Domínguez, J. F. & Manchon Gomez, R., 'Recherches sur les mots campidoctor et campiductor: de l'Antiquité au Moyen Âge tardif', *Bulletin Du Cange*, 58 (2000), pp.5–44

Donner, F. M. *The Expansion of the Early Islamic State* (London: Routledge, 2007)

Doorninck F. H. van Jr, 'The Seventh Century Byzantine Ship at Yass1ada and Her Final Voyage: Present Thoughts', in D. N. Carlson, J. Leidwanger, S. M. Kampbell (eds), *Maritime Studies in the Wake of the Byzantine Shipwreck at Yassiada, Turkey*, (College Station: Texas A & M University Press, 2015), pp.205–216

Drapeyron, L., *L'Empereur Héraclius et l'Empire byzantin au VIIe siècle* (Paris: Ernest Thorin, 1869)

Duncan-Jones, R. P., 'Pay and Numbers in Diocletian's Army', *Chiron*, 8 (1978), pp.541–560

Durand, M., Guelton, M. H., et al, 'Les costumes des élégants d'Antinoé conservés au Musée des Tissus de Lyon: approche historique, analyses techniques et analyses de colorants', *Techne*, 41 (2015), pp.32–45.

Durliat, J., *Les dédicaces d'ouvrages de défense dans l'Afrique Byzantine* (Rome: PEFR, 49, 1981).

Durliat, J., *De la ville antique à la ville Byzantine: le problème des subsistances* (Rome: CEFR, 136, 1990)

Dussaud, R., *Topographie historique de la Syrie antique et médiévale* (Paris: OpenEdition Books, 2015)

Eastmond, A., *The Glory of Byzantium and Early Christendom* (London: Phaidon, 2013).

Elsig, P. and Morand M. Cl. (eds), *Le Musée d'histoire du Valais, Sion. Collectionner au cœur des Alpes* (Sion, Paris: Somogy Édition d'Art, Musée d'histoire, 2013)

Emion, M., '*Christum in scutis notat*: le bouclier au chrisme des gardes impériaux dans l'Antiquité tardive', *Journée des doctorants du GRHis*, Université de Rouen-Normandie, 7 mai 2014

Esposito, G., 'The Isola Rizza Dish', *Medieval Warfare*, 4/6 (2014), p.58

Faider-Feytmans, G. & France-Lanord, A., 'Le casque mérovingien de Trivières', *Revue Belge d'archéologie et d'Histoire de l'Art*, t. 20, fasc. 4 (1951), pp.265–272

Fasano Guarini, F., 'Au XVIe siècle: comment naviguent les galères', *Annales*, 16–2 (1961), pp.279–296

Feissel, D., 'Les itinéraires de Procope et la métrologie de l'antiquité tardive', *AnTard*, 10 (2002), pp.383–400

Ferjančić, B., 'Invasions et installation des Slaves dans les Balkans' in *Villes et peuplement dans l'Illyricum protobyzantin*. Actes du colloque de Rome (12–14 mai 1982), (Rome: PEFR, 1984), pp.85–109

Fleschenberg, O. Schissel von, 'Spätantike Anleitung zum Bogenschiessen', *Wiener Studien*, 59 (1941), pp.10–24, 60; (1942), pp.43–70

Fleury, Ph., 'Vitruve et la nomenclature des machines de jet romaines', *REL*, 59 (1981), pp.216–234.

Fossella, J., 'Waiting Only for a Pretext: A New Chronology for the Sixth Century Byzantine Invasion of Spain', *Estudios bizantinos*, 1 (2013), pp.31–38.

Fotiou, A., 'Recruitment Shortages in Sixth Century Byzantium', *Byzantion*, 58 (1988), pp.65–77.

Foulon, E., 'Hypaspistes, peltastes, chrysaspides, argyraspides, chalcaspides', *REA*, 98 (1996), pp.53–63.

Frank, R. I., *Scholae Palatinae: The Palace Guards of the Later Roman Empire* (Rome: American Academy, Papers and Monographs of the American Academy in Rome, 23, 1969)

Freshfield, E. H., 'Notes on a Vellum Album Containing Some Original Sketches of Public Buildings and Monuments, drawn by a German Artist Who Visited Constantinople in 1574', *Archaeologia*, 72 (1921/1922), pp.87–104

Frendo, J. D. C., *History and Panegyric in the Age of Heraclius: The Literary Background to the Composition of the Histories of Theophylact Simocatta*, *DOP*, 42 (1988), pp.143–156

Fresne du Cange, Ch. du, et al, *Glossarium mediæ et infimæ latinitatis* (Niort: L. Favre, 1883–1887)

Galland-Hallyn, P., 'La *Johannide* (*De Bellis Libycis*). Corippus et le sublime dans la 'dernière' épopée romaine' in Droin J., Roth A. (eds), *La croisée des études libyco-berbères: mélanges offerts à Paulette Galand-Pernet et Lionel Galand* (Paris: Geuthner, 1993), pp.73–87

Gascou, J., 'Militaires étrangers en Égypte Byzantine', *BIFAO*, 75 (1975), pp.203–206

Gascou, J., 'L'institution des bucellaires', *BIFAO*, 76 (1976), pp.143–156

Gascou, J., 'Deux Inscriptions Byzantines de Haute-Égypte (reedition from I. Thebes-Syène 196 r° and v°)', Collège de France, Centre de recherche d'histoire et civilisation de Byzance, *Travaux et Mémoires*, 12 (1994), pp.323–342

Ghilardi, M., Goddard, Ch. J., Porena, P. (eds), *Les cités de l'Italie tardo-antique (IVe-VIe siècle). Institutions, économie, société, culture et religion* (Rome: CEFR, 2006)

Gibbons, A., 'Why 536 was the "worst year to be alive"', *Science Magazine*, 362 (2018), pp.733–734

R. Ginouvès, 'La mosaïque des mois à Argos', *Bulletin de Correspondance Hellénique*, 81 (1957), pp.216–268

Glad, D., 'The Empire's Influence on Barbarian Elites from the Pontus to the Rhine (Fifth-Seventh Centuries): A Case Study of Lamellar Weapons and Segmental Helmets' in S. Ivanišević, M. Kazanski, *The Pontic Danubian in the Period of the Great Migration*, Centre de Recherche d'Histoire et Civilisation de Byzance, Monographies 36-Arheološki Institute Beograd,

Posebna Izdanja, Knijiga, 51, (Paris-Belgrade: Collège de France/ CNRS, 2012), pp.349–362

Goddard, Chr. J. et al, 'D'Ulpiana à Iustiniana Secunda, d'une cité à l'autre dans l'Antiquité tardive (prospection géophysique 2019–2020)', *Revue archéologique. Bulletin de la Société française d'Archéologie classique*, 73 (2022), pp.153–162

Goeje, M. J. De, *Mémoire sur le Fotouho's-Sham attribué à Abou Ismail al-Baçri* (Leiden: *Mémoires d'histoire et de géographie orientales*, 2, 1864)

Goffart, W. A., *Barbarians and Romans AD 418–584: The Techniques of Accommodation*, (Princeton NJ: Princeton University Press, 1980)

Goffart, W. A., *The Narrators of Barbarian History AD 550–800. Jordanes, Gregory of Tours, Bede and Paul the Deacon*, (Princeton NJ: Princeton University Press, 1988)

M. P. S. Gomez, 'The Byzantine Balkan Path in the Gothic Campaigns of 536 and 551', (Murcia: Universidad Catolica San Antonio-Online edition Academia.edu., 2014)

Gonis N., 'Payments to Bucellarii in Seventh Century Oxyrhynchus' in J. L. Fournet, A. Papaconstantinou, *Mélanges Jean Gascou*, Travaux et Mémoires, 20/1 (Paris: Collège de France, Centre de recherche d'histoire et civilisation de Byzance, 2016), pp.175–192

Gračanin, H., 'The Gepids and Southern Pannonia in the Age of Justinian I' in T. Vida, D. Quast, Z. Racz, I. Koncz (eds), *Kollaps – Neuordnung – Kontinuität. Gepiden nach dem Ungtergang des Hunnenreiches. Tagung der Internationalen Konferenz and der Eötvös Lorand Universität, Budapest, 14–15 Dezember 2015*, (Mainz, Budapest: Institut für Archäologiewissenschaften, Eötvös Lorand Universität, Budapest Institut für Archäologie des Forschungszentrums für Humanwissenschaftender Ungarischen Akademie der Wissenschaften, Leibniz-Forschungsinstitut für Archäologie, Römisch-Germanisches Zentralmuseum, 2019), pp.185–274

Graf, D. F., 'The *Via Militaris* and the *limes Arabicus*' in W. Groenman-van Waateringe, B. L. van Beek, W. J. H. Willems, S. L. Wynia (eds), *Roman Frontier Studies 1995, Proceedings of the XVI International Congress of Roman Frontier Studies* (Oxford: Oxbow, 1997), pp.123–133

Greatrex, G., *Rome and Persia at War, 502–532* (Cambridge: Francis Cairns, 2006)

Greatrex, G., Lieu, S. N. C. (eds), The Roman Eastern Frontier and the Persian Wars, Part II, AD 363–630. A Narrative Sourcebook, (London: Routledge, 2002)

Greatrex, G., 'Moines, militaires et défense de la frontière orientale au VIe s.' in Lewin, A. S., Pellegrini, P., Fiema, Z. T., Janniard, S. (eds), *The Late Roman Army in Near East from Diocletian to the Arab Conquest*. Proceedings of a colloquium held at Potenza, Acerenza and Matera, Italy, May 2005, BAR International Series 1717 (Oxford: BAR, 2007), pp.285–297

Greatrex, G., 'Perceptions of Procopius in Recent Scholarship' in Histos, 8 (2014), pp.76–121

Grotowski, P. L., *Arms and Armour of the Warrior Saints. Tradition and Innovation in Byzantine Iconography (843–1261)*, The Medieval Mediterranean 87 (Leiden: BRILL, 2010)

Guilland, R., 'Les Logothètes: Études sur l'histoire administrative de l'Empire byzantin', *REB*, 29 (1971), pp.5–115

Guillou, A., 'Prise de Gaza par les Arabes au VIIe siècle', *BCH*, 81 (1957), pp.396–404

Hahn, W., *Moneta Imperii Byzantini*, vol.1, *Von Anastasius I. bis Justinianus I. (491–565)*, vol.2, *Von Justinus II bis Phocas (565–610)*, vol. 3, *Von Heraclius bis Leo III (610–720)*, (Vienna: Veröffentlichungen der Numismatischen Kommission X = Österr. Akad. der Wiss., phil.-hist. Kl., Denkschriften 148, 1973, 1975 and 1981)

Haldon, J. F., '*Solenarion*-The Byzantine Crossbow', *Historical Journal of the University of Birgminham*, 12 (1970), pp.155–157

Haldon, J. F., *Byzantine Praetorians: an administrative, institutional and social survey of the Opsikion and tagmata, c. 580–900*, Poikila Byzantina 3 (Bonn: Dr. Rudolf Habelt, Freie Universität Berlin, Byzantinisch-neugriegechischtes Seminar, 1984)

Haldon, J. F., *Byzantium in the Seventh Century: The Transformation of a Culture* (Cambridge: Cambridge University Press, 1997)

Haldon, J. F., 'Some Aspects of Early Byzantine Arms and Armour' in D. Nicolle (ed.), *A Companion to Medieval Arms and Armour* (Woodbridge: The Boydell Press, 2002), pp.65–86.

Haldon, J. F., *Warfare, State and Society in the Byzantine world, 565–1204*, Warfare and History (London: UCL Press, 2003)

Haldon J. F. (ed.), *Byzantine Warfare* (Aldershot: Ashgate Publishing, 2007)

Haldon, J. F., *The Byzantine Wars* (Brimscombe Port Stroud: The History Press, 2008)

Haldon, J. F., 'The Army and Military Logistics' in I. P. Stephenson (ed.), *The Byzantine World* (London: Routledge, 2010), pp.47–60

Halifeoglu, F. M., 'Castle Architecture in Anatolia: Fortifications of Diyarbakir', *Frontiers of Architectural Research*, vol. 2/2 (2013), pp.209–221

Hallot-Charmasson, M., 'Saints guerriers ou guerriers saints? Les saints militaires à Byzance des origines à 1204)' in M. Hallot-Charmasson (ed.), *Médiation, paix et guerre au Moyen Âge. Actes du 136e Congrès national des sociétés historiques et scientifiques, 'Faire la guerre, faire la paix', Perpignan, 2011* (Paris: Éditions du CTHS, Actes des congrès nationaux des sociétés historiques et scientifiques, 136–3, 2012), pp.51–62

Harl, K. W., *Coinage in the Roman Economy, 300 B.C. to AD 700* (Baltimore: The John Hopkins University Press, 1996)

Harris, W. V., *Roman Power: A Thousand Years of Empire* (Cambridge: Cambridge University Press, 2016)

Heather, P. J., *Empires and Barbarians. Migration, Development and the Birth of Europe*, (London: Macmillan, 2009)

Herrmann, P., *Itinéraires des voies romaines de l'Antiquité au Moyen Âge* (Paris: Errances 2007)

Hoffmann, D., *Das Spätrömische Bewegungsheer und die Notitia Dignitatum*, vol. 1 (Düsseldorf: Rheinland-Verlag, 1968)

Hombert, M., 'Bulletin papyrologique, XXVIII (1954 to 1959), 2ème partie', *REG*, t. 79, fasc. 374–375, January-June (1966), pp.99–278

Howard-Johnston, J., 'Heraclius' Persian Campaigns and the Revival of the East Roman Empire 622–630', *War in History*, 6 (1999), pp.1–44

Hoyland, R. G., *Seeing Islam as Others Saw It: A Survey and Evaluation of Christian, Jewish and Zoroastrian Writings on Early Islam*, Studies in Late Antiquity and Early Islam series 13 (Princeton NJ: Darwin Press, 1998)

Hoyland, R. G., *In God's Path: The Arab Conquests and the Creation of an Islamic Empire* (Oxford: Oxford University Press, 2015)

Iorga, N., *Histoire de la vie Byzantine, tome 1, l'Empire œcuménique (527–641)*, (Bucarest: Privately Published by the Author, 1934)

Ivanišević, V., Kazanski, M., Mastykova, A. (eds), *Les nécropoles de Viminacium à l'époque des Grandes Migrations*, Centre de Recherche d'Histoire et Civilisation de Byzance, Monographies, 22, Association des Amis du Centre d'histoire et civilisation de Byzance, (Paris: Collège de France-CNRS, 2006)

Ivanišević, V. and Kazanski, M., 'Illyricum du Nord et les Barbares à l'époque des Grandes Migrations (V^e-VIe siècles)', *Starinar*, 64 (2014), pp.131–160

Ivanišević, V., 'Une capitale revisitée: Caričin Grad (Justiniana Prima)', *Comptes rendus des séances de l'Académie des Inscriptions et Belles-Lettres*, 161–1 (2017), pp.93–115

James, S., 'The *Fabricae*: State Arms Factories of the Later Roman Empire' in J. C. Coulston, *Military Equipment and the Identity of Roman Soldiers. Proceedings of the Fourth Roman Military Equipment Conference*, BAR International Series, 394 (Oxford: BAR, 1988), pp.257–331

Janin, R., 'Citharizum' in A. Baudrillart, A. De Meyer, É. Van Cauwenbergh (eds), *Dictionnaire d'Histoire et de Géographie ecclésiastiques*, vol. XII, fasc. 67–72 (Paris: Letouzey et Ané, 1953), col. 997

Janin, R., *Constantinople Byzantine. Développement urbaine et répertoire topographique* (Paris: Institut français d'Études Byzantines, 1964)

Janniard, S., 'Procope, les Huns et les transformations tactiques de la cavalerie romaine au VIe siècle' in G. Greatrex & S. Janniard (eds), *Le monde de Procope/ The World of Procopius*, (Paris: O&M, 28, 2018), pp.205–214

Jarry, J., 'La conquête du Fayoum par les Musulmans d'après le Futūḥ Al-Bahnasa', *Annales Islamologiques*, 9 (1970), pp.9–20

Jones, A. H. M., *The Later Roman Empire, 284–602. A Social, Economic and Administrative Survey*, 3 volumes (Oxford: Blackwell, 1964). Abridged version in French, *Le déclin du monde antique, 284–610* (Paris: Sirey, 1970)

Jones, A. H. M., Martindale, J. R. and Morris, J., *The Prosopography of the Later Roman Empire* (Cambridge: Cambridge University Press, vol.1 [A.D. 260–395], 1971; vol. 2 [A.D. 395–527] 1980; vol. 3 [A.D. 526–641], 1992.)

Kaegi, W. E., *Byzantium and Early Islamic Conquests* (Cambridge: Cambridge University Press, 1992)

Kaegi, W. E., *Heraclius, Emperor of Byzantium* (Cambridge: Cambridge University Press, 2003)

Kaplan, M., *Byzance. Villes et campagnes* (Paris: Picard, 2006)

Karelin, D. A., 'Imaging of the Late Roman Castrum. Hypothetical Computer Reconstruction of Nag el-Hagar Fortress in Egypt', *AMIT*, 2/15, (2011) pp.1–20

Karelin, D. A., 'The Reconstruction of the Diocletianic Fortress in Babylon of Egypt: Architectural Decorations and Details' in A. V. Zakharova., S. V. Maltseva, E. I. Staniukovich-Denisova (eds), *Actual Problems of Theory and History of Art: Collection of articles*, 9, Lomonosov Moscow State University (St Petersburg: NP-Print, 2019) pp.180–188

Kawar, I., 'Procopius on the Ghassanids', *Journal of the American Oriental Society*, 77, 2 (1957), pp.79–87

Kazanski, M., Vallet, F., (eds), *L'armée romaine et les Barbares du IIIe au VIIe siècle*, Colloque international organisé à Saint-Germain-en-Laye, 1990 (Chelles: Association française d'Archéologie Mérovingienne et la Société des Amis du Musée des Antiquités Nationales, t. 5 des Mémoires publiés par l'Association française d'Archéologie Mérovingienne, 1993)

Kazanski, M., 'La cavalerie slave à l'époque de Justinien', *Archaeologia Baltica*, 11 (2009), pp.229–239, Russian version, 'О раннеславянской коннице', *Stratum Plus*, 5 (2009), pp.457–471

Kazanski, M., 'Les casques du type Baldenheim en Europe orientale: les origines' in M. Kazanski & P. Perin (eds), *Autour du règne de Clovis, Les grands dans l'Europe du Haut Moyen Âge, Histoire et archéologie* (Leuven: *AFAM*, 31, 2021), pp.230–229

Kazhdan, A. P., Talbot, A. M., Cutler, A., Gregory, T. E., Ševčenko, N. P. (eds), *The Oxford Dictionary of Byzantium*, 3 vols (Oxford: Oxford University Press, 1991)

Keating, P. *Belisarius Military Master of the West, Book One: Nika* (London: Vanguard Press, 2021)

Kennedy, H., *The Armies of the Caliphs. Military and Society in the Early Islamic State* (Abingdon: Routledge, 2006)

Kennedy, H., *The Great Arab Conquests: how the spread of Islam changed the world we live in* (London: Weidenfeld & Nicholson, 2007)

Kern, E. '*Non ignota cano:* histoire et mémoire dans 'la dernière épopée romaine', la *Johannide* de Corippe', *Schedæ*, fasc.1 (2007), pp.97–106

Keser-Kayaalp, E., Erdogan, N., 'Recent research on Dara/Anastasiopolis' in E. Rizos (ed.), *New Cities in Late Antiquity: Documents and Archaeology* (Turnhout: Brepols, 2017), pp.153–175

Khalidi, T., *Arabic historical though in the Classical Period*, Cambridge Studies in Islamic Civilisation (Cambridge: Cambridge University Press, 2004)

Khoperia, N., 'The Byzantine Lazic Phalanx at the Battle of the Hippis River (550 CE)', *The Journal of Politics and Democratisation-Online Publication*, 4/2, January (2020), pp.17–24

Kislinger, E., 'Ein Angriff zu viel: zur Verteidigung der Thermopylen in justinianischen Zeit', *BZ*, 91 (1998), pp.45–58

Kiss, P. A., 'Huns, Germans, Byzantines? The origins of the narrow bladed long seaxes', *Acta Archaeologica Carpathica*, 49 (2014), pp.131–164

Kolias, T. G., *Byzantinische Waffen. Ein Beitrag zur byzantinischen Waffenkunde von den Anfängen bis zur lateinischen Eroberung* (Vienna: Verlag der Österreichischen Akademie der Wissenschaften, *Byzantina Vindobonensia* 17, 1988)

Kondić, Vl., 'Les formes des fortifications protobyzantines dans la région des Portes de Fer' in Collectif, *Villes et peuplement dans l'Illyricum protobyzantin. Actes du colloque de Rome (12–14 mai 1982)*, (Rome: PEFR, 77, 1984), pp.131–161

Konrad, M., *Der spätrömische Limes in Syrien. Archäologische Untersuchungen an den Grenzkastellen von Sura, Tetrapyrgium, Cholle und in Resafa* (Mainz: Verlag Philipp von Zabern, Deutsches Archäologisches Institut, *Resafa* 5, 2001)

Kraemer, C. J., *Excavations at Nessana, III, Non-literary papyri* (Princeton NJ: Princeton University Press, 1958)

Krischen, F., *Die Landmauer von Konstantinopel*, t. 1. Zeichnerische Wiederherstellung mit begleitendem Text (Berlin: De Gruyter, 1938)

Lassus, J., *La forteresse Byzantine de Thamugadi, fouilles à Timgad 1938–1956* (Paris: Éditions du CNRS, Études d'Antiquités africaines, 1981)

Kubik, A. L., 'Introduction to Studies on Late Sasanian Protective Armour. The Yarysh-Mardy1 Helmet', *Historia I Świat*, 5 (2016), pp.77–105

Kubik, A. L., Radyuš, O. A., Vyazov, L. A., 'On one series of the VI Century AD Iron One-Piece Asian Helmets', *Bulletin of the Institute of Oriental Studies,* 3 (1) (2023), pp.52–82

Lécrivain, Ch., 'Les soldats privés au Bas-Empire', *MEFR*, 10 (1890), pp.267–283

Lebedynsky, I., *Les Scythes. La Civilisation des steppes (VIIe-IIIe siècles av. J.-C.)*, (Paris: Errances 2001)

Lebedynsky, I., *De l'épée scythe au sabre mongol: Les armes blanches des Steppes* (Paris: Errances-Actes Sud, 2021)

Le Bohec, Y., 'Écuyers et marins militaires sous le Haut-Empire romain', *Ktèma*, 21 (1996), pp.313–320

Lehmann, Ph. W., 'Theodosius or Justinian? A Renaissance Drawing of a Byzantine Rider', *The Art Bulletin*, vol. 41, no. 1 (March, 1959), pp.39–57

Lendon, J. E., *Soldiers and Ghosts: A History of Battle in Classical Antiquity* (New Haven: Yale University Press, 2005)

Lendon, J. E., *Soldats et fantômes. Combattre pendant l'Antiquité*, translated into French by Villeneuve G. (Paris: Tallandier, 2009)

Lepie, H., Münchow, A., *Elfenbeinkunst aus dem Aachener Domschatz* (Pandersberg: Imhof Verlag, 2006)

Lewin, A. S., Pellegrini, P., Fiema, Z. T., Janniard, S. (eds), *The Late Roman Army in Near East from Diocletian to the Arab Conquest: Proceedings of a colloquium held at Potenza, Acerenza and Matera, Italy, May 2005*, BAR International Series 1717 (Oxford: BAR, 2007)

Llewellyn, P., *Rome in the Dark Ages* (London: Constable and Company Ltd, 1993)

Lo Jacono, Cl., 'La bataille d'Aǧnadain selon Ibn Aʿt am al-Kūfī's Kitab al-futūḥ' in R. Traini (ed.), *Études en l'honneur de Francesco Gabrieli à l'occasion de son quatre-vingtième anniversaire*, vol. 2 (Rome: 1984), pp.447–457

Lombardi, F. V., 'Lo scontro franco-bizantino fra Pesaro nel 554 d.C. (Agatia II, 2–3)', *Studia Oliveriana*, 12 (1992), pp.55–62

Lot, F., 'La *Notitia Dignitatum utriusque imperii* ses tares, sa date de composition, sa valeur', *REA* (1936), pp.285–338

Luchitskaya, S., 'L'Empereur Héraclius vu par les chroniqueurs occidentaux du XIIe siècle', *Cahiers de Recherches Médiévales et Humanistes*, 37 (2019), pp.75–96

Maas, M., *John Lydus and the Roman Past. Antiquarianism and Politics in the Age of Justinian* (London: Routledge, 1992)

Maas M. (ed.), *The Cambridge Companion to the Age of Justinian* (Cambridge: Cambridge University Press, 2005)

Macdowall, Simon, *Late Roman Infantryman, 236–565*, Warrior Series 9 (London: Osprey Publishing, 1994)

Macdowall, Simon, *Late Roman Cavalryman, 236–565*, Warrior Series 15, (London: Osprey Publishing, 1995)

Marciak, M., *Sophene, Gordyene, and Adiabene: Three Regna Minora of Northern Mesopotamia Between East and West* (Leiden: Brill, 2017)

Marciniak, M., *Draco – historia smoczego sztandaru – History of the Dragon standard, University of Varsaw*, Master's Degree in archaeology in the field of general anthropology n° 209 672 (Uniwersytet Warszawski Instytut Archeologii, 2010)

Maiuri, M., 'L'assedio di Narsete a Cuma nel racconto dello storico Agathias', *La Parola del Passato*, 4 (1949), pp.41–46

Maksimović, L., 'L'administration de l'Illyricum septentrional à l'époque de Justinien', in H. Ahrweiler, *Philadelphie et autres études* (Paris: Éditions de la Sorbonne, *Byzantina Sorboniensa*, 1984), pp.143–157

Maksymiuk, K., *Geography of Roman-Iranian Wars: Military operations of Rome and Sasanian Iran* (Siedlce: Uniwersytet Przyrodniczo-Humanistyczny w Siedlcach, 2015)

Maneva, E., 'Le casque à fermoir d'Héraclée', *Archaeologia Iugoslavica*, 24 (1987), pp.101–111

Mason, H. J., *Greek Terms for Roman Institutions. A Lexicon and Analysis, American studies in papyrology*, 13 (Toronto: Hakkert, 1971)

Maspéro, J., *Organisation militaire de l'Égypte Byzantine* (Paris: Champion, 1912)

Matvieiev, A., 'Kitab Futuh el-Sham of (Pseudo-)Muhammad ibn Umar al-Waqidi as a Source for Studying the Battle on the River Yarmuk (636)', *Vox Patrum*, 77 (2021), pp.51–80

Meier, M., 'Prokop, Agathias, die Pest und das Ende der antiken Historiographie', *Historiche Zeitschrift*, 278 (2004), pp.281–310

Merrills, A., 'Understanding Late Antique North Africa' in A. Merrills (ed.), *Vandals, Romans and Berbers. New Perspectives on Late Antique North Africa* (London: Routledge, 2006), pp.1–28

Merrills, A., *War, Rebellion, Epic in Byzantine Africa. A Historical Study of Corippus' Iohannis* (Cambridge: Cambridge University Press, 2023)

(Michele Daviau, M. P., Chadwick, J. R., Steiner, M., eds), 'Excavation and Survey at Khirbat al-Mudayna and Its Surroundings: Preliminary Report of the 2001, 2004 and 2005 Seasons', in *Annual of the Department of Antiquities of Jordan* 50 (2006), pp.249–283

Mihaescu, H., 'Torna, torna, fratre', *Byzantina*, 8 (1976), pp.21–35

Mitchell, S., *A History of the Later Roman Empire, AD 284–641* (Oxford: Blackwell, 2007)

Milligen, A. van, *Byzantine Constantinople. The Walls of the City and adjoining Historical Sites* (London: John Murray, 1899)

Modéran, Y., 'Corippe et l'occupation Byzantine de l'Afrique: Pour une nouvelle lecture de la Johannide', *Antiquités Africaines*, XXII (1986), pp.195–212

Modéran, Y., 'Koutzinas-Cusina. Recherche sur un Maure du VIe siècle' in A. Mastino (ed.), *L'Africa romana 7. Atto del VII convegno di studio, Sassari, 1989* (Sassari: Edizioni Galizzi, 1990), pp.393–407

Modéran, Y., 'Cusina', *Encyclopédie berbère*, 14 (Aix-en-Provence: 1994), pp.2158–2159

Modéran, Y., 'Les frontières mouvantes du royaume vandale' in Cl. Lepelley, X. Dupuis (eds), *Frontières et limites géographiques de l'Afrique du Nord antique, Hommage à Pierre Salama* (Paris: 1999), pp.241–264

Modéran, Y., *Encyclopédie berbère*, 23 (Aix-en-Provence: 2000), pp.3565–3567

Modéran, Y., *Les Maures et l'Afrique romaine (IVe-VIIe siècle)*, (Rome: PEFR, 2003)

Mollat, M., 'Problèmes maritimes de l'histoire des croisades', *Cahiers de Civilisation Médiévale*, 10–39–40 (1967), pp.345–359

Moorhead, J., 'Italian Loyalties During Justinian's Gothic War', *REB*, 53 (1983), pp.575–596.

Morizot, P., 'Aurès' in *Encyclopédie berbère*, 7 (Aix-en-Provence: 1990), pp.1103–1113

Morizot, P., 'Recherches sur les campagnes de Solomon en Numidie méridionale', *CRAI*, January-February (1993), pp.83–106

Morizot, P., 'Timgad et son territoire' in *L'Afrique, la Gaule et son territoire à l'époque romaine, Mélanges à la mémoire de Marcel Le Glay* (Brussels: *Latomus*, 226, 1994), pp.220–243

Morizot, P., *Romains et Berbères face à face* (Arles: Errances, Les Hesperides, 2015).

Morrisson, C. (ed.), *Le monde Byzantin. L'Empire romain d'Orient (330–641)* (Paris: PUF, Nouvelle Clio, 2006)

Mrav, Z., 'Maniakon. The Golden Torc in Late Roman and Early Byzantine Army' in T. Vida, Ph. Rance et al, *The Frontier World. Roman, barbarians and Military Culture* (Budapest: Eötvös Lorand University, Martin Optiz Kiado, 2015), pp.287–303

Nagy, K., 'Notes on the Arms of the Avar Heavy Cavalry' in *Proceedings of the First International Conference on the Medieval History of the Eurasian Steppe*, Szeged, May 11—16, 2004, Part II, (Szeged: Akadémiai Kiado, *Acta Orientalia Academiae Scientiarum Hungaricae*, 58, 2, 2005), pp.135–148

Narkiss, B., 'Scribes and Artists of the Ashburnham Pentateuch' in *Tributes to Jonathan J. G. Alexander. The Making and Meaning of Illuminated Medieval & Renaissance Manuscripts, Art & Architecture* (London: H. Miller, 2006)

Nelis-Clément, J., *Les Beneficiarii: militaires et administrateurs au service de l'empire: Ier s. a.C.-VIe s. p.C.* (Bordeaux: Ausonius-De Boccard, 2000)

(Nicholson, O., ed.), *The Oxford Dictionary of Late Antiquity*, 2 volumes (Oxford: Oxford University Press, 2018)

Nicolle, David, *Yarmuk 636 AD: The Muslim Conquest of Syria* (Oxford: Osprey Publishing, 1994), Campaign Series, 31

O'Donnell, J. J. 'Liberius the Patrician', *Tradition*, 31 (1981), pp.31–72

Oikonomidès, N., 'Les premières mentions des thèmes dans la chronique de Théophane', *Zbornik radova Vizantološkog Instituta*, 16 (1975), pp.1–8

Onur, F., 'The Anastasian Military Decree from Perge in Pamphylia: Revised 2nd Edition', *Gephyra*, 14 (2017), pp.133–212

Pacha Miran, F., *Le décor de la Bible syriaque de Paris (BnF syr. 341) et son rôle dans l'histoire du livre chrétien* (Paris: Geuthner, 2020)

Palmer, A., 'Une chronique syriaque contemporaine de la conquête arabe: essai d'interprétation théologique et politique' in P. Canivet (ed.), *La Syrie de Byzance à l'Islam (VIIe-VIIIe siècles)*, (Damascus: Institut français d'études Arabes de Damas, 1992), pp.31–46

Palmer, A., *The Seventh Century in the West-Syrian Chronicles* (Liverpool: Liverpool University Press, 1993)

Parani, M., *Reconstructing the Reality of Images: Byzantine Material Culture and Religious Iconography (11th–15th centuries)*, (Leiden: Brill, 2003).

Paret, R., 'The Legendary Futūḥ Litterature' in F. M. Donner, *The Expansion of the Early Islamic State* (London: Routledge, 2007), pp.163–176

Pargoire, J., 'Les LX soldats martyrs de Gaza', *REB*, 50 (1905), pp.40–43

Parnell, D. A., 'A Prosopographical Approach to Justinian's Army', *Medieval Prosopography*, 27, 1 (2012), pp.1–75

Parnell, D. A., 'Barbarians and Brothers-in-Arms. Byzantines on Barbarian Soldiers in the Sixth Century', *BZ*, 108, 2 (2015), pp.809–826

Parnell, D. A., *Justinian's Men: Careers and Relationships of Byzantine Army Officers, c. 518–610*, New Approaches to Byzantine History and Culture (London: Palgrave Macmillan, 2017).

Parnell, D. A., 'Procopius on Romans, non-Romans, and battle casualties' in G. Greatrex, S. Janniard (eds), *Le monde de Procope/ The World of Procopius,* (Paris: O&M, 28, 2018), pp.249–262

Paulsen, P., *Alamannische Adelsgräber von Niederstotzingen (Kreis Heindeinheim)*, (Stuttgart: Müller & Gräff, Kommissions Verlag, 1967)

Pietri, Ch., 'Le serment du soldat chrétien. Les épisodes de la *Militia Christi* sur les sarcophages', *MEFR*, 74–2 (1962), pp.649–664.

Pillon, M., 'Armée et défense de l'Illyricum Byzantin de Justinien à Héraclius (527–641). De la réorganisation justinienne à l'émergence des 'armées de cité'', *Erytheia*, 26 (2005), pp.7–85.

Polh, W. *Die Avaren. Ein Steppenwolk im Mitteleuropa 567–822 n. Chr* (Munich: C.H. Beck, 1988)

Pomey, P., 'À propos de la voile latine: la mosaïque de Kelenderis et les *Stereometrica* (II, 48–49) d'Héron d'Alexandrie', *Archeonautica*, 19 (2017), pp.9–25

Popović, Vl., 'Les témoins archéologiques des invasions avaro-slaves dans l'Illyricum byzantin', *MEFR*, 87–1 (1975), pp.445–504

Popović, Vl., 'La descente des Koutrigurs, des Slaves et des Avars vers la mer Égée: le témoignage de l'archéologie', *Comptes rendus des séances de l'Académie des Inscriptions et Belles-Lettres*, 122–3 (1978), pp.596–648

Poulter, A., 'The Use and Abuse of Urbanism in the Danubian Provinces During the Later Roman Empire' in J. Rich (ed.), *The City in Late Antiquity* (London, New York: Routledge, 2002), pp.106–109

Pralong, A., 'Remarques sur les fortifications Byzantines de Thrace orientale' in H. Ahrweiler, *Géographie historique du monde méditerranéen* (Paris: Éditions de la Sorbonne, 1988), pp.179–200

Pringle, D., *The Defence of Byzantine Africa from Justinian to The Arab Conquest. An account of the military history and archaeology of the African provinces in the sixth and seventh centuries*, BAR International Series 99 (Oxford: BAR, 2001)

Pryor, J. H. & Jeffrey, H., *The Age of the Dromōn: The Byzantine Navy Ca 500–1204*, The Medieval Mediterranean, Peoples, Economies and Cultures 400–1500, 62, (Leiden-Boston: Brill, 2006).

Puech, V., 'Les officiers de l'armée d'Afrique sous Justinien', *RM2E – Revue de la Méditerranée, édition électronique*, t. II.2 (2015), pp.57–82

Rance, Ph., 'The *Fulcum*, the Late Roman and Byzantine Testudo: The Germanisation of Roman Infantry Tactics', *Greek, Roman and Byzantine Studies*, 44 (2004), pp.265–326

Rance, Ph., 'Drungus, Δροῦγγος and Δρουγγιστί – a Gallicism and Continuity in Roman Cavalry Tactics', *Phoenix*, 58 (2004), pp.96–130

Rance, Ph., 'Narses and the Battle of Taginæ (Busta Gallorum) 552: Procopius and Sixth Century Warfare', *Historia*, 54 (2005), pp.424–472

Rance, Ph., 'Campidoctores Vicarii vel Tribuni: The Senior Regimental Officers of the Late Roman Army and Rise of the Campidoctor' in Lewin, A. S., Pellegrini, P., Fiema, Z. T., Janniard, S. (eds), *The Late Roman Army in Near East from Diocletian to the Arab Conquest: Proceedings of a colloquium held at Potenza, Acerenza and Matera, Italy, May 2005*, BAR International Series 1717 (Oxford: BAR, 2007), pp.395–409.

Rance, Ph., '*sculca, sculcator, exculcator* and *proculcator*: The Scouts of the late Roman Army and a Disputed Etymology', *Latomus*, 73 (2014), pp.474–501.

Rapport, M. *Nationality and Citizenship in Revolutionary France* (Oxford: Oxford University Press, 2000)

Ravegnani, G., *Soldati di Bisanzio in Età Giustinianea* (Rome: Jouvence, 1998)

Ravegnani, G., *I bizantini e la guerra. L'età di Giustiniano* (Rome: Jouvence, Storia, 51, 2004)

Ravegnani, G., 'Le unità dell'esercito bizantino nel VI secolo tra continuità e innovazione' in S. Gaspari (ed.), *Alto Medioevo Mediterraneo* (Florence: Firenze University Press, 2005), pp.185–205

Ravegnani, G., 'Soldati di Bisanzio in Italia nelle epigrafi del VI secolo in G. Cresci Marrone', A. Pistellato, *Studi in ricordo di Fulviomario Broilo* (Padova, S.A.R.G.O.N., vol. 2, 2007), pp.523–530

Reichenkron, G., 'Zur romischen Kommando-sprache bei byzantinischen Schriftstellern', *BZ*, 54 (1961), pp.18–27

(Reinink, G. J. & Stolte, B. H. eds), *The Reign of Heraclius (610–641), Crisis and Confrontation* (Leuven: Paris; Dudley MA: Peeters, 2002)

Rémondon, R., 'Soldats de Byzance d'après un papyrus trouvé à Edfou', *Recherches de Papyrologie*, I (1961), pp.41–93

Rich, J., *The City in Late Antiquity* (London: Routledge, 1996).

Richardot, P. H., 'Du Ve au XVIe siècle: un millénaire stratégique' in *Méditerranée, Les constantes géostratégiques*, Actes du Colloque du Groupe des Écoles du Commissariat de la Marine et Fondation Méditerranéenne pour les Études Stratégiques, Toulon, 25–26 avril 1996, (Paris: Publisud, 1997), pp.87–143

Richardot, P. H., 'Le plus vieux limes: la défense de l'Afrique romaine', *Revue Internationale d'Histoire Militaire*, 76 (1997), pp.15–37

Richardot, P. H., *La fin de l'Armée romaine 284–476, 3e édition revue et augmentée avec une traduction de la Notitia Dignitatum* (Paris: Economica, 2005)

Richardot, P. H., *Les erreurs stratégiques des Gaulois face à César* (Paris, Economica, 2006)

Richardot, P. H., 'La bataille antique: représentation et modèle', *Prétorien*, 9, avril-juin (2009), pp. 19–27

Richardot, P. H., 'La pacification de l'Afrique Byzantine, 534–546' in Coutau-Bégarie (ed.), *Stratégies irrégulières* (*Stratégique*, 93–96, 1, 2009), pp. 129–158.

Richardot, P. H., *L'Âge des guerriers ou l'aube du Moyen Âge 476–711* (Le Rove: Centre Littéraire d'Impression Provençal, 2016).

Rodgers, W. L., *Naval Warfare under Oars 4th to 16th Centuries* (Annapolis: Naval Institute Press, 1990)

Roisl, H. N., 'Totila und die Schlacht bei den Busta Gallorum, Ende Juni/Anfang Juli 552', *Jahrbuch der Österreichischen Byzantinistk*, 30 (1981), pp.25–50

Rougé, J., 'Sur un mot de Cassiodore: Exculcatoriae-Sculcatoriae-Sulcatoriae' in *Latomus*, 21 (1962), pp.384–390

Ruysschaert, J., 'Lectures des illustrations du Virgile Vatican et du Virgile romain', *Monuments et Mémoires de la Fondation Eugène Piot*, 73 (1991), pp.25–51

Sahas, D. J., 'Face to Face Encounter Between Patriarch Sophronius of Jerusalem and the Caliph 'Umar Ibn al-Khattab: Friends or Foes?' in E. Grypeou, M. N. Swanson, D. R. Thomas (eds), *The Encounter of Eastern Christianity with Early Islam* (Leiden: Brill, 2006), pp.33–44

Sarantis, A., 'War and Diplomacy in Pannonia and the North-West Balkans During the Reign of Justinian: The Gepid Threat and Imperial Responses', *DOP*, 63 (2009), pp.15–40

Sarantis, A., 'The Justinianic Heruli: from allied barbarians to Roman provincials' in F. Curta (ed.) *Neglected barbarians* (Turnhout: Brepols, 2011), pp.361–402

Schlumberger, G., 'L'ivoire Barberini' in *Monuments et Mémoires de la Fondation Eugène Piot*, 7–1 (1900), pp.79–94

Scott, S., *The Response of the Royal Army to the French Revolution: The Role and Development of the Line Army 1787–93* (Oxford: Clarendon Press, 1978).

Shahid, I. *Byzantium and the Arabs in the Sixth century*, vol.1, part 1, *Political and Military History* (Washington: Dumbarton Oaks Research Library and Collection, 1995)

Speidel, M. P., 'Raising New Units for the Late Roman Army: Auxilia Palatina', *DOP*, 50 (1996), pp.163–170

Speidel, M. P., 'Who fought in the Front' in G. Alföldy, B. Dobson, W. Eck (eds), *Kaiser Heer und Gesellschaft in der Romischen Kaiserzeit. Gedenkschrift für Eric Birley* (Stuttgart: Franz Steiner Verlag, 2000), pp.473–482

Stadler, P., 'Avar Chronology Revisited, and the Question of Ethnicity in the Avar Qaganate' in F. Curta, R. Kovalev (eds), *The Other Europe in the Middle Ages. Avars, Bulgars, Khazars and Cumans* (Leiden: Brill, 2009), pp.47–82

Stein, E., '*Ordinarii* et *Campidoctores*', *REB*, 8 (1933), pp.379–387

Stephenson, I. P., (ed.), *The Byzantine World* (London: Routledge, 2010).

Stephenson, I. P., *Romano-Byzantine Infantry Equipment* (Stroud: Tempus, 2006)

Stewart, M. E., 'Contest of Andreia in Procopius' Gothic Wars', *Parekbolai*, 4 (2014), pp.21–54

Stewart, M. E., 'The Danger of the Soft Life: Manly and Unmanly Romans in Procopius' Gothic War', *Journal of Late Antiquity*, 10.2 (2017), pp.473–502

Stiebel, G. D., 'A Spangenhelm-type helmet' in E. Mazar, *The Temple Mount Excavations in Jerusalem 1968–1978. Directed by B. Mazar. Final Report II. The Byzantine Period*, (Jerusalem: The Hebrew University of Jerusalem, Qedem, Monographs of the Institute of Archaeology, The Institute of Archaeology 2003), pp.43–46

Stiernon, D., 'Bulletin de théologie mariale Byzantine', *REB*, 17 (1959), pp.201–250

Stratos, A., 'Byzance et la Perse', *La Nouvelle Revue des Deux Mondes,* April (1981), pp.32–46

Tarver, W. T. S., 'The Traction Trebuchet: A Reconstruction of *an Early Medieval Siege Engine*', *Technology and Culture,* 36, 1 (1995), pp.136–167

Torallas-Tovar, S., 'Los *Riparii* en los papiros del Egipto tardoantiquo', *Aquila Legionis,* 1 (2001), pp.123–149

Treadgold, W., *Byzantium and its Army, 284-1081* (Stanford: Stanford University Press, 1995)

Treadgold, W., *The Early Byzantine Historians* (Basingstoke, New York: Palgrave Macmillan, 2007)

Trombley, F. R., 'The Operational Methods of the Late Roman Army in the Persian War of 572–591' in Lewin, A. S., Pellegrini, P., Fiema, Z. T., Janniard, S. (eds), *The Late Roman Army in Near East from Diocletian to the Arab Conquest: Proceedings of a colloquium held at Potenza, Acerenza and Matera, Italy, May 2005,* BAR International Series 1717 (Oxford: BAR, 2007), pp.321–356

Trousset, P. 'Les limites Sud de la réoccupation Byzantine', *Ant tard,* 10 (2003), pp.143–150

Tsangadas, B. *The Fortifications and Defense of Constantinople* (New York: Columbia University Press, 1980)

Turnbull, S., *The Walls of Constantinople, AD 324–1453* (London: Osprey Publishing, 2004), Fortress Series 25

Vagalanski, L., 'Ein neuer spätantiker Segmenthelm aus Voivoda, Schumen Gebiet (Nordost)', *Archaelogica Bulgarica,* 2 (1998), pp.96–106

Valensi, L., 'La réorganisation de l'Égypte Byzantine au temps de Justinien Ier', *Bulletin de l'Association Guillaume Budé,* LH–11 (1952), pp.55–71

Amela Valverde, L., *Varia Historicorum,* I (Seville: Punto Rojo Libros, 2021)

Weitzmann, K., 'Prolegomena to a Study of the Cyprus Plates', *Metropolitan Museum Journal,* vol. 3 (1970), pp.97–111

Viscidi, F., *I prestiti latini nel greco antico e bizantino* (Padua: Olschki, Università di Padova. Pubblicazioni della Facoltà di lettere e filosofia, 22, 1944).

Vogt, M., *Spangenhelme: Baldenheim und verwandte Typen* (Mainz: Verlag des Römisch-Germanischen Zentralmuseums, Kataloge vor – und frühgeschichtlicher Altertümer, 39, 2006).

Whately, C., 'Some Observations on Procopius' Use of Numbers in Descriptions of Combat in Wars Books 1–7', *Phoenix,* 69, 3/4 (2015), pp.394–411

Whately, C. *Battles and Generals: Combat, Culture, and Didacticism in Procopius' Wars* (Leiden: Brill, History of Warfare Series, 111, 2016)

Whately, C. *Procopius on Soldiers and Military Institutions in the Sixth-Century Roman Empire* (Leiden: Brill, 2021)

Wheeler, E. L., 'The legion as phalanx in the Late Empire, Part 2', *REMA,* 1 (2004), pp.147–175

Wiewiorowski, J., 'The Defence of the Long Walls of Thrace (Μακρά Τείχη τῆς Θράκης) under Justinian the Great (527–565 AD)', *Studia Ceranea,* 2 (2012), pp.181–194

Whitby, M., 'The Long Walls of Constantinople', *REB*, 55 (1985), pp.560–583

Whitby, M., *The Emperor Maurice and his Historian: Theophylact Simocatta on Balkan and Persian Warfare* (Oxford: Oxford University Press, 1988)

Whitby, M., 'Recruitment in Roman Armies from Justinian to Heraclius (ca. 565–615)' in A. Cameron & L. I. Conrad. (eds), (1995), pp.61–124

Wiesehöfer, J. 'CIRCESIUM' in *Encyclopaedia Iranica,* vol. V, fasc. 6 (1991), pp.595–596.

Williams, S. and Friell, G., *The Rome That Did Not Fall: The Survival of the East in the Fifth Century* (London: Routledge, 1999)

Woods, D., 'The 60 Martyrs of Gaza and the Martyrdom of Bishop Sophronius of Jerusalem', *ARAM*, 15 (2003), pp.129–150

Woods, D., 'Jews, rats and the Battle of Yarmuk' in Lewin, A. S., Pellegrini, P., Fiema, Z. T., Janniard, S. (eds), *The Late Roman Army in Near East from Diocletian to the Arab Conquest: Proceedings of a colloquium held at Potenza, Acerenza and Matera, Italy, May 2005*, BAR International Series 1717 (Oxford: BAR, 2007), pp.372–373, 374, n. 47.

Vryonis, S. Jr. (ed.), 'The evolution of Slavic society and the Slavic invasions in Greece: the first major Slavic attack on Thessaloniki, AD 597', *Hesperia. Journal of the American School of Classical Studies at Athens*, 50 (1981), pp.378–390

Zarini, Z., *Berbères ou barbares? Recherches sur le livre second de la Johannide de Corippe*, Nancy (Paris: de Boccard, 1997)

Zarini, V., 'Images de guerre dans la poésie officielle de l'Antiquité tardive: l'exemple de la Johannide de Corippe', *Images romaines, Études de littérature ancienne*, IX (1998), pp.161–173

Zeller, A., *Soldats perdus. Des armées de Napoléon aux garnisons de Louis XVIII* (Paris: Perrin, 1977)

Zinski, Z., 'Ein völkerwanderungszeitlicher Helm aus Sinj', *Starohrvatska prosvjeta* 3712 (1982), pp.7–34

Zuckerman, C., 'The early Byzantine strongholds in eastern Pontus', Centre de recherche d' histoire et civilisation de Byzance, *Travaux et Mémoires*, 11 (1991), pp.473–486

Zuckerman, C., 'Le δευτερόν βάνδον Κωνσταντινιακῶν dans une épitaphe de Pylai', *Tyche*, 10 (1995), pp.233–235

Zuckerman, C., *Du village à l'Empire: autour du Registre fiscal d'Aphroditô (525/526)*, (Paris: Association des Amis du Centre d'Histoire et de Civilisation de Byzance, Monographies, 16, 2004)

Zuckerman, C., 'L'armée' in C. Morrisson (ed.), *Le monde Byzantin. L'Empire romain d'Orient (330-641)* (Paris: PUF, Nouvelle Clio, 2006), pp.143–182

Zuckerman C. (ed.), *Constructing the Seventh Century* (Paris: Collège de France, CNRS, Centre de recherche d'histoire et civilisation de Byzance, 2013)

Unpublished

Comfort, A. M., 'Roads on the Frontier Between Rome and Persia: Euphratesia, Osrhoene and Mesopotamia from AD 363 to 602' (Doctoral thesis, University of Exeter, 2009), https://ore.exeter.ac.uk/repository/handle/10036/68213

Emion, M., *Des soldats de l'armée romaine tardive: les protectores (IIIe-VIe siècles ap. J.-C.)*, thèse de Doctorat en Histoire sous la direction de Pierre Cosme (Rouen: Université de Rouen-Normandie, École doctorale Histoire, Mémoire, Patrimoine, Langage ED 558, 2017)

Lillington-Martin, Chr., 'Forts on frontiers facing 'βάρβαροι' et alii', paper was presented at the Late Antique and Byzantine Archaeology and Art Seminar, St. John's College, University of Oxford on 28 May 2015,

https://www.academia.edu/1175514/Roman_Persian_frontier_fortlet_Mindouos_?auto=download

Shams, A., 'The Treasures of the Holy Monastery of Saint Catherine at Mount Sinai: from the treasury of Sixth Century CE to the museum of Twenty First Century CE', Management and Development of Cultural Heritage (MDCH), PhD Student, IMT Institute for Advanced Studies, Lucca, Italy (2011)

About the author

Philippe Richardot is a specialist in military history and the author of eleven books and nearly 200 articles. His main subject of study is the late Roman army and the warriors of the early Middle Ages, but he also places himself in the broader perspective of comparative military history. A graduate of the regional sessions of the Hautes Etudes de l'Armement and of the Institut des Hautes Etudes de la Défense nationale (France), he has also been a member of the Scientific Committee of the Centre d'Histoire et de Prospective Militaires de Lausanne-Pully (Switzerland) and research director at the Institut für vergleichende Tactik in Vienna-Postdam (Austria-Germany). He regularly writes for the *Revue Militaire Suisse* for nearly three decades, and for three years has directed dissertations at the Ecole de Guerre (Paris).

About the artist

Renato Dalmaso was born in Sao Paulo in 1981, where he currently lives with his wife and daughter. Self-taught in drawing and painting, he began his career in illustration at the age of 37, after deciding to change his professional path. Today he illustrates for several publishers in Brazil and around the world. He has been contributing his illustrations and covers to Helion & Company since 2021. In Brazil, he illustrated several graphic novels, such as *Elisio, A Journey To Hell* and *Jambocks!*, about the participation of the Expeditionary Force and the Brazilian Air Force in World War II. He also illustrated comic books about soccer, telling the story of the Sao Paulo FC and CR Flamengo clubs. In parallel with his work as a book illustrator, he is working on developing his new comic book series, which will tell the story of the Portuguese Great Navigations, in the 16th century.